Duane L. Faw's

PARAMONY

A PARALLEL and HARMONY of

The URANTIA® Book

and

The BIBLE

A limited "Experimental Edition" of the PARAMONY was distributed in 1983 with a request for additions and suggestions. The response was gratifying, and this second commercial edition incorporates additions and ideas submitted by users.

Published in USA by: Duane L. Faw, Publisher, 23301 Bocana, Malibu, CA 90265

Distributed by Jesusonian Foundation, P. O. Box 18764, Boulder, CO 80308

For information about study groups, social functions, and fellowship of *The Urantia Book* readers contact The Fellowship, 529 Wrightwood, Chicago, IL 60614.

Religion   God   Jesus

Library of Congress Catalog Card Number 86-91357

ISBN   0-940215-00-4

DEDICATION

This book is respectfully dedicated to our religious guardians, the "angels of the churches," with the prayer that it will facilitate their work by fostering greater recognition and appreciation by mankind of the continuum of truth throughout the ages and of the unity of Deity throughout the universes.

Revelation 1:20

The URANTIA Book 1255:24—33

SOMETHING to THINK ABOUT

Could it be that each person's religion is nothing more nor less than the composite, the totality, of one's personal relationship with Deity?

If so, one's religion is not the church, sect, denomination——or even the broad classification given to those whose experiences with deity have common characteristics (such as Christianity, Judaism, Islam, Buddhism, etc.). Nor is it a system of beliefs. Rather, it is a unique personal relationship with God (Deity personified) which each individual must establish for himself or herself, alone.

How "personal" is one's relationship with Deity if it is based vicariously upon the experiences of others? Is there a significant difference between having faith in God and having faith in the representations of others about God? What must one know "about" God before one can "know" God? Is it essential to one's salvation to choose the correct "Holy Book"? Or to follow the correct religious leader? Or to accept an orthodox interpretation of "inspired" writings? How does membership in human institutions affect one's personal relationship with God?

The most exciting and self—satisfying challenge before anyone is to develop a unique soul—creating _personal_ relationship with God. Certainly, reading inspired books (books written by inspired authors), listening to the experiences of inspired persons, and belonging to truth—seeking organizations can help, but can any or all of these substitute for the development of one's own personal experiences with Deity? Cannot the essential personal relationship be developed by living each day as a loyal and loving son or daughter of God no matter what book one reads, what person one hears, or what organization one joins or avoids?

I propose that there is no secret formula, no magic knowledge, no social group, no single creed which opens the door of eternity. Rather, it is the dedication of one's self to finding and doing that which—_for that person_—is the will of the Creator, together with active and living faith in the mercy of a loving and understanding Deity, which results in the development of a soul of eternal value.

If this is correct, then is it not the role of religious leaders to hold up the challenge, to inspire the dedication, to support the efforts and facilitate the progress of those who choose to become faith—children of the Universal Father/Mother of all? And cannot this better be done by expanding, rather than by limiting, the ways in which man—kind can perceive and relate to Deity? What better way to fulfill the vision of Isaiah and work toward the goal of Jesus than to help "set the spiritual captives free" of burdensome theological bondage?

TABLE of CONTENTS

FOREWORD

Everyone is interested in God. Theologians exchange ideas *about* God. Pilgrims search *for* God. Devotees strive for a closer personal relationship *with* God. Evangelists seek more effective ways by which to *represent* God. And skeptics hope to confirm *whether or not* God exists. All have this in common: each looks for a deeper understanding of cosmic reality and a greater revelation of Deity than has yet been found.

For each of the above, *The URANTIA Book* is required reading. No religionist of any sort can be aware of all viable concepts about God without first being exposed to the unique pronouncements contained within the 2097 pages of this remarkable book.

Upon reading *The URANTIA Book* some are convinced that it is an epochal revelation of God to mankind, and accept it as containing the "revealed truth." On the other extreme, some consider it to be heretical, if not diabolical, a stumbling-block on the road to truth, and summarily reject it. But many, perhaps most, see it as revealing many attractive and intriguing concepts about Deity worthy of serious consideration. And some selectively incorporate various of its teachings into their own personal religion.

People whose native tongues are of European or Middle-Eastern origin have been influenced to some degree by religion originating in the teachings of Moses, the sayings of Jewish prophets and the life and teachings of Jesus Christ. They relate in some manner to a common source document: The BIBLE. It is only natural that, upon reading *The URANTIA Book*, they would wish to compare its teachings with those contained in The BIBLE.

Christians, whose beliefs are largely derived from matters reported in the New Testament, may wish to compare New Testament teachings with parallel reports in *The URANTIA Book*. Persons of Jewish background, holding beliefs based upon documents contained in the Old Testament, may wish to compare Old Testament writings with language of *The URANTIA Book*.   Even those of Islamic faith, who recognize both Moses and Jesus as prophets, may wish to com—pare traditions reported in both The BIBLE and the Koran with the treatment of such traditons in *The URANTIA Book*.

Before publication of the PARAMONY there was no easy and practical way to "go" from a familiar or interesting passage in one book to the treatment of the same or similar matter in the other.   Clyde Bedell's CONCORDEX was helpful, but time consuming.   The PARAMONY is designed to facilitate this "location" process.

The PARAMONY evolved from the author's personal research into concepts, incidents and language common to both books.   *The URANTIA Book* recounted a remarkable number of incidents, events and concepts already known from The BIBLE; and The BIBLE, read in context of *The URANTIA Book* teachings, revealed far more useful information about cosmology, Deity and the Divine Plan than traditional study methods had shown.   By applying concepts in *The URANTIA Book* to traditional Biblical language, The BIBLE seemed to "come alive."   Not only were many beautiful teachings about the universe, the role and nature of Deity, and the Divine purpose and destiny of mankind exposed from their hiding places in the ancient text of The BIBLE, but also there were revealed many new and sig—nificant meanings to well—known Bible passages not heretofore suspected.   This is particularly true of stories recounting the life and teachings of Jesus.   The beloved Bible, which had proved to be sufficient to lead generations to the grace of God, now became more beautiful, more convincing and more valuable than ever before.

The author's first thought was to share the joy of discovery of new and enhanced Bible truths with those who already loved The BIBLE. However, it has become obvious that the PARAMONY also serves other purposes.   By placing insights from *The URANTIA Book* alongside wording of The BIBLE, it highlights similarities and differences in theology emanating from the two books.   This may facilitate a new look at old doctrines, dogma, rituals and tradi—tions; and help to re—evaluate them.   By shedding new light on old teachings, it offers help and hope to those to whom Bible teachings have been poorly or inaccurately presented, and who therefore discount such teachings in their traditional context.   And the PARAMONY facilitates scholarly study of The BIBLE, no matter for what purpose.

The PARAMONY is nothing more pretentious than a mechanical tool to assist anyone wishing to compare language in *The URANTIA Book* with language in The BIBLE relating to the same matter. It contains no theology of its own.

In form, the PARAMONY is a cross—reference between *The URANTIA Book* and The BIBLE. When the same material appears in both books, the PARAMONY shows where it appears in each. One can go from matter in *The URANTIA Book* to similar matter in The BIBLE, or vice versa. In this capacity it provides a traditional PARALLEL between similar passages in the two books.

The PARAMONY displays material in the chronological order of the source document. Sections I and II display parallel Biblical material in the time sequence of *The URANTIA Book*. This results in a traditional HARMONY of materials treated in both books. Similarly, Section III of the PARAMONY produces four more "harmonies" of incidents and teachings in the life of Jesus which are reported in different sequences in the four Gospels of the New Testament. Collectively, Sections II and III of the PARAMONY provide to New Testament scholars an extremely useful and valuable tool by which to harmonize the Four Gospels.

The PARAMONY contains no original material. It is a study aid, a tool, for use by scholars, teachers, theologians, skeptics and casual readers to correlate teachings of the two books. It is not intended to be a commentary on either.

Yet, some judgment is required to determine which language, incidents and teachings in one book refer to the same or similar recitations in the other. This judgment is originally made by the author in the process of determining what to include and what to omit in a cross—reference. Further judgment is required when cross references are classified as being to the "same matter" (underlined), "referenced matter" (in bold type), or "comparable similar matter" (in lighter type.) These classifications are really only the author's opinion. There exists no official interpretation of the meaning of any portion of *The URANTIA Book*, and the PARAMONY is not to be used to imply even an unofficial interpretation. It is important for each user of the PARAMONY to exercise his or her independent judgment on such matters.

The author has borrowed from every available source in compiling this work. Included are documents by Dr. William S. Sadler, William Sadler, Jr., Winona R. Jewell, Helen Steen, Bill Brehio, Jacques Weiss, Randy Moser, Ruth Renn, Dave Brandl, Herb Millen, Tom Toth and many others. Great assistance and support was provided by Harry McMullan III, Julia Fenderson and Randy Moser.

The PARAMONY is never finished. We will constantly find new and important cross—references as we learn more and more about these two great books. When readers find errors or omisssions, they are requested to forward them to the author for inclusion in the next edition.

As a personal note, the author has been deeply impressed by new insights into The BIBLE which come from a study of *The URANTIA Book*. The BIBLE has become more meaningful, more useful and more loved as a result of the study.

Duane L. Faw, JD
Brigadier General, USMC(Retired)
Professor of Law Emeritus

ABOUT THE PARAMONY

I: WHAT IS A PARAMONY?

This book is a PARAMONY. In fact, it is *the* PARAMONY. There is no other. PARAMONY is simply the name given to this book.

A document which identifies similar passages contained in two or more writings is called a PARALLEL because it "parallels" passages in one writing with similar passages in the others.

A document which arranges in chronological order incidents reported in two or more writings is called a HARMONY becauses it "harmonizes" the incidents into a single non—conflicting choronological sequence.

This book is designed to PARALLEL and to HARMONIZE the various incidents, teachings and quotations reported in both *The URANTIA Book* and The BIBLE.

The title of this work, "PARAMONY," is a word coined from parts of the two words which signify these two major functions: "PARA" to signify its function as a PARA—llel, and "MONY" to signify its function as a har—MONY. By joining the two halves, we have PARA as the beginning and MONY as the ending, hence: PARAMONY.

This book, by whatever name, is designed to facilitate comparison of similar passages and materials found in both *The URANTIA Book* and The BIBLE.

   *It tells where material covered in one book can be found in the other.

   *It arranges in sequential order events reported in a different order in both books, or reported in one book but not the other.

   *As part of this process it displays in a chronological order various events in the life of Jesus, and places in context various statements of Jesus, which are reported by topic and in fragments in the four Gospels.

   *And it also reflects many parallel Bible passages and quotations for better study of The BIBLE.

In basic form the PARAMONY is a cross—reference between passages in *The URANTIA Book* and The BIBLE. Because of its format, it is also a cross—reference between many Bible passages.

*If information in *The URANTIA Book* also appears in The BIBLE, the PARAMONY will cite all relevant Bible references to it. Citations to Bible passages are contained in Sections I and II of the PARAMONY. The absence of a citation in Section I or II of a particular line of *The URANTIA Book* indicates that matters covered in the absent line do not appear in The BIBLE.

*If information in The BIBLE also appears in *The URANTIA Book* the PARAMONY will cite all relevant URANTIA Book references to it. Citations to URANTIA Book passages can be found in Sections III and IV of the PARAMONY. The absence of a citation in Section III or IV of any verse of The BIBLE indicates that matters covered in the absent verse do not appear in *The URANTIA Book.*

*As an intended by—product, the technique employed has pro—duced five separate "Harmonies" of the Four Gospels of the New Testament, each using a different document as its "source" or "base". These are so useful and significant that they are given a special format. See Sections II and III of the PARAMONY.

*When a passage in *The URANTIA Book* appears at more than one place in The BIBLE, all such places are shown. By this technique, Sections III and IV of the PARAMONY have been made to provide a valuable cross—reference to similar passages within The BIBLE as well as similar passages within *The URANTIA Book.*

II: USES FOR THE PARAMONY

A. AS A PARALLEL:

The PARAMONY will be used most frequently to determine whether or not a passage contained in either *The URANTIA Book* or The BIBLE is also contained in the other book and, if so, where it is located in the other. This is done by the following steps.

1. Select the passage in which you are interested from either book.

2. Determine the correct citation of the selected passage as used in the PARAMONY. (See III, below.)

3.	Enter the PARAMONY by locating the citation in the proper Section (I, II, III or IV).

    a.	For citations from *The URANTIA Book*, use Section I or II and look under the first column.

    b.	For citations from any of the four Gospels, use Section III, find the proper Book and look under the first column.

    c.	For citations from the remainder of The BIBLE, use Section IV, find the proper Book, and look under the first column.

4.	If the citation of the passage does _not_ appear in the PARAMONY at the place indicated above, the matter is _not_ covered in the other book. Your inquiry has been answered.

5.	If the citation of the passage *appears* in the PARAMONY, the matter _is_ contained in the other book. The citation(s) to the other book will appear in column(s) to the right. Again, your inquiry has been answered.

6.	Using the PARAMONY citations, look up the cited passages in the other book and read them.

The foregoing steps should reveal all the parallel passages between *The URANTIA Book* and the BIBLE which are known to the author at the time of publication.

Sections III and IV also contain parallel passages from different places in The BIBLE which are useful for Bible study without refer—ring to *The URANTIA Book*.

B:	AS A HARMONY:

The PARAMONY will also be used to indicate the order or sequence of events recounted in both *The URANTIA Book* and The BIBLE.

Each book is generally assumed to present events in chronological order (with notable exceptions), yet some events appear in a different order in one book than in the other. If we postulate that *The URANTIA Book* presents matters in proper chronology, Sections I and II rearrange the order of appearance of the same matters in The BIBLE. Conversely, if we postulate that matters are reported in proper chronology in The BIBLE, Sections III and IV rearrange the order of appearance of the same matters in *The URANTIA Book*.

This characteristic is particulaly useful in studying the chronology of events and teachings in the life of Jesus. Sections II and III of the PARAMONY are specially formatted to "harmonize" the life and teachings of Jesus. Section II harmonizes them by using *The URANTIA Book* as the information or data base (as having the correct chronology); Section III harmonizes them four times, using each of the four Gospels as a separate data base.

It should be noted that the PARAMONY is an extremely useful Bible study resource without reference to *The URANTIA Book*.

C: TO CLASSIFY CROSS-REFERENCES:

Cross-references between matters reported in two or more books are of interest for several different reasons. Each book may report the same incident or teaching, although not necessarily in the same language. Or one may quote from or refer to the other. Or each may treat common matters in such a way as to reinforce, contradict or modify the meaning of the other. Thus, not all cross-references have the same purpose. It is often helpful to know why a cross-reference has been made.

The PARAMONY attempts to classify each cross-reference so that the reader may determine why it has been included and decide its value or interest before looking it up in the "other" book. The three classes are:

a. SAME: both books recite the same incident. This class-ification is usually of high interest, and is indicated by underlining in bold type the citation of the "other" book. In Sections I and II, Bible passages, only, are underlined.

Examples: Ps 23:1-6; or 15:10-22.

In Sections III and IV, *The URANTIA Book* passages, only, are underlined.

Example: 1905: 3-6.

b. REFER: one book quotes from, or refers to an incident contained in, the other. This classification is considered to be of intermediate interest, and is indicated by citing the "other" book in a bold type, and with no underlining.

Examples: **He 11:10-13, 16: 8-11 or 1620: 1-10**

c.   COMPARE: one book relates matter which, although not the same as the other, is significant to reinforce, modify or contradict the other.   This classification is often of the least interest, and is shown by citing the "other" book in lighter type.

Examples: Ge 17: 1, 9:17-28 or 1968: 5-14

It is hoped that, by classifying all entries and by printing the citiations to "other" books in distinctive type, the PARAMONY will be more useful.   This allows the user to determine which class(es) of cross—references to pursue.

It should be noted that some classifications are a matter of opinion. The classifications employed in the PARAMONY reflect only opinions of the author, and are not authoritative.

D.   TO LOCATE SIMILAR PASSAGES IN A SINGLE BOOK:

Similar passages in The BIBLE are contained in Sections III and IV. For each passage cited in the first column the PARAMONY will also cite parallel Bible passages (if any) in the column(s) to the right of citations to *The URANTIA Book*.

Some similar passages in *The URANTIA Book* can be found by locating, in Section I or II, a Bible reference to the passage, and then looking at the Bible reference in Section III or IV.   Similar passages in *The URANTIA Book* (if any) will appear under the proper column.

III: HOW TO CITE PASSAGES

A.   THE NEED FOR PROPER CITATIONS OF PASSAGES

The PARAMONY contains no text.   It operates solely by the use of citations.   In order to use it, one must convert a passage in the book one is reading (*The URANTIA Book* or The BIBLE) into a citation, locate such citation in the PARAMONY, find one or more corresponding citations to the other book, and then convert the latter citations into passages by locating them in the other book.

The user is interested only in the passages; but must use citations to get from passages in one book into relevant passages of the other. It is therefore necessary to employ the correct citations.

B.   CITATIONS OF PASSAGES IN *The URANTIA Book*

Passages in *The URANTIA Book* are cited by page and line, separated by a colon: [PAGE:LINE(S)] 0000:00—00.

> Each PAGE has 1 to 4 digits: 1 (p. 1) to 2097 (p. 2097).
> Each LINE has 1 or 2 digits: 1 (line 1) to 50 (line 50).
>
> > Example: 1222:14—15 means page 1222, lines 14 and 15.
>
> When a passage is on more than one line, the first and last lines are separated by a dash (—).
>
> > Example: 1056:45—1057:12 means page 1056, line 45, through page 1057, line 12.

Lines are counted down from the top. All lines are counted except those on which the page number appears.   For illustration, see Figures 1 and 2.

C: CITATIONS OF PASSAGES IN THE BIBLE

Passages in The BIBLE are cited by book, chapter and verse.   Books are abbreviated, and separated by a space from chapters.   Chapters are separated by a colon from verses: [BOOK CHAPTER:VERSE(S)] BK 00:00—00.

> Each BOOK has been assigned a two—letter abbreviation used throughout the PARAMONY. In addition, when the name of a book includes a number, a single arabic number is added. See Figures 3 and 4 for a complete list of book abbreviations.
>
> CHAPTERS and VERSES are numbered as they appear in the King James version for canonical books and in the Catholic

Bible for apocryphal books.

Example: Ge 17:1–12 means Genesis, 17th chapter,
1st through 12th verses.

When a passage contains more than one verse, the first and
last verses are cited, divided by a dash (–).

Example: Mt 7:9–8:15 means Matthew, 7th chapter,
9th verse, through 8th chapter, 15th verse.

Citations to separate verses in the same chapter are divided
by a comma and no space.

Examples: Ex 5:6,48 means Exodus, 5th Chapter, 6th
and 48th verses; and Mk 16:12,18–24 means Mark, 16th
chapter, 12th verse and verses 18 through 24.

Citations to separate chapters in the same book are divided
by a semicolon, with or without a space.

Example: Da 5:8; 11:12 means Daniel, 5th chapter,
8th verse and 11th chapter, 12th verse.

In Sections II and III the four Gospels (Matthew, Mark, Luke and
John) are cited in their respective columns by chapter and verse,
only. No book is shown. In all other places, the above format
is used.

IV: HOW TO READ CITATIONS

Citations in the PARAMONY are arranged in columns and in lines.
Columns represent documents. Lines represent parallel passages. The
first (or left) column represents the source document from which a
passage is taken. In Section I, the third column also represents the
source document. All other columns cite relevant passages in other
documents. When the number of relevant passages exceeds the space
available on one line, additional lines are used as needed.

If difficulty is experienced in determining which citations are on
which line or column, rotate the page and look along the line or
column. The ambiguity will clear up.

COUNTING LINES CORRECTLY

HELPFUL SUGGESTION: It helps in locating the correct line to make neat marks on the outer margin of the pages: a period or very short mark on lines numbered 5, 15, 25, etc.; and a slightly longer mark on lines numbered 10, 20, 30, etc. On pages marked in this manner it is easy to locate any line without having to "number" the lines.

On pages numbered at the TOP, neither the heading nor the number is counted as a line. The "first" line (line 1) is the line immediately below the number. Each line containing printing, no matter how short, is counted. Spaces between lines, no matter how wide, are ignored. See the following illustrations:

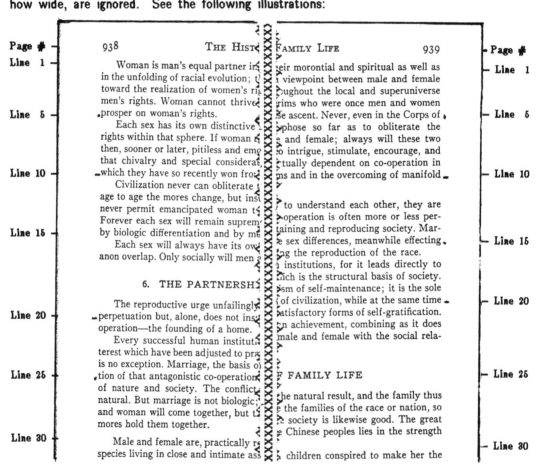

FIGURE 1: Line Counting on Pages Numbered at the TOP.*

*Pages from **The URANTIA Book**, copyrighted in 1955 by URANTIA® Foundation, 533 Diversey Parkway, Chicago, IL 60614.

On pages numbered at the BOTTOM, every line above the number is counted as a line, including those showing the number and name of the Paper. Each line containing printing, no matter how short, is counted. Spaces between lines, no matter how wide, are ignored. See the following illustration:

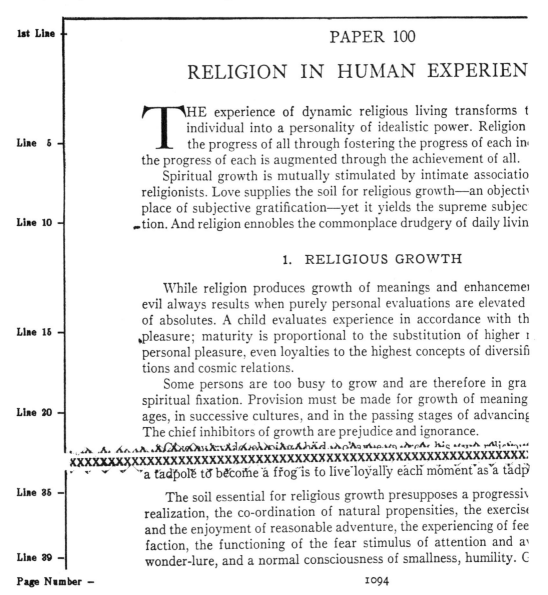

FIGURE 2: **Line Counting on Pages Numbered at the BOTTOM.***

*Pages from The URANTIA Book, copyrighted in 1955 by URANTIA® Foundation, 533 Diversey Parkway, Chicago, IL 60614.

Figure 3: ABBREVIATIONS for BOOKS of The BIBLE
(Key to Meaning of Abbreviations)

Ac	= Acts of the Apostles	3Jo	= Third John
Am	= Amos	Js	= Joshua
As	= Assumption of Moses	1Ki	= First Kings
Ba	= Baruch	2Ki	= Second Kings
BD	= Bel & the Dragon	La	= Lamentations of Jeremiah
Ca	= Canticles, also called Song of Solomon	Le	= Leviticus
1Ch	= First Chronicles	Lk	= Gospel of Luke
2Ch	= Second Chronicles	1Mc	= First Maccabees
Cl	= Colossians	2Mc	= Second Maccabees
1Co	= First Corinthians	Mi	= Micah
2Co	= Second Corinthians	Mk	= Gospel of Mark
Da	= Daniel	Ml	= Malachi
De	= Deuteronomy	Mt	= Gospel of Matthew
Ec	= Ecclesiastes	Na	= Nahum
1Ed	= First Esdras	Ne	= Nehemiah
2Ed	= Second Esdras	Nu	= Numbers
Ek	= Ezekiel	Ob	= Obadiah
En	= First Enoch	1Pe	= First Peter
Ep	= Ephesians	2Pe	= Second Peter
Es	= Esther	Ph	= Philemon
Ex	= Exodus	PM	= Prayer of Manasseh
Ez	= Ezra	Pp	= Philippians
Ga	= Galatians	Ps	= Psalms
Ge	= Genesis	Pv	= Proverbs
He	= Hebrews	Re	= Revelation
Hg	= Haggai	Ro	= Romans
Hk	= Habakkuk	Ru	= Ruth
Ho	= Hosea	1Sa	= First Samuel
Is	= Isaiah	2Sa	= Second Samuel
Ja	= James	Si	= Sirach, also called Ecclesiasticus
Jb	= Job		
Jd	= Jude	1Th	= First Thessalonians
Je	= Jeremiah	2Th	= Second Thessalonians
Jg	= Judges	Ti	= Titus
Jh	= Jonah	1Tm	= First Timothy
Jl	= Joel	2Tm	= Second Timothy
Jn	= Gospel of John	To	= Tobit
1Jo	= First John	Wi	= Wisdom of Solomon
2Jo	= Second John	Zc	= Zechariah
		Zp	= Zephaniah

Figure 4: ABBREVIATIONS of BOOKS of the BIBLE
(Abbreviation Assigned to Each Book)

Acts of the Apostles	= Ac	Jude	= Jd
Amos	= Am	Judges	= Jg
Assumption of Moses	= As	Kings, First	=1Ki
Baruch	= Ba	Kings, Second	=2Ki
Bel & the Dragon	= BD	Lamentations of Jeremiah	= La
Canticles	= Ca	Leviticus	= Le
Chronicles, First	=1Ch	Luke, Gospel of	= Lk
Chronicles, Second	=2Ch	Maccabees, First	=1Mc
Colossians	= Cl	Maccabees. Second	=2Mc
Corinthians, First	=1Co	Malachi	= Ml
Corinthians, Second	=2Co	Mark, Gospel of	= Mk
Daniel	= Da	Matthew, Gospel of	= Mt
Deuteronomy	= De	Micah	= Mi
Ecclesiastes	= Ec	Nahum	= Na
Ecclesiasticus	= Si	Nehemiah	= Ne
Enoch, First	= En	Numbers	= Nu
Ephesians	= Ep	Obadiah	= Ob
Esdras, First	=1Ed	Peter, First	=1Pe
Esdras, Second	=2Ed	Peter, Second	=2Pe
Esther	= Es	Philemon	= Ph
Exodus	= Ex	Philippians	= Pp
Ezekiel	= Ek	Prayer of Manasseh	= PM
Ezra	= Ez	Proverbs	= Pv
Galatians	= Ga	Psalms	= Ps
Genesis	= Ge	Revelation	= Re
Habakkuk	= Hk	Romans	= Ro
Haggai	= Hg	Ruth	= Ru
Hebrews	= He	Samuel, First	=1Sa
Hosea	= Ho	Samuel, Second	=2Sa
Isaiah	= Is	Sirach	= Si
James	= Ja	Song of Solomon	= Ca
Jeremiah	= Je	Thessalonians, First	=1Th
Job	= Jb	Thessalonians, Second	=2Th
Joel	= Jl	Timothy, First	=1Tm
John, Gospel of	= Jn	Timothy, Second	=2Tm
John, First	=1Jo	Titus	= Ti
John, Second	=2Jo	Tobit	= To
John, Third	=3Jo	Wisdom of Solomon	= Wi
Jonah	= Jh	Zechariah	= Zc
Joshua	= Js	Zephaniah	= Zp

INDEX

to CITATIONS in the PARAMONY

(See INDEX to SECTION FOUR on next page.)

INDEX To SECTION FOUR

Citations from the remainder of The BIBLE*
(including the Apocrypha & Pseudepigrapha)
*New Testament Books shown in Italics.

SECTION ONE

Parts I, II, and III of *The URANTIA Book* Cross Referenced to The BIBLE.

* * * * *

FOREWORD

The URANTIA Book Page and Line	The BIBLE Book, Chapter, Verse	The URANTIA Book Page and Line	The BIBLE Book, Chapter, Verse
8:42	Mt 6:10;7:21;12:50 Mt 26:39,42,44 Mk 3:35;14:36-39 Lk 8:21;11:2;22:42	8:42	Jn 4:34;5:30;6:38 Jn 7:17;14:23-24 Jn 15:10,14;17:4

PAPER 1: The Universal Father

21: 8-10	Ge 1:1 Ne 9:6 2Ki 19:15 Ps 115:15-16 Is 37:16 Lk 19:50	22:15-16 22:28-30	(Same as 21:30-31) Ps 68:5;89:26 Ps 103:13
21:10-11	Ps 33:6	22:40	Ac 17:28
21:11-12	Ps 104:2	23:14	Ja 1:17
21:18-20	Is 45:18	23:14-15	Ac 17:25 Ro 6:23
21:30	Is 57:15	23:24	Mt 5:16,48;6:1-9
21:30-31	Ge 17:1 Le 19:2 De 18:13 Mt 5:48 2Co 13:11 Ja 1:4		Mt 7:11,21;11:25 Mt 16:17;18:35;23:9 Mk 11:25-26 Lk 10:21;11:2

The URANTIA Book Page and Line	The BIBLE Book, Chapter, Verse	The URANTIA Book Page and Line	The BIBLE Book, Chapter, Verse
23:27-29	Ge 46:3 Ex 3:14	27:40-42	Is 40:12
23:31	Ge 21:33	27:42-43	Is 40:22
	Is 40:28 Ps 90:2	27:43-45	Is 40:26
23:31-32	Is 57:15	27:45-46	Ro 1:20
	2Ed 8:20	28: 5- 6	Jn 3:16 Ro 5:6-21
24: 9	Ps 100:3		He 9:11-20;13:12
24:10	Jb 23:3		2Co 5:14-21
24:11	Ps 143:10		1Jo 4:9
25: 1- 2	Jn 4:24	28: 6	Nu 14:8 De 10:15
25: 3- 4	1Tm 1:17		Pv 8:31
25: 4	Ac 17:28-29	28:12-13	Jn 14:9
25: 6	Ge 1:26-27;9:6	28:14-15	Mt 11:27 Lk 10:22
25:10-11	Jb 9:11		Jn 1:18;6:45-46
25:17-18	Ex 33:20		Jn 8:26;12:49-50
25:17-18	Ex 33:20		Jn 14:7-9,20
26:17	Jn 4:24	28:19-20	Jn 14:10-11
26:17	1Jo 4:8,16	28:20	Jn 1:1;5:18;10:30
26:27	1Co 3:16; 6:19		Jn 10:38;14:9-11,20
	2Co 6:16		Jn 17:11,21-22
26:29	Je 31:3	28:28-31	Jn 10:14
	Jn 3:14-15;6:44		1Jo 4:19
	Jn 8:28;12:32	28:29	Jn 14:21
26:29-31	Re 3:20		1Co 13:12
26:36-37	Ge 3:19 Ec 3:20	28:30-31	Ja 2:23
26:36-38	Ec 12:7	29:33	Is 63:9
27: 8	2Ch 19:7	29:42	Ac 17:28
	Ac 10:34	30:40	Jn 4:24
	Jb 34:19	31: 2- 3	Mt 16:16-17
	Ro 2:11		Jn 6:57
	Ga 2:6 Ep 6:9	31:36	De 4:35,39;6:4
27:21-22	Ps 94:9	31:36	Mk 12:29,32
27:38-39	1Tm 6:16		1Co 8:4-6 Ro 3:30
			Ga 3:20 Ep 4:6 Ja 2:19

PAPER 2:   The Nature of GOD

33:35	Jb 37:23	33:38	1Ki 8:12 2Ch 6:1
33:35-36	Ps 77:19	33:39	Jb 5:9; 9:10
33:36	Ps 147:5; 145:3	33:39-34: 2	Jb 36:26

The URANTIA Book Page and Line	The BIBLE Book, Chapter, Verse	The URANTIA Book Page and Line	The BIBLE Book, Chapter, Verse
34: 2- 3	De 10:4 1Ki 8:27	37:25-26	Ob 16
	2Ch 2:6; 6:18	38: 8- 9	Ps 86:15
	Ne 9:6 Ps 148:4		Ps 145:8
34: 3- 4	Ro 11:33	38: 9-10	Jl 2:32 Ac 2:21
34: 5	1Co 8:6 1Pe 4:19		Ro 10:13
34: 6- 7	Is 44:6	38:10	Is 55:7
	Re 1:8,11,17	38:10-11	Ps 103:17
	Re 21:6; 22:18	38:11-12	1Ch 16:34,41
34: 8	2Sa 22:31		2Ch 5:13; 7:3-6
34: 8- 9	1Sa 29:11		Ps 107:1;118:1-4
34:12:13	Re 1:18		Ps 136:1-26
34:13-14	Mt 19:26	38:12-13	Je 9:24
	Mk 10:27; 14:36	38:13-14	La 3:33
	Lk 1:37; 18:27	38:14	2Co 1:3
34:26	Is 46:10	38:45	1Jo 4:8,16
34:30-31	Is 57:15	39: 1- 2	Mt 5:45
	2Ed 8:20	39: 4- 5	Jn 16:27
34:32-33	Ex 3:14	39: 7	Mt 16:24-25
35:28-29	Ac 17:28		Mk 8:34-35
35:36	Jn 5:26		Lk 9:23-24
35:37	1Jo 5:11		Jn 3:15-16
35:38	Ac 17:25		Re 22:17
35:38-39	Ml 3:6	39: 7- 8	1Tm 2:4
35:40-41	Ja 1:17	39: 8- 9	2Pe 3:9
35:42-43	Is 46:10	39:12-13	He 12:10
35:43-44	Ep 3:11	39:14	Is 63:9
35:47-36:1	Ec 3:14	39:16	Is 55:7
36: 1	Ge 6:6 Ex 32:14	39:16-18	Is 43:25
	Nu 23:19	39:18-19	Is 56:5 Jn 1:12
	Am 7:3,6 Zc 8:14		Ro 8:14-17
	1Sa 15:29		Ga 3:26; 4:6
36: 3- 4	Ps 90:4		1Jo 3:1
36:39	Ps 145:17	39:38	Ps 36:37+
36:40	Ek 14:23		Je 31:3
36:40-41	Ps 19:9	41: 1	Ro 2:4
36:43-44	2Ch 19:7 Jb 34:19	41: 2	Ja 1:17
	Ac 10:24 Ro 2:11	41: 3	Na 1:7 De 33:27
	Ga 2:6 Ep 6:9	41: 3- 4	Ex 34:6
37: 1- 2	Jb 4:8 Ga 6:7	41: 5	Ps 34:8 Na 1:7

The URANTIA Book Page and Line	The BIBLE Book, Chapter, Verse	The URANTIA Book Page and Line	The BIBLE Book, Chapter, Verse
41: 6	Ps 111:4;145:8	41: 6- 7	Ps 147:3
41: 6	Ps 68:20	41: 7- 8	Ps 46:1

PAPER 3: The Attributes of GOD

44: 5- 6	Jn 3:15-16	48:46	Jb 36:4
	Jn 5:24-25;39-40	48:46	Pv 15:3
	Jn 6:10,47;10:10	48:47-49:1	Mt 10:29 Lk 12:6
	Jn 11:25-26	49: 1- 2	Mt 10:30 Lk 12:7
	1Jo 5:11-12	49: 2- 3	Ps 147:4
44:26-27	Ex 20:4 De 5:8	49: 6- 8	Ex 3:7
	Js 2:11	49: 8-10	Ps 33:13-14
44:27-28	Ps 139:7	49:10-11	Jb 23:10
44:29-30	Je 23:23-24	49:11-13	Ps 139:2-3
44:31	Ep 1:23; 4:10	49:13-14	He 4:13
44:32	1Co 12:6	49:15	Ps 103:14
44:33-34	1Ki 8:27 De 10:14	49:16-17	Mt 6:8 Is 65:24
	2Ch 2:6; 6:18	50:19	2Ed 8:20 Is 57:15
	Ne 9:6 Ps 148:4	50:32-33	Ge 1:26-27;9:6
44:34	Cl 3:11 Ep 4:6	50:34	1Jo 4:8,16
45: 3- 5	Ps 19:6	51: 4- 5	Ps 24:1
45: 6- 7	1Jo 4:13		1Co 10:26,28
45:11-12	Je 23:23	51: 5	Da 2:21
45:14	1Jo 4:4; 5:19	51: 5- 6	Da 4:17,25,32
45:14-15	1Jo 4:16		Da 5:21
45:34-35	Cl 1:16-17	51:10-11	Jn 10:29
46:32-33	2Ch 19:7 Ac 10:34	51:15-16	Ep 4:6
	Ro 2:11 Ep 6:9	51:16-17	Cl 1:17
46:37	Re 19:6	52: 1- 4	Mt 6:10;7:21;12:50
46:38-39	Da 4:35		Mt 26:39,42,44
46:40	Ro 13:1		Mk 3:35;14:36-39
46:42	Mt 19:26		Lk 8:21;11:2;22:42
	Mk 10:27; 14:36		Jn 4:34;5:30;6:38
	Lk 1:37; 18:27		Jn 7:17;14:23-24
46:46	Ja 4:12		Jn 15:10,14
47:10	Jb 28:26;38:25	52: 1- 4	1Co 12:12-27
48:43	1Jo 3:20	53:24	Is 63:9
48:45-46	Jb 37:16		

PAPER 4:   GOD's Relation to the Universe

The URANTIA Book Page and Line	The BIBLE Book, Chapter, Verse
55: 1	1Co 1:9; 10:13
55: 1	Ps 119:172
55: 1- 2	Ps 36:5
55: 2- 4	Ps 119:89-90
55: 4	1Pe 4:19
55: 4	Ps 89:2; 119:86
55: 6- 7	De 33:27
55: 7- 8	Ps 91:1
55: 8- 9	Ps 121:4
55: 9-10	Ro 8:28
55:10-11	Ps 34:15
	1Pe 3:12
55:12	He 1:3
55:12	He 1:3
55:14	Ne 9:6
55:15-16	Jb 26:7
55:24-25	Ps 104:30
55:26-27	Jb 26:7
57:36-38	Ex 20:5; 34:14
	De 4:24;5:9;6:15

The URANTIA Book Page and Line	The BIBLE Book, Chapter, Verse
57:44-45	Ex 22:24+
	Nu 11:33+
	De 29:27-28
58: 6	Ge 6:6
	Ex 32:14
	Nu 23:19
	1Sa 15:29,35
	Am 7:3,6
	Zc 8:14
58:35	Ml 3:6 Ja 1:17
59:42-43	Jn 1:12-13
	1Jo 5:4
60:15	Is 28:2; 29:6
60:15-16	Na 1:2-6
60:16	1Ch 13:10
	Ac 5:1-10
60:16-17	Ek 5:16-17
60:17	Ge 6:17
60:31-32	He 9:22

PAPER 5:   GOD's Relation to the Individual

64:33	Ps 110:1
	Mt 22:43-44
	Mk 12:35-36;16:19
	Lk 20:42-44
	Ro 8:34 Cl 3:1
	1Pe 3:22 He 10:12
64:34	Jn 1:18
65: 5	Mt 7:20 Lk 6:44
66:46-47	Lk 2:14
	Jn 14:27; 16:33

66:46-47	Pp 4:7
67:31	1Ch 28:9
	Je 9:24; 31:34
67:32	Pp 3:8
	2Pe 1:8; 3:18
67:32-33	Is 56:5 Jn 1:12
	Ro 8:14-17
	Ga 3:26; 4:6
	1Jo 3:1-2

PAPER 6: The Eternal Son

The URANTIA Book Page and Line	The BIBLE Book, Chapter, Verse	The URANTIA Book Page and Line	The BIBLE Book, Chapter, Verse
73:37	Ps 2:7 Jn 1:14	74:18-19	Jn 17:5
	Jn 1:18;3:16-18	74:42-43	Jn 14:9
	He 1:5; 5:5	75:25,35	1Jo 4:8,16
	1Jo 4:9 Ac 13:33	75:47	1Jo 4:8,16
74: 4	Jn 4:24	78:15-16	Ge 1:26
74:10-11	Jn 1:1; 5:18	78:32-33,42	1Co 13:12
	Jn 10:30,38	79: 3	Ro 8:27
	Jn 14:9-11,20	80: 3- 5	Jn 1:1; 5:18
	Jn 17:11,21-22		Jn 10:30,38
74:11-12	Jn 1:3 He 1:2		Jn 14:9-11,20
74:14-16	1Jo 1:1		Jn 17:11,21-22

PAPER 7: Relation of Universal Son to the Universe

The URANTIA Book Page and Line	The BIBLE Book, Chapter, Verse	The URANTIA Book Page and Line	The BIBLE Book, Chapter, Verse
81:37-38	Is 40:12	86: 3	Ge 17:1 Le 19:2
82:24-29	Je 31:3		De 18:3 Mt 5:48
	Jn 3:14-15;6:44	86: 3	2Co 13:11 Ja 1:4
	Jn 8:28; 12:32	86:11-12	Ge 17:1 Le 19:2
84:12-20	Je 31:3		De 18:13 Mt 5:48
	Jn 3:14-15;6:44		1Co 13:11 Ja 1:4
	Jn 8:28; 12:32	86:15-16	Jn 14:6
84:46	1Co 13:1	87:38-39	Jb 38:7
85:18-19	Ge 1:26	89:17-18	Jn 14:6 He 10:12

PAPER 8: The Infinite Spirit

The URANTIA Book Page and Line	The BIBLE Book, Chapter, Verse	The URANTIA Book Page and Line	The BIBLE Book, Chapter, Verse
93:46	Mt 11:27 Lk 10:22	96: 4- 5	Jd 24
	Jn 1:18; 6:45-46	96:10	Ge 1:2
	Jn 8:26; 16:6	96:11-14	Jn 4:22
	Jn 12:49-50	96:28	1Co 2:10
	Jn 14:6-9,20	96:30-31	1Co 12:11
	Jn 17:6,25-26	96:32	Ro 15:30
	He 10:12	96:32-33	Ep 4:30
94:12	Jn 1:14	96:36-37	Re 2:7,11,17,29
95:21-23	1Pe 3:12 Ps 34:15		Re 3:6,13,22
95:39	Is 48:16	96:37-38	Ro 8:26-27
95:39-40	Ge 1:2 Jb 33:4	96:39	Ro 8:14

6

PAPER 9:   Relation of the Infinite Spirit
to the Universe

The URANTIA Book Page and Line	The BIBLE Book, Chapter, Verse
98:32	Cl 1:17

PAPER 10:   The Paradise Trinity

The URANTIA Book Page and Line	The BIBLE Book, Chapter, Verse	The URANTIA Book Page and Line	The BIBLE Book, Chapter, Verse
108:10-15	Mt 8:29 Ac 2:33	110:40	Ge 1:26
	1Co 12:4-6	111: 4	Jn 1:1-2,14
	1Jo 5:7		Re 19:13
109:22	Ps 2:7	115:15-18	Mt 28:19 Ac 2:33
	Jn 1:14,18		1Co 12:4-6
	Jn 3:16,18		1Jo 5:7
	Ac 13:33	115:16	De 4:35,39; 6:4
	He 1:5; 5:5		Mk 12:29,32
	1Jo 4:9		Ro 3:30 Ga 3:20
109:28-33	Mt 11:27 Lk 10:22		1Co 8:4-6 Ep 4:6
	Jn 1:18;6:45-46		Ja 2:19
	Jn 8:26;12:49-50	115:19	Is 44:6
	Jn 14:7-9,20		Re 1:8,11,17
	Jn 17:6,25-26		Re 21:6; 22:18

PAPER 11:   The Eternal Isle of Paradise

The URANTIA Book Page and Line	The BIBLE Book, Chapter, Verse	The URANTIA Book Page and Line	The BIBLE Book, Chapter, Verse
118:29-30	Is 57:15	121:47-122:2	Is 64:4 1Co 2:9
120:41-43	Jn 14:2	125:29-30	Cl 1:17

PAPER 12:   The Universe of Universes

The URANTIA Book Page and Line	The BIBLE Book, Chapter, Verse	The URANTIA Book Page and Line	The BIBLE Book, Chapter, Verse
137:43	Ml 3:6 Ja 1:17	139: 8- 9	Ac 17:28
138: 1- 2	Ml 3:6 Ja 1:17	139:26	Jn 4:24
138:22	2Ch 19:7 Jb 34:19	139:43-44	Je 31:3
	Ac 10:34 Ro 2:11		Jn 3:14-15;6:44
	Ga 2:6 Ep 6:9		Jn 8:28;12:32
139: 7- 8	Ac 17:27	140:44	Jn 4:24
139: 8	1Jo 4:12		

PAPER 13: The Sacred Spheres of Paradise

The URANTIA Book Page and Line	The BIBLE Book, Chapter, Verse	The URANTIA Book Page and Line	The BIBLE Book, Chapter, Verse
144:30-31	Jn 1:18	148:46-47	Ac 7:55-56
147: 3	He 1:14	149: 3- 4	Ge 17:1 Le 19:2
148:45-46	Jn 1:18		De 18:13 Mt 5:48
			2Co 3:11 Ja 1:4

PAPER 14: The Central and Divine Universe

153:28-29	Ps 90:4 2Pe 3:8	153:37-40	Jb 23:12-14

PAPER 15: The Seven Superuniverses

PAPER 16: The Seven Master Spirits

184: 2	Re 1:4; 3:1 Re 4:5; 5:6	191:40-43	Ro 15:5 1Co 1:10 Pp 1:27;2:2;4:2
189: 9-16	Re 1:4; 3:3		1Pe 3:8; 4:1
	Re 4:5; 5:6	195:44	1Co 13:32
191:34-40	1Co 2:16 Pp 2:5	196:10	Jn 14:7-9

PAPER 17: The Seven Supreme Spirit Groups

PAPER 18: The Supreme Trinity Personalities

209:13	Da 7:9,13,22		

PAPER 19: The Co-ordinate Trinity-origin Beings

PAPER 20: The Paradise Sons of God

223: 8- 9	Jn 1:2	223:18-21	Jn 1:2
223:14	Jn 1:2	227: 8- 9	Jn 1:18

The URANTIA Book Page and Line	The BIBLE Book, Chapter, Verse	The URANTIA Book Page and Line	The BIBLE Book, Chapter, Verse
227:18-27	Mt 24:27-37,42	229:46	Mt 10:27;20:22
	Mt 25:13 Jn 14:3		Mt 26:39
	Mk 13:32-33		Mk 10:38;14:36
227:29-34	Jn 1:1; 5:18		Lk 18:27;22:42
	Jn 10:30,38	232:33-35	Ps 2:7
	Jn 14:9-11,20		Jn 1:14,18;3:16
	Jn 17:11,21-22		Ac 13:33 1Jo 4:9
227:33	Jn 1:14		He 1:5; 5:5
228:24-29	Jn 3:16	232:42-44	Mt 11:27 Mk 10:22
	Ro 5:6-21		Jn 1:18; 6:45-46
	2Co 5:14-21		Jn 8:26;12:49-50
	He 9:11-28;13:12		Jn 14:7-9;20
	1Jo 4:9		Jn 17:6,25-26
229:24	Jn 14:9	233: 4- 5	(Same as 232:42-44)

PAPER 21:   The Paradise Creator Sons

234:2	Ep 3:9	239:45-46	Cl 3:1 He 10:12
	Cl 1:15-16		1Pe 3:22
234: 3- 4	Jn 1:3 He 1:2	240: 7	Jn 19:30
234: 7	Jn 1:14,18; 3:16	240:11-12	1Tm 6:15
	Jn 3:18 Ac 13:33	240:11-12	Re 17:14; 19:16
	He 1:5; 5:5	240:14	Mt 28:18
	1Jo 4:9 Ps 2:7	241:41-42	Ek 11:19;36:26-27
235: 6	(Same as 234:7)		Jl 2:28 Lk 24:19
235:37-38	Jn 1:3 He 1:2		Jn 14:16-18,26
239:45-46	Ps 110:1 Mt 22:44		Jn 15:26;16:7,13-14
	Mk 12:36; 16:19		Ac 2:2-4,6-18
	Lk 20:42 Ro 8:34	242:24-26	Jn 14:6

PAPER 22:   The Trinitized Sons of God

PAPER 23:   The Solitary Messengers

PAPER 24:   Higher Personalities of the Infinite Spirit

| 269:45-47 | Is 64:4 1Co 2:9 |

9

PAPER 25: The Messenger Hosts of Space

The URANTIA Book Page and Line	The BIBLE Book, Chapter, Verse	The URANTIA Book Page and Line	The BIBLE Book, Chapter, Verse
274:33-35	Mt 25:21,23 Lk 19:17	283:27	Ge 2:18

PAPER 26: Ministering Spirits of the Central Universe

285: 2	He 1:14	291:26-27	Mt 19:26
286:40	Jn 4:32		Mk 10:27; 14:36
290:20	Ge 17:1 Le 19:2		Lk 1:37;18:27
	De 18:13 Mt 5:48	295:10-11	(Same as 290:20)
	2Co 13:11 Ja 1:4	297: 5- 6	(Same as 290:20)

PAPER 27: Ministry of the Primary Supernaphim

299:40-42	Re 22:3-4	301:30-31	Ex 20:10 De 5:4
299:42-43	Re 22:5	301:42	2Co 3:2
299:44-46	Re 21:4	301:45	Pp 4:3 Re 20:12
300: 3	He 9:23		

PAPER 28: Ministering Spirits of the Superuniverses

310:43	Ja 1:5	316:39	Ac 20:35
311:12	Lk 9:55	316:40	Mt 19:30; 23:11
312: 2	Ex 30:25-32		Mt 20:16,26-27
313:31	Lk 9:55		Mk 9:35; 10:31
313:34	1Co 2:10		Mk 10:43-44
314:41-44	Da 7:9-10		Lk 9:48;13:30;14:11
315:24	Lk 19:12-26		Lk 18:14; 22:26
	Mt 25:14-28	317:10-11	Pv 16:32
316:17-18	Da 5:27	317:11	Ja 3:8

PAPER 29: The Universe Power Directors

PAPER 30: Personalities of the Grand Universe

The URANTIA Book Page and Line	The BIBLE Book, Chapter, Verse	The URANTIA Book Page and Line	The BIBLE Book, Chapter, Verse
341:11	Ep 4:8	341:46-47	Jn 14:2

PAPER 31: The Corps of Finality

348:21	Ge 17:1 Le 19:2	348:21	2Co 13:11
	De 18:13 Mt 5:48		Ja 1:4

PAPER 32: The Evolution of Local Universes

357:14-17	Jn 1:1-3	363:42	2Tm 2:19
359:31-32	Ge 1:26	365:29-31	2Tm 4:7
361:17-18	Jn 1:1; 5:18	365:32-33	Ek 11:19;36:26-27
	Jn 10:30,38		Jl 2:28 Lk 24:49
	Jn 14:9-11,20		Jn 14:16-18,25
	Jn 17:11,21-22		Jn 15:26;16:7,13-14
361:18-19	Jn 14:9		Ac 2:2-4,16-18
363:28-29	He 11:27		

PAPER 33: Administration of the Local Universe

366:15	Ps 2:7	366:15	1Jo 4:9
	Jn 1:14,18;	367: 5- 6	(Same as 1361:17-18)
	Jn 3:16,18	367:22	Mt 28:18
	Ac 13:33	368:45-46	Mt 28:18
	He 1:5; 5:5	370:19-20	Re 19:14

PAPER 34: The Local Universe Mother Spirit

375:28-29	Mt 28:18	378:29-34	Re 4:4,10;5:8,14
376:10-11	Ps 104:30	378:35-36	Re 4:5
376:20	Ge 2:7	378:41	Is 11:3
378:21-29	Re 1:4;3:1;4:5;5:6	378:42-43	Re 4:6-8
378:24-27	Is 11:2	379:36	Jl 2:28

11

The URANTIA Book Page and Line	The BIBLE Book, Chapter, Verse	The URANTIA Book Page and Line	The BIBLE Book, Chapter, Verse
379:36	(Same as 365:32-33)	381:27	Ep 3:19
380:33	Jn 3:5,8	381:27-28	Ro 8:14
380:36-37	Ti 3:5	381:37-38	Ro 8:16
380:39-40	Jn 6:63	381:44-45	Ga 5:22-23 Ep 5:9
380:40	2Co 3:6	382: 1- 3	Ro 14:17
380:43-44	1Th 1:5	382:11-14	Jn 14:16-18,26
381: 2- 3	1Co 3:16; 6:19		Jn 15:26
	2Co 6:16		Jn 16:7,13-14
381: 5- 9	Is 55:1 Mt 5:6	382:14	Jn 16:13
	Jn 4:10,13-14	382:46-383:2	Ro 8:2
	Jn 6:35; 7:37-38	383: 2	Jn 1:12-13
	Re 7:16-17		1Jo 5:4
381:24-25	Ep 3:16	383:17	Is 30:21

PAPER 35: The Local Universe Sons of God

389:27-28	Ge 14:18 He 7:1-2		

PAPER 36: The Life Carriers

401:31	Re 1:4;3:1;4:5;5:6	402:39	Is 11:2
401:40-42	Is 11:2	402:44	Is 11:2
402:23	Is 11:2	403:41-45	Jn 1:4
402:32,36	Is 11:2	404:17	Ge 2:7

PAPER 37: Personalities of the Local Universe

407:17-18	Ge 16:7+ Ex 3:2+	409:24	1Th 4:16
	Mt 1:20; 28:2	409:26	Jd 9
	Lk 1:11 Ac 5:19+	409:33	Ps 69:28
409:10	Mt 15:13 Jn 14:3	411: 5	Ge 17:1 Le 19:2
	Mt 24:27-37,42		De 18:13 Mt 5:48
	Mk 13:32-33		2Co 13:11 Ja 1:4

PAPER 38: Ministering Spirits of the Local Universe

The URANTIA Book Page and Line	The BIBLE Book, Chapter, Verse	The URANTIA Book Page and Line	The BIBLE Book, Chapter, Verse
418: 6- 7	Ps 110:1 Mt 22:44	419:33-34	2Pe 2:11
	Mk 12:36; 16:19	419:37-39	Re 19:10;22:8-9
	Lk 20:42 Ro 8:34	421:36-37	Mt 26:53
	Cl 3:1 He 10:12	421:44	Re 19:4
	1Pe 3:22	421:45	2Sa 5:10
418:18	Is 6:2,6		Ps 80:4,7,14,19
419:12-13	Mt 22:30 Mk 12:25	422: 2- 3	He 1:6
419:13-15	Lk 20:35-36	422: 4	2Th 1:7 Re 10:1
419:25	Mt 10:30 Lk 12:7		

PAPER 39:   The Seraphic Hosts

431:19	1Co 15:44	438:35-38	Ek 1:19-21;
435:45-46	Mt 16:19		Ek 10:16-17
437:11-12	Ge 3:8	438:41-43	Ek 1:4,22,27
437:32-33	Lk 2:14		Ek 10:9
437:38	Lk 2:14	439: 2- 3	Ek 1:4,13-14
438:23	Ex 25:20+	439: 6- 7	Ek 1:12; 10:19
	Is 6:2	441: 7	Ps 8:5
	Ek 10:5		He 2:7
438:27-30	Ek 1:6,11,23;10:21		

PAPER 40:   The Ascending Sons of God

445:20-21	Ps 8:5 He 2:7	448: 8-10	Ro 8:14-17
447:38-39	Is 9:2 Mt 4:16	448:11-13	Is 56:5
	Lk 1:79; 2:32	448:13-14	Ga 4:6
	Jn 1:4-9; 5:35	449:14	Ge 17:1 Le 19:2
	Jn 8:12; 9:5		De 18:13 Mt 5:48
	Jn 12:35-36,46		2Co 13:11 Ja 1:4
	1Jo 2:8	449:40	Mt 18:21-22
447:40	Jn 1:12		Lk 6:37; 17:3-4
448: 5- 6	1Jo 3:1	454:17-19	2Ch 19:7 Jb 34:19
448: 6- 7	Jn 1:12		Ac 10:34 Ro 2:11
448: 7- 8	1Jo 3:1-2		Ga 2:6 Ep 6:9
448: 8	Ga 3:26		

PAPER 41:   Physical Aspects of the Local Universe

The URANTIA Book Page and Line	The BIBLE Book, Chapter, Verse	The URANTIA Book Page and Line	The BIBLE Book, Chapter, Verse
466:33-34	Mt 19:30; 23:11 Mt 20:16:26-27 Mk 9:35;10:31;43:44	466:33-34	Lk 9:48; 13:30 Lk 14:11; 18:14 Lk 22:26

PAPER 42:   Energy—Mind and Matter

467:27-28	Cl 1:17	484:19-23	1Co 2:16 Pp 2:5

PAPER 43:   The Constellations

486:27	Re 4:6; 15:2	491:34-35	De 32:8
487: 7-11	Re 4:6; 15:2	491:39	Da 4:17,25,32
488:15	Ge 14:18-22		Da 5:21
	Nu 24:16+	491:43-44	Ge 14:18-20+
	De 32:8 Ps 9:2		Nu 24:16 De 32:84
	Da 4:17,25,32		Ps 9:2;110:4 PM 7
	Da 5:21 PM 7		Da 4:17,25,32;5:21
	Mk 5:7 He 7:1+		Mk 5:7 He 7:1-3
488:30-32	Ps 46:4	491:45-46	Ge 14:20 He 7:1
488:37-39	Ps 91:1	492: 7	Ez 28:13;31:8-9
488:41-42	Da 4:17,25,32	492:11	Ge 2:15;3:23-24
	Da 5:21	492:14-16	Ps 24:3-4
489:41-43	Is 14:13-14	495:20-21	He 12:22-23
489:43-44	He 12:22-23	495:32	Mt 22:30
490: 4- 5	Is 14:13-14		Mk 12:25
490:15-16	Jb 1:6; 2:1		Lk 20:36
490:28	Lk 10:18		

PAPER 44:   The Celestial Artisans

501: 4	Is 64:4 1Co 2:9	503:20	1Co 13:12
501:42	He 11:10		

PAPER 45: The Local System Administration

The URANTIA Book Page and Line	The BIBLE Book, Chapter, Verse	The URANTIA Book Page and Line	The BIBLE Book, Chapter, Verse
511:35-36	Jb 1:6; 2:1	513:41	De 4:35-39; 6:4
513: 9-13	Re 4:4,10;5:8,14		Mk 12:29,32
513:13-15	Re 4:2		1Co 8:4-6 Ro 3:30
513:29	Ge 2:7 Ac 17:25		Ga 3:20 Ep 4:6
513:31	Is 9:2 Mt 4:16		Ja 2:19
	Lk 1:79; 2:32	513:43	Ge 1:1
	Jn 1:4-9; 5:35		Jn 1:1-4;6:32-35
	Jn 8:12; 9:5	513:45	De 10:17
	Jn 12:36-36,46	514: 7- 8	Ge 5:24 He 11:5
	1Jo 2:8	514:11	Ex 5:1+
513:33-34	Jn 4:24	514:12-13	2Ki 2:11
513:38	Jn 3:2	514:15-16	(Same as 493:43-44)
513:40	Jn 14:6	514:24-25	Jn 1:6-8

PAPER 46: The Local System Headquarters

519:33	Re 21:23	525:24	He 12:22
521:44	Re 4:6; 15:2	529:18	Ro 6:23 Ge 2:17

PAPER 47: The Seven Mansion Worlds

530: 3- 4	Jn 14:2	538:14	Re 2:17
532:39-40	Jn 6:39-40	538:27-28	Re 7:14
	Jn 11:24-26;13:36	538:39	Re 13:16-18;14:9
	Jn 14:3; 17:24		Re 16:2; 19:20
533: 3-11	(Same as 532:39-40)	539:27-31	Re 4:6; 15:2
534:44	Re 4:6; 15:2	539:30-33	Re 5:8;14:2;15:2
538:10-11	Mt 3:17 Mk 1:11	539:36-40	He 12:22-23
	Lk 3:22		

PAPER 48: The Morontia Life

542:24-25	He 10:34	549:11-12	Ro 12:3 Ga 6:3
542:26	He 11:10	552:30	Ro 2:4
542:27	He 11:16	552:31	1Jo 4:18
548: 7- 8	Ro 8:28	552:33-47	Ps 23:1-6

The URANTIA Book Page and Line	The BIBLE Book, Chapter, Verse	The URANTIA Book Page and Line	The BIBLE Book, Chapter, Verse
553:20-21	De 10:14 Ne 9:6	553:26	1Ki 8:27
	Ps 148:4		2Ch 2:6; 6:18
553:22-23	2Co 12:2	553:46-48	Pp 2:5 1Co 2:16

PAPER 49:   The Inhabited Worlds

568:21	(Same as 532:39-40)	568:45-0569:1	Mt 24:31
568:30	Is 26:19 Da 12:2		Mk 13:27
568:35-37	Mt 27:52	569:15-17	Je 51:29

PAPER 50:   The Planetary Princes

574: 6- 7	Da 4:17,25,32	578:38-43	Jn 20:29
	Da 5:21	579: 3	Jn 20:29

PAPER 51:   The Planetary Adams

583: 5- 7	Ge 2:8-14	584: 8- 9	He 7:1-4
583:30-31	Ge 3:8-19	584: 9-10	Mt 2:1-2
584: 8	Ge 2:8		Lk 2:7-11
584: 8- 9	Ge 14:18		Jn 1:14

PAPER 52:   Planetary Mortal Epochs

590:29	Re 7:2-3	596:21-24	Jd 9 AM (All)
590:33	Is 9:2 Mt 4:16	596:31-32	Ek 11:19;36:26-27
	Lk 1:79; 2:32		Jl 2:28 Lk 24:49
	Jn 1:4-9; 5:35		Jn 14:16-18,26
	Jn 8:12; 9:5		Jn 15:26;16:7,13-14
	Jn 12:35-36,46		Ac 2:2-4; 16:18
	1Jo 2:8		Ac 2:17
591:33	Is 9:6	596:38	Mt 16:27; 24:30
593:38-39	Ac 17:26		Mt 25:31
596:14	He 10:20 Jn 14:6		Mk 8:38; 13:26
596:17	He 10:20 Jn 14:6		Lk 9:26; 21:27

The URANTIA Book Page and Line	The BIBLE Book, Chapter, Verse	The URANTIA Book Page and Line	The BIBLE Book, Chapter, Verse
597:13	Is 9:6	597:21-22	Mt 10:34 Lk 12:51
597:14	Lk 2:14	599:46-48	Re 21:1-2
597:20	Mt 24:6 Mk 13:7	600: 2- 6	Is 66:22-23
597:20-21	Mt 24:6-7	600: 7-10	1Pe 2:9
	Mk 13:7-8	600:17-21	2Pe 3:13-14
	Lk 21:9-10		

PAPER 53:   The Lucifer Rebellion

601:21-22	Ek 28:15	608:44-45	Re 12:7
601:23-24	Ek 28:14	608:48-609:1	Re 12:8
601:30-32	Jd 9 AM (All)	609:11	Re 12:8
601:36-37	Ek 28:17	609:28-29	Jb 1:6; 2:1
602:38-40	Is 14:12	609:35-610:3	Mt 4:3-11 Mk 1:13
602: 1- 2	1Ch 21:1 Jb 1:6-7	609:38-39	Lk 10:18
	Ps 109:6 Is 14:12	609:44-45	Mt 4:10;16:23
	Zc 3:1-2 Mk 1:13		Mk 8:33 Lk 4:8
	Mt 4:3-11	610: 4- 5	Jn 12:31;14:30;16:11
	Lk 4:3-11	610: 7- 8	Jn 12:31;14:30;16:11
602: 5- 6	Jn 12:31;14:30	610: 9	2Co 4:4
	Jn 16:11	610:24-25	Ep 6:16
602: 9	Re 9:11	610:25-26	1Jo 5:18
602:11	Mt 9:34;10:25;12:24	610:33	1Pe 3:19
	Mk 3:22,30	611:10	Ep 6:12
	Lk 11:15	611:11-20	Re 20:1-3
602:14-15	Re 20:1-2	611:34-35	Ek 28:16-19
602:16-18	Jd 6	611:42	Re 12:8
605:34	Mt 28:18	611:43-44	Ek 28:19
606: 7- 9	Re 12:7-8	611:45	Ob 16
608:17-19	Re 12:3-4	611:48	Pv 13:15
		612: 1- 2	Ro 6:23 Ge 2:17

PAPER 54:   Problems of The Lucifer Rebellion

613:37-38	1Pe 2:16	616:38-41	Ro 8:28
	Ga 5:13	619: 3-10	Ep 4:25
616: 5	Lk 15:11-32	619: 4- 5	1Co 12:26

PAPER 55:   The Spheres of Light and Life

The URANTIA Book Page and Line	The BIBLE Book, Chapter, Verse	The URANTIA Book Page and Line	The BIBLE Book, Chapter, Verse
622: 6- 7	Re 3:12; 21:1-4	623: 2- 5	Ge 5:24 He 11:5
622:19-20	Re 3:12; 21:2	631:10-11	2Co 5:17 Re 21:4-5

PAPER 56:   Universal Unity

The URANTIA Book Page and Line	The BIBLE Book, Chapter, Verse	The URANTIA Book Page and Line	The BIBLE Book, Chapter, Verse
637: 8- 9	Ge 17:1 Le 19:2	646: 4- 5	Ac 17:28 Ep 4:6
	De 18:13 Mt 5:48		1Co 8:6; 12:6
	2Co 13:11 Ja 1:4		1Co 15:28
638:19	Cl 1:17		Cl 1:17; 3:11
640:20-21	De 4:35-39; 6:4		He 2:10-11
	Mk 12:29-32	647:29-30	Ro 14:7
	Ro 3:29-30	647:31-32	Mt 19:26; 23:11
	1Co 8:4-6		Mt 20:16,26-27
	Ep 4:6 Ja 2:19		Mk 9:30;10:31,43-44
640:33-35	Mt 28:19 Ac 2:33		Lk 9:48;13:30;14:11
	1Co 12:4-6 1Jo 5:7		Lk 18:14; 22:26
644: 8- 9	Jn 5:19	648:23	1Jo 4:8,16
	Jn 3:32; 8:38		

PAPER 57:   The History of Urantia

654: 1- 3	Jn 1:3 He 1:2	659:41-44	Ge 2:6
655:28	Ge 1:3	660:13-15	Ge 1:6,9

PAPER 58:   Life Establishment on Urantia

667:33	Ge 1:11	669:15	Ge 1:20

PAPER 59:   The Marine—Life Era on Urantia

679:10-26	Ge 1:21

PAPER 60: Urantia During the Early Land—Life Era

The URANTIA Book Page and Line	The BIBLE Book, Chapter, Verse	The URANTIA Book Page and Line	The BIBLE Book, Chapter, Verse
686:21-37	Ge 1:24		

PAPER 61: The Mammalian Era on Urantia

700:11	Ge 1:26-27; 2:7	691:24-30	Ge 1:20-22

PAPER 62: The Dawn Races of Early Man

707:41	Ge 1:26-27; 2:7		

PAPER 63: The First Human Family

716:23-24	Ex 20:24	716:25	He 9:22

PAPER 64: The Evolutionary Races of Color

PAPER 65: The Overcontrol of Evolution

PAPER 66: The Planetary Prince of Urantia

750:38-39	Pv 17:6	751:47	Ge 3:19

PAPER 67: The Planetary Rebellion

754:15-16	2Co 11:14	756:11	Re 12:7
754:22-24	Jn 8:44	758: 5	Ge 4:16
755:37	2Co 4:4		

PAPER 68: The Dawn of Civilization

The URANTIA Book Page and Line	The BIBLE Book, Chapter, Verse	The URANTIA Book Page and Line	The BIBLE Book, Chapter, Verse
763:29-30	Ge 4:14-15	766:32-33	Jb 28:28
766:32-33	Ps 111:10	766:47	Is 9:6
	Pv 1:7; 9:10	769:32-33	Ge 3:19

PAPER 69: Primitive Human Institutions

773:32-33	Ge 3:18	779:12	Js 2:10 Jg 21:11
	2Th 3:10	779:13	Nu 31:7
775:19	Nu 35:6,11	779:19-21	De 21:10-14
779: 8-10	Js 8:1-29	781:46-47	De 19:14
779:10-11	De 3:1-7	781:47	De 27:17

PAPER 70: The Evolution of Human Government

784:35	2Ch 20:15 Ps 24:8	795:16-25	Nu 5:12-31
784:36-39	Nu 31:3-18	795:36-37	Ex 21:24 Le 24:20
784:37-39	Jg 21:10-11		De 19:21 Mt 38:42
784:40-41	Nu 31:1-2	795:39-40	De 32:35 Ps 94:1
785: 1- 2	Jg 4:16		Ro 12:19 He 10:30
785: 4- 5	1Sa 18:25	796:16-17	Nu 35:31
785: 8-10	1Sa 17:1-51	796:25-26	Ge 38:24 Le 21:9
787:38-39	Le 19:34	796:45	Ex 20:13 De 5:17

PAPER 71: Development of The State

PAPER 72: Government on a Neighboring Planet

PAPER 73: The Garden of Eden

822:20	Ge 6:4	825:39	Ge 2:9,17
823:19-20	Ge 2:6	825:40-41	Ge 3:22,24
823:27	Ge 2:10		Re 2:7;22:2,14
824:34	Ge 3:24; 4:16	826:24-25	Ge 3:5
825:31-32	Re 22:2		

PAPER 74: Adam and Eve

The URANTIA Book Page and Line	The BIBLE Book, Chapter, Verse	The URANTIA Book Page and Line	The BIBLE Book, Chapter, Verse
828: 8-15	Ge 5:2	836:28-29	Ge 35:11 He 7:5,10
831:31-32	Ge 2:19-20	836:44-45	Ge 1:1-31
831:39	Ge 3:24; 4:16	837: 3- 4	Ge 2:2-3
832:45	Ge 2:2-3	837: 6- 9	Ge 1:14-18
835:23	Ge 3:24; 4:16	837:10-17	Ge 2:21-23
836:16-17	Ge 1:26-27; 9:6	837:14-17	Ge 2:7,21-23
836:20-21	Is 26:8	837:48-49	Ge 4:16-17

PAPER 75: The Default of Adam and Eve

841: 2-19	Ge 3:1	843: 9-11	Ge 3:8-11
842:24-29	Ge 3:8-19	844:16-18	Ge 3:15
842:37-38	Ge 2:17	844:28-31	Ge 3:23-24
842:39-44	Ge 3:1-4	844:41	Pv 13:15
842:45-48	Pv 14:12	845:29-35	Ge 3:22-24
843: 1- 2	Ge 3:6		

PAPER 76: The Second Garden

848: 3- 4	Ge 3:19	849:20-22	Ge 4:17
848: 7- 8	Ge 4:2	849:46-0850:1	Ge 5:3
848:11-14	Ge 4:3-5	850: 3	Ge 5:6
848:33-35	Ge 4:8	850: 4	Ge 5:9
849: 8- 9	Ge 4:13-14	851: 9	Ge 2:16;3:2
849:12-16	Ge 4:15		Ge 1:29
849:17	Ge 4:16	851:34-41	Ge 6:2
		852:40	Ge 5:5

PAPER 77: The Midway Creatures

856:38-41	Ge 6:4	858: 3- 6	Ge 5:5-27; 9:29
857:48-49	Ge 5:5-31; 9:29	858: 5	Ps 90:10
	Ge 11:10-26	858:11	Ge 11:1-9

The URANTIA Book Page and Line	The BIBLE Book, Chapter, Verse	The URANTIA Book Page and Line	The BIBLE Book, Chapter, Verse
859:41	Ge 4:16	863:27	Mk 3:30,32
859:43-44	Ge 6:2		Lk 11:15
862:13-14	Ge 6:4	863:42-44	Mt 4:24
863:27	Mt 9:34; 10:25	865:26-28	Ac 5:19; 12:7
	Mt 12:24	865:28-30	Ac 12:7-10

PAPER 78: The Violet Race After the Days of Adam

874:41-0875:17	Ge 6:5-8:19	876:38	Is 20:1

PAPER 79: Andite Expansion in The Orient

PAPER 80: Andite Expansion in The Occident

PAPER 81: Development of Modern Civilization

900:31-33	Ge 3:17-19	900:33-35	Ge 4:2-5

PAPER 82: The Evolution of Marriage

917:33-34	Ge 29:18-20	919: 1- 3	Ge 16:6
	Ru 4:10	919: 3- 4	De 25:5-6
918:46	Ge 20:12		Mt 22:24 Mk 12:19
918:46-47	Le 18:9		Lk 20:28

PAPER 83: The Marriage Institution

924: 5	Ge 29:18-20	926:12-14	Mt 22:24
926:12-14	Ge 38:6-10		Mk 12:19
	De 25:5-6		Lk 20:28

PAPER 84: Marriage and Family Life

The URANTIA Book Page and Line	The BIBLE Book, Chapter, Verse	The URANTIA Book Page and Line	The BIBLE Book, Chapter, Verse
932: 1- 2	Ge 2:7	935:36-38	Le 12:2-8
932:41-43	Le 17:11		Lk 2:22-24
934: 3	Ps 23:1	936: 8-11	Le 15:19-20
935:24-25	Ge 3:1-17	940:29-30	Pv 17:6

PAPER 85: The Origins of Worship

944:30-31	Ge 28:18	946:23	Ex 4:3-4; 7:9-12
944:31	Ge 31:19,32-35		Nu 21:8-9
945: 9-10	Js 24:27		2Ki 18:4 Jn 3:14
945:24-27	Ge 22:14	946:38	Ge 22:7-8
	Ex 3:1,12		Ex 12:3-5
	Ex 18:3,11-23	946:38-39	Ca 5:2; 6:9
	Ex 24:12-18	947: 1- 2	Mt 3:6,11
	Nu 10:33 De 11:29		Mk 1:4-5,8
	Ps 121:1; 72:4		Lk 3:3,7,16
	Is 2:2; 8:18		Jn 1:25-33
	Je 3:23	947: 2- 3	Jn 5:2-4
	Jn 4:20-21	947:10	Ge 9:9-17
945:37-38	1Co 15:35-38	947:16	Ex 3:2;13:21-22
946: 3	Ge 21:33		Ex 19:18
	2Ki 17:10-16		Nu 9:15-16
	2Ki 21:3,7		De 4:12+
	2Ch 33:19	947:17-19	Ex 19:9,16
946: 4	Pv 3:18; 11:30	947:19-21	1Sa 7:10
	Pv 13:12; 15:4		2Sa 22:14-15

PAPER 86: Early Evolution of Religion

951:13-18	Ec 9:11-12	954:40-42	De 13:1-5
953: 6	Ge 2:7	955: 3- 5	Jn 20:22
953:41-42	Lk 16:19-31	955: 5- 6	Ps 33:6
954: 8	Ge 25:8+ Jb 3:11	955:16	Ge 4:10
	Je 15:9 La 1:19	955:18	Le 3:17; 7:22-25
	Jn 4:34; 17:4	955:19-20	Mt 6:22-23
	Jn 19:30,42		Lk 11:34

PAPER 87: The Ghost Cults

The URANTIA Book Page and Line	The BIBLE Book, Chapter, Verse	The URANTIA Book Page and Line	The BIBLE Book, Chapter, Verse
962:15-17	Ac 17:22-23	964:37	Mt 3:6,11
962:35-36	De 15:9;28:54,56		Mk 1:4,8
962:36-38	Pv 23:6		Lk 3:7,16
964:34	Mt 3:6,11		Jn 1:26,28
	Mk 1:4-5,8	965:11	Ge 31:13
	Lk 3:3,7,16		Nu 6:2-8
	Jn 1:25-33	965:11-12	Nu 30:2-15
			De 29:10-15

PAPER 88: Fetishes, Charms and Magic

The URANTIA Book	The BIBLE	The URANTIA Book	The BIBLE
968: 3	Ge 3:1-5	969:17-19	Le 26:1
968:11-12	2Sa 24:1-4	969:21-23	Ex 37:1-9
	1Ch 21:1-7		De 10:5
969: 3- 4	Ex 25:8-9; 33:7		2Ki 18:4
	Ex 40:1-33		He 9:4
969: 5- 6	Ge 28:22	971:43-44	Ex 20:7
969:17-19	Ex 20:4 De 5:8		De 5:11

PAPER 89: Sin, Sacrifice, and Atonement

The URANTIA Book	The BIBLE	The URANTIA Book	The BIBLE
974:12-16	Le 1:1-9:24	976:16-17	2Sa 12:16,21-23
974:24-27	Le 11:1-47		Es 4:16 Ps 35:13
974:34-35	Le 10:1-2		Is 58:3-6 Mt 9:14
975: 5- 7	Ex 20:3-17		Mk 2:18-20 Lk 5:33
	De 5:7-21	976:25-27	Ac 2:44-47
975:12-13	Le 11:7-8		1Tm 6:8-11
975:32-34	Ge 2:17; 3:2-3	976:29-32	Ge 37:34
975:40-41	Ro 6:23		1Ki 21:27
975:46-47	Ge 1:27; 2:7-22		Es 4:1-4 Jh 3:5
975:47-48	Ge 3:16-19		Is 37:1-2; 58:5
976: 3- 4	Le 26:14-39	977: 6	1Co 7:9
976:11	Le 13:45+	977:10-11	1Co 7:1

The URANTIA Book Page and Line	The BIBLE Book, Chapter, Verse	The URANTIA Book Page and Line	The BIBLE Book, Chapter, Verse
977:11	1Co 7:7	981:44-45	Ex 13:12-13
977:11-12	1Co 7:8		Ex 21:30
977:14-15	1Co 7:6	981:45-47	Le 27:1-34
977:47-0978:1	Ge 8:21 Le 1:9+	982: 5- 6	Ex 12:7,12-13
	Ex 29:18,25,41		Ex 12:22-23
	Ez 6:13 Ep 5:2	982: 9-12	Ex 2:1-10
978:30-31	Ex 29:1 Le 1:3+	982:46-47	Ge 17:10-14+
978:37-38	Le 6:16,29+	983: 8-11	Ge 6:18; 15:18+
980:28	Ge 22:1-10	983:32-33	Ja 5:16
980:41-44	Jg 11:30-39	984:10	He 13:20
980:45	Ps 24:8	984:14-16	1Co 5:7 Ep 5:2
981:11-12	Js 6:26		He 7:27;9:11-28
981:22-26	1Ki 16:34		He 10:10-18
981:35	Ge 3:19 Ec 3:20		He 13:12
981:36	Ge 22:1-10	984:17-18	1Co 11:23-27

PAPER 90: Shamanism—Medicine Men and Priests

986:28-29	Ex 2:16; 28:1-3+	988: 9-11	1Sa 28:7-19
	Nu 18:1-10	988:22-25	Mt 2:2
	2Ki 17:13	990:19	Jb 6:4
986:33-34	Nu 3:5-10+		Ps 38:1-2
	1Sa 9:8-10	992:26	Ps 3:2
	2Sa 15:27	992:29-30	Nu 19:1-22
987:42-44	Ex 22:18 Le 20:27	992:38-39	He 7:5
988: 5- 7	2Sa 5:24	992:43	Mt 16:19
	1Ch 14:15		

PAPER 91: The Evolution of Prayer

1001:36	Mt 6:11 Lk 11:3	1001:37	Mt 6:10 Lk 11:2

PAPER 92: The Later Evolution of Religion

The URANTIA Book Page and Line	The BIBLE Book, Chapter, Verse	The URANTIA Book Page and Line	The BIBLE Book, Chapter, Verse
1004:20	1Jo 4:8,16	1009:32-33	Mk 12:29,32
1004:30-32	Ex 20:25		Ro 3:30 Ja 2:19
	De 27:5-6		1Co 8:4-6
1004:35-36	Ex 12:8		Ga 3:20 Ep 4:6
1006: 3- 4	Jd 3	1011:32-33	Ge 1:1 2Ki 19:15
1009:32-33	De 4:35,39; 6:4		Is 37:16 Ne 9:6
			Ps 115:15-16

PAPER 93:   Machiventa Melchizedek

The URANTIA Book Page and Line	The BIBLE Book, Chapter, Verse	The URANTIA Book Page and Line	The BIBLE Book, Chapter, Verse
1015: 7- 9	He 7:3	1018:12-13	Ge 22:2-13
1015:12-13	Ge 14:18	1018:25	De 7:6
1015:12-23	Ge 14:18-20,22	1019:10	Ge 11:32
	Nu 24:16 De 32:8	1019:12-14	Ge 12:1-2
	Ps 9:2; 110:4	1019:16	Ge 12:4-5
	Da 4:17,25,32	1019:17-18	Ge 12:8
	Da 5:21 PM 7	1019:23-25	Ge 12:9-10
	Mk 5:7 He 7:1-3	1019:28-29	Ge 13:1-2
1015:26-30	Ge 14:18 He 7:1-2	1019:37-38	Ge 13:5-12
1015:40	He 7:3	1020: 1- 3	Ge 13:17-18
1116:14	Ge 14:18	1020: 8- 9	Ge 14:1-12
	Ps 76:1-2	1020: 9-11	Ge 14:13-15
	He 7:1	1020:12-15	Ge 14:16-20
1016:16-17	Ge 14:20 He 7:4-9	1020:26-28	Ge 15:1-3
1016:18-25	(Same as 1015:21-23)	1020:37	Ge 15:18-21
1016:25	Nu 24:16 De 26:8	1020:37-19	Ge 15:4-5
	2Sa 22:14 Ps 9:2+	1020:39-40	Ge 5:6
1016:37	Da 4:17,25,32	1020:40-42	Ge 15:12-16
	Da 5:21	1021: 5- 6	Ge 15:2-4;17:19
1017: 9-10	Ps 110:4		Ge 21:2-3
	He 5:6-10;6:20	1021: 6-10	Ge 17:1-9
	He 7:17,21	1021:14-15	Ge 17:10-13
1017:35	Ge 15:6 Ro 4:3	1021:17-18	Ge 18:1-5
	Ga 3:6 Ja 2:23	1021:18-22	Ge 18:16-19:29
1018: 6- 7	Ge 14:18	1022:37-39	Ge 20:1
1018:11	Ge 15:9-10	1022:40-42	Ge 20:2

The URANTIA Book Page and Line	The BIBLE Book, Chapter, Verse	The URANTIA Book Page and Line	The BIBLE Book, Chapter, Verse
1023: 1- 2	Ge 12:12-13	1023:35-36	Ge 22:11,15
	Ge 20:2-11	1023:40-41	Ge 25:1
1023: 4- 5	Ge 21:22-32		1Ch 1:32
1023: 5- 7	Ge 22:1-2	1023:42-43	Ge 17:1,17,24
1023:10-11	Ge 23:2,17-20	1023:43-45	Ge 17:17
1023:12-14	Ge 24:1-4	1024: 4- 6	Ge 14:18-20
1023:15	Ge 25:8	1024:13-16	He 7:1-3
1023:21-22	Ge 37:19	1024:17-18	Ps 110:4
1023:25-26	Ge 41:41		He 5:6,10; 6:20
1023:32-33	Ge 12:7; 13:14		He 7:17-21,25
	Ge 15:1,18	1025:25-26	Is 9:6
	Ge 17:1; 18:1	1025:26	1Co 15:45

PAPER 94: The Melchizedek Teachings in The Orient

PAPER 95: The Melchizedek Teachings in The Levant

1042:19-23	Ex 20:8-10	1046:31-32	Pv 23:5
	Ex 31:13-16;35:3	1046:46	Pv 15:1-33
	De 5:12-14		Pv 17:1-28
	Ne 10:31		Pv 20:1-30
1042:30	Is 46:1 Je 51:44	1046:46-47	Pv 22:17-24:22
	BD 2:22	1047: 1- 3	Ps 1:1-6
1042:30-31	Je 50:2	1047:16-17	Mt 2:14
1042:36-37	Jg 2:13; 10:6	1051: 8	Mt 24:14; 28:19
	1Sa 12:10		Mk 13:10; 16:15
	1Ki 11:50		Lk 24:47
1043:10	2Ki 23:13		Jn 20:21 Ac 1:8
1043:38-39	Jb 1:1-42:17	1051:11	Mt 13:55
1044:42-46	Jn 9:6		Mk 6:3 Lk 4:42
1046:21	Pv 22:1-4		Jn 1:45 6:42
1046:27-29	Pv 1:8		

PAPER 96: Yahweh—God of The Hebrews

The URANTIA Book Page and Line	The BIBLE Book, Chapter, Verse	The URANTIA Book Page and Line	The BIBLE Book, Chapter, Verse
1052:24-26	Ge 17:2-9	1055: 6	2Ki 16:6+
1053: 6- 7	Ex 6:3; 34:23	1055: 6	De 7:6+
	Ps 83:18+	1055:27-29	Ex 2:1-10
1053:10-14	Ge 14:18-22+	1056:16-17	Ex 14:8-9
	Nu 24:16 De 32:8	1057: 7- 9	Ex 19:18
	Ps 9:2 PM 7	1057:11	De 7:21; 10:17
	Da 4:17,25,32		De 28:58 Ex 24:17
	Da 5:21	1057:15	Ex 20:5+
	Mk 5:7 He 7:1+	1057:16-17	Nu 16:22; 27:16
1053:15	Ge 17:1; 35:11+	1057:17-18	De 33:27
1053:24	Ge 31:13 De 4:24+	1057:19-21	De 4:31; 7:8
1053:28	Ge 1:1-31+	1057:23-24	De 32:4
1053:39	Ge 1:2+	1058:17-21	De 7:12-15
1053:39	Ge 18:27+	1058:21-22	De 8:18
1053:39	Ge 16:7+	1058:22-24	De 15:6
1053:39	Ge 49:25+ PM 1	1058:27-28	De 4:35,39; 6:4
1053:39-40	2Ki 19:22+		Mk 12:29,32
1053:40	Nu 24:16+		Ro 3:30 Ga 3:20
1053:40	Js 3:11,13+		1Co 8:4-6
1053:40	Da 7:9,13,22+		Ep 4:6 Ja 2:19
1053:40	Ex 5:1+	1058:29	Ex 15:11
1053:41	Ge 1:1+	1058:30-32	De 4:15
1053:41	Ac 19:20+	1058:34-36	De 10:17
1053:41	Ps 68:4+	1058:37-38	De 28:1-37
1053:41	1Sa 1:3+		De 32:39
1053:41-42	Mt 5:16,48;6:1-9	1058:39-40	De 7:6-11+
	Mt 7:11,21;11:25		De 10:12-13
	Mt 16:17; 18:35	1058:42	Ge 49:25
	Mt 23:9		Ex 6:3
	Mk 11:25-26	1058:42	Ex 15:3
	Lk 10:21; 11:2	1058:42	Ps 24:8
1053:43	Ex 6:3 Ps 83:18	1058:43	Ex 15:6
	Is 12:2; 26:4+	1058:43-44	De 23:14
1054:17-19	1Ki 20:23	1058:45	Ex 7:13+
1054:46	Ex 3:8,17+	1058:45-46	De 30:7
1055: 6	Ge 45:21+	1059:34-35	Js 1:5
1055: 6	Ge 40:15+	1059:38-39	Js 24:19

The URANTIA Book Page and Line	The BIBLE Book, Chapter, Verse	The URANTIA Book Page and Line	The BIBLE Book, Chapter, Verse
1059:40-41	Jb 37:23	1060:35-36	1Sa 17:14 Jg 9:23
	Ba 1:15-2:10	1060:37-38	Jb 5:12-13
1059:43-44	Js 24:19	1060:39-41	Jb 33:26
1059:44-45	Jb 4:17	1060:42-43	Jb 33:24
1059:45-46	Jb 11:7	1058:42	Ge 49:25
1059:46-47	Jb 36:26	1061: 1- 2	Jb 32:2+
1059:47	Jb 37:23		

PAPER 97: Evolution of the God Concept Among the Hebrews

1062:18	Ac 3:24	1064:23	1Ki 22:7-28
1062:33-34	1Sa 7:3-4		2Ch 18:6-27
1062:36-37	1Sa 15:32-33	1064:37-38	Le 25:23
1062:38-39	1Sa 2:8	1065: 8- 9	1Ki 18:17-40
1063: 6- 7	Ge 6:6 Ex 32:24	1065:12-13	1Ki 21:1-16
	Nu 23:19	1065:37	De 7:6; 14:2
	1Sa 15:29	1065:38	Am 4:13
	Am 7:3,6 Zc 8:14	1065:38-40	Am 5:8
1063:19	1Sa 12:22	1065:42-44	Am 9:2
1063:19-20	2Sa 23:5	1065:44-45	Am 9:4
1063:22-23	2Sa 7:22	1065:47	Am 8:7
1063:26-28	1Sa 2:7-8	1065:48	Am 9:9
1063:35-36	1Sa 2:2	1066: 1	Am 4:13
1063:36	Ps 89:6	1066: 2	Am 5:21-24
1063:38-39	1Sa 2:3	1066: 8	Ho 6:6
1063:39	1Sa 2:10	1066: 9-11	Ho 2:19-20
1063:39-40	2Sa 22:26	1066:11-12	Ho 14:4
1063:42-43	2Sa 24:14	1066:13-14	Ho 10:10
1063:43-44	1Sa 14:6	1066:15-16	Ho 2:23
1064: 1- 5	1Ch 29:11	1066:17-18	Ho 14:4
1064: 5- 7	1Ch 29:12	1066:19-20	Ho 1:7
1064:15	1Ki 17:1	1066:20	Ho 13:4
1064:18-19	1Ki 18:40	1066:34	Is 28:17
1064:20	1Ki 16:30-33	1066:34-36	Is 14:3
	1Ki 21:25-26	1066:36-37	Is 30:21
1064:22	1Ki 19:16,19-20	1066:37-38	Is 12:2
1064:22-23	2Ki 2:1-15	1066:38-41	Is 1:18

The URANTIA Book Page and Line	The BIBLE Book, Chapter, Verse	The URANTIA Book Page and Line	The BIBLE Book, Chapter, Verse
1066:43-44	Is 60:1	1069:33-34	Is 57:15
1066:44-47	Is 61:1	1069:34-35	Is 44:6
1066:47-1067:2	Is 61:10		Re 1:8,11,17
1067: 2- 3	Is 63:9		Re 21:6; 22:18
1067: 8- 9	Mi 3:11	1069:35-36	Is 59:1
1067:10-12	Mi 4:4-5	1069:38	Is 49:15
1067:13-18	Mi 6:6-8	1069:39	Is 41:17
1067:27-28	Je 21:3-7	1069:41	Is 43:7
1067:28-29	Je 32:27	1069:42	Is 43:21
1067:31-32	Je 10:6-7	1069:42-43	Is 43:25
1067:40-41	Je 31:3	1069:45-46	Is 66:1
	Jn 3:14-15; 6:44	1070: 5- 6	Is 57:15
	Jn 8:28; 12:32	1070: 7- 9	Is 58:11
1067:41-42	La 3:33	1070: 9-10	Is 59:19
1067:43	Je 12:1	1070:46-48	Ec 1:1-18
1067:43-45	Je 32:19		Ec 2:12-17
1067:47-1068:1	Je 27:6	1071: 3	Is 6:11
1068: 1- 2	Je 38:2-3	1071: 4- 5	De 7:6-15
1068: 2- 3	Je 38:6	1071: 7- 8	De 11:26-28
1068:45	Is 40:15	1071:10	Is 31:33
1068:46-47	Is 55:9	1071:14-16	Da 2:31-45
1069: 3	Is 45:12	1071:26-27	Da 4:17,25,32
1069: 4	Is 45:18		Da 5:21
1069: 4- 5	Is 44:6	1071:41-43	Jg 3:5-6
	Re 1:8,11,17	1071:44-45	Nu 21:1-3
	Re 21:6; 22:18	1072: 3- 5	1Sa 11:1-11
1069: 6- 7	Is 51:6	1072: 6- 7	1Sa 11:15
1069: 7- 8	Is 51:8	1072:11-12	1Sa 10:1
1069: 8	Is 41:10	1072:17-18	1Sa 27:2-3
1069: 9	Is 45:21	1072:18-19	1Sa 29:1-11
1069:11-12	Is 43:1	1072:19-20	1Sa 31:1-9
1069:12-13	Is 43:2	1072:19-20	1Ch 10:1-14
1069:13	Is 43:4	1072:21-22	1Sa 22:1-2
1069:14-16	Is 49:15-16	1072:26	1Sa 28:18
1069:16-17	Is 51:16	1072:28-30	2Sa 2:1-4
1069:16-17	Is 51:16	1072:36-37	2Sa 2:1-4
1069:20-22	Is 40:11	1072:38-42	1Sa 16:1-13
1069:22-23	Is 40:29	1072:46	1Sa 18:22-27
1069:23-25	Is 40:31	1072:47	1Sa 25:42

The URANTIA Book Page and Line	The BIBLE Book, Chapter, Verse	The URANTIA Book Page and Line	The BIBLE Book, Chapter, Verse
1072:47	2Sa 3:3	1074:12-14	2Ki 10:15-28
1072:49	2Sa 11:27	1074:15-16	2Ki 14: 8-29
1073: 4- 5	2Sa 5:3	1074:21-24	2Ki 17:4-6
1073: 6- 7	2Sa 5:6-7	1074:24-25	Is 10:20
1073: 8- 9	2Sa 5:17-25	1074:26	Is 5:8
1073:10	2Sa 5:10	1074:28-29	2Ki 11:12-18
1073:14-15	2Sa 5:20	1074:28-29	2Ch 23:11-17
1073:17-19	2Sa 21:1-2	1074:32-33	2Ch 25:27; 26:1
1073:19-20	1Sa 23:1-5	1074:36	Is 31:5
1073:21-23	2Sa 21:3-9	1074:37	Je 6:1-8;15:5-6
1073:24-25	2Sa 6:1-17	1074:38-40	2Ki 21:1-18
	1Ch 15:25-16:2		2Ch 33:1-20
1073:26-27	2Sa 8:11-12	1074:44-46	2Ki 23:29-30
1073:31	2Sa 11:14-17		2Ch 35:20-24
1073:31-34	2Sa 15:2-6	1075: 3	Je 46:2
1073:39	1Ki 7:8	1075: 7- 8	Je 38:2-3
1073:39-41	1Ki 9:15	1075: 8-11	2Ki 25:1-17
1073:41-42	1Ki 9:26-27		Je 39:1-9
1073:42	1Ki 11:3	1075:37-38	De 32:1-43
1073:49	1Ki 16:23-24	1076: 6- 9	Ba 2:9-5:8
1074: 5- 8	1Ki 21:1-16	1076:26-27	Ek 18:1-9
1074: 8- 9	1Ki 21:17-24	1076:27-28	Ek 43:18-46:24

PAPER 98: Melchizedek Teachings in The Occident

1083:43-44	2Co 5:19 Ro 5:10	1085: 7- 8	Da 4:17,25,32
1085: 7-8	Ge 14:18-20		Da 5:21 PM 7
	Nu 24:16 De 32:8		Mk 5:7 He 7:1-3
	Ps 9:2; 110:4		

PAPER 99: The Social Problems of Religion

1091: 9-10	Ge 17:1 Le 19:2	1091:16-17	Ga 3:26;4:6
	De 18:13 Mt 5:48		1Jo 3:1-2
	2Co 13:11 Ja 1:4	1091:20	Ga 5:22 Ep 5:9
1091:16-17	Ro 8:1-17; 9:26	1091:32	Ro 14:22
	Is 56:5 Jn 1:12	1091:34-35	He 11:1

PAPER 100: Religion in Human Experience

The URANTIA Book Page and Line	The BIBLE Book, Chapter, Verse	The URANTIA Book Page and Line	The BIBLE Book, Chapter, Verse
1095:20-21	Mt 6:25-34	1102:38-39	Mt 7:8
1099: 7- 8	Ac 9:3-9,20		Lk 11:10
1101: 6- 8	Lk 2:14 Pp 4:7	1102:40-41	Jn 14:2
	Jn 14:27; 16:33	1102:48	Lk 2:49
1101:10-12	Ro 8:38-39	1103: 3	Is 53:3
1101:34	Jn 19:5	1103: 4	Mt 5:12
1101:39	Jn 14:6	1103: 5- 6	Ps 23:4
1102:18-19	Mt 16:24-25	1103: 8	Jn 2:4
	Mk 8:34-35	1103:14	Mt 10:31 Lk 5:10
	Lk 9:23-24		Lk 8:50; 12:7,32
	Jn 3:15-16		Lk 12:32
	Re 22:17	1103:19	Mt 5:16; 6:1-9
1102:20	Mt 27:43		Mt 7:11,21;11:25
1102:27	Ac 10:38		Mt 16:17;18:35;23:9
1102:29	Mt 9:2; 14:27		Mk 11:25-26
	Mk 6:50 Jn 16:33		Lk 10:21; 11:2
1102:35-36	Ac 20:35	1103:23	Jn 8:46
1102:36-37	Mt 10:8	1103:30-32	2Co 5:17

PAPER 101: The Real Nature of Religion

The URANTIA Book Page and Line	The BIBLE	The URANTIA Book Page and Line	The BIBLE
1104:14-15	Is 9:2 Mt 4:16	1112:45	Jn 9:39
	Lk 1:79; 2:32	1113: 7- 8	Jn 3:15-16
	Jn 1:4-9; 5:35		Jn 5:24-25,39-40
	Jn 8:12; 9:5		Jn 6:40,47;10:10
	Jn 12:35-36,46		Jn 11:25-26
	1Jo 2:8		1Jo 5:11-12
1105: 3- 4	He 12:14	1113:28	Jn 14:6 He 10:20
1107: 6- 7	Ps 19:1	1113:29	1Pe 1:4
1107:17-18	Ro 8:16	1114:25-26	Mt 22:21
1108:45	Jb 13:15		Mk 12:17
1112:41-42	Jn 1:12		Lk 20:25
1112:43-44	Jn 8:32		

PAPER 102: The Foundations of Religious Faith

The URANTIA Book Page and Line	The BIBLE Book, Chapter, Verse	The URANTIA Book Page and Line	The BIBLE Book, Chapter, Verse
1118: 7-11	Ec 1:1-8;2:11-26	1122:26-28	Ex 3:14
1118:35-36	Mt 18:3-4	1123:10-11	1Co 2:6 Pp 2:5
	Mk 10:15 Lk 10:17	1125:20-21	Jn 13:34-35
1121:10-11	He 11:27		Jn 15:12

PAPER 103: The Reality of Religious Experience

1130:43-44	Jn 3:3-8	1134:28-29	Mt 10:39;16:25
1131:47	Ep 4:22,24		Mk 8:35 Jn 12:25
	Cl 3:9-10		Lk 9:24;17:33
1131:48	Ac 20:35	1135: 7- 8	2Co 3:17

PAPER 104: Growth of the Trinity Concept

1144:43-45	1Co 12:4-6	1150:42	Ro 11:36
1144:48-1145:2	Mt 28:19 Ac 2:33		Cl 1:17
	1Co 12:4-6 1Jo 5:7		He 2:10

PAPER 105: Deity and Reality

1152:21	Ex 3:13-14	1155:21	Ac 17:28

PAPER 106: Universe Levels of Reality

1165:23-24	Jn 14:9	1165:24-25	De 18:13 Mt 5:48
1165:24-25	Ge 17:1 Le 19:2		2Co 13:11 Ja 1:4

PAPER 107: Origin and Nature of Thought Adjusters

1176:17	Ge 17:1 Le 19:2	1181: 7- 8	Lk 1:79; 2:32
	De 18:13 Mt 5:48		Jn 1:4-9;5:35;8:12
	2Co 13:11 Ja 1:4		Jn 9:5;12:25-36,46
1176:24	Jn 14:9	1181:14	1Co 3:16; 16:9
1181: 7- 8	Is 9:2 Mt 4:16		2Co 6:16

PAPER 108: Mission & Ministry of Thought Adjusters

The URANTIA Book Page and Line	The BIBLE Book, Chapter, Verse	The URANTIA Book Page and Line	The BIBLE Book, Chapter, Verse
1187:18-20	Ac 1:8; 2:1-21	1191:45	Re 2:17; 3:12
1188:41	Re 2:17; 3:12	1193: 5- 6	Lk 17:21
1190:17-18	Je 31:3	1193:14-17	Ep 4:23-24
	Jn 3:14-15;6:44	1193:18	Ge 1:26-27; 9:6
	Jn 8:28; 12:32	1193:28-31	1Co 15:42-50
1191:32-33	Jn 6:39		

PAPER 109: Relation of Adjusters to Universe Creatures

1199: 1- 3	Mt 13:12; 25:29	1199:10-21	1Co 2:6-16
	Mk 4:25	1199:33-34	Mt 6:24 Lk 16:13
	Lk 8:18; 19:26	1200:41	(Same as 8:42)

PAPER 110: Relation of Adjusters to Individual Mortals

1203: 5- 6	Is 63:9	1206:35-37	Lk 6:21; 12:31
1204:14-16	1Co 3:16-17;6:19	1206:38-39	De 6:4-5 Mt 22:37
	2Co 6:16		Mk 12:30 Lk 10:27
1204:21-27	1Co 6:17		Jn 14:15,23-24
1204:46-47	Ep 2:8		Jn 15:10
1205: 1- 2	Mt 16:24-25	1206:40-42	Le 19:18
	Mk 8:34-35		Mt 5:43-44; 7:12
	Lk 9:23-24		Mt 19:19; 22:39
	Jn 13:15-16		Mk 12:31 Ja 2:8
	Re 22:17		Lk 6:27-35;10:27-28
1205:20-21	Ro 12:2 Ep 5:23		Jn 13:34-35;15:12,17
	Pp 2:1-6		Ro 13:9 Ga 5:14
1206:35-37	Is 55:1-3	1212:24	2Ki 2:11
	Mt 5:6; 6:33		

PAPER 111: The Adjuster and The Soul

1221:33-34	(Same as 8:42)	1223: 7- 8	Pv 16:18
1222:14-15	Ge 1:31 Ps 19:11		

PAPER 112:   Personality Survival

The URANTIA Book Page and Line	The BIBLE Book, Chapter, Verse	The URANTIA Book Page and Line	The BIBLE Book, Chapter, Verse
1227:25	Ro 14:7	1237:24	2Tm 4:7
1234: 8-11	Jn 13:3	1240: 3- 4	Ge 3:19
1235:36-39	1Co 13:12		Ps 103:14

PAPER 113:   Seraphic Guardians of Destiny

1241:12	He 2:2	1241:20-22	Lk 17:2
1241:13	Ac 7:53	1247:32-33	Mt 24;31 Mk 13:27
1241:20-22	Mt 18:6-10	1247:38	Ac 24:15
	Mk 9:42-47	1248:18-19	He 2:7

PAPER 114:   Seraphic Planetary Government

1250: 3	Da 4:17,25,32	1255:24	Re 1:20
	Da 5:21	1255:34	Re 8:2,6
1251: 7- 9	Re 4:4	1255:38	Da 4:17,25,32
1251:31-43	Re 4:4,10		Da 5:21
	Re 5:8-9,14	1259:18	Jn 16:27
	Re 7:11; 14:3		

PAPER 115:   The Supreme Being

PAPER 116:   The Almighty Supreme

1269:31	Re 1:4; 3:1	1269:31	Re 4:5; 5:6

PAPER 117:   God The Supreme

1279:37-39	Jn 15:917:18-23	1287: 1	Is 30:21
1281:29	Jn 14:6 He 10:20	1289:21	1Jo 4:7
1281:44	Ge 1:26-27; 9:6	1290:43-45	2Ch 19:7 Jb 34:19
1283:11-12	Ac 17:28		Ac 10:34 Ro 2:11
1285:26-28	1Jo 4:19		Ga 2:6 Ep 6:9
1286:19-20	1Co 3:6-9		

PAPER 118: Supreme and Ultimate—Time and Space

The URANTIA Book Page and Line	The BIBLE Book, Chapter, Verse	The URANTIA Book Page and Line	The BIBLE Book, Chapter, Verse
1303: 7	Mt 6:10;7:21 Mt 12:30; 26:39 Mt 26:42,44 Mk 3:35;14:36,39 Lk 8:21;11:2 Lk 22:42	1303: 7 1306:39 1306:44-46	Jn 4:34;5:30 Jn 6:38;7:17 Jn 14:23-24 Jn 15:10,14;17:4 Lk 17:21 Ro 8:28

PAPER 119: The Bestowals Of Christ Michael

1310:26-31	Ps 110:4 He 5:6,10;6:20 He 7:17-21	1317: 9-13 1317:19-26	Mt 16:16 Mk 1:1 Jn 1:34; 3:15-16 Mt 2:1-11
1311:49-1312:2	Re 15:3	1317:34-1318:3	1Pe 3:22
1313:17	He 4:15	1318:29-30	(Same as 1303:7)
1314:13-14	He 4:15	1319: 6- 8	Mt 24:27-37,42
1314:45-46	He 4:15		Mt 25:13
1316:16	Lk 2:49		Mk 13:32-33
1316:42-44	Lk 2:9-14		Jn 14:3

SECTION TWO

Part IV of *The URANTIA Book*
(The LIFE and TEACHINGS of JESUS)
Cross Referenced to The BIBLE.

PAPER 120:   The Bestowal of Michael on Urantia

The URANTIA Book Page:Line	MATTHEW Chap:Verse	MARK Chap:Verse	LUKE Chap:Verse	JOHN Chap:Verse	Other BOOKS Chap:Verse
1323: 3				1:1-18	
1324:21-22	6:10	3:35	8:21	4:34;5:30	
	7:21	14:36-39	11:2	6:38;7:17	
	12:50		22:42	14:23-24	
	26:39,42,44			15:10,14;17:4	
1324:23-32	11:27		10:22	1:18;5:30	
				6:45-46;8:26	
	—	—		12:49-50	
				14:7-9,20	
				17:6,25-26	
1327:10	(Same as 1324:21-22, above.)				
1327:26-27	5:14-16		16:8	12:36	Is 14:12 Ep 5:8 1Th 5:5
1328: 3- 4	27:52-53			5:25-29	
1328: 4- 5			24:49	14:16-18,26	Ek 11:19
				15:26	Ek 36:26-27
	—	—		16:7-11	Jl 2:28
	—	—		16:13-14	Ac 2:2-4,16-18
1328:14-15			4:18		Is 61:1
1328:22-25	(Same as 1328:4-5, above)				

The URANTIA Book Page:Line	MATTHEW Chap:Verse	MARK Chap:Verse	LUKE Chap:Verse	JOHN Chap:Verse	Other BOOKS Chap:Verse
1328:38-41	(Same as both 1324:21-22 and 1324:23-32, above)				
1328:39-40				4:34;5:30	
	—	—		6:38	
1328:41-42				8:26;12:49-50	
1331: 9-10	(Same as 1324:21-22, above.)				
1331:18-20				1:1;5:18	
	—	—		10:30-38	
				14:9-11,20	
				17:11,21-22	
1331:21-22	11:27		10:22	1:18;6:45	
				8:26;12:49-50	
	—	—		14:7-9	
				17:4,25-26	

PAPER 121: The Times of Michael's Bestowal

1332:28					Pp 3:5
1332:29	—	—		—	Ac 21:37
1332:29-30					Ac 22:24-29
1333:40-41	—	—		—	Ac 10:2,7,22
					Ac 17:4,17
	—	—		—	Ac 22:12
1333:44-45					Ac 11:26
1334: 4- 8	—	—	3:15		
1334:23					1Pe 2:9
1334:27-30	—	—	1:5		
1336:10					Ac 17:28
1336:14	—	—		—	Pp 4:11
1340:24-25					Je 31:33
	—	—		—	Ek 18:31
1340:24-27			24:49	14:16-18,26	Ek 11:19;18:31
	—	—	15:26		Ek 36:26-27
			16:7,13-14		Jl 2:28
	—	—		—	Ac 2:2-4,16-18
1340:26-27					Ps 51:10
	—	—		—	Ek 36:26-27

The URANTIA Book Page:Line	MATTHEW Chap:Verse	MARK Chap:Verse	LUKE Chap:Verse	JOHN Chap:Verse	Other BOOKS Chap:Verse
1341:41-43	1:22-23				Is 7:14
	2:5-6	—		—	Mi 5:2
	2:15				Ho 11:1
	2:17-18	—		—	Je 31:15
	2:23				Is 11:1
	4:14-16	—		—	Is 9:1-2
	8:17				Is 53:3-4
	12:17-21	—		—	Is 42:1-4
	13:35				Is 6:9-10
	21:4-5	—		—	Zc 9:9
	26:15				Zc 11:12
	27:9-10				Zc 11:12
	27:35	15:24	23:34	19:23-24	Ps 22:18
1341:43	1:1,6,17				
1342:16-17			2:40		Ac 15:11
1342:17-18	9:10-11	9:2-15	5:29-30;7:34		
	11:19		15:2		

PAPER 122: Birth and Infancy of Jesus

1344:26-33	1:1-16		3:23-38	
1345:15-20	1:18-21;24-25		1:27;2:4-5	
1345:22-26			1:5-7	
1345:27-38	—		1:11-17	—
1345:30-31			1:8-10	
1345:43-44	—		1:24	—
1345:44-1346:5			1:18-21	
1345:47			1:24	
1346:6-7	1:18-21		1:26-27	
1346:7-16			1:39-40	
1346:12-13	—		1:56	—
1346:17-20			1:57-66	
1346:24-29	—		1:80	—
1346:31-44			1:26-38	
1346:35-36	1:21			
1347:17-19	1:18-21			
1347:21-29	1:20-25			
1347:32-36			1:32-33	

39

pp. 1347 to 1353

The URANTIA Book Page:Line	MATTHEW Chap:Verse	MARK Chap:Verse	LUKE Chap:Verse	JOHN Chap:Verse	Other BOOKS Chap:Verse
1347:37	1:6-16		1:27		
1347:38-42			2:4		
1347:39-42	1:14-16		3:23-24		
1347:43-1348:5	1:22-23				
1348: 5- 6	22:41-46	12:35-37	20:41-44		Ps 110:1
1348: 6- 7	1:22-23				Is 7:14
1348: 7-11	1:2-16		3:23-37		
1349:20-23	1:18-21,24-25		1:27;2:4-5		
1350:22	1:18-21,24-25		1:27;2:4-5		
1350:22-30			2:1		
1350:25-26	—	—		—	1Ch 21:1,7
					2Sa 24:1-4,10
1350:31-41	—	—	2:5		
1351:16-20			2:7		
1351:29-34	1:25		2:6-7		
1351:35-37			2:21		
1352: 7-12			2:8-18,20		
1352: 9-19	2:1-12				
1352:19-21	2:11				
1352:22	2:2,7,9-10				
1352:37					Ex 13: 2
					Nu 3:13
1352:37-47	—	—	2:22-24		
1352:38-40					Ex 13:15
	—	—		—	Ex 34:20
					Nu 3:47-48
1352:40-47	—	—		—	Nu 18:16
					Le 12:2-8
1353: 1- 5	—	—	2:25-26,36		
1353: 8-14			2:27-28		
1353:12-14	—	—	1:67		
1353:15-34			1:68-79		
1353:17-18	—	—			Ps 132:17
1353:35-39			2:29-32		
1353:38-39	4:16		1:79	1:4-9;5:35	1Jn 2:8
			2:32	8:12;9:5	Is 9:2
				12:35-36,46	
1353:40-43	—	—	2:33		
1353:45-1354:7	2:3-8				

40

The URANTIA Book Page:Line	MATTHEW Chap:Verse	MARK Chap:Verse	LUKE Chap:Verse	JOHN Chap:Verse	Other BOOKS Chap:Verse
1354: 7	2:12				
1354:18-19		—		—	Le 12:6-8
1354:20-24	2:16				
1354:29-38	2:13-15				
1354:37-38	2:19-21				

PAPER 123:   The Early Childhood of Jesus

1356: 1- 2	2:19-21				
1356:14-20	2:22-23				
1356:22-24			2:39		
1356:32-33	—		—	2:39	
1356:39-40			2:40		
1357: 5- 6	13:55	6:3			
	27:56	15:40		—	Ga 1:19
1357:47-48	13:56	6:3			
1362: 1- 2	13:55	6:3			
	27:56	15:40			
1363: 2				1:46	
1363:27-30	—	—		—	Is 61:1
1363:39					1Ki 17:1-19:21
				—	2Ki 1:3-2:11
1365: 9-10	13:55	6:3			

PAPER 124:   The Later Childhood of Jesus

1367:18	13:56	6:3			
1370:11	13:55	6:3			
1372:30-31					De 6:6-9
1372:33-34	—	—		—	Ps 121:8
1373: 4- 5					Ex 20:12
	—	—		—	De 5:16
1373:30					Ps 82:6
1374: 4-1375:35			2:42		

PAPER 125: Jesus at Jerusalem

The URANTIA Book Page:Line	MATTHEW Chap:Verse	MARK Chap:Verse	LUKE Chap:Verse	JOHN Chap:Verse	Other BOOKS Chap:Verse
1378:27-29	21:12-13	11:15-17	19:45-46	2:14-16	
1379: 4					Ac 3:2,10
1379:14	—	—		—	1Mc 4:52-59
1379:14					Es 9:17-32
1381: 5-27	—		—	2:43-44	
1381:41-42				2:45	
1383:46-1384:7	—		—	2:46-48	
1384:21-24				2:49	
1384:37-39				2:50-51	

PAPER 126: The Two Crucial Years

The URANTIA Book Page:Line	MATTHEW Chap:Verse	MARK Chap:Verse	LUKE Chap:Verse	JOHN Chap:Verse	Other BOOKS Chap:Verse
1387:10-11					Je 32:35
1387:15	—	—		—	2Ki 23:29
					2Ch 35:20-24
1387:16	—	—		—	Jg 4:10-16
1387:17-18					Ge 37:23-28
1387:46-47			2:52		
1389:21-22	13:56	6: 3			
1389:46-47			2:49		
1390: 3- 5	8:20+	2:10+	5:24+	1:51+	En 46:1-71:17
1390:14-15					Da 7:13-14
1390:24-31	8:20+	2:10+	5:24+	1:51+	En 46:1-71:17
1390:45			2:49		
1391:41-47					Is 61:1-3
1392: 1- 3	—	—		—	Am 5:14-15
1392: 4- 6					Is 1:16-17
1392: 7-13	—	—		—	Mi 6:6-8
1392:14					Is 40:18
1392:14	—	—		—	Is 40:22
1392:15-17					Is 40:26
1392:18	—	—		—	Is 40:29
1392:19-21					Is 41:10
1392:21-22	—	—		—	Is 41:13
1392:23-25					Is 43:10-11
1393:23			13:32		

PAPER 127: The Adolescent Years

The URANTIA Book Page:Line	MATTHEW Chap:Verse	MARK Chap:Verse	LUKE Chap:Verse	JOHN Chap:Verse	Other BOOKS Chap:Verse
1401: 2					He 11:27
1403:15	—	—	2:49		
1403:18-19					He 4:15
1403:33-35	21:8-9	11:8-10	19:36-38	12:12-13	Ac 1:4
1403:35-36	27:35-36	15:40-41	8:2-3	19:25	
			23:27,49		
	—	—	24:10		
1403:37					Ca 5:16
1403:37-38	—	—	—		Ca 5:10
1404:46-47					Ex 12:1-28

PAPER 128: Jesus' Early Manhood

The URANTIA Book Page:Line	MATTHEW Chap:Verse	MARK Chap:Verse	LUKE Chap:Verse	JOHN Chap:Verse	Other BOOKS Chap:Verse
1407: 8-10					He 2:14-18;4:15
1407:12-13					He 2:9-10
1407:27	8:20+	2:10+	5:24+	1:51+	En 46:1-71:17
1407:27-28					He 2:14-18;4:15
1407:30-32	—	—		1:14	
1407:34-35					He 4:15
1408: 6- 8	—	—	—		He 4:14-15
1408:14-18					Pp 2: 5- 8
1408:20-22	—	—	—		He 5:7
1408:48-49					Is 44:6
	—	—	—		Re 1:8,11,17
					Re 21:6; 22:13
1409: 1	—	—	—		1Co 2:8
1409: 2					Ac 3:14
1409: 2	—	—	20:28		
1409: 3					Pp 2:9
1409: 4- 5	—	—	—		Cl 2:3
1409: 5					Ep 1:23
1409: 5- 6	—	—	1:1-2,14		Re 19:13
1409: 6- 7					Cl 1:17
1409: 7	—	—	—		Ac 4:24
1409: 8					Ac 10:42

43

The URANTIA Book Page:Line	MATTHEW Chap:Verse	MARK Chap:Verse	LUKE Chap:Verse	JOHN Chap:Verse	Other BOOKS Chap:Verse
1409: 8	—	—	—	Ro 6:23
1409: 8					He 13:20
1409: 9	—	—	—	He 2:10
1411:26					Ep 2:12
1411:37-39	—	—	—	Ac 7:57-60
1411:44-46					Ac 7:58
1414: 8- 9	24:1-2	13:1-2	21:5-6 19:44		
1414:48					Ep 2:12
1415:36					Ex 12:16 Le 23:7
1417: 5- 7	6:10 7:21 12:50 26:39,42,44	3:35 14:36-39	8:21 11:2 22:42	4:34;5:30 6:38;7:17 14:23-24 15:10,14;17:4	
1417: 8- 9					Cl 2:3
1417:23-24				2:4	

PAPER 129: The Later Adult Life of Jesus

1420:27-32	8:5-13		7:1-10		
1425:21					Is 53:3
1425:27-28	—	—			He 2:14-18;4:15
1426:10				14:6	He 10:20

PAPER 130: On the Way to Rome

1428:14-15					Jh 1:3
1428:41	—	—	—		Ac 9:36-42
1428:42-43					Ac 9:43
1429: 7				—	1Jo 4:8,16
1429:21-23	13:24-30				
1430:42-45					Ac 8:40
1430:45-46	—	—	—		Ac 10:7
1430:46					Ac 10:1-48
1430:47-48	—	—	—		Ac 23:31-33
					Ac 24:27
1436:16-18	—	—	—		Ti 1:10-16

The URANTIA Book Page:Line	MATTHEW Chap:Verse	MARK Chap:Verse	LUKE Chap:Verse	JOHN Chap:Verse	Other BOOKS Chap:Verse
1438:30-31					Ti 1:5
1438:34-38	27:32	15:21	32:26		
1439: 3- 4					Pv 18:24
1440:22-23	7:7-8		11:9-10	14:13-14	Je 29:13
				15:7-16	
	—	—		16:23-24	
1440:24-25					Je 24:7
1440:26-28	—	—		—	Jb 33:27-28

PAPER 131:   The World's Religions

The URANTIA Book Page:Line	MATTHEW Chap:Verse	MARK Chap:Verse	LUKE Chap:Verse	JOHN Chap:Verse	Other BOOKS Chap:Verse
1444: 5- 6					Ge 1:1-31
	—	—		—	Ba 3:32-36
1444: 6- 7					De 4:35,39
1444: 7- 8					De 6:5
1444: 9-10	—	—		—	Is 11:9
1444:10-12					Ps 19:1-3
1444:12	—	—		—	Ps 92:5
1444:13					Ps 104:24
1444:13	—	—		—	Ps 145:3
1444:14					Ps 147:4
1444:15	—	—		—	Ps 147:5
1444:16-17					Is 55:9
1444:17-18	—	—		—	Da 2:22
1444:18					Ps 103:8
1444:18-19	—	—		—	Ex 34:6
1444:19-20					Ps 25:8-9
1444:20-21	—	—		—	Ps 34:8 Na 1:7
1444:21					Je 17:7
1444:21-22	—	—		—	Ps 46:1
1444:23-24					Ps 103:17
1444:24-25	—	—		—	Ps 111:4; 145:8
1444:25-26					Ps 145:9
1444:26	—	—		—	Ps 147:3
1444:27					Ps 139:7
1444:28-30	—	—		—	Is 57:15
1444:30-31					Je 23:24
1444:31	—	—		—	Ps 96:11

pp. 1444 and 1445

The URANTIA Book Page:Line	MATTHEW Chap:Verse	MARK Chap:Verse	LUKE Chap:Verse	JOHN Chap:Verse	Other BOOKS Chap:Verse
1444:31-32	—	—	—	1Ch 16:31
					Ps 96:10
1444:32	—	—	—	1Ch 16:34
					Ps 136:1-3,26
1444:33-34	—	—	—	Ps 97:6
1444:34-35					Ps 100:3
1444:35-36	—	—	—	Ps 100:5
1444:36					Ps 22:28
	—	—	—	Da 4:17,25,32
					Da 5;21
1444:36-37	—	—	—	Ps 72:19
1444:37-38					Ps 107:8,15,21,31
1444:39-40	—	—	—	Ps 8:5
1444:40-41					Ps 1:6
1444:41	—	—	—	Ps 111:10
					Jb 28:28
1444:41-42	—	—	—	Pv 1:7; 9:10
1444:42-43	5:48				Ge 17:1 Le 19:2
	—	—	—	De 18:13
					2Co 13:11 Ja 1:4
	—	—	—	De 18:13
1444:43-44					Pv 16:18
1444:44	—	—	—	Pv 16:32
1444:44-46					Is 30:15
1444:46-1445:1	—	—	—	Is 40:31
1445: 1- 2					Is 14:3
1445: 2- 4	—	—	—	Is 41:10
1445: 5					Is 63:16
1445: 5- 6	—	—	—	Ne 9:6
1445: 6- 7					Ps 36:6
1445: 7- 8	—	—	—	Ps 36:8-9
1445: 8-10					Ps 92:1-2
1445:10-11	—	—	—	Ps 145:13
1445:11-15					Ps 23:1-4
1445:15-16	—	—	—	Ps 23:6
1445:17-18					Is 12:2
1445:18-20	—	—	—	Pv 3:5-6
1445:20					De 7:9
1445:20-21	—	—	—	Hk 2:4

46

The URANTIA Book Page:Line	MATTHEW Chap:Verse	MARK Chap:Verse	LUKE Chap:Verse	JOHN Chap:Verse	Other BOOKS Chap:Verse
1445:21					Ge 4:7
1445:21-22	—	—		—	Jb 4:8 Ga 6:7
1445:22					Ps 37:1
1445:23	—	—		—	Ps 66:18
1445:23-24					Pv 8:36
1445:24-25	—	—		—	Ec 12:14
1445:25-26					Pv 23:7
1445:27	—	—		—	Ps 145:18
1445:27-28					Ps 30:5
1445:28-29	—	—		—	Pv 17:22
1445:29					Ps 84:11
1445:29-30	—	—		—	Ec 12:13
1445:30-33					Is 45:18,21-22
1445:33	7:7-8		11:9-10	14:13-14 15:7,16 16:23-24	Je 29:13
1445:34-35	—	—			Ps 37:11
1445:35	—	—		—	Pv 22:8 Jb 4:8 Ga 6:7
1445:35-36	—	—		—	Ho 8:7
1445:37-39					Is 1:18
1445:39	—	—		—	Is 48:22; 57:21
1445:39-40					Je 5:25
1445:40	—	—		—	Ps 43:5
1445:41					Ps 35:9 Is 61:10
1445:41-42	—	—		—	De 33:27
1445:42-44					Ps 34:18-19
1445:44-45	—	—		—	Ps 37:5
1445:45-46					Ps 91:1
1445:47	19:19;22:39	12:31	10:27-28		Le 19:18 Ro 13:9 Ga 5:14 Ja 2:8
1445:47-48	7:12		6:31		To 4:15
1445:49-50	—	—		—	Pv 4:18
1445:50-1446:2					Da 12:3
1446: 2- 4	—	—		—	Is 55:7
1446: 5- 6					Ps 119:165
1446: 6-10	—	—		—	Ex 20:3-17 De 5:7-21
1446:11	22:37	12:30	10:27	—	De 6:5 Le 19:18

47

The URANTIA Book Page:Line	MATTHEW Chap:Verse	MARK Chap:Verse	LUKE Chap:Verse	JOHN Chap:Verse	Other BOOKS Chap:Verse
1446:11-12	19:19;22:39	12:31	10:27-28		Le 19:18 Ro 13:9 Ga 5:14 Ja 2:8
1446:12-13	—	—	—	Ho 13:14
1446:13					Ps 103:17-18
1446:14	—	—	—	Ho 1:10
1446:14-15					Je 31:3
1446:15-16	—	—	—	De 7:6 Da 2:44 Ps 23:6
1453:36-37	22:37	12:29-30 12:32	10:27	—	De 4,35-39;6:4-5 Ro 3:30 Ga 3:20
	—	—	—		1Co 8:4-6 Ep 4:6 Ja 2:19
1453:37	19:19;22:39	12:31	10:27-28		Le 19:18 Ro 13:9 Ga 5:14 Ja 2:8
1453:38	11:25		10:21		
1453:38					Cl 1:17
1453:38-39	—	—	—	1Co 3:16; 6:19 2Co 6:16 1Jo 4:12-13
	—	—			
1453:39			20:36		Ro 8:16+
1453:40-41					1Pe 4:19
1453:41	19:26	10:27 14:36	1:37 18:27	5:30	
1453:41-42				1:3	Ac 14:15 He 1:2
1453:43				14:7	1Jo 4:7
1453:43-44	(Same as 1417:5-6, above.)				
1453:45-47					1Co 2:9-16
1454: 2- 5	7:11		11:13		
1454: 6	18:14				2Pe 3:9
1454:10-11					Ml 3:6 Ja 1:17
1454:14-15	—	—		14:20 15:4-7	
1454:16-17	—	—			2Co 6:18
1454:17-19				4:23-24	
1454:20-21	5:38-45		6:27-31		
1454:22-23	7:7-8		11:9-10	14:13-14 15:7,16 16:23-24	Je 29:13
1454:24-25	—	—		15:10-11	

The URANTIA Book Page:Line	MATTHEW Chap:Verse	MARK Chap:Verse	LUKE Chap:Verse	JOHN Chap:Verse	Other BOOKS Chap:Verse
1454:27	–	–		–	2Co 9:15
1454:27-28					Ps 107:8,15
	–	–		–	Ps 107:21,31
1454:30-31					1Jo 3:2
1454:31-32	–	–		–	Ro 5:1
1454:32-33					Ro 15:13
					1Pe 1:8
	–	–		–	Re 2:10
1454:33-34					
1454:35					1Th 5:21
1454:35-36	7:12		6:31		To 4:15
1454:37				1:12	
1454:40	–	–		–	Jl 2:32
					Ac 2:21
1454:40-41	7:21	3:35	8:21		
	12:50				
1454:42-43	6:1-6				
1454:43	7:1-2		6:37		
1454:44	5:43-44		6:27,35		
1454:47	5:45				
1454:50		–		–	He 5:9

PAPER 132: The Sojourn at Rome

1458:33-35	4:16		1:79 1:4-9;5:35 Is 9:2		
			2:32 8:12;9:5 1Jo 2:8		
			12:35-36,46		
1461:45-46	–	–		–	Cl 4:10 Ph 24
					1Pe 5:13
1464:37-38	7:12		6:31		To 4:15 Ga 5:14

PAPER 133: The Return From Rome

1468:30					2Ch 19:7 Jb 34:19
	–	–		–	Ac 10:34 Ro 2:11
					Ga 2:6 Ep 6:9
1471:39-40	–	–		–	Ti 3:12
1471:48	–	–		–	1Co 1:14 Ac 18:8

The URANTIA Book Page:Line	MATTHEW Chap:Verse	MARK Chap:Verse	LUKE Chap:Verse	JOHN Chap:Verse	Other BOOKS Chap:Verse
1472:12-13	—	—		—	Ac 18:1-5
1472:22-23					Ac 18:7
1473:41-42	—	—		—	Ac 19:29;20:4
					Ro 16:23
	—	—		—	1Co 1:14
					3Jo 1:1
1473:48-50	—	—		—	Ac 18:2,18,26
					Ro 16:3
	—	—		—	1Co 16:19
					2Tm 4:19
1474:10-13	—	—		—	1Co 3:1-2
					1Pe 2:2
1474:14-15	22:21	12:17	20:25		
1474:22-23					2Co 13:5
1474:27	—	—		10:34-35	
1474:33					Ro 8:9
1474:37-42	5:10-12		6:35		
	6:19-20		12:33-34		
1474:40-42	—	—		14:2	
1474:42-43					He 11:10
1474:44-45	7:2		6:38		
1475: 4- 7	6:12,14-15	11:25-26	6:36-38		
	7:1-2;18:21-35		11:4		
1475: 7					Ge 18:25
1475: 9	-	-		-	Ps 82:6
1478:12-13					Pv 18:16
1478:16-19	-	-		-	Ac 19:1-10
1481:10					Ec 9:10
1481:21-22	-	-		-	Ge 11:27-28
1481:22					Es 1:2+
1481:28-31	-	-		-	Pv 4:7-8

PAPER 134: The Transition Years

1486:37-38					1Jo 4:7-11,16,19
1486:40-42	—	—		4:24	
1487: 7					Ep 4:3-6
1487:11	—	—		4:24	

The URANTIA Book Page:Line	MATTHEW Chap:Verse	MARK Chap:Verse	LUKE Chap:Verse	JOHN Chap:Verse	Other BOOKS Chap:Verse
1488: 9					Da 4:17,25,32
					Da 5:21
1490:30-32	24:6-7	13:7-8	21:9-10		
1491:32-34			2:14		
1492:18-19		–			Ac 11:25-26
1492:33-36	4:1		4:1		
1493:14-15	4:2-4	1:13	4:2-4		
1493:33-1494:6	4:3-11	1:12-13	4:1-13		
1495:16-17					1Sa 31:1-4

PAPER 135:   John The Baptist

The URANTIA Book Page:Line	MATTHEW Chap:Verse	MARK Chap:Verse	LUKE Chap:Verse	JOHN Chap:Verse	Other BOOKS Chap:Verse
1496: 3- 4			1:57		
1496: 3- 9	–		–	1:11-24	
1496:10			1:59		
1496:10-23	–		–	1:80	
1496:18-20			1:5		
1496:28-36			1:15		
1497: 5-11	3:4	1:6	1:80;3:4		
1497:30-33	3:1		3:2		
1498:12-14					Da 2:31-33
1498:19-22	-	-		-	Da 2:44
1498:22-25					Da 7:14
1498:25-28	-	-		-	Da 7:27
1498:31-33					Da 7:13-14
1499:15-48	-		-	3:2	
1499:24-27					Ml 4:5-6
1500:27	6:10	3:35	8:21	4:34;5:30	
	7:21	14:36-39	11:2	6:38;7:17	
	12:50		22:42	14:23-24	
	26:39,42,44			15:10,14;17:4	
1500:41-42	24:35	13:31	31:33		Is 65:17;66:22
					2Pe 3:10 Re 21:1-2
1501:22-28	–	–		–	En 46:1-6;48:1-7
					En 62:1-5;63:11
					En 69:27-29;71:14,17
1501:27-28	3:2;4:17	1:15			
	10:7				

pp. 1501 to 1505

The URANTIA Book Page:Line	MATTHEW Chap:Verse	MARK Chap:Verse	LUKE Chap:Verse	JOHN Chap:Verse	Other BOOKS Chap:Verse
1501:29-35	3:3	1:2-3	3:4-6	1:2-3	Is 40:3-5
1501:35	3:7		3:7		
1501:37-42	3:1		3:3		
1502: 1			2:25		
1502: 2				—	Ac 1:6
1502: 3	3:2;4:17;10:7	1:15			
1502: 7- 8			1:17		
1502:11-14	3:6,11	1:4-5,8	3:3,7,16	1:25-33	
1502:11-24	3:5-6	1:4-5			
1502:12-17	3:11	1:4,8	3:3,16	1:25-28,33	
1502:21-22				1:28	
1502:25-33	3:3	1:3	3:4-6	1:22-23	
1502:28-29					Is 40:3-5
1502:34-44	3:7-10		3:7-9		
1502:37-38	23:33				
1502:39-44	7:16-20			15:2	
1502:42-44	3:8-10 7:16-20 12:33		3:8-9 6:43-44 13:6-9	15:2,5-8,16	
1502:44-46					Js 4:1-9
1502:47-1503:2			3:10-14		
1503: 3- 4	3:2;4:17;10:7	1:15			
1503: 6-19	—	—		1:31	
1503:20-28			3:15-18		
1503:24-28	3:11-12	1:7-8		1:27	
1503:31	3:11	1:4,8	3:3,16	1:25:28,33	
1503:35-36				1:28	
1504:11-17		1:9-11		1:28	
1504:11-42	3:13-17	1:9-11	3:21-22		
1504:42-44		1:12-13	4:2		
1504:44	4:1-2				
1504:45-48				1:32-34	
1504:47-48	—	—		1:34	
1505: 4- 7				1:32-34	
1505:21-25	—	—		1:19-21	
1505:25-30				1:24-26	
1505:35-36	—	—			Js 12:7-24
1505:45-1506:3				1:15	
1505:45-1506:8	—	—		1:29-32	

The URANTIA Book Page:Line	MATTHEW Chap:Verse	MARK Chap:Verse	LUKE Chap:Verse	JOHN Chap:Verse	Other BOOKS Chap:Verse
1506: 2- 3		1:7		1:15,20	
1506: 6	3:16	1:10	3:22		
1506: 7- 8	3:17	1:11	3:22		
1506:11-12	4:12	1:14			
1506:14-16				1:43	
1506:27-29	14:3-4	6:18	3:19		
1506:31-40			3:19-20		
1506:36-40	14:3	6:17			
1506:38-42	4:12	1:14			
1507: 9-13				3:25-26	
1507:13-19	–		–	3:27-30	
1507:19-25				3:31-36	
1507:36-45	11:2-6		7:18-23		
1508: 7-15	14:3-5				
1508: 7-18		6:20			
1508:14-15		6:19			
1508:23-45	14:6-12	6:21-29			
1508:25-27		6:19			

PAPER 136: Baptism and The Forty Days

1509: 3- 5			3:15		
1509:10-13	11:11		7:28		
1509:17			8:1		
1509:24					Is 42:1
	–	–	–	–	Ek 34:23-24
					Ek 37:24-25
1509:24	–	–	–	–	Da 7:13-14
1509:25					Da 3:25
1509:27	–	–	4:25		
1510:19					Ge 6:6 Ex 32:14
	–	–	–	–	1Sa 15:29 Am 7:3,6
					Zc 8:14
1510:26-27	3:2,11 4:17;10:7	1:4,8,15	3:3,16	1:25-28,33	
1510:35-36					Da 7:13-14
1510:41-43				1:1-5,14	
1510:45-46	3:13-17	1:9-11	3:21-22		
1510:46	3:2;4:17;10:7	1:15			

53

The URANTIA Book Page:Line	MATTHEW Chap:Verse	MARK Chap:Verse	LUKE Chap:Verse	JOHN Chap:Verse	Other BOOKS Chap:Verse
1511: 7					Da 9:11
1511:37-38	3:16	1:10	3:22		
1511:39-41	3:17	1:11	3:22	1:34	
1511:42-43	3:16	1:10	3:22	1:32	
1511:46-48	6:9-10		11:2		
1511:47-48	6:10	3:35	8:21	4:34;5:30	
	7:21	14:36-39	11:2	6:38;7:17	
	12:50		22:42	14:23-24	
	26:39,42,44			15:10,14;17:4	
1511:48	3:16	1:10	3:21		
1512: 5	3:17	1:11	3:22		
1512:22			3:23		
1512:23-29			3:1		
1512:30-34	4:1-11	1:12-13	4:1-13		
1514:24-26	4:2	1:13	4:2		
1514:27-28	4:3	1:13	4:2		
1514:35	(Same as 1511:47-48, above.)				
1514:38-39	4:1-11	1:12-13	4:1-13		
1515:25-26	4:1	1:12-13	4:1-2		
1516: 5	26:53				
1517:46-48	4:2-4		4:2-4		
1518:24-25	4:4		4:4		De 8:3
1518:26-28	4:3-4		4:3-4		
1518:31-32	27:42	15:31			
1519:27-33	4:5-6		4:9-11		
1519:34-38	4:5-7		4:9-11		Ps 91:10-12
1519:46	14:25	6:48		6:19	
1520: 6- 7	27:39-44	15:29-32	25:35		
1520:20-21	8:4	1:44	5:14		
	9:30	5:43	8:56		
		7:36;8:26			
1520:21-23	12:38;16:1	8:11	11:16	2:18;6:30	
1521: 2- 5	4:5-7		4:9-11		
1521:13-14					Ac 14:22
1522: 1-18	4:8-10		4:5-8		De 6:13-14;10:20
1522:33-34	4:8-10		4:5-8		
1522:43-47				1:14,18	Ps 2:7-9 He 1:5
				3:16,18	Ac 13:33 He 5:5
				1Jo 4:9	

PAPER 137: Tarrying Time in Galilee

The URANTIA Book Page:Line	MATTHEW Chap:Verse	MARK Chap:Verse	LUKE Chap:Verse	JOHN Chap:Verse	Other BOOKS Chap:Verse
1524: 9				1:40	
1524: 9-1525:2	4:18-20	1:16-18	5:1-9	1:40-42	Ac 1:13
	10:2	3:16-18	6:14		
1524:25-28				1:41	
1524:36-1525:2	16:17-18			1:42	
1525: 7-46		4:21-22	1:19-20		Ac 1:13
			6:14		
1526: 4- 6				1:43	
1526: 8-10	_	_		1:35-37	
1526:11-12					Da 7:13
1526:22-44	_	_		1:43-44	
1526:45-1527:13				1:45-51	
1527:26-27	_	_		2:2	
1528:31-32				2:1	
1529:31-1530:5	_	_		2:3-4	
1530: 6-16				2:5	
1530:25-30	_	_		2:6-8	
1531: 4- 8				2:9-10	
1531: 9-17	_	_		2:11	
1531:24-27				2:12	
1532:34-35	_	_		2:12	
1532:41-45					Is 66:1-2
1532:45-1533:3	_	_		_	Is 66:5-8
1533: 4- 7					Is 66:12-14
1533:23-25	_	_	17:20-21		
1533:26				15:14-15	
1533:29-31	_	_		16:33	Ac 14:22 Re 7:14
1534: 9				1:38,49	
				3:2;6:25	
	_	_		15:14-15	
1534:11-12					
1534:41-42	_	_			Da 12:1-2
1535: 8- 9				4:9	
1535:18			8:1		
1535:31-37	4:12,17	1:14,15			
1536: 3					Ex 19:6
1536: 3- 4	_	_		_	Is 33:22
1536: 4- 5					Ps 84:3

The URANTIA Book Page:Line	MATTHEW Chap:Verse	MARK Chap:Verse	LUKE Chap:Verse	JOHN Chap:Verse	Other BOOKS Chap:Verse
1536: 5	—	—		—	Ps 47:2
1536: 5- 6					Ps 138:2
1536: 6	—	—		—	Ek 3:12
1536: 6					Ps 10:16
1536: 8-1537:23	3:2 / 4:17;10:7	1:15			
1536: 9-10					1Co 12:13
1536:10	—	—		—	2Ch 19:7 Jb 34:19 / Ac 10:34 Ro 2:11 / Ga 2:6 Ep 6:9
1536:16	—	—		18:36	
1536:24-26	6:33		12:31		
1536:26-28	18:3	10:15	18:17		
1536:29-30	24:23	13:21			
1536:34-36	3:11	1:4,8	3:3,16	1:25-28 / 1:33	Ac 1:5 / Ac 11:16
1536:37					Ga 3:28 Cl 3:11
1536:38-39	19:30 / 20:16,26-27 / 23:11	10:31 / 10:43-44	9:48;13:30 / 14:11;18:14 / 22:26-27		
1536:39-42			22:28-30		
1536:43-44	13:8,23	4:8,20	8:8		
1536:47-49					Ro 14:17
1537: 2	5:48	—		—	Ge 17:1 Le 19:2 / De 18:13
		—		—	2Co 13:11 Ja 1:4
1537:6-9	19:29				
1537:11-12	3:2;4:17 / 10:7	1:15	21:31		
1537:17-19	9:13	2:17	5:32		
1537:21-22					Ep 2:8
1537:29-30		3:21			

PAPER 138: Training the Kingdom's Messengers

1538:19	13:57	6:4	4:24	4:44	
1540:16-21	9:9	2:14	5:27-28		
1540:31-1541:14	9:10-13	2:15-17	5:29-32		

The URANTIA Book Page:Line	MATTHEW Chap:Verse	MARK Chap:Verse	LUKE Chap:Verse	JOHN Chap:Verse	Other BOOKS Chap:Verse
1540:34	11:19		7:34		
1541:38-40					1Co 12:13
1543:22-23					He 9:8;10:20
1544:47	4:19	1:17	5:10		
1545:21	3:17	1:11	3:22		
1545:24				2:1-11	
1545:35-37		—		3:3-8	
1545:39	3:7		3:7		
1546:37-38		3:21			
1547:33	—	—		12:6;13:29	

PAPER 139: The Twelve Apostles

The URANTIA Book Page:Line	MATTHEW Chap:Verse	MARK Chap:Verse	LUKE Chap:Verse	JOHN Chap:Verse	Other BOOKS Chap:Verse
1548: 2	10:2-4	3:16-19	6:13-16		Ac 1:13
1548:20-21					Ac 4:13
1548:31	—	—		1:42 21:15-17	
1548:34-35	4:18,21	1:16	5:10		
1549:10-12				1:40-42	
1549:28	—	—			Ac 2:41
1549:35	10:2		6:14	1:40;6:8	
1550:23	4:18-20	1:16-18		1:40-42	
1550:26-27	4:18-20	1:16	5:10		
1550:28-29				1:40-42	
1550:29	10:2		6:14		
1550:29		3:16	6:14		
1550:31-32	16:18		6:37 17:3-4	1:42	
1551: 1- 2		—		21:7	
1551: 4- 6	18:21-22				
1551: 6- 8	26:69-75	14:66-72	22:55-62	18:15-18 18:25-27	
1551: 9-11				13:8-9	
1551:15-17	26:69-72	14:66-70	22:56-57	18:16-17	
1551:21-22					Ac 8:14-25
	—	—	—		Ac 15:5-12
1551:22-25					Ga 2:11-14
1551:32	26:58	14:54	22:54		

pp. 1552 to 1561

The URANTIA Book Page:Line	MATTHEW Chap:Verse	MARK Chap:Verse	LUKE Chap:Verse	JOHN Chap:Verse	Other BOOKS Chap:Verse
1552:22-23		3:17			
1552:25-26	4:21-22	1:19-20	5:10		
1553: 9		3:17			
1553: 9-11			9:54		
1553:21-30	20:21-22	10:35-39			
1553:28-30				—	Ac 12:1-2
1553:40-43	4:21-22	1:19-20	5:10		
1554: 1				13:23;19:26 20:2;21:20	
1554:22	—	—		13:23;19:26 20:2;21:20	
1554:37-42	—	—		—	1Jo 3:11,23 1Jo 4:7,11-12 1Jo 4:16-21
1554:37-42	—	—		—	2Jo 5
1555: 3- 4			9:54-56		
1555: 4- 5		9:38	9:49-50		
1555:19-23	—	—		19:26-27	
1555:25-27				21:7	
1555:35-36	—	—		—	Re 1:9
1555:40-41					Pv 15:1
1556: 6- 8	—	—		1:43-44	
1556:10				1:43	
1557: 2	—	—		1:44 12:21	
1557:21-23	—	—		1:45-46	
1557:30-36				12:20-22	
1557:36-38	—	—		—	Ac 8:5-6,12
1557:38-40					Ac 8:14-17
1558: 8- 9	—	—		1:45-49	
1558:15				21:2	
1558:19-20				1:47	
1558:25-26	—	—		1:46	
1558:42-43				10:10	
1559:13	10:3	3:18	6:14		Ac 1:13
1559:21-23	9:9	2:14	5:27-28		Ac 1:13
	10:3	3:18	6:15		
1560: 7-10	9:9	2:14	5:27-28		
1561: 3				20:25	

58

The URANTIA Book Page:Line	MATTHEW Chap:Verse	MARK Chap:Verse	LUKE Chap:Verse	JOHN Chap:Verse	Other BOOKS Chap:Verse
1562:23-24	—	—		11:16	
1563: 6				21:1-2	
1563:15	10:3	3:18	6:15-16		Ac 1:13
1563:37	10:3	3:18	6:16		Ac 1:13
1564:13-15	19:20-22	10:21-22	18:22-23		
1564:23-24				14:22	
1564:34	10:4	3:18	6:15		Ac 1:13
1565:11			2:14		
1566:18	—	—		—	Ca 5:16
1566:18-19					Ca 5:10
1566:32	—	—		—	Pv 14:12
1566:32					Pv 16:25
1567: 3- 5	—	—		3:15-16	1Jo 5:11-12
				5:24-25	Re 3:8
	—	—		5:39-40;6:40,47	
				10:10;11:25-26	
1567: 4	16:24-25	8:34-35	9:23-24	3:15-16	Re 22:17
1567:18-21	26:7-13				
1567:24-25	26:14-16	14:10	22:3-6		
1567:41-44	27:3-5				

PAPER 140: The Ordination of The Twelve

The URANTIA Book Page:Line	MATTHEW Chap:Verse	MARK Chap:Verse	LUKE Chap:Verse	JOHN Chap:Verse	Other BOOKS Chap:Verse
1568: 3-13	5:1				
1568:28-30			1:33		
1568:30-34	8:11-12		13:28-30		
1569: 1			2:14		
1569: 6- 8	3:8-10		3:8-9	15:2,5-8	Ga 5:22-23
	7:16-20		6:43-44	15:16	Ep 5:9
	13:6-9		13:6-9		
1569: 8-10	6:10;7:21	3:35	8:21	4:34;5:30	
	12:50	14:36-39	11:2	6:38;7:17	
	26:39,42,44		22:42	14:23-24	
				15:10,14;17:4	
1569:10	5:16,48	11:25-26	10:21		
	6:1-9;7:11,21		11:2		
	11:25;16:17				
	18:35;23:9				

pp. 1569 to 1571

The URANTIA Book Page:Line	MATTHEW Chap:Verse	MARK Chap:Verse	LUKE Chap:Verse	JOHN Chap:Verse	Other BOOKS Chap:Verse
1569:11-13	6:33		12:31		
1569:13-15	24:30-31				
1569:15-17	24:26-27		17:20-21		
1569:18-20	20:26-27	10:43-44	22:26		
	23:11	9:35	9:48		
1569:21				15:15	
1569:24-25	16:28	9:1	9:27		
1570: 8-26	5:2				
1570:10-12					He 11:16
1570:16-17	_	_	12:48		
1570:23-24			4:18		Is 61:1
1570:27-28	5:3		6:20		
1570:29-30	5:6		6:21		
1570:31	5:5				Zp 2:3
1570:32	5:8				
1570:35-36	5:4		6:21		
1570:37	5:7				
1570:38	5:9				
1570:39-42	5:10-12		6:22-23		
1570:43-45	5:13				
1570:44-45		9:50	14:34-35		
1570:46-1571: 2	5:14-16		11:33-36		
1570:46-47		4:21	8:16		
1571: 1- 2	5:16	4:21	8:16;11:33		
1571: 2	5:16,48	11:25-26	10:21		
	6:1-9;7:11,21,25		11:2		
	16:17;18:35;23:9				
1571: 3- 4					2Co 5:20
1571: 5- 7	5:39		6:29		
1571: 7- 8					1Co 6:1-7
1571:10-11	5:43-44		6:27-28,35		
1571:10-12				13:34;15:12	
1571:11-12	7:12		6:31		To 4:15
1571:13-14	5:45				
1571:15-16			6:36		
1571:16-17	5:16;5:48	11:25-26	10:21		Ge 17:1 Le 19:2
	6:1-9;7:11,21,25		11:2		De 18:13
	16:17;18:35;23:9				2Co 13:11 Ja 1:4
1571:18-19			6:37		

The URANTIA Book Page:Line	MATTHEW Chap:Verse	MARK Chap:Verse	LUKE Chap:Verse	JOHN Chap:Verse	Other BOOKS Chap:Verse
1571:18-23	7:1-5				
1571:20-23			6:41-42		
1571:25-26			6:39		
1571:29-30	7:6				
1571:31-37	7:15-20				
1571:32-37	3:8-10		3:8-9	15:2,5-8,16	
	7:16-20		6:43-44		
	12:33		13:6-9		
1571:37-39	6:21		6:45;12:34		
1571:40-43	7:21-23				
1571:43-46	7:24-27		6:47-49		
1571:47-48	7:28-29	1:22			
1572: 7- 9	5:13	9:50	14:34-35		
1572:13-16	5:14-16	4:21	8:16;11:33		
1572:27	(Same as 1571:32-37, above.)				
1572:29-30	7:19				
1573: 6- 7	5:48				Ge 17:1 Le 19:2
	—	—	—		De 18:13
					2Co 13:11 Ja 1:4
1573:10-18				13:34;15:9-12	
				14:15,23-24	
1573:19-21	5:48				Ge 17:1 Le 19:2
	—	—	—		De 18:13
					2Co 13:11 Ja 1:4
1573:42	5:3		6:20		
1573:46-47			18:10-14		
1574: 6- 7	5:6		6:21		
1574:19-20	5:5				Zp 2:3
1574:21	6:10;7:21	3:35	8:21	4:34;5:30	
	12:50	14:36-39	11:2	6:38;7:17	
	26:39,42,44		22:42	14:23-24	
				15:10,14;17:4	
1574:25	5:8				
1574:45	5:48				Ge 17:1 Le 19:2
	—	—	—		De 18:13
					2Co 13:11
1575: 3	5:4		6:21		
1575: 6- 8			6:32;19:41	11:35	
1575:12-13					Nu 12:3

The URANTIA Book Page:Line	MATTHEW Chap:Verse	MARK Chap:Verse	LUKE Chap:Verse	JOHN Chap:Verse	Other BOOKS Chap:Verse
1575:16	5:7				
1575:23	5:9				
1575:26-27				14:1,27	
1575:32-33	16:25	8:35	9:24	12:25	
	10:39		17:33		
1575:34-37	5:10-12		6:22-23		
1575:39-40				15:13	
1576:14-16	18:3-4	9:37		3:3	
		10:15	18:17	3:7	
1576:18-21	5:17				
1576:22-25	5:20				
1576:27-32	5:21-22				
1576:28					Ex 20:13 De 5:17
1576:28-29	–	–	–		Le 24:17,21
					Nu 35:30
1576:29	–	–	–		1Sa 16:7
1576:34					Ex 20:14 De 5:18
1576:34-36	5:27-28				
1576:39-1577:2	5:31-32	10:2-12	16:18		
	19:3-9				
1577:13-14				10:16	
1577:16-21	5:38-42				De 19:21
1577:17					Ex 21:24 Le 24:20
					De 19:21
1577:18-19	–	–	–		2Tm 2:24
1577:21-26		–		6:60-69	
1577:29-30	6:1-4				
1577:30-32	6:6-8				
1577:31-32	6:8	–	–		Is 65:24
1577:32-33	6:16				
1577:33-36	5:10-12		6:35		
	6:19-21		12:33-34		
1577:37-40	6:22-23		11:34		
1577:44-46	6:24		16:13		
1577:47-50	6:25-26		12:22-23		
	6:31				
1577:47-1578:4			12:22-31		
1578: 1- 4	6:25-26,32-34		12:22-23		

The URANTIA Book Page:Line	MATTHEW Chap:Verse	MARK Chap:Verse	LUKE Chap:Verse	JOHN Chap:Verse	Other BOOKS Chap:Verse
1580: 1	5:38-40				Ex 21:24 Le 24:20 De 19:21
1580: 7	5:43-44	—	6:27,35	—	
1580: 8- 9	18:14				Ro 12:17,21 1Th 5:15 1Pe 3:9
1580:10-11	6:25-34	—	12:22-34	—	
1580:16-17	22:21	12:17	20:25		
1580:29-32			10:29-37		
1580:37-39		—	14:12-14		
1580:42	7:1-2		6:37		
1580:47	10:16				
1581:26-27			12:15		
1581:28-29	16:26	8:36	9:25		
1581:44-45					Ac 20:35
1582: 8	6:10;7:21 12:50 26:39,42,44	3:35 14:36-39	8:21 11:2 22:42	4:34;5:30 6:38;7:17 14:23-24 15:10,14;17:4	
1582:19-20	10:31		12:7;5:10 8:50;12:32		
1582:33-34	3:8-10 7:16-20 12:33		3:8-9 6:43-44 13:6-9	15:2,5-8,16	
1582:40-42		—	—		1Co 15:45-49
1583: 2- 4	6:1-3				
1583:10-11	13:31-32	4:31-32	13:19		
1583:14-15	13:45-46				
1583:38	5:48	—	—	—	Ge 17:1 Le 19:2 De 18:13 2Co 13:11 Ja 1:4
1584: 1- 3	10:1	3:13-14	9:1-2		
1584: 4- 6	10:7-8 24:14 28:19-20	13:10 16:15	24:47	20:21	Ac 1:8
1584: 7- 8	10:9-10	6:8-9	9:3;10:4-7		
1584: 8- 9			10:3		
1584: 8-17	10:16-22				
1584:10-17	24:9-13 —	13:9-13 —	21:12-17 12:11-12		

63

The URANTIA Book Page:Line	MATTHEW Chap:Verse	MARK Chap:Verse	LUKE Chap:Verse	JOHN Chap:Verse	Other BOOKS Chap:Verse
1584:18					Ro 1:16
1584:28-29	5:48				Ge 17:1 Le 19:2
	—	—	—		De 18:13
					2Co 13:11 Ja 1:4
1584:31-32	3:2,6,11	1:4-5,8	3:3,7,16	1:25-33	Ac 13:24
1585: 9-23	18:2-5				
1585:11	7:15				
1585:11-12	7:6				
1585:13-15	19:14	10:14-15	18:16-17		
1585:29-30	—	—		13:34	
1585:29-30				15:12	
1585:30	7:12		6:31		To 4:15

PAPER 141: Beginning the Public Work

1588:25-28	3:2;4:17				
	10:7;1:15				
1588:26-28	10:7		17:20-21		
1590: 4	27:54	15:39	23:47		
1590:11				—	Ac 10:38
1590:13-16	11:28-30				
1590:20	5:39				
1590:27-30	—	—		—	Ps 94:1-15
1590:31					Zc 14:9+
1590:31	—	—		—	Is 63:16
					Is 64:8
1590:44-45	10:1,8		9:2;10:9		
1591:15-16	—	—	24:49	14:16-18	Ek 11:19
			14:26;15:26	Ek 36:26-27	
	—	—	16:7,13-14	Jl 2:28	
					Ac 2:2-4,16-18
1591:16-17	16:27;24:30	8:38	9:26		Ac 1:8
	25:31	13:26	21:27		
1591:30					Ep 4:3
1591:35-36	—	—		—	Ep 4:13
1591:41-45					1Co 12:4-30
1592:46	—	—	3:3-7		
1593: 5					2Tm 2:24

The URANTIA Book Page:Line	MATTHEW Chap:Verse	MARK Chap:Verse	LUKE Chap:Verse	JOHN Chap:Verse	Other BOOKS Chap:Verse
1593:11-13	3:6,11	1:4-5,8	3:7,16	1:25-33	Ac 1:5
1593:34	—	—		14:6	
1594: 1- 2				8:32	
1594: 2- 3	—	—		1:14	
1594: 3- 4	(Same as 1591:15-16, above.)				
1594:12-13	11:5		4:18;7:22 14:13		Is 61:1
1594:14-16	—	3:21			
1594:23-24				3:2	
1594:33-34	6:10;7:21 12:50 26:39,42,44	3:35 14:36-39	8:21 11:2 22:42	4:34;5:30 6:38;7:17 14:23-24 15:10,14;17:4	
1594:47-48				1:14	
1594:48	—	—			1Tm 2:5
1595:38				2:23	

PAPER 142: The Passover at Jerusalem

The URANTIA Book Page:Line	MATTHEW Chap:Verse	MARK Chap:Verse	LUKE Chap:Verse	JOHN Chap:Verse	Other BOOKS Chap:Verse
1596:26-27	3:8-10 7:16-20 12:33		3:8-9 6:43-44 13:6-9	15:2,5-8,16	Ga 5:22-23 Ep 5:9
1596:28-29	—	—		2:23	
1597: 7-10					Ex 4:14;20:5
	—	—	—		Ex 22:24;32:10 Ex 34:14
	—	—	—		De 5:9;32:35
1597: 9-10					Is 35:4
1598:21-27		5:7			Ge 14:9-20
	—	—	—		Nu 24:16 De 32:8 Ps 9:2 PM 7 Da 4:17,15,32 Da 5:21 He 7:1+
	—	—	—		
1598:23-24	—	—	—		Ge 11:31
1598:24-25					Ge 14:18-22
1598:34-35	—	—	—		Ge 1:1
1599:10-12					2Sa 24:1
1599:16-17	—	—	—		1Ch 21:1

The URANTIA Book Page:Line	MATTHEW Chap:Verse	MARK Chap:Verse	LUKE Chap:Verse	JOHN Chap:Verse	Other BOOKS Chap:Verse
1599:24-37					Ex 34:11-27
1599:26-37	—	—		—	Ex 23:10-19
1599:38					Ex 19:16-18
	—	—		—	De 5:4-5
1599:38-40					Ex 20:1-17
	—	—		—	De 5:6-21
1599:41-42					De 5:15
1599:43-45					Ex 20:11
1600: 1- 3	19:19	12:29-31	10:27-28		De 6:5 Le 19:18
	22:37-40				Ro 13:9 Ga 5:14
	—	—		—	Ja 2:8
1600:23					Ex 20:4 De 5:8
1600:33-36	(Same as 1600:1-3, above.)				
1601: 8-10	3:8-10		3:8-9	15:2,5-8,16	Ga 5:22-23
	7:16-20		6:43-44		Ep 5:9
	12:33		13:6-9		
1601:18-37				1:12-13	Ro 8:9-16
1601:27-29	—	—		1:12-13	1Jo 5:4
1601:30-32				1:12-13	Is 32:15-17
1601:36-37	—	—		13:34;15:12,17	
1601:45-1602:9				3:1-2	
1602:16-19	—	—		3:2	
1602:20-23				3:3-4	
1602:24-30	—	—		3:5-8	
1602:31-37				3:9-13	
1603: 6- 7	—	—		19:38-42	
1603:37-40				1:12	Is 56:5
	—	—		—	Ro 8:14-17
					Ga 3:26;4:6
	—	—		—	1Jo 3:1-2
1604:35-36	5:48				Ge 17:1 Le 19:2
	—	—		—	De 18:13
					2Co 13:11 Ja 1:4
1605:29-31	—	—		3:22	
1606:19-21				4:1-3	

PAPER 143: Going Through Samaria

The URANTIA Book Page:Line	MATTHEW Chap:Verse	MARK Chap:Verse	LUKE Chap:Verse	JOHN Chap:Verse	Other BOOKS Chap:Verse
1608: 1	6:10;7:21	3:35	8:21	4:34;5:30	
	12:50	14:36-39	11:2	6:38;7:17	
	26:39,42,44		22:42	14:23-24	
				15:10,14;17:4	
1608: 1- 2	11:27		10:22	1:18;6:45-46	
				8:26;12:49-50	
	—	—		14:7-9,20	
				17:6,25-26	
1608: 5- 8	—	—	—	He 12:5-11
1608: 8-15				1Jo 4:7-19
1608:18-19	11:5		4:18;7:32		Is 61:1
			14:13		
1608:20	—	—	—	2Ch 19:7 Jb 34:19
					Ac 10:34 Ro 2:11
					Ga 2:6 Ep 6:9
1608:22	24:14	13:10	24:47	20:21	Ac 1:8
	28:19-20	16:15			
1608:25					2Co 13:11 Mi 7:18
1608:28-34					Ro 8:35-39
1609:11-14	—	—	—	1Pe 2:23
1609:22-23					Pv 16:32
1609:24-25	9:14	2:18	5:33		
1609:26-27					2Co 5:17
1609:27-29	—	—	13:35		
1609:28-29					Ro 8:21
1609:30-34	—	—	—	Ro 12:2
1609:35-36					2Pe 1:4
1609:36-38	—	—	—	1Co 3:16;6:19
					2Co 6:16
1609:38-41	—	—	—	2Co 3:17
1609:44-46					Je 17:9
1610: 3- 8	—	—	—	Ro 3:27-28
					Ro 8:14-17
1610: 4- 5	—	—	—	Ga 2:16
1610: 4-12					Ro 5:1-2
1610:10-12	—	—	—	2Co 7:1
1610:13					Ga 3:26

The URANTIA Book Page:Line	MATTHEW Chap:Verse	MARK Chap:Verse	LUKE Chap:Verse	JOHN Chap:Verse	Other BOOKS Chap:Verse
1610:15-16	—	—		—	Ro 2:4
1610:18					Ep 2:8
1610:19-20	—	—		—	Ro 8:21 Is 56:5
1610:21-23		—			Ro 8:1-17
1610:24-27	—	—		—	Ga 5:22-23
					Ep 5:9
1611:46-48	—	—		4:3	
1612:30-37		—		4:4-6	
1612:31-34	—	—		4:8	
1612:40-42				4:7	
1612:42-1613:3		—		4:9	
1613: 3- 8	5:6			4:10-14;6:35 Is 55:1	
				7:37-38 Re 7:16-17	
1613: 9-14	—	—		4:13-15	
1613:19-29				4:16-18	
1613:34-43	—	—		4:19-20	
1613:47-1614:8				4:21-24	
1614: 9-15	—	—		4:25-26	
1614:25-29				4:27	
1614:31-37	—	—		4:28-30	
1615: 1				4:29	
1615: 2- 3	—	—		4:18	
1615:12-18				4:31-32	
1615:18-30	—	—		4:33-38	
1615:22-23				5:17,36;9:4	
				17:4;19:30	
	—	—		4:39-41	
1615:31-34				4:39-41	
1615:33-34	—	—		3:22,26	
1616: 6-11		—			Ac 8:3-13

PAPER 144: At Gilboa and in The Decapolis

1618:21-32			11:1		
1619: 2-15			11:5-10		
1619:13-15	7:7-8		11:9-10	14:13-14 Je 29:13	
	—	—		15:7,16	
				16:23-24	
1619:16-24	7:9-11		11:11-13		

The URANTIA Book Page:Line	MATTHEW Chap:Verse	MARK Chap:Verse	LUKE Chap:Verse	JOHN Chap:Verse	Other BOOKS Chap:Verse
1619:23	5:16,46 6:1-9;7:11,21 11:25;16:17 18:35;23:9	11:25-26	10:21 11:2		
1619:25-35			18:1-5		
1619:36-38	17:20				1Co 13:2
1619:40-45			11:1		
1619:46-1620:10	6:9-13		11:2-4		
1620: 1	(Same as 1619:23, above.)				
1620:12			11:1		
1620:21-23	6:6				
1621: 5-11	18:2-5	10:15	18:15-17		
1625: 3- 4				10:16	
1625:18-23	—	—		3:22,26	
1625:23-26				4:2	
1625:30-35	3:11	1:48	3:3,16	1:25-28,33	
1626:38-42	11:2-3		7:19-20		
1626:43-45	11:4-5		7:21-22		
1626:45-1627:8	11:7-10		7:24-27		
1627: 6- 8				1:6-7	
1627: 7- 8					Ml 3:1
1627: 9-12	11:11		7:28		
1627:13-14			7:29		
1627:20-27	11:16-19		7:31-35		
1627:28-31	11:25-26				
1627:31-33	11:28-29				
1627:32-33			2:14	14:27;16:33	Pp 4:7
1627:35-40	14:9-12	6:26-29			

PAPER 145: Four Eventful Days at Capernaum

The URANTIA Book Page:Line	MATTHEW Chap:Verse	MARK Chap:Verse	LUKE Chap:Verse	JOHN Chap:Verse	Other BOOKS Chap:Verse
1628: 3- 4		1:21	4:31		
1628:27-35			5:1-3		
1628:27-1629:11	4:18-22	1:16-20			
1628:36-1629:11			5:4-11		
1629:18-19		1:21	4:31		
1629:26-27					Ex 23:25
1629:28-32	—	—		—	Is 60:1-3

The URANTIA Book Page:Line	MATTHEW Chap:Verse	MARK Chap:Verse	LUKE Chap:Verse	JOHN Chap:Verse	Other BOOKS Chap:Verse
1630: 4-12	—	—		—	Je 31:29-34
1630:16-19					Je 17:9-10
1630:22-25	—	—		—	Ek 18:2-4
1630:26-27					Ek 36:26
1630:42-44	7:28-29	1:22	4:31-32		
1630:45-1631: 2		1:23-26	4:33-35		
1631:14-19		1:27-28	4:36-37		
1631:22-27	8:14-15	1:29-31	4:38-39		
1632: 1-1633:15	8:16	1:32-34	4:40-41		
1634:18-19		1:34			
1634:42-45	—	1:35	4:42		
1635: 8-11		1:36-37			
1635:20-28	—		4:42		
1635:25-26		1:37			
1635:41-1636: 3		1:38	4:43		
1636: 9-10		1:39	4:44		

PAPER 146:   First Preaching Tour of Galilee

The URANTIA Book Page:Line	MATTHEW	MARK	LUKE	JOHN	Other BOOKS
1637: 2	4:23				
1637:24					Ex 32:1-35
					De 9:16-21
1638:22-27	—	—		—	Zc 7:11-13
1638:28-29				—	Pv 28:9
1638:34-41	6:14-15	11:25-26			
1638:35	(Same as 1619:23, above.)				
1638:36-41	6:12,14-15	11:25-26	6:37		
	18:21-35		11:4		
1639: 3- 7					Pv 1:24-29
1639: 8-10	7:1-2		6:36-37		
1639:11-12					Pv 21:13
1639:18-23	7:7-8		11:9-10	14:13-14	Je 29:13
	—	—		15:7,16	
				16:23-24	
1639:34-36	—	—		—	Ps 37:4-5
1639:37					Ps 72:12
1639:37	—	—			Ps 102:17
1639:39-42	(Same as 1639:18-23, above.)				

The URANTIA Book Page:Line	MATTHEW Chap:Verse	MARK Chap:Verse	LUKE Chap:Verse	JOHN Chap:Verse	Other BOOKS Chap:Verse
1640: 1- 2	5:44		6:28		
1640: 4					He 12:9
1640: 8	6:6				
1640:15-17					Ps 51:10
1640:19	—	—		—	Ps 141:3
1640:19-22					Ja 3:8
1640:28-31		—		4:24	
1640:32-34	6:7				
1640:38-41					Ps 92:1-2,4
1640:42-46	—	—		—	Pp 4:6
1640:46-48					Ps 69:30-31
1642: 3	—	—		5:26	
1642: 7- 8				5:24	
1642:18-24	—	—	24:49	14:16-18	Ek 11:19
				14:26;15:26	Ek 36:26-27
	—	—		16:7,13-15	Jl 2:28
1642:20-22					Ro 8:16
1642:22-24	—	—			Ro 8:14
1642:25-30				17:2-3	
1643:17-18		1:39	4:44		
1643:27-41	8:1-3	1:40-42	5:12-13		
1643:42-45	8:4				
1643:42-1644: 3		1:43-45	5:12-15		
1644:24				4:43	
1644:25-45	—	—		4:45-53	
1644:47-48				4:54	
1645:19-36	—		7:11-15		
1645:39-42			7:16		
1646: 1- 3	-		7:17		
1646:10-12					1Sa 28:7-25

PAPER 147: The Interlude Visit to Jerusalem

The URANTIA Book Page:Line	MATTHEW Chap:Verse	MARK Chap:Verse	LUKE Chap:Verse	JOHN Chap:Verse	Other BOOKS Chap:Verse
1647:27-36	8:5-6		7:1-5		
1647:37-1648: 6	8:7-9		7:6-8		
1648: 7- 9	8:10				
1648: 7-13			7:9-10		
1648:11-13	8:13				

71

The URANTIA Book Page:Line	MATTHEW Chap:Verse	MARK Chap:Verse	LUKE Chap:Verse	JOHN Chap:Verse	Other BOOKS Chap:Verse
1649: 2-12				5:1-4	
1649:30	—	—		4:36;5:17,36	
				9:4;17:4;19:30	
1649:39-43	—	—		3:15-16	1Jo 5:11-12
				5:24-25,39-40	
	—	—		6:40,47;10:10	
				11:25-26	
1649:40-41				6:40	
1649:47-1650:5	12:1-14	7:1-7	11:37-41	5:5,9	Ex 20:8-11
				5:16-18	De 5:12-15
1650:16-17		—		—	To 4:15
1650:40-41	7:12		6:31		
1651:29-33			7:36		
1651:43-1652:9	—	—	7:36-38		
1652:10-19			7:39-43		
1652:19-31	—	—	7:44-48		
1652:32-36			7:49-50		
1652:43-45	—	—			Re 3:8
1653:21				14:6	He 10:20
1653:26-37	5:17-20				
1654:29-49	12:1-2	2:23-24	6:1-2		
1654:49-1655:12	12:3-8	2:25-28	6:3-5		
1655: 2- 5			6:3-4		1Sa 21:3-6
1655:28-47	9:14-17	2:18-22	5:33-38		
1655:37-38	5:14-16		16:8	12:36	1Th 5:5 Ep 5:8
1656: 3- 9			5:39		
1656:14-17	—	—		—	Is 58:3-4
1656:18-24					Is 58:5-7
1656:25-37	—	—		—	Is 58:8-12

PAPER 148: Training Evangelists at Bethsaida

1660: 2- 4				3:5-6	
1660:31-34	—	—		—	Ro 5:12-19
1660:35-36					Ge 4:16-17
1660:36-38	—	—		—	Ge 6:1-2
1660:39					Ro 3:23
1660:48-1661:2		—		—	Ro 5:12-19

The URANTIA Book Page:Line	MATTHEW Chap:Verse	MARK Chap:Verse	LUKE Chap:Verse	JOHN Chap:Verse	Other BOOKS Chap:Verse
1661: 5- 6					Ps 82:6
1661: 6- 7	—	—		—	2Sa 7:14
1661: 7					1Ch 28:6
1661: 7- 9	—	—		—	Is 43:6-7
1661: 9-10					Ho 1:10
1661:39-48	—	—		—	He 12:5-10
1662:12-14					Pv 3:11-12
1662:14	—	—		—	La 3:33
1662:15					Ps 119:67
1662:15-16	—	—		—	Ps 119:71
1662:16-17					Ex 3:7
1662:17-18	—	—		—	De 33:27
1662:18-19					Ps 9:9
1662:19-20	—	—		—	Ps 41:3
1662:20-22					Ps 103:13-14
1662:22-23	—	—		—	Ps 147:3
1662:23-24					Is 25:4
1662:24-25	—	—		—	Is 40:29
1662:26					Is 42:3
1662:27-28	—	—		—	Is 43:2
1662:28-30			4:18		Is 61:1-2
1662:30	—	—		—	Jb 5:17-18
1662:30-31					Jb 5:6
1662:38-40	—	—		—	Jb 1:1-42:17
1662:40-43					Jb 1:1-5
1662:45-47	—	—		—	2Ch 19:7 Jb 34:19
					Ac 10:34-35
	—	—		—	Ro 2:11 Ga 2:6
					Ep 6:9
1663: 2	—	—		—	Ga 6:7
1663:10					Jb 42:6
1663:13-14	—	—	2:14	14:27;16:33	Pp 4:7
1663:15-22					Jb 4:1-5:27
1663:24-30	—	—		—	Jb 8:1-22
1663:31-39					Jb 9:1-10:22
1663:48-1664:1	—	—		—	Jb 11:1-20
1664: 3					Jb 14:1
1664: 4- 5	—	—		—	Jb 15:1-35
1664: 5- 6					Jb 18:1-21

73

The URANTIA Book Page:Line	MATTHEW Chap:Verse	MARK Chap:Verse	LUKE Chap:Verse	JOHN Chap:Verse	Other BOOKS Chap:Verse
1664: 6	—	—		—	Jb 20:1-29
1664: 6- 9					Jb 21:34
	—	—		—	Jb 23:1-24:25
1664: 9-11					Jb 27:1-31:40
1664:15	—	—		—	Jb 19:25
1664:21-22					Jb 38:1
1664:24	—	—		—	1Ki 19:12
1664:24-25					Is 30:21
1664:25-26	—	—		—	1Jo 4:12-13
1664:27-28					La 3:33
1665: 7-35	12:9-14	3:1-6	6:6-11		
1666:30-38		2:1-2	5:17		
1666:39-1667:12	9:2-3	2:3-5	5:18-20		
1667:13-27	9:3-8	2:6-12	5:21-26		

PAPER 149:   The Second Preaching Tour

1669:10-14		3:7-8			
1669:14-16	8:4	1:44	5:14		
		5:43	8:56		
	9:30	7:36			
1669:20		5:30	8:46		
1669:20-22			6:19		
1671:10-11	4:16		1:79;2:32	1:4-9;5:35	Is 9:2
	—	—		8:12;9:5	1Jo 2:8
				12:35-36,46	
1671:20-26	27:55-56	15:40-41	8:1-3	19:25	Ac 1:14
			23:27-49		
	—	—	24:10		
1671:35-38			13:1-5		
1671:42-43	15:16-20	7:14-23			
1672: 3- 5	8:21-22		9:59-60		
	19:20-22	10:21-22	18:22-23		
1673:12-15					Ja 1:20
1673:17	—	—		—	Jb 5:2
1673:18					Jb 18:4
1673:18-19	—	—		—	Pv 14:29
1673:20					Pv 15:1

The URANTIA Book Page:Line	MATTHEW Chap:Verse	MARK Chap:Verse	LUKE Chap:Verse	JOHN Chap:Verse	Other BOOKS Chap:Verse
1673:21					Pv 19:11
1673:21-22	–	–		–	Pv 25:28
1673:22					Pv 27:4
1673:23	–	–		–	Pv 29:22
1673:23-24					Ec 7:9
1674:26-27	–	–		–	Pv 20:27
1674:27-28					Ps 16:6
1674:28-29	–	–		–	Ps 37:16
1674:29-30					Pv 14:14
1674:30-33	–	–		–	Pv 15:13-17
1674:33-34					Pv 16:8
1674:34-35	–	–		–	Pv 17:22
1674:35-36					Ec 4:6
1674:42-43	–	–		–	Pv 28:1
1674:43-44					Is 57:20-21
1675: 6	–	–		–	Ps 34:9,11
1675:18					Ps 34:11
1675:31-32	–	–		–	Ro 2:4
1675:43-44					Ps 111:10 Jb 28:28
	–	–		–	Pv 1:7; 9:10
1676: 8- 9					Ec 12:13
1676:17-18	–		–	20:17	
1676:45					Mi 6:8
1676:46-47					Is 57:15
1676:48-1677:2	18:3	10:15	18:17		
1677: 3- 4					Je 12:2
1677: 5- 7	–	–		–	Mi 3:11
1677: 8- 9					Ps 28:3
1677: 9-10	–	–		–	Ps 5:9; 12:2
1677:10-11					Zc 13:6

PAPER 150: The third Preaching Tour

1678: 9			6:13		
1678:19-25			8:1		
1678:28-1679:10	27:55-56	15:40-41	8:2-3	19:25	Ac 1:14
			23:27,49		
	–	–	24:10		

75

pp. 1679 to 1686

The URANTIA Book Page:Line	MATTHEW Chap:Verse	MARK Chap:Verse	LUKE Chap:Verse	JOHN Chap:Verse	Other BOOKS Chap:Verse
1679:11-15			8:3		
1679:23-25	—	—			Ga 3:28
1679:36-38					1Tm 2:11-12
1680:21-29	(Same as 1671:20-26, above.)				
1680:28-29			8:3		
1680:34-36	2:1-10				
1681:28-32			10:2		
1681:28-38			9:1-2		
1681:29-32	9:37-38				
1681:32-35	10:1	6:7	9:1-2		
1681:35-38	10:2-4				
1681:35-38		3:16-19	6:13-16		
1681:39-42	3:2;4:17 10:5-7	1:15			
1681:43-45			6:40	13:16;15:20	
1681:43-47	10:24-26				
1681:47-1682:7	10:26-28	4:22	8:17;12:2-5		
1682: 1- 3	10:26-28	4:22	8:17;12:2-3		
1682: 4- 7			12:4-5		
1682: 8-11	10:29-31		12:6-7		
1682:11-18	10:34-36		12:51-53		
1682:19-20	10:37		14:26		
1682:21-23		6:12-13	9:6		
1682:32-1683:3					Ro 3:21-4:5
1682:34-35	—	—		—	Is 45:24
1682:35-36					Is 51:5
1682:36-38	—	—		—	Is 61:10
1682:39					Je 23:6;33:16
1682:39-41	—	—		—	Zc 3:4
1682:41-42					Hk 2:4
1682:44-48	—	—		—	Ep 2:8
1682:46-48					Ro 3:28;5:1 Ga 2:16; 3:24
1683:36-43		6:1	4:16		
1684:37-38	13:54	6:2	4:16		
1685:45-49			4:17		
1685:50-1686:6		—			De 30:11-14
1686: 7-11			4:17-19		
1686: 8-11	—	—			Is 61:1-2

76

The URANTIA Book Page:Line	MATTHEW Chap:Verse	MARK Chap:Verse	LUKE Chap:Verse	JOHN Chap:Verse	Other BOOKS Chap:Verse
1686:12-16			4:20-22		
1686:15-16	13:54	6:2	4:22		
1686:28-35	13:55-57	6:3-4	4:22-24		
			1:45;6:42		
1686:30-31	13:55	6:3	4:22	1:45;6:42	
1686:33-35				4:44	
1686:40-44	13:58	6:5			
1686:45-1687:14			4:28-30		
1687: 3					Pv 15:1
1687:16-17		1:21	4:31		

PAPER 151: Tarrying and Teaching by The Seaside

1688:21-36	13:1-3	4:1-2			
1688:26-29			8:4		
1688:37-1689:8	13:3-9	4:3-9	8:5-8		
1689: 9-13	13:10	4:10	8:9		
1689:14-31	13:11-15,35	4:11-12	8:10-11	12:37-40	Ho 6:9-10
1689:21-22					Ac 28:25-27 Is 6:9
1689:23-24	13:12;19:26	4:25	8:18;19:26		
1689:29-31					Is 6:10
1689:37-45	13:18-23	4:13			
1689:46-1690:17	13:18-23	4:14-20	8:11-15		
1692: 8-10	5:15-16	4:21	8:16;11:33		
1692: 8-16		4:21-25	8:16-18		
1692:10-13	10:26-27	4:22	8:17;12:2-3		
1692:15-16	13:12;25:29	4:25	8:18;19:26		
1693:20-27		4:26-29			
1693:31-43	13:24-30				
1693:44-1694:2	13:31-32	4:30-32	13:18-19		
1694: 3- 5	13:33		13:20-21		
1694: 6- 8	13:44				
1694: 9-11	13:45-46				
1694:12-15	13:47-48				
1694:16-19		4:33-34			
1694:21-25	8:18	4:35	8:22		
1694:26-43	8:23-24	4:36-38	8:22-23		

The URANTIA Book Page:Line	MATTHEW Chap:Verse	MARK Chap:Verse	LUKE Chap:Verse	JOHN Chap:Verse	Other BOOKS Chap:Verse
1695: 3-27	8:25-27	4:38-41	8:24-25		
1695:35-39		5:1	8:26		
1695:35-48	8:28				
1695:40-48		5:2-4	8:27		
1695:44-48			8:29		
1696: 1- 8		5:5			
1696: 9-11	8:29	5:6-7	8:28		
1696:15-18		5:8	8:29		
1696:15-28	8:30-33				
1696:18-25		5:15	8:35		
1696:26-28		5:11-14	8:32-33		
1696:26-35		5:9-14	8:30-34		
1696:42-1697:3	8:34	5:16-19	8:36-37		
1697: 5-12		5:18-20	8:38-39		

PAPER 152: Events Leading Up to The Capernaum Crisis

The URANTIA Book Page:Line	MATTHEW Chap:Verse	MARK Chap:Verse	LUKE Chap:Verse	JOHN Chap:Verse	Other BOOKS Chap:Verse
1698: 4-16		5:21-24	8:40-42		
1698: 8-16	9:18-19				
1698:16-37	9:20-22	5:25-34	8:43-48		
1699: 9-22		5:35-42	8:49-55		
1699:13-22	9:23-25				
1699:23-24		5:43	8:55		
1699:32-33		5:43	8:56		
1699:34-35	9:27				
1699:35-36	9:26				
1700:15-17				6:4	
1700:20-32	14:13-14	6:31-34	9:10-11	6:1-3	
1701:14-35	14:15-17	6:35-38	9:12-13	6:5-9	
1701:36-49	14:18-21	6:39-44	9:14-17	6:10-13	
1702:20-25				6:14	
1702:34-36	—	—		6:26	
1702:36-37				18:36	
1702:42					Ja 1:17
1702:44-1073:7	14:22-23	6:45-46			
1703: 1- 2				6:15	
1703: 5- 7				6:16-17	

The URANTIA Book Page:Line	MATTHEW Chap:Verse	MARK Chap:Verse	LUKE Chap:Verse	JOHN Chap:Verse	Other BOOKS Chap:Verse
1703:11-38	14:24-33	6:47-51		6:17-21	
1703:40-41	14:34	6:53			
1703:43-45				6:22	
1704:11-12	–	–		–	Ex 14:13
1704:12-13					Ps 4:5
1704:13-14	–	–		–	Ps 27:14
1704:14-15					Ps 55:22
1704:15-16	–	–		–	Ps 62:8
1704:16-17					Ps 91:1
1704:17-18	–	–		–	Ps 118:9

PAPER 153: The Crisis at Capernaum

1707:26-28				6:59	
1709:10-27	–	–		–	De 28:15-53
1709:29-48					Je 26:4-15
1710: 1- 3					Je 38:4-6
1710:15-16	11:27		10:22	1:18;6:45-46 8:26;12:49-50	
	–	–		14:7-9,20 17:6,25-26	
1710:25-26	–	–			Js 24:15
1710:27-29				6:23-24	
1710:29-43	–	–		6:26-27	
1710:43-45				6:28-29	
1710:46-1711:2		–		6:30-33	
1710:48-49					Ex 16:14-15
1711: 1- 4	5:6;26:26	14:22	22:19	6:35,48 6:51,58	Is 52:2 Re 7:16-17
1711: 3-13				6:34-40	
1711: 4- 5	5:6		–	4:10,13-14 6:35;7:37-38	Is 55:1 Re 7:16-17
1711:12-13	–	–		3:15-16 5:24-25,39-40	1Jo 5:11-12
	–	–		6:40,47;10:10 11:25-26	
1711:14-16	(Same as 1711:1-4, above.)				
1711:17-25				6:41-42	

79

pp. 1711 to 1716

The URANTIA Book Page:Line	MATTHEW Chap:Verse	MARK Chap:Verse	LUKE Chap:Verse	JOHN Chap:Verse	Other BOOKS Chap:Verse
1711:22-24	13:55-56	6:3	4:22		
1711:26-37				6:43-47	
1711:31-32	—	—		6:45	Is 54:13
1711:38-40				6:58	
1711:38-44	(See also 1711:1-4, above.)				
1711:38-44				6:48-51	
1711:46-48	—	—		6:52	
1712: 5- 8				6:52	
1712: 8- 9	(Same as 1711:4-5, above.)				
1712: 8-20	(See also 1711:1-4, above.)			6:53-58	
1712:10-11				1:14	
1712:21-42	15:1-9	7:1-13	11:37-41		
1712:29					Ex 20:12 De 5:16
1712:36-38					Is 29:13
1712:43-1713:14	15:10-20	7:14-23			
1713: 1-14	12:33-37 15:11	7:15			
1713:25-28					Ac 10:9-16
1713:40-48	12:22 9:32-33		11:14		
1714: 7-13	12:23-24 9:34;10:25	3:22 3:30	11:15		
1714:14-19	12:25-30	3:23-27			
1714:14-25			11:17-23		
1714:14-32	12:25-32				
1714:28-32		3:28-29			
1714:33-40	12:33-36				
1714:36-38	3:8-10 7:16-20 12:33		3:8-9 6:43-44 13:6-9	15:2,5-8,16	
1714:41-43	16:1	8:11	11:16	6:30	
1714:41-47	12:38-39	8:11-12			
1714:44-47	16:4		11:29		
1715: 4-24				6:60	
1715:25-36	—	—		6:61-62	
1715:30-31					Re 3:15-16
1715:37-1716: 1		—		6:63-70	

80

PAPER 154: Last Days at Capernaum

The URANTIA Book Page:Line	MATTHEW Chap:Verse	MARK Chap:Verse	LUKE Chap:Verse	JOHN Chap:Verse	Other BOOKS Chap:Verse
1717: 9-16		6:14	9:7		
1717:17-23	14:1-2	6:14-16	9:7-9		
1721: 4- 6	12:46	3:31	8:19		
1721:42-48	12:46-47	3:31-32	8:19-20		
1722:14-19	12:48-50	3:33-35			
1722:17-19			8:21		
1722:31-35			11:27-28		
1722:45	10:36		12:52-53		
1723:35-37	8:20		9:58		

PAPER 155: Fleeing Through Northern Galilee

The URANTIA Book Page:Line	MATTHEW Chap:Verse	MARK Chap:Verse	LUKE Chap:Verse	JOHN Chap:Verse	Other BOOKS Chap:Verse
1725:11-18					Ac 4:25-28
1725:12-15	—	—	—		Ps 2:1-3
1725:19-21					Ps 2:4-5
1725:21-22	—	—	—		Ps 2:8
1725:26-27					Ro 2:9
1725:27	—		—		Ps 2:11
1725:28				1:12	Is 56:5 1Jo 3:12
	—	—	—		Ro 8:14-17
					Ga 3:26;4:6
1725:29	—	—	—		Ps 2:11
1725:29-30					Ps 2:12
1725:33-34	—	—	—		Ps 2:12
1725:35-36					Ps 46:6
1726:32-40	11:21	10:13			
1727:10-11				—	Ro 14:17
1727:29-30	25:40				
1731: 4- 6	11:13				
1731: 6- 8			—	—	2Ch 19:7 Jb 34-19
					Ac 10:34-35
	—	—	—		Ro 2:11 Ga 2:6
					1Pe 1:17 Ep 6:9
1731:11-21	—	—	—		1Pe 2:9-10
1731:43					Is 26:3
1733: 3- 6	18:4;19:14	10:14-15	18:16-17		

81

PAPER 156: The Sojourn at Tyre and Sidon

The URANTIA Book Page:Line	MATTHEW Chap:Verse	MARK Chap:Verse	LUKE Chap:Verse	JOHN Chap:Verse	Other BOOKS Chap:Verse
1734: 3- 5	15:21	7:24			
1734:17-21		7:25-26			
1734:17-28	15:22				
1734:22-26		7:24			
1734:30-1735:4	15:23				
1735: 5-14	15:24-27	7:27-28			
1735:21-25	15:28	7:29-30			
1736:10-12	(Same as 1731:6-8, above.)				
1736:20-21	24:35	13:31	21:33		
1736:24-26					Pp 3:13-14
1736:26-28	—	—	—		1Co 3:1-2 1Pe 2:2 He 5:13-14
1736:32	—	—	—		1Jo 1:9
1736:33					Ac 24:16
1736:41-42	23:24				
1738: 9-14	7:24-27		6:47-49		
1738:25	6:13		11:4		
1738:34					Ex 7:13 +
1738:37-41	—	—	—		Ge 22:1 Ja 1:13-14
1739: 8- 9					2Co 5:17 Ep 4:22-24
	—	—	—		Cl 3:9-10
1739:12-13					Ro 12:21
1739:20	5:6		6:21		
1739:37-38	5:46				
1739:38-39					1Co 13:1-8
1740:19-20	22:21	12:17	20:25		
1740:37-38	10:8				
1740:43-44		—	—		Ga 6:9 2Th 3:13

PAPER 157: At Caesarea—Philippi

	MATTHEW	MARK	LUKE	JOHN	
1743:27-36	17:24-25				
1744: 2-28	17:25-27				
1744:37-1745:4	12:38-39 16:1-4		11:16	2:18;6:30	
1744:40-45		8:11	11:29		
1744:48-1745:2			12:54-57		

The URANTIA Book Page:Line	MATTHEW Chap:Verse	MARK Chap:Verse	LUKE Chap:Verse	JOHN Chap:Verse	Other BOOKS Chap:Verse
1745: 2- 4		8:12			
1745:10-11	16:6-12	8:15	12:1		
1745:16-17		8:18			
1745:29-30	16:13	8:27	9:18		
1745:45-47	16:13	8:27	9:18		
1746:10-14	16:14	8:28	9:19		
1746:12-13		6:14-15			
1746:14-20	16:15-16	8:29	9:20		
1746:17-21		1:1		1:34;3:15-16	
1746:22-23	16:17				
1746:24-25	16:20	8:30	9:21		
1747:19-33	16:18-20				
1747:32-33		8:33	9:21		
1748: 2- 3	16:16	1:1;8:29	9:20	1:34;3:15-16	
1748: 8-12	16:16-18				
1749: 8- 9				10:10	
1750: 5- 6	10:38 16:24	8:34 10:21	9:23 14:27		
1750:10-11	9:13	2:17	5:32		
1750:11	20:28	10:45			
1750:12-13	18:11		19:10		
1750:14-15	11:27		10:22	1:18;6:45-46 8:26;12:49-50 14:7-9,20 17:6,25-26	
1750:15	—	—		3:14-15;6:44 8:28;12:32	Je 31:3
1750:16-17	16:24-25	8:34-35	9:23-24	3:15-16 5:24-25,39-40 6:40,47;10:10 11:25-26	1Jo 5:11-12 Re 22:17
1750:21	—	—		8:58	
1750:21-23				16:28	
1750:26		—		18:36	
1750:27-29	8:20		9:58		
1750:30	—	—		1:1;5:18;10:30 14:9-11,20 17:11,21-22	
1750:30-31	—	—		14:9	

The URANTIA Book Page:Line	MATTHEW Chap:Verse	MARK Chap:Verse	LUKE Chap:Verse	JOHN Chap:Verse	Other BOOKS Chap:Verse
1750:32					He 13:5
1751:25	16:6,11	8:15	12:1		

PAPER 158: The Mount of Transfiguration

The URANTIA Book Page:Line	MATTHEW Chap:Verse	MARK Chap:Verse	LUKE Chap:Verse	JOHN Chap:Verse	Other BOOKS Chap:Verse
1752:16-21	17:1	9:2	9:28		
1753:31-38	17:2-3	9:2-4	9:29-32		
1753:41-48	17:4	9:5-6	9:33		
1753:49-1754:7	17:5-8	9:7-8	9:34-36		
1754: 9-12	17:9	9:9			
1754:21-22					Ml 4:5-6
1754:21-29	17:10-13	9:11-13			
1754:25-27	11:14				
1754:33-35		9:10	9:36		
1755:18-19	17:5	9:7	9:35		
1755:29-35		9:14	9:37		
1756:26-27	16:19				
1757: 2-18		9:15-18			
1757: 8-18	17:14-16		9:38-40		
1757:11-13		9:22			
1757:19-25	17:17	9:19	9:41		
1757:25-37		9:20-24			
1757:26-30			9:42		
1757:34-35	19:26	10:27 14:36	1:37;18:37		
1757:38-44	17:18	9:25-27	9:42-43		
1758: 9-15	17:19	9:28			
1758:16-27	17:20				
1758:17-27		9:29			
1758:28				18:36	
1758:33-35	19:30 20:26-27 23:11-12	9:35 10:31 10:43:44	9:48;13:30 14:11;18:14 22:26		
1759:10-15	17:22-23	9:31	9:43-44		
1759:15-17		9:32	9:45		
1759:19-31		9:30			
1759:39-46	16:21	8:31			
1759:43-46	17:22-23	9:31	9:22,44		

84

The URANTIA Book Page:Line	MATTHEW Chap:Verse	MARK Chap:Verse	LUKE Chap:Verse	JOHN Chap:Verse	Other BOOKS Chap:Verse
1760: 1- 4	16:22	8:32			
1760:10-15	16:23	8:33			
1760:17-26	16:24-28	8:34-38	9:23-27		
1760:17-19	8:34 10:21-38	10:21	14:27		
1760:19-20	10:39 16:25	8:35	9:24 17:33	12:25	
1760:20-22	16:26	8:36	9:25		
1760:22-25	16:27	8:38	9:26		
1760:25-26	16:28	9:1	9:27		
1761: 6-13		9:33-34			
1761: 9-13	18:1		9:46		
1761:13-19	18:3-4	10:15	18:17		
1761:13-20		9:36-37	9:47-48		
1761:13-29	18:2-10				
1761:19-20	10:40-42 18:5	9:37	9:48 10:16	13:20	
1761:20-21		9:35			
	(See also 1758:33-35, above.)				
1761:21-23			17:2		
1761:21-29		9:42-47			

PAPER 159: The Decapolis Tour

1762:21-32	18:12-14		15:3-7		
1762:33-1763:5	18:15-17				
1763: 5-19	18:18-20				
1763:20-1764:7	6:12 6:14-15	11:25-26	6:37 11:4		
1763:20-35	18:21-27		17:3-4		
1763:36-43	18:28-30				
1763:43-1764:3	18:31-35				
1764: 2	5:16,48 6:1,9;7:11,21 11:25;16:17 18:35;23:9	11:25-26	10:21 11:2		
1764: 6- 7	10:8				
1764:21-22					Ge 4:24

85

pp. 1764 to 1771

The URANTIA Book Page:Line	MATTHEW Chap:Verse	MARK Chap:Verse	LUKE Chap:Verse	JOHN Chap:Verse	Other BOOKS Chap:Verse
1764:24-29		9:38	9:49		
1764:29-36		9:39-40	9:50		
1764:38-40	10:42	9:41			
1764:42	12:30		11:23		
1765: 8-12	8:28-32	5:1-13	8:26-33		
1765:31-32					Re 3:20
1766:14	11:30				
1766:20-21					1Tm 6:12 2Tm 4:7
1766:31	—	—	—		Is 53:3
1768: 8-10					1Sa 15:3
1768:18-21	—	—	—		De 4:2 Pv 30:6
1768:26-27					Ga 1:6-9 Re 22:18-19
1769:24	—	—	—		Ps 51:10
1769:25					Ps 23:1
1769:26	19:19;22:39	12:31	10:27-28		Le 19:18 Ro 13:9 Ga 5:14 Ja 2:8
1769:27-28	—	—	—		Is 41:13
1769:29					Is 2:4 Mi 4:3
1769:42-44	6:10;7:21 12:50 26:39,42,44	3:35 14:36-39	8:21 11:2 22:42 15:10,14;17:4	4:34;5:30 6:38;7:17 14:23-24	Ja 1:22-25;2:17 1Jo 3:18
1770: 4- 5	19:19;22:39	12:31	10:27		Le 19:18 Ro 13:9 Ga 5:14 Ja 2:8
1770: 5- 7					Le 19:18
1770: 8-12	5:39		6:29		
1770:20					Ro 12:21
1770:22-23	16:24 10:38	8:34 10:21	9:23 14:27		
1770:24					Ac 10:38
1770:29-30			6:29		
1770:29-34	5:38-40				
1770:32	5:38-42				Ex 21:24 Le 24:20 De 19:21
1770:41-46	5:41	—	—		
1770:47					Je 36:3
1770:48-1771:1	18:11-14		15:3-10;19:10		
1771: 2- 3	5:38-48;7:12		6:27-38;6:31		To 4:15
1771: 9-10	15:14		6:39		

PAPER 160: Rodan of Alexandria

The URANTIA Book Page:Line	MATTHEW Chap:Verse	MARK Chap:Verse	LUKE Chap:Verse	JOHN Chap:Verse	Other BOOKS Chap:Verse
1774:28	(Same as 1769:42-44, above.)				
1775:44-45					Ge 2:18
1776:41	5:4		6:21		
1777:15			2:14		
1777:21	4:4		4:4		De 8:3
1781:47-50		12:29-30		—	Ex 20:3 De 5:7
					De 4:35-39 Ro 3:30
	—	—		—	1Co 8:4-6 Ga 3:20
					Ep 4:6 Ja 2:19
1782: 9-10	10:39	8:35	9:24	12:25	
	16:25		17:33		
1782:10-11	10:34		12:51		
1782:21-22				4:24	
1782:22					1Jo 4:8,16

PAPER 161: Further Discussions with Rodan

1784:27				1:1;5:18;10:30,38	
	—	—		14:9-11,20	
				17:11,21-22	
1784:43-44	5:48				Ge 17:1 Le 19:2
	—	—		—	De 18:13
					2Co 13:11 Ja 1:4
1786:28-29	—	—		1:34	
1786:33					Ac 10:38
1786:33	(Compare to 1784:27, above)				
1786:35-36	—	—		8:58	
1786:36-37				16:15	
1786:38-39	—	—		10:30	
1786:39-40				14:9	

PAPER 162: At The Feast of The Tabernacles

1788: 3-15			9:51-53		
1788:16-23	—	—	9:54-56		
1788:37-40				7:2-4	
1789: 4- 5	—	—		7:6	

87

The URANTIA Book Page:Line	MATTHEW Chap:Verse	MARK Chap:Verse	LUKE Chap:Verse	JOHN Chap:Verse	Other BOOKS Chap:Verse
1789:14-16				7:1	
1789:49-1790:2		—		7:8-10	
1790: 4- 6				7:11	
1790:10-16	—	—		7:12-13	
1790:16-18				7:15	
1790:25-39	—	—		7:14-19	
1790:38					Ex 20:13 De 5:17
1790:40-1791:14		—		7:20-26	
1791:15				7:25	
1791:15-26	—	—		7:27-29	
1791:27-33				7:30-31	
1791:34-44	—	—		7:32	
1791:47				7:30	
1792: 4- 5	—	—		3:15-16	1Jo 5:11-12
			5:24-25,39-40		
	—	—	6:40,47;10:10		
			11:25-26		
1792: 6-10	—	—		7:33-34	
1792: 7- 9				8:21	
1792:11-14	—	—	7:35-36;8:22		
1792:15-36	—	—		7:45-52	
1792:37-38				7:53-8:1	
1792:40-48	—	—		8:3-9	
1793: 1- 6				8:2-5	
1793: 7-12	—	—		8:6	
1793:25-37				8:6-11	
1793:43	—	—	—		Le 23:39-43
1794: 5					Nu 10:1-7
1794:39	—	—	—		Ps 113:1-118:29
1794:43					Ps 82:5-8
1795: 1	4:16		1:79;2:32	1:4-9;5:35	Is 9:2
				8:12;9:5	1Jo 2:8
				12:35-36,46	
1795: 1-16	—	—		8:12-19	
1795:17-18	—	—	8:21;7:33-34		
1795:18-27				8:23-26	
1795:28-32	—	—		8:28-30	
1795:32-33				8:20	
1795:35-43	—	—		7:37-39	

The URANTIA Book Page:Line	MATTHEW Chap:Verse	MARK Chap:Verse	LUKE Chap:Verse	JOHN Chap:Verse	Other BOOKS Chap:Verse
1795:41					Is 12:2-3
1796: 4- 7	—	—		—	Is 44:3
1796:13					He 12:9
1796:19-23	—		—	7:40-44	
1796:27-38				8:31-36	
1796:39-1797: 1			—	8:37-41	
1797: 1- 9				8:42-45	
1797:10-18	—		—	8:46-50	
1797:19-30				8:51-56	
1797:31-38			—	8:57-59	
1797:41-1798:15			10:38-42		

PAPER 163: Ordination of The Seventy at Magadan

The URANTIA Book Page:Line	MATTHEW Chap:Verse	MARK Chap:Verse	LUKE Chap:Verse	JOHN Chap:Verse	Other BOOKS Chap:Verse
1800: 8-11			10:1		
1800:29-1801:3			10:2-7		
1800:30-32	9:37-38				
1800:33-34	10:16		10:3		
1800:34-35	10:9-10	6:8-9	9:3; 10:4		
1800:36-38	10:11-13	6:10	10:5-7		
1800:37-1801:3		6:10			
1800:38-39	10:11-13	6:10	9:4; 10:5-7		
1801: 3- 4			2:14		
1801: 6- 8	3:2; 4:17	1:15 10:7-8			
1801: 6-13			10:8-11		
1801: 9-13	10:14-15	6:11	9:5		
1801:13-14	10:40; 18:5	9:37	9:48	13:20	
1801:13-15			10:16		
1801:18-20			10:1		
1801:31-39	8:19-22		9:57-60		
1801:40-45			9:61-62		
1801:46-1802:15	19:16-20				
1802: 5-15			10:17-20	18:18-21	
1802: 9-11	19:18-19	10:19	18:20		Ex 20:3-17 De 5:7-21
1802:16-24	19:20-21				
1802:17-24		10:21	18:22		
1802:25-26	19:22	10:22	18:23		

The URANTIA Book Page:Line	MATTHEW Chap:Verse	MARK Chap:Verse	LUKE Chap:Verse	JOHN Chap:Verse	Other BOOKS Chap:Verse
1803: 5- 8	19:24	10:25	18:25		
1803: 7- 8	6:24		16:13		
1803:26-33	19:23-24	10:23-25	18:24-25		
1803:34-40	19:25-26	10:26-27	18:26-27		
1803:38-40		14:36	1:37		
1804: 5- 6	19:27				
1804: 5-10			18:28-30		
1804: 5-11		10:28-31			
1804: 6-11	19:29-30				
1804:10-11	19:30	9:35	9:48;13:30		
	20:16,26-27	10:31	14:11;18:14		
	23:11	10:43-44	22:26		
1804:14-24	20:1-7				
1804:25-34	20:8-12				
1804:35-39	20:13-15				
1805:10-11	22:37-40	12:30-31	10:27-28		De 6:5 Le 19:18
		12:33			Ro 13:9 Ga 5:14 Ja 2:8
1805:21					Is 6:8
1805:33	−	−	10:4		
1806:38-46			10:17		
1807: 4- 9	−	−	10:17-18		
1807: 9-15			10:20		
1807:16-27	11:25-26		10:21-22		
1807:18-19	5:16,48	11:25-26	10:21		
	6:1-9;7:11,25		11:2		
	11:26;16:17				
	18:35;23;9				
1807:28-33	13:16-17		10:23-24		
1807:34-43	11:20-23		10:13-15		
1808: 6- 7					Ga 6:9 2Th 3:13
1808: 9-11	11:28-29				

PAPER 164: At The Feast of Dedication

1809:21-28	19:19	12:28-31	10:25-28		Le 19:18 De 6:5
	22:34-40				Ro 13:9 Ga 5;14 Ja 2:8
1809:29-32			10:29		
1809:35	15:26-27	7:27-28			

The URANTIA Book Page:Line	MATTHEW Chap:Verse	MARK Chap:Verse	LUKE Chap:Verse	JOHN Chap:Verse	Other BOOKS Chap:Verse
1810: 3-19			10:30-37		
1810:22	—		10:29		
1811:16		8:22-25			
1811:18-20				9:1	
1811:26-28	—	—		9:2	
1812: 5-12				9:3-5	
1812: 8-11	—	—		4:34;5:17,36	
				9:4;17:4;19:30	
1812:16-21	—	—		9:6-7	
1812:24-27				9:8-9	
1812:28-35	—	—		9:10-12	
1813:13-16				9:14	
1813:32-40		—		9:13-15	
1813:41-1814:5				9:16	
1814: 7- 9	—	—		9:17	
1814:10-12				9:18	
1814:13-24	—	—		9:19-23	
1814:25-34				9:24	
1814:35-40	—	—		9:25-26	
1814:41-48				9:27-29	
1814:49-1815:9		—		9:30-33	
1815: 9-13				9:34	
1815:28-43	—	—		10:22-31	
1815:37				10:3-4	
1815:41	—	—		1:1;5:18	
				10:30,38	
	—	—		14:9-11,20	
				17:11,21-22	
1815:44-48		—		10:32-33	
1815:48-1816:8				10:36-39	
1816:12-18	—	—		9:35-38	
1816:26-27				10:40	

PAPER 165: The Perean Mission Begins

1817:33-34				10:41	
1818:10-11	—	—		10:40	
1818:31-33				9:41	

91

pp. 1818 to 1822

The URANTIA Book Page:Line	MATTHEW Chap:Verse	MARK Chap:Verse	LUKE Chap:Verse	JOHN Chap:Verse	Other BOOKS Chap:Verse
1818:34-43	—	—		10:1-5	
1818:36-37				10:8	
1818:47-48	—	—		10:8	
1819: 7- 9				10:6-7	
1819: 9-10	—	—		10:8	
1819:10-13				10:9	
1819:14-19	—	—		10:10-12	
1819:19-23				10:14-15	
1819:24-28	—	—		10:16	
1819:29-37				10:17-18	
1819:38-43	—	—		10:19-21	
1819:44-45				10:42	
1819:47-48	—	—	12:1		
1820: 2-10			12:1-2		
1820: 4- 5	16:6,11	8:15			
1820: 7-12	10:26-27	4:22	8:17;12:2-3		
1820:11-18			12:3-5		
1820:14-15	10:28		12:4-5		
1820:16-18					Jd 24
1820:19-24	10:29-31		12:6-7		
1820:25-28	10:32-33		12:8-9		
1820:29-32			12:10		
1820:33-37	—	—	12:11-12		
1820:41					Ac 20:32;26:18 1Pe 1:3-4 Cl 3:24
1820:44-45	16:24-25	8:34-35	9:23-24	3:15-16	Re 22:17
1820:46-47				10:42	
1821: 3-12	—	—	12:13-15		
1821:18-25			12:16-19		
1821:26-34			12:20-21		
1821:43-46	19:24	10:25	18:25		
1821:44-47	5:10;6:19-20		6:35;12:33		
1822: 1	6:21		12:34		
1822:25-29					Pv 13:7-8 Si 11:18-19
1822:30	—	—		—	Ex 20:17 De 5:21
1822:30-31	—	—		—	De 31:20;32:15-17
1822:32					Ps 10:3
1822:32-33	—	—		—	Ps 37:16

The URANTIA Book Page:Line	MATTHEW Chap:Verse	MARK Chap:Verse	LUKE Chap:Verse	JOHN Chap:Verse	Other BOOKS Chap:Verse
1822:33-34					Ps 62:10
1822:34-35	—	—	—		Je 9:23
1822:35-36					Ek 33:31
1822:37-38	16:26	8:36	9:25		
1823:15-17	6:31				
1823:15-25	6:25-27		12:22-26		
1823:26-30	6:28-30		12:27-28		
1823:36-39	6:31-32		12:29-30		
1823:39-43	6:33-34		12:31		
1823:44-48	5:10-12		6:35		
	6:19-21		12:32-34		
1824: 3-10			12:35-38		
1824:11-14	24:43-44		12:39-40		
1824:18-19			12:41		
1824:20-27	24:45-47		12:42-44		
1824:28-31	24:48-51		12:45-46		
1824:33-40			12:48-53		
1824:43-44	28:19-20	16:15	24:47	20:21	Ac 1:8
	24:14	13:10			

PAPER 166:   Last Visit to Northern Perea

The URANTIA Book Page:Line	MATTHEW Chap:Verse	MARK Chap:Verse	LUKE Chap:Verse	JOHN Chap:Verse	Other BOOKS Chap:Verse
1825:17-30			11:37-38		
1826: 8- 9	23:25				
1826: 8-12			11:39		
1826: 9-12	23:28				
1826:13-15			11:40		
1826:15-17	—	—	11:41		
1826:17-21			11:42		
1826:18-19	23:23				
1826:22-24	23:6-7	12:38-39	11:43		
1826:25-28			11:45		
1826:28-32			11:46		
1826:32-36	23:29-31				
1826:32-38			11:47-51		
1826:36-38	23:35-36				
1826:38-41			11:52		
1826:40-41	23:13				

pp. 1826 to 1834

The URANTIA Book Page:Line	MATTHEW Chap:Verse	MARK Chap:Verse	LUKE Chap:Verse	JOHN Chap:Verse	Other BOOKS Chap:Verse
1826:44-46	23:27				
1826:47-1827:4			11:53-54		
1827:15-28		—	17:11-13		
1827:45-1828:4			17:14-16		
1828: 7-11	—	—	17:17-19		
1828:27-29			13:22-23		
1828:32-33				—	Nu 26:65
1828:36-42	7:13-14				
1828:43-46			13:24		
1829: 5-23			13:25-27		
1829:14-23	7:21-23				
1829:17-18					2Tm 4:7 1Tm 2:12
1829:23		—	—		Ps 6:8
1829:26-31	8:11				
1829:26-32			13:28-30		
1829:31-32	19:30;20:16	9:35	9:48;13:30		
	20:26-27	10:31	14:11;18:14		
	23:11	10:43-44	18:14;22:26		
1829:36-37				3:3,5	
1829:38-42	—	—			Re 3:20
1829:43-45			10:7,9		
			14:6		He 10:20
1829:44-45	16:24-25	8:34-35	9:23-24	3:15-16	1Jo 5:11-12
			5:24-25,39-40		Re 22:17
	—	—	6:40,47;10:10		
			11:25-26		
1830:23-24	5:45				
1830:24-30			13:1-5		
1830:39-45	3:8-10;12:33	3:8-9;6:43-44	15:2		
	7:16-20	13:6-9	15:5-8,16		
1831: 8					2Ch 19:7 Jb 34:19
	—	—		—	Ac 10:34 Ro 2:11
					Ga 2:6 Ep 6:9

PAPER 167: The Visit to Philadelphia

1833:26-28			14:1		
1833:33-39	—	—	14:7		
1834: 3- 4			14:1		

94

The URANTIA Book Page:Line	MATTHEW Chap:Verse	MARK Chap:Verse	LUKE Chap:Verse	JOHN Chap:Verse	Other BOOKS Chap:Verse
1834: 6- 7			14:2		
1834: 6-32	12:1-14				
1834:18-23			14:3-4		
1834:24-26	–	–	14:4		
1834:29-32			14:5-6		
1834:33-44			14:7-11		
1834:42-44	(Same as 1829:31-33, above.)				
1834:44-49			14:12-14		
1835: 2- 4	–	–	14:15		
1835: 7-26			14:16-24		
1835: 7-27	22:1-10				
1835:40-1836:7			13:10-13		
1836:11-17	–	–	13:14		
1836:18-26			13:15-17		
1836:39-41	–	–		11:1-3	
1836:45-47				11:4	
1837: 1- 2	–	–		11:5	
1837:21-22				11:6	
1837:23-24	–	–		11:7	
1837:28-31				11:8	
1837:32-35	–	–		11:9-10	
1837:39-40				11:11	
1837:41-46	–	–		11:12-15	
1838: 1- 6				11:15-16	
1838:10-13	–	–	18:9		
1838:19-28			18:10-14		
1838:27-28	(Same as 1829:31-32, above.)				
1838:29-32	19:3	10:2			
1838:41-42	7:7-8		11:9-10	14:13-14	Je 29:13
			15:7-16;16:23-24		
1838:43-1839:11	19:4-12	10:3-5			
1839:23-25		10:10			
1839:29	19:4	10:6			Ge 1:26-27
1839:29-34	19:4-5	10:6-8			
1839:33-34	19:4-5	10:6-8			Ge 2:24 Ep 5:31
1839:40-48	19:13	10:13	18:15		
1840: 1- 2	19:14				
1840: 1- 4	18:3-4	10:14-15	18:16-17		
1840: 5- 7	19:15	10:16			

The URANTIA Book Page:Line	MATTHEW Chap:Verse	MARK Chap:Verse	LUKE Chap:Verse	JOHN Chap:Verse	Other BOOKS Chap:Verse
1841: 3- 4					Ge 6:2,4
	—	—			Jb 1:6; 2:1
1841: 5				14:2	
1841:16-17	—	—		1:51	Ge 28:12
1841:18-19				10:16	
1841:22-23	—	—		—	1Co 3:16; 6:19
					2Co 6:16
1841:27-28	4:11	1:13			
1841:30-32			15:7		
1841:32-33	—	—	15:10		
1841:38				14:2	

PAPER 168: The Resurrection of Lazarus

1842: 3	—	—		11:20	
1842: 3- 6				11:17	
1842:20-21	—	—		11:4	
1842:23-24				11:18-19	
1842:32-1843:7		—		11:20-24	
1843: 8-13				11:25-27	
1843: 9-10	—	—		3:15-16	1Jo 5:11-12
				5:24-25,39-40	
	—	—		6:40,47;10:10	
				11:25-26	
1843:14-20	—	—		11:28-31	
1843:29-32				11:32-33	
1843:47-48	—	—		11:34	
1844: 1- 5				11:35-38	
1844: 6-23	—	—		11:35	
1844:28				11:4	
1844:29	—	—		11:34	
1845: 9				11:39	
1845:20-28	—	—		11:39-40	
1845:30-32				11:41	
1845:43	—	—		11:25	
1846: 4- 9				11:41-43	
1846:11-15	—	—		11:44	
1846:34				11:25	
1846:44-1847:2		—		11:45-47	

The **URANTIA** Book Page:Line	MATTHEW Chap:Verse	MARK Chap:Verse	LUKE Chap:Verse	JOHN Chap:Verse	Other BOOKS Chap:Verse
1847: 8- 9				11:47	
1847:34-38	—	—		11:48	
1847:39-41				11:49-50;18:14	
1847:42-47				11:53-54	
1848:12	—	—		11:4	
1848:17-19					1Co 14:14-15
1849: 2				14:23-24	Ep 6:18
1849: 3- 4	6:5-13	11:24	11:2-4		Ro 8:26-27
1849:13-14					Ja 5:15-16
1849:19-20	7:7-8		11:9-10	14:13-14	Je 29:13
				15:7-16	
				16:23-24	

PAPER 169: Last Teaching at Pella

1850:15-19			15:2		
1850:18-19	11:19		7:34		
1850:20-21				5:18	
1850:20-21				10:30-39	
1850:22-23	12:1-2	2:23-28	6:1-5	5:5-16	
	12:9-14	3:1-5	6:6-11	9:14	
	15:1-9	7:1-7	11:37-41		
			13:10-17		
			14:1-6		
1850:24-25	9:34;10:25	3:22	11:15		
	12:24	3:30			
1850:31-32					Is 55:6
1850:34-1851:5	18:12-13		15:3-7		
1851: 7- 8	11:19		7:34		
1851:14	18:11		19:10		
1851:15-22	—	—	15:8-10		
1851:35-47			15:11-12		
1851:48-1852:6			15:13-16		
1852: 7-13	—	—	15:17-19		
1852:16-24			15:20-22		
1852:25-29	—	—	15:23-24		
1852:30-36			15:25-27		
1852:37-45		—	15:28-30		
1852:47-1853:2			15:31-32		

The URANTIA Book Page:Line	MATTHEW Chap:Verse	MARK Chap:Verse	LUKE Chap:Verse	JOHN Chap:Verse	Other BOOKS Chap:Verse
1853: 6- 7	18:12-13		15:3-7		
1853: 9-10			15:8-10		
1853:12-13	_	_	15:11-32		
1853:22-24			16:8-9		
1853:26-34	5:10-12		6:35		
	6:19-21		12:33-34		
1853:35-41			16:1-2		
1853:42-1854:10		_	16:3-8		
1854:11-17	5:14-16		16:8-9	12:36	Ep 5:8 1Th 5:5
1854:18-24	_	_	16:10-12		
1854:25-27	6:24		16:13		
1854:28-29	_	_	16:14		
1854:29-31			16:15		
1854:46-1855:22		_	16:19-31		
1855:44				1:1;5:18	
	_	_		10:30,38	
				14:9-11,20	
	_	_		17:11,21-22	
1855:44-45				14:9	
1855:45-46				16:30	1Jo 3:20
1855:46-47	11:27		10:22	1:18;6:45-46	
	_	_		8:26;12:49-50	
				14:7-9,20	
	_	_		17:6:25-26	
1855:47				14:7	
1855:47-48	_	_		7:16,29	
				8:42;12:49	
1856: 2- 3	_	_		4:24	
1856:21-24			17:21		
1856:24-25	_	_		4:24	
1857:12-13				16:28	
1857:15	_	_		14:9	
1857:24				4:24	

PAPER 170: The Kingdom of Heaven

1858:23-31	3:2	1:15			
	4:17;10:7				

The URANTIA Book Page:Line	MATTHEW Chap:Verse	MARK Chap:Verse	LUKE Chap:Verse	JOHN Chap:Verse	Other BOOKS Chap:Verse
1858:26					Ps 22:28;103:19
1858:26	—	—	—		Ps 145:11-13 Da 4:3
1858:27-28	—	—	—		2Sa 7:12-16 Ps 89:19-37
	—	—	—		Is 9:6-7;11:1-10 Ob 21 Mi 4:1-10
1858:28-29	3:1-2				
1858:30	4:17,23 10:7	1:15	9:2		Ac 28:31
1858:32-33					Zc 14:6-9
1859:10-11	—	—	17:21		
1859:18			17:21		
1859:36-38		—		8:32	
1859:39-40	11:5		4:18;7:22 14:13		Is 61:1
1859:41-42	5:3-7:23		6:20-38		
1859:44-45				3:5-21	
1860: 1				6:27	
1860: 3- 5	5:10-12 6:19-20		6:22-23 6:35		
1860: 6- 8				1:12-13	Ga 4:4-7
1860:16-17	16:27 24:30;25:31	8:38 13:26	9:26 21:27		
1860:23-24	6:10		11:2		
1860:37-39	13:31-33	4:30-32	13:18-21		
1860:39-40	24:29-31	13:24-27	21:25-28		
1861: 7	18:3-4	10:15	18:17		
1861:12	5:6		6:21	4:10-14 7:37-38	
1861:23	—	—		3:15-16	1Jo 5:11-12
	—	—		5:24-25,39-40 6:40,47;10:10 11:25-26	
1861:24-25	—	—	17:21		
1861:25-26					Ep 3:14-15
1861:27	12:50	3:35	8:21;12:32	6:38-40	Ep 3:14-15
1861:28				15:14-15	
	—	—		12:44-48	

The URANTIA Book Page:Line	MATTHEW Chap:Verse	MARK Chap:Verse	LUKE Chap:Verse	JOHN Chap:Verse	Other BOOKS Chap:Verse
1861:29	5:9		20:36	10:7-16	1Jo 1:3-7
1861:29-30				1:12;12:26	Is 56:5
	—	—	—		Ro 8:14-17
					1Jo 3:1-2 Ga 26:4,6
1861:30		—		—	Ro 8:21
1861:37-40	5:20				
1861:41-42	18:3-4	10:15	18:17		
1862: 5- 6	6:12	11:25-26	6:37		
	6:14-15		11:4		
	18:22-35				
1862: 8	19:19	12:31	10:27-28		Le 19:18 Ro 13:9
	22:39				Ga 5:14 Ja 2:8
1862:13-14	19:30	9:35	9:48;13:30		
	20:16,26-27	10:31	14:11;18:14		
	23:11	10:43-44	22:26		
1862:30			17:21		
1863:43-47	24:29-31	13:24-27	21:25-28		
1864: 8-11					Cl 2:17
	—	—	—		He 8:5; 10:1
1864:25-27			1:68		Ga 3:13;4:4-5
	—	—	24:21		Cl 1:14 Ti 2:14
					1Pe 1:19 He 9:11-15
1864:29-33	—	—		—	Ep 5:21-32
1864:34-35			17:21		
1865:14-16	5:6		6:21		
1865:29-31					Da 7:27
1865:45-46	12:50	3:35	8:21		
1866: 7- 8	3:2;4:17	1:15			
	10:7				

PAPER 171: On The Way to Jerusalem

1867:15-16			17:21		
1867:23-31	20:20-21	10:35-37			
1867:32-1868:5	20:22-23	10:38-40			
1868: 6-17	20:24-28	10:41-45			
1869:29-33			14:25		
1869:30				1:28	

The URANTIA Book Page:Line	MATTHEW Chap:Verse	MARK Chap:Verse	LUKE Chap:Verse	JOHN Chap:Verse	Other BOOKS Chap:Verse
1869:34-40	10:37-38	14:26			
1869:37-41	18:38	8:34	9:23		
	16:24	10:21	14:27		
1869:41			14:27		
1869:42-1870:1			14:28-30		
1870: 1- 6			14:31-32		
1870:10-12	–	–	14:33		
1870:16-24			14:34-35		
1870:17-20	5:13	9:50	16:34-35		
1871:15-16				11:25	
1871:29-41	20:17-19	10:32-34	18:31-33		
1871:43-48			18:34		
1872: 5- 8	–	–	13:31		
1872:18-21			13:32		
1872:22-30			13:33-35		
1872:25-30	23:37-39				
1872:38-43	20:19	10:34	18:33		
1873: 1	9:27-30				
1873: 2- 3	20:29				
1873: 2- 5		10:46	18:35		
1873:16-20	20:30-31	10:47-48	18:36-39		
1873:21-31	20:32-34	10:49-52	18:40-43		
1873:34-46			19:1-4		
1874: 1- 6	–	–	19:5-6		
1874: 7-17			19:7-8		
1874:20-24	18:11	–	19:9-10		
1874:29-30				1:14	
1874:46-47				9:1	
1875:13-14	9:20-22	5:25-34	8:43-48		
1875:20				9:1	
1875:23	–	–	–		Ac 10:38
1875:27-31			19:11		
1875:40-43	–	–	19:11-12		
1875:43-45			19:14		
1876: 7-12	–	–	19:13		
1876:13-15			19:15		
1876:16-31	25:19-27		19:15-23		
1876:32-36	25:28-30		19:24-26		
1877: 9-10			19:28		

PAPER 172: Going into Jerusalem

The URANTIA Book Page:Line	MATTHEW Chap:Verse	MARK Chap:Verse	LUKE Chap:Verse	JOHN Chap:Verse	Other BOOKS Chap:Verse
1878:16-18				11:57	
1878:23-25	–	–		12:9	
1878:27-28				11:55-56	
1878:34-36	26:6	14:3			
1878:34-39				12:1-2	
1879: 3					Js 6:20
1879:10-21	26:7-8	14:3-5		12:3-5	
1879:11-15				11: 2	
1879:22-29				12:7-8	
1879:22-37	26:10-13	14:6-9			
1879:38-39	26:10-13	14:6-9		12:7-8	
1879:42-44	26:7	14:3		12:3	
1880: 3- 7				12:10-11	
1881:12-18	21:4-5			12:14-15	
1881:16-18	21:4-5			12:14-15	Zc 9:9
1881:27-32	21:1-3	11:1-3	19:28-31		
1881:33-38	21:6-7	11:4-7	19:32-35		
1881:39-46				12:17-18	
1882: 6-13	21:7-9	11:7-10	19:35-38	12:12-14	
1882:12-13					Ps 118:26
1882:16-27	–	–	19:41-44		
1882:40-45			19:39-40		
1882:46-50		–		12:19	
1883: 9-11	21:10-11				
1883:13-15		11:11			
1883:26-34	–	12:41-44	21:1-4		
1883:35-40		11:11			
1883:41				12:16	
1884:49-50	21:4-5		–	12:14-15	Zc 9:9
1885:38-39	21:4-5			12:14-15	Zc 9:9

PAPER 173: Monday in Jerusalem

The URANTIA Book Page:Line	MATTHEW	MARK	LUKE	JOHN	Other BOOKS
1888: 3- 5				2:13	
1888: 4- 5		11:12			
1888:17-18	21:12	11:15	19:45		

The URANTIA Book Page:Line	MATTHEW Chap:Verse	MARK Chap:Verse	LUKE Chap:Verse	JOHN Chap:Verse	Other BOOKS Chap:Verse
1888:23-25				2:14	
1888:26-27	—	—			Le 22:18-25
1888:33-35				2:14	
1889:10-13				2:14	
1890:11-25	21:12-13	11:15-17	19:45-46	2:15-16	
1890:24-25					Is 56:7 Je 7:11
1890:26-32	21:15-16				
1890:32					Ps 8:2
1890:36-42		11:18	19:47-48		
1891:28-32	21:23	11:27-28	20:1-2	2:18	
1892: 6- 9	21:24-25	11:29-30	20:3-4		
1892:10-24	21:25-27	11:31-33	20:5-8		
1893: 5-12	21:28-31				
1893:13-20	21:31-32				
1893:35-1894:10	21:33-40	12:1-9	20:9-15		
1894:11-13	21:41	12:9			
1894:11-17			20:16		
1894:18-24		12:10			
1894:18-30	21:42-44		20:17-18		
1894:23-24					Ps 118:22
1894:29-30					Da 2:34-35
1894:31-33	21:45-46		20:19		
1894:31-35		12:12			
1894:38-1895:12	22:1-7				
1894:40-44			14:16-20		
1895:13-21	22:8-10		14:21-24		
1895:21-27	22:11-13				
1895:28-29	22:14				
1895:30-34				2:18	
1895:34-36	—	—		2:19	
1895:36-41				2:20-22	
1895:42-44	21:17	11:19			

Paper 174: Tuesday Morning in The Temple

1897:13-14	16:18				
1897:14-15					2Co 10:7
1897:16-17	5:43-44		6:27,35		
1897:18	—	—		7:24	

The URANTIA Book Page:Line	MATTHEW Chap:Verse	MARK Chap:Verse	LUKE Chap:Verse	JOHN Chap:Verse	Other BOOKS Chap:Verse
1897:19-20					2Co 5:20
1897:20-21	—	—		—	He 3:14
1897:23					Cl 2:18
1897:24	—	—		—	1Co 15:58
					1Pe 5:8-9
1897:25-26	—	—			2Co 5:7
1897:26			4:34;5:17-36		
	—	—		9:4;17:4;19:30	
			17: 4		
	—	—	19:30		
1897:33			24:49	14:16-18	Ek 11:19;36:26-27
	—	—		14:26;15:26	Jl 2:28
				16:7,13-14	Ac 2:2-4,16-18
1897:33-34	6:33		12:31		
1897:36					Ga 6:9 2Th 3:13
1899: 2-10	22:15	12:13	20:20		
1899:13-26	22:16-21	12:14-17	20:21-25		
1899:27-30	22:22	12:17	20:26		
1900: 2-12	22:23-28	12:18-23	20:27-33		
1900: 4- 6					De 25:5-6
1900:17-29	22:29-32	12:23-27	20:34-38		
1900:27	22:32	12:26	20:37		Ex 3:6 Ac 7:32
1900:29-30					Ac 17:28
1900:31-35			20:39-40		
1900:34-35	22:33				
1900:43-44	22:32	12:26	20:37		Ex 3:6
1901: 2- 9	22:34				
1901:10-20	19:19	12:28-31	10:25-28		Le 19:18 Ro 13:9
	22:35-40				Ga 5:14 Ja 2:8
1901:14-16	22:37	12:29	10:27		De 4:35,39;6:4-5
					Ro 3:30
	—	—		—	1Co 8:4-6 Ga 3:20
					Ep 4:6 Ja 2:19
1901:18	—	—		—	Le 19:18 Ro 13:9
					Ga 5:14 Ja 2:8
1901:24-31	—	12:32-34			
1901:39		12:34			
1901:40-1902:6	22:41-46	12:35-37			
1901:45-1902:3			20:41-44		

The URANTIA Book Page:Line	MATTHEW Chap:Verse	MARK Chap:Verse	LUKE Chap:Verse	JOHN Chap:Verse	Other BOOKS Chap:Verse
1902: 2- 3	22:43-44	12:35-36	20:42-44		Ps 110:1
1902:15-16		12:37			
1902:18-35				12:20-22	
1902:38-1903: 8		–		12:37-43	
1902:45-46					Is 53:1
1902:47-1903:1	13:35	4:11-12		12:37-40	Is 6:10
					Ho 6:9-10
1903:21-35				12:44-50	
1903:36-43	10:39;16:25	8:35	9:24;17:33	12:23-26	
1903:46-1904: 2				12:27-28	
1904: 3- 7	–		–	12:28	
1904: 8-11				12:29	
1904:12-18	–		–	12:30-31	
				14:30;16:11	
1904:20-21	–		–	3:14-15;6:44	Je 31:3
				8:28;12:32	
1904:21-22	–		–	12:34	
1904:23-28	5:14-16		16:8	12:35-36	Ep 5:8 1Th 5:5
1904:32-35				12:36	

PAPER 175: The Last Temple Discourse

The URANTIA Book Page:Line	MATTHEW Chap:Verse	MARK Chap:Verse	LUKE Chap:Verse	JOHN Chap:Verse	Other BOOKS Chap:Verse
1905: 3- 6	23:1				
1905:22-23				1:41-44	
1905:23-24	8:2-3	1:40-43	5:12-13		
	8:5-13		5:18-20		
	9:2	2:3-5	7:2-10		
	9:20-22	5:25-34	8:43-48		
	9:28-30				
	15:22-28	7:25-30			
	20:29-34	10:46-52	18:35-43		
1906:38-49	23:2-4				
1906:40					Da 4:17,25,32
					Da 5:21
1906:47-49			11:46		
1907: 1- 5	23:5-7				
1907: 1- 8		12:38-40	20:46-47		
1907: 3- 5			11:43		

105

The URANTIA Book Page:Line	MATTHEW Chap:Verse	MARK Chap:Verse	LUKE Chap:Verse	JOHN Chap:Verse	Other BOOKS Chap:Verse
1907: 5- 8	23:14	12:40	20:47		
1907: 9-11	23:9				
1907:12-14	19:30;20:16	9:35	9:48;13:30		
	20:26-27	10:31	14:11;18:14		
	23:11-12	10:43-44	22:26		
1907:16	5:16,48	11:25-26	10:21		
	6:1-9;7:11-21		11:2		
	11:25;16:17				
	18:35;23;9				
1907:24-27	23:13		11:52		
1907:30-33	23:15				
1907:34-37	23:14				
1907:38	23:16				
1907:38-40	15:14		6:39		
1907:41-50	23:16-19				
1908: 1- 5	23:23-24		11:42		
1908: 6-10	23:25-26		11:39-40		
1908:14-18	23:27-28				
1908:19-26	23:29-32		11:47-48		
1908:27-29	23:33				
1908:30-41	23:34-36		11:49-51		
1908:42-44					2Ed 1:30-32
1908:42-49	23:37-39		13:34-35		
1908:50	24:1				
1909: 1					Ro 10:12
1909:35	—	—	—	2Ch 19:7 Jb 34:19	
				Ac 10:34 Ro 2:11	
	—	—	—	Ga 2:6 Ep 6:9	
1909:35-36					Ro 1:16
1910:42-46			12:42		
1911: 6- 7	21:12-13	11:15-17	19:45-46	2:13-16	
1911:20-22	23:1-39		11:39-53		
1911:23-27	26:3-5				

PAPER 176: Tuesday Evening on Mount Olivet

1912: 3-10	24:1-2	13:1-2	21:5-6		
1912:10-13	24: 3				
1912:21-24	24:3	13:3-4			

The URANTIA Book Page:Line	MATTHEW Chap:Verse	MARK Chap:Verse	LUKE Chap:Verse	JOHN Chap:Verse	Other BOOKS Chap:Verse
1912:22-24			21:7		
1912:29-1913:6	24:4-14	13:5-13	21:8-17		
1912:33-1913:1	10:17-20 24:9-13	13:5-13	21:8:17		
1913: 1- 6	10:21-22	13:12-13	21:6-18		
1913:26-31	24:15-18	13:14-16	21:20-21		
1913:31-32	24:21	13:19	21:20-22		
1913:31-35			21:22-24		
1913:35-38	24:23-25	13:21-23			
1913:46-47					Re 3:12;21:2
1913:48-49	24:3				
1914: 1					Is 65:17;66:22 Re 21:1
1914: 2	24:35	13:31	21:33		2Pe 3:10
1915: 1- 4	16:27 24:30;25:31	8:38 13:26	9:26 21:27		
1915: 5- 6	24:36,42 25:13	13:32-33		14:3	
1915:11-12	24:34	13:30	21:32		
1915:13-15	24:27-37 24:42;25:13	13:32-33		14:3	
1915:15-19	24:32-33	13:28-29	21:29-31		
1915:20-24	24:27-37 24:42;25:13	13:32-33		14:3;17:24	
1915:30-40	24:15-51				
1915:39-40		13:33-37	20:36		
1915:40-42	25:1-13				
1916:25-27	24:27-37 24:42;25:13	13:32-33		14:3	
1916:37-1917:2	25:14-18				
1917: 2-14	25:19-23				
1917:14-26	25:24-28				
1917:27-28	13:12;25:29		4:25;19:26	8:18	
1917:30					2Pe 3:18
1917:30-32	3:8-10 7:16-20 12:33		3:8-9 6:43-44 13:6-9	15:2,16 15:5-8	Ga 5:22-23 Ep 5:9
1917:32-34	25:40				
1917:49	25:21,23				

The URANTIA Book Page:Line	MATTHEW Chap:Verse	MARK Chap:Verse	LUKE Chap:Verse	JOHN Chap:Verse	Other BOOKS Chap:Verse
1918: 2- 8	25:24-26				
1918:20-21	10:8				
1918:45	28:18				
1918:45-47			24:49	14:16-18	Ek 11:19;36:26-27
	—	—		14:26;15:26	Jl 2:28
				16:7,13-14	Ac 2:2-4,16-18
1918:47-48	24:27-37	13:32-33		14:3,28	
	24:42;25:13				

PAPER 177: Wednesday, The Rest Day

1923:12	5:16,48	11:25-26	10:21		
	6:1-9;7:11-21		11:2		
	11:25;16:17				
	18:35;23;9				
1924:12-13	23:38		13:35		
1924:17	23:2				
1924:24-28	26:14	14:10	22:4		
1924:28-34	26:3-4	14:1	22:2		
1924:45-46	9:34	3:22,30	11:15		
	10:25;12:24				
1925:43-46	26:5	14:2	22:2		
1925:47-49	26:15	14:10			
1926: 3-12	26:16	14:11	22:4-6		

PAPER 178: Last Day at The Camp

1929:33-35	22:21	12:17	20:25		
1930:18-20					Ga 6:10
1930:33-34	10:16				
1931:23-24	7:12		6:31		To 4:15
1931:43-44	13:31-33	4:31-32	13:19,21		
1932:19				13:34-35	
	—	—		15:12,17	
1932:20					2Tm 2:14,24
1932:20-21	5:44		6:27-28		
1933:12-14	26:17	14:12	22:8-9		

The URANTIA Book Page:Line	MATTHEW Chap:Verse	MARK Chap:Verse	LUKE Chap:Verse	JOHN Chap:Verse	Other BOOKS Chap:Verse
1933:22-28	26:18	14:13-15	22:10-12		
1933:29-32	26:19	14:16	22:13		
1934:23					1Co 3:9
1934:25-26				16:16,28	
1934:28-30	24:14	13:10	24:47	20:21	Ac 1:8
	28:19-20	16:15			
1934:31-32	24:1-2	13:1-2	21:5-6		
1934:32-33	24:15-21	13:14-19	21:20-24		
1934:41-42	26:53				
1934:46-47				14:2-3	
1935: 1	—	—		—	He 11:10
1935: 4- 5					Re 3:21
1935: 6-10	—		—		Ac 14:22
1935: 9-10				14:2,12,28	
				16:10,16	

PAPER 179: The Last Supper

The URANTIA Book Page:Line	MATTHEW Chap:Verse	MARK Chap:Verse	LUKE Chap:Verse	JOHN Chap:Verse	Other BOOKS Chap:Verse
1937: 9-23			22:24		
1937:35-38	26:20	14:17	22:14		
1937:45-1938:5			22:15-16		
1938: 6-11			22:17-18		
1938: 8-11	26:29	14:25	22:20		
1938:12-21				13:1-3	
1938:20-21	—	—			Ep 6:12
1938:33-42				13:4-6	
1939: 1- 3	16:15-16	8:29	9:20		
1939: 9-13				13:6-8	
1939:21-31	—	—		13:8-9	
1939:32-34				13:10	
1939:34	—	—		13:11	
1939:38-40				13:12	
1939:42-49	—	—		13:12-17	
1940: 3- 5			22:24		
1940:11-17			22:25-27		
1940:13-15	19:30	9:35	9:48;13:30		
	20:16,26-27	10:31	14:11;18:14		
	23:11	10:33-36	22:26		

The URANTIA Book Page:Line	MATTHEW Chap:Verse	MARK Chap:Verse	LUKE Chap:Verse	JOHN Chap:Verse	Other BOOKS Chap:Verse
1940:17-19			22:28-30		
1940:28-35	26:21	14:18		13:21	
1940:36-39	26:22	14:19		13:22	
1940:40-44	26:24	14:21	22:21-22		
1940:44-45	26:23	14:18,20			
1940:46	26:22		22:23		
1940:47-1941:1	26:25				
1941: 1- 4				13:25-26	
1941:10-12	—	—		13:23-24	
1941:16-21				13:19	
1941:22-28				13:27-30	
1941:41-47	26:27-29	14:23-25	22:20		1Co 11:25-26
1942: 9-14	26:26	14:22	22:19		1Co 11:23-24
1942:11-12	5:6			6:35,48	Is 55:2
				6:51,58	Re 7:16-17
1942:44-46	—	—	22:19		1Co 11:24-26
1943: 5-11					1Co 11:26
1943:12-14	26:30	14:26			

PAPER 180:   The Farewell Discourse

The URANTIA Book Page:Line	MATTHEW	MARK	LUKE	JOHN	Other BOOKS
1944: 5-11			22:35-36		
1944:13-14	—	—		13:31	
1944:14-16				13:33,36	
1944:16-20	—	—		6:39-40;11:24-26	
				13:36;14:3;17:24	
1944:23-31	—	—		13:34-35	
				15:12,17	
1944:32-37		—		15:11	
1944:38-1945: 4				15:12-15	
1945: 5- 9	—	—		15:16-17	
1945:11				14:23-24	
1945:21	—	—		1:12	Is 56:5 Ro 8:14-17
					Ga 3:26; 4:6
					1Jo 3:1-2
1945:24-33	—	—		14:20;15:1-4	
1945:33-37	—			15:5	
1945:37-40				15:7	

The URANTIA Book Page:Line	MATTHEW Chap:Verse	MARK Chap:Verse	LUKE Chap:Verse	JOHN Chap:Verse	Other BOOKS Chap:Verse
1945:37-44	7:7-8		11:9-10	14:13-15	Je 29:13
	−	−		15:7-16	
1945:40-44				15:8	
1945:40-47	3:8-10		3:8-9	15:2,5-8,16	
	7:16-20;12:33		6:43-44;13:6-9		
1945:42-44				13:35	
1945:45-47	−	−		14:15,12-24	
				15:9-10	
1946: 1- 2	2:23	−		−	Is 11:1 Je 23:5
					Zc 3:8; 6:12
1946: 6- 7		−		15:16	
1946:21-26	3:8-10		3:8-9	15:2-8,16	
	7:16-20;12:33		6:43-44;13:6-9		
1946:25-28	−	−		15:8-9	
1946:27-28				13:34	
	−	−		15:12	
1946:40-47				15:18-20	
1946:48-1947:1		−		15:21	
1947: 4-13				15:22-25	
1947:13	−	−		−	Ps 35:19
					Ps 69:4
1947:14-17	−	−	24:49	14:16-18	Ek 11:19;36:26-27
				14:26;15:26	Jl 2:28
	−	−		16:7,13-14	Ac 2:2-4,16-18
1947:18-25				14:1-2	
1947:26-34	−	−		6:39-40;14:3	
				11:24-26	
	−	−		13:36;17:24	
1947:35-37				14:5	
1947:38-41	−	−		14:6-7	
1947:42-44				14:8	
1947:42-47	11:27		10:22	1:18;6:45-46	
				8:26;12:49-50	
	−	−		14:7-9,20	
				17:6,25-26	
1947:45-1948:3		−		1:1;5:18	
				10:30-38	
	−	−		14:9-11,20	
				17:11,21-22	

pp.1947 to 1952

The URANTIA Book Page:Line	MATTHEW Chap:Verse	MARK Chap:Verse	LUKE Chap:Verse	JOHN Chap:Verse	Other BOOKS Chap:Verse
1947:50-1948:1	6:10	3:35	8:21	4:34;5:30	
	7:21;12:50	14:36-39	11:2	6:38;7:17	
	26:39,42,44		22:42	14:23-24	
				15:10,14;17:4	
1948: 2- 3	—	—		10:37-38	
1948: 9-24			24:49	14:16-18	Ek 11:19;36:26-27
	—	—		14:26;15:26	Jl 2:28
				16:7,13-14	Ac 2:2-4,16-18
1948:24-26	—	—		16:7	
1948:27-33				14:19-21	
1948:34-36	(Same as 1948:9-24, above.)				
1948:37-43				14:25-26	
1948:44-49	—	—		14:22	
1949: 6- 9				13:34;14:23	
		—		15:12	
1949:43	7:12		6:31		To 4:15
1950:17-18	19:19	12:31	10:27-28		Le 19:18 Ro 13:9
	19:22-39				Ga 5:14 Ja 2:8
1951:15-29	—	—		16:1-4	
1951:23-24				13:24;15:12	
1951:29-30	10:21	13:12	21:16		
1951:34-43				16:5-8	
1951:44-46	—	—		16:12-13	
1951:45-48			24:49	14:16-18	Ek 11:19;36:26-27
	—	—		14:26;15:26	Jl 2:28
				16:7,13-14	Ac 2:2-4;16:18
1951:46	—	—		14:2	
1952: 1- 4				16:14-15	
1952: 5- 7	26:32	14:28		16:16	
1952: 8-12				16:17-18	
1952:13-25				16:19-22	
1952:16-17	16:21	8:31	9:22		
	17:23	9:31			
	20:18-19	10:34	18:33		
1952:26-28				16:23-24,26	
1952:29-31	—	—		16:25	
1952:31-35				16:27-28	
1952:36-37	—	—		16:29-30	

PAPER 181: Final Admonitions and Warnings

The URANTIA Book Page:Line	MATTHEW Chap:Verse	MARK Chap:Verse	LUKE Chap:Verse	JOHN Chap:Verse	Other BOOKS Chap:Verse
1953:22-26			24:49	14:16-18	Ek 11:19;36:26-27
	–	–		14:26;15:26	Jl 2:28
				16:7,13-14	Ac 2:2-4,16-18
1953:27-35	–	–		14:2-3	
1953:28-29					1Ki 8:27 De 10:14
	–	–	–		2Ch 2:6; 6:18
					Ne 9:6 Ps 148:4
1953:33			16:8	12:26	Ep 5:8 1Th 5:5
1953:33-35	5:48				Ge 17:1 Le 19:2
					De 18:13 Ja 1:4
	–	–			2Co 3:18;13:11
1953:36-38				14:23-24	
	–	–		14:15;15:10	
1954: 1- 4				1:9-13	
1954: 2	–	–	24:49	14:16-18	Ek 11:19;36:26-27
				14:26;15:26	Jl 2:28-29
		–		16:7,13-14	Ac 2:2-4,16-18
1954: 3- 6	5:6		4:10,13-14		Is 55:1
	–	–	6:35		Ac 2:38-39
			7:37-38		Re 7:16-17
1954: 7-10			2:14	14:1,27;16:33	Pp 4:7
1954:11-13	26:32	14:28		14:28;16:16-22	
1954:14-15				14:16-18	Ek 11:9
					Ek 36:26-27
1954:15-16				14:29	
1954:16-17	–	–		14:28,31	
1954:19-27				16:32-33	
1954:28-47	–	–	2:14	14:27;16:33	Pp 4:7
1954:44					Is 53:3
1955: 4	–	–		14:1,27	
1955: 7- 9			2:14	14:27;16:33	Pp 4:7
1955:20-21	–	–		19:26-27	
1955:30-32				4:34;5:17,36	
	–			9:4;17:4;19:30	
1955:37		3:17			
1955:38-40	–	–	9:54		
1955:41-42				13:34-35;15:12	

pp. 1956 to 1960

The URANTIA Book Page:Line	MATTHEW Chap:Verse	MARK Chap:Verse	LUKE Chap:Verse	JOHN Chap:Verse	Other BOOKS Chap:Verse
1956: 5- 6					Ro 12:18
1956: 7- 8	—	—			2Tm 2:14,24-25
1956:39-41				18:36	
1957: 4- 5	22:21	12:17	20:25		
1957:13-14					Ac 4:33
1957:14-15	28:20				
1957:21	26:52				
1957:21-23		10:30	18:30		
1957:26-27					Ro 6:23
1957:35-37	24:14	13:10	24:17	20:21	Ac 1:8
	28:19-20	16:15			
1957:36-37				1:12	Is 56:5 Ro 8:14-17
	—	—		—	Ga 3:26; 4:6
					1Jo 3:1-2
1957:43-44	9:9	2:14	5:27-28		
1957:45-46					Ga 3:28
1958: 7- 9	—	—	24:49	14:16-18	Ek 11:19;36:26-27
				14:26;15:26	Jl 2:28
	—	—		16:7,13-14	Ac 2:2-4,16:18
1958:12					2Ch 19:7 Jb 34:19
	—	—		—	Ac 10:34 Ro 2:11
					Ga 2:6 Ep 6:9
1958:17	—	—		1:12	Is 56:5 Ro 8:14-17
					Ga 3:26; 4:6
					1Jo 3:1-2
1958:19-22	20:20-22	10:35-39			
1958:24-25	20:24	10:41			
1958:25-26	20:23	10:39			Ac 12:1-2
1958:26-27			21:19		
1958:33-34	20:23	10:39			Ac 12:1-2
1959:22-24	—	—	24:49	14:16-18	Ek 11:19;36:26-27
				14:26;15:26	Jl 2:28
	—	—		16:7,13-14	Ac 2:2-4,16:18
1959:42				10:16	
1960:24	—	—		6:5-7	
1960:36-37					Is 64:4
					1Co 2:9
1960:37-38	18:3	10:15	18:17		
1960:41				14:9	

The URANTIA Book Page:Line	MATTHEW Chap:Verse	MARK Chap:Verse	LUKE Chap:Verse	JOHN Chap:Verse	Other BOOKS Chap:Verse
1961:24-27	—	—	24:49	14:16-18	Ek 11:19;36:26-27
				14:26;15:26	Jl 2:28
		—		16:7,13-14	Ac 2:2-4,16:18
1961:33-34	5:48				Ge 17:1 Le 19:2
	—	—	—		De 18:13
					2Co 13:11 Ja 1:4
1961:45				13:34;15:12	
1961:49	24:14	13:10	24:47	20:21	Ac 1:8
	28:19-20	16:15			
1962:13-19	26:31-32	14:27-28		14:28;16:16-22	
1962:15-16					Zc 13:7
1962:18-19	26:32	14:28		20:17	
	28:7,10	16:7			
1962:20-22	26:33,35	14:29	22:33	13:37	
1962:24-27	26:34	14:30	22:34	13:38	
1962:28-29			22:32		
1962:32	16:21:17:23	8:31;9:31	9:22		
1962:32-33				16:16-22	
1962:33-35	—	—	22:32		
1962:36				13:34;15:12	
1962:37-38		14:26			

PAPER 182: In Gethsemane

The URANTIA Book Page:Line	MATTHEW Chap:Verse	MARK Chap:Verse	LUKE Chap:Verse	JOHN Chap:Verse	Other BOOKS Chap:Verse
1963:30-1964: 2				17:1-5	
1963:37-49	—	—		4:34;5:17,36	
				9:4;17:4;19:30	
1964: 3-23	—	—		17:6-12	
1964:24-25				17:12	
1964:27-39	—	—		17:13-19	
1964:40-1965: 2				17:20-23	
1964:45	—	—		13:34;15:12	
1965: 2- 8				6:39-40;11:24-26	
				13:36;14:3;17:24	
1965: 8-12	11:27		10:22	1:18;6:45-46	
				8:26;12:49-50	
				14:7-9,20	
	—	—		17:6,25-26	

115

pp. 1965 to 1970

The URANTIA Book Page:Line	MATTHEW Chap:Verse	MARK Chap:Verse	LUKE Chap:Verse	JOHN Chap:Verse	Other BOOKS Chap:Verse
1965:25					Ex 3:6
1965:26					Ex 3:14
1965:29	5:6;26:26	14:22	22:19	6:35,48	Is 55:2
				6:51,58	
1965:30	5:6			4:10,13-14	Is 55:1
				6:35	Re 7:16-17
				7:37-38	
1965:31	4:16		1:79	1:39;5:35	Is 9:2
			2:23	8:12;9:5	1Jo 2:8
	—	—		12:35-36,46	
				1:4-9	
1965:32	—	—			Hg 2:7
1965:33				10:7,9	
1965:33-34	—	—		3:25-16	1Jo 5:11-12
				5:24-25,39-40	
	—	—		6:40,47;10:10	
				11:25-26	
1965:35	—	—		10:11,14	
1965:37				11:25	
1965:39	—	—		14:6	
1965:41				15:1,5	
1965:42	-	-			1Tm 1:1
1966:35-37				17:12	
1968: 5-14	26:36-39	14:32-35	22:42		
1968:16-20	26:40	14:37			
	26:38	14:34			
1968:21-24	6:10	3:35	8:21	4:34;5:30	
	7:21;12:50	14:36,39	11:2	6:38;7:17	
	26:39,42,44		22:41-42	14:23-24	
				15:10,14;17:4	
1968:25-26			22:43		
1968:27-30	26:43	14:40	22:40		
	26:41	14:38	22:45-46		
1968:31-41	26:44-46	14:41-42			
1968:32-33	26:41	14:38	22:40		
1969:13-16			22:44		
1969:20-23	26:53				

PAPER 183: The Betrayal and Arrest of Jesus

The URANTIA Book Page:Line	MATTHEW Chap:Verse	MARK Chap:Verse	LUKE Chap:Verse	JOHN Chap:Verse	Other BOOKS Chap:Verse
1971:19-20				18:1	
1971:32-33			22:31-32		
1972: 5- 7	6:10	3:35	8:21	4:34;5:30	
	7:21;12:50	14:35,39	11:2	6:38;7:17	
	20:22;26:39		22:42	14:23-24	
	26:42,44			15:10,14;17:4	
1973: 7-11				18:2	
1973:29-36	26:47	14:43		18:3	
1973:33-36			22:47		
1974: 4- 6	26:48	14:44			
1974:11-20				18:4-6	
1974:28-32			22:47-48		
1974:30-32	26:49-50	14:45			
1974:34-38				18:7-8	
1974:41-1975:1	26:50-52			18:10-11	
1974:41-50		14:46-47	22:49-51		
1975: 1- 3	26:53				
1975: 4- 7				18:12	
1975: 7-10	26:55	14:48-49	22:52-53		
1975:11-14	26:56	14:50			
1975:14-22		14:51-52			
1975:31-32				18:15	
1975:32	26:58	14:54	22:54		
1975:32-34		14:51-52			
1976:34	26:31	14:27			Zc 13:7
1977: 5-11				18:13	
1977:30-43	—	—		18:15-16	
				19:25-27	
1977:44-46	—	—			Is 53:7 Ac 8:32

PAPER 184: Before The Sanhedrin Court

1979:25-39				18:19-23	
1979:44-50	26:63-64	14:61-62	22:70		
1980: 1- 5	26:57	14:53		18:24	
1980: 7-16				18:15-16	

The URANTIA Book Page:Line	MATTHEW Chap:Verse	MARK Chap:Verse	LUKE Chap:Verse	JOHN Chap:Verse	Other BOOKS Chap:Verse
1980: 7-18	26:58	14:54	22:54-55		
1980:17-18				18:18	
1980:31-38	26:69-70	14:66-68	22:56-57	18:17	
1980:39-43			22:58	18:26-27	
1980:44-48		14:68-70			
1980:44-1981:2	26:71-72				
1980:48-1981:2		14:71			
1981: 3- 8	26:73-74	14:70	22:59-60	18:25	
1981:13-14			22:60	18:27	
1981:13-15	26:74-75	14:72			
1981:14-20			22:61		
1981:24-25	26:75	14:72	22:62		
1982: 5- 7			22:66		
1982:23-24			22:66		
1982:27-33	26:59-60	14:55-56			
1982:37-40	26:60-61	14:57-59			
1982:39-40				2:19	
1982:43-45	26:62-63	14:60-61			
1983:11-12				2:19	
1983:20-27	26:63-64	14:61-62	22:66-67,70		
1983:28-30			22:71		
1983:28-32	26:65-66	14:63-64			
1983:45-49	26:67	14:65	22:63		
1984:16-22	26:67-68	14:65	22:63-65	18:22	
1985: 9-12				1:1;5:18	Ep 4:5
	—	—		10:30,38	
				14:9-11,20	
	—	—		17:11;21-22	
1985:11-12				10:30	
1985:22-46	27:1	15:1			
1986:10-11			22:67-68		
1986:12-14	27:2	15:1	23:1	18:28	

PAPER 185: The Trial Before Pilate

1987:17-24				18:28	
1989:26-33	—	—		18:29-30	
1989:34-42				18:31	

The URANTIA Book Page:Line	MATTHEW Chap:Verse	MARK Chap:Verse	LUKE Chap:Verse	JOHN Chap:Verse	Other BOOKS Chap:Verse
1990:25-33			23:2		
1990:25-44	27:12-14	15:3-5			
1991: 2- 4				18:33	
1991:13-14	27:11	15:2	23:3		
1991:13-22				18:33-35	
1991:23-28				18:36	
1991:30-32	27:11	15:2	23:3		
1991:30-36				18:37-38	
1991:47-1992:2		_	23:4	18:38	
1992: 2- 7			23:5		
1992: 8-17	_	_	23:6-7		
1992:12-13			23:12		
1992:29-32	_	_	23:8		
1992:33-37			23:9		
1992:38-42	_	_	23:10-11		
1993: 4-13			23:13-16		
1993:15-16		15:8			
1993:17-19	27:15	15:6	23:17	18:39	
1993:25-29	27:16	15:7	23:19	18:40	
1993:30-34	27:17				
1993:32-34		15:9		18:39	
1993:34-38		15:11	23:18	18:40	
1993:45-47	27:18	15:10			
1994:13-20	27:19				
1994:22-24	27:20	15:11			
1994:25-28	27:22	15:12-13	23:20-21		
1994:31-34	27:23	15:14	23:22		
1994:35-38	27:21				
1995: 4- 6	27:26	15:15	23:23-25	19:1,16	
1995: 8-18	27:27-31	15:16-20			
1995:12-17				19:2-3	
1995:19-21	_	_	23:22	19:6	
1995:19-23				19:4-5	
1995:29-31	_	_	23:23	19:6	
1995:36-43				19:7-9	
1995:46-1996:10		_		19:9-11	
1996:14-28				19:12-15	
1996:40-43		15:15	23:23-25		
1996:40-47	27:24-25			19:6	

PAPER 186: Just Before The Crucifixion

The URANTIA Book Page:Line	MATTHEW Chap:Verse	MARK Chap:Verse	LUKE Chap:Verse	JOHN Chap:Verse	Other BOOKS Chap:Verse
1997:26-28			23:25	19:14,16	
1997:38-1998:34	27:3-4				
1998:11-13	26:14-15 27:3	14:10	22:40		
1998:35-36	27:5				
1998:43-50	27:5				
1998:49-50					Ac 1:18
1999: 5- 6	26:60-62	14:56-61			
1999: 6- 9	26:63-64	14:61-62	22:67,70		
1999: 9-10			23:9		
1999:10-12	27:11	15:2	23:3	18:33-37	
1999:12-13	7:6				
2000:12-14	26:67-68	14:65	22:63-65	18:22	
2000:15-21				19:5	
2001:14	16:21;17:23 20:19 27:63	8:31 9:31 10:34	9:22 18:33 24:7		
2001:27	27:24				
2001:29-31	27:26	15:15	23:24-25	19:16	
2001:31-34	27:31	15:20			
2001:37-38	27:31	15:20			
2001:47-2002:3			23:32		
2003: 7					He 9:28
2003: 7- 9					Ro 5:6-9

PAPER 187: The Crucifixion

The URANTIA Book Page:Line	MATTHEW Chap:Verse	MARK Chap:Verse	LUKE Chap:Verse	JOHN Chap:Verse	Other BOOKS Chap:Verse
2004:12-14			23:32		
2004:15-20	–	–		10:17-18	
2004:21-22				19:16-17	
2004:22-25	–	–	23:27		
2004:31-37				19:16-17	
2005: 3-17				19:19-22	
2005: 7- 9	27:37	15:24	23:38	19:19-20	
2005:33-45	27:55-56	15:40-41	23:27-30 8:2-3;23:49;24:10	19:25	Ac 1:4

120

The URANTIA Book Page:Line	MATTHEW Chap:Verse	MARK Chap:Verse	LUKE Chap:Verse	JOHN Chap:Verse	Other BOOKS Chap:Verse
2006:14-20	27:32	15:21	23:26		
2006:28-29		15:21			
2006:32-33	27:33	15:22			
2006:32-34			23:33		
2006:36-46	27:35	15:24	23:33	19:18	
2007: 7-11	27:34	15:23			
2007:15-16	27:38	15:27		19:18	
2007:15-18			23:33-34		
2007:22-24	27:37	15:26	23:38		
2007:22-36				19:19-20	
2007:37-38	27:56				
2007:44-49	27:35	15:24	23:34	19:23-24	
2007:46-49					Ps 22:18
2008: 8- 9		15:25			
2008:14-19	27:55-56	15:40-41	23:47-49	19:25	Ac 1:14
			8:2-3;24:10		
2008:20-25			23:35,37		
2008:20-28	27:39-44	15:29-32			
2008:30-33	27:36				
2008:33-40			23:36		
2008:45-2009:9		_	23:39-43		
2009:43-2010:4				19:26-27	
2010: 9-13	27:45	15:33	23:44-45		
2010:21-38	27:46	15:34			
2010:28-29					Ps 20:6
2010:29	_	_	_		Ps 21:8
2010:30					Ps 22:1
2010:35-36					Ps 22:1
2010:39-42	27:48	15:36		19:28-29	
2010:46-2011:2			23:49		
2011: 3- 5	27:50	15:37	23:46	19:30;14:34 5:17,36 9:4;17:4	
2011: 5- 7	27:54	15:39	23:47		
2011:19		15:42	23:54	19:42	
2011:19-29				19:31-34	
2011:34	27:45	15:33	23:44-45		

PAPER 188: The Time of The Tomb

The URANTIA Book Page:Line	MATTHEW Chap:Verse	MARK Chap:Verse	LUKE Chap:Verse	JOHN Chap:Verse	Other BOOKS Chap:Verse
2012:18-26	27:57-58	15:42-45	23:50-52	19:38	
2013: 6-11				19:41-42	
2013:10-11	_	_	23:53		
2013:17-28			23:53	19:39-41	
2013:17-33	27:59-60	15:46			
2013:38-44			23:55-56		
2013:38-47	27:61	15:47			
2014: 5-18	27:62-64				
2014:19-27	27:65-66				
2015: 3			23:46		
2017:44-45	6:12,14-15	11:25-26	6:37		
	18:23-25		11:4		
2018:18	5:39				
2018:36-37					1Tm 6:12 2Tm 4:7
2018:43	_	_	23:34		
2018:46-47					Ac 7:60
2018:49-2019: 2				15:13	
2019:19-25	_	_		3:14-15;6:44	Je 31:3
				8:28;12:32	
2019:39-40					Is 53:3-5; 63:9

PAPER 189: The Resurrection

2020:11-12				10:17-18	
2020:29-31				10:17-18	
2023:15-24	28:2-4				
2023:24-36	28:11-15				
2024:13-43	27:52-53				
2025:30-35			24:1		
2025:30-39	28:1	16:1-2		20:1	
2025:45-47		16:3-4	24:2	20:1	
2026:10-23			24:3		
2026:32-49	28:5-6,9	16:5-6,9	24:4-8	20:11-16	
2027: 4- 7	28:7,10	16:7		20:17	
2027: 8-10	28:8	16:8	20:2		
2027: 8-11		16:10-11			

The URANTIA Book Page:Line	MATTHEW Chap:Verse	MARK Chap:Verse	LUKE Chap:Verse	JOHN Chap:Verse	Other BOOKS Chap:Verse
2027: 8-17	–		24:9-12		
2027:12				20:18	
2027:13-14	–	–		20:3	
2027:27-34				20:4-9	
2027:29-34			24:12		
2027:46-2028:2	28:7,10	16:7		20:10-17	
2028: 1- 2	26:32	14:28			

PAPER 190: Morontia Appearances of Jesus

2029: 9				5:39-40	
2029:9-12	–	–		6:39-40;11:24-26 13:36;14:3;17:24	
2029:20-21	–	–	–		1Co 15:12-20
2031:34-35					Ac 10:41
2032: 5-13	–	–	–		1Co 15:7
2033:14-15					Ga 3:28 Cl 3:11
2033:16-17					Ro 8:21
2033:17-18	28:19-20 24:14	16:15 13:10	24:47	20:21	Ac 1:8
2033:20	28:20				
2034: 1					Ga 3:28 Cl 3:11
2034: 2- 3	28:19-20 24:14	16:15 13:10	24:47	20:21	Ac 1:8
2034: 3					Ep 1:13
2034: 4					1Co 1:9
2034:27-37		16:12	24:13-16		
2034:38-2035:7			24:17-24		
2035: 8-42			24:25-27		
2035:12				18:36	
2035:18-19	16:21 17:22-23 20:18-19	8:31 9:31 10:33-34	9:22 18:31-33		
2035:22					Ge 28:14; 12:3
2035:22-23	–	–	–		Ps 72:12-13
2035:23-24					Ps 72:17
2035:24-25	–	–	–		Is 32:2
2035:25-26					Is 40:11

123

The URANTIA Book Page:Line	MATTHEW Chap:Verse	MARK Chap:Verse	LUKE Chap:Verse	JOHN Chap:Verse	Other BOOKS Chap:Verse
2035:26-28					Is 42:7
2035:28-29	4:16		1:79	5:35	Is 9:2
			2:32	8:12;9:5	1Jo 2:8
				12:35-36,46	
2035:29-31	–		4:18;24:27		Is 61:1
2035:31-32					Is 61:3 Je 31:13
2035:32-33	–	–		–	Hg 2:7
2035:33					Is 61:7
2035:34-35	–	–		–	Ml 4:2
2035:35					Ps 28:8
2035:35	1:21				
2035:36	18:11		19:10		
2035:36-37	5:5-6				
2035:38				3:15-16	1Jo 5:11-12
	–	–		5:24-25,39-40	
				6:40-47;10:10	
	–	–		11:25-26	
2035:38-39			24:49	15:26	Ek 11:19;36:26-27
	–	–		14:16-18,26	Ac 2:2-4,16-18
				16:7,13-14	Ac 1:4 Jl 2:28
2035:39-40	5:6	–		4:10,13-14	Is 55:1
				6:35;7:37-38	Re 7:16-17
2035:40-41	4:23;9:35				
2035:42					He 2:3
2035:43-2036:5			24:28-32		
2036: 6-13		16:13	24:33-35		

PAPER 191: Appearances to The Apostles and Other Leaders

The URANTIA Book Page:Line	MATTHEW Chap:Verse	MARK Chap:Verse	LUKE Chap:Verse	JOHN Chap:Verse	Other BOOKS Chap:Verse
2037:35		16:7			
2039: 3-14	–	–		20:24	
2039:18-19					1Co 15:5
2039:30-31	–	16:7			
2039:35-36			22:31-32		
2040:18-22	–	–		20:19	1Co 15:5
2040:18-23			24:36-38		
2040:18-29	–	16:14			

The URANTIA Book Page:Line	MATTHEW Chap:Verse	MARK Chap:Verse	LUKE Chap:Verse	JOHN Chap:Verse	Other BOOKS Chap:Verse
2040:24-27			24:44-46		
2040:30	–	–		20:24	
2040:37-38				20:20	
2041:41	–	–		13:34;15:2	
2042: 2- 3			16:8	12:26	1Th 5:5 Ep 5:8
2042: 4- 6					Ga 6:10
2042: 6- 7				13:34-35	
2042: 8- 9	24:14 28:19-20	13:10 16:15	24:47	20:21	Ac 1:8
2042:11-12	10:8				
2042:12-13	28:20				
2042:13-14			2:14	14:27 16:33	Pp 4:7
	–	–			
2042:28-47				20:25	1Co 15:5
2042:44-2043:2		–			1Co 15:7
2042:47-2043:3				20:26	
2043: 3- 6	24:14	16:15	24:47-48	20:21	Ac 1:8
2043: 4- 5	28:19	13:10			
2043:12-14					Ac 2:1-4
2043:15	3:11	1:8	3:16	1:33	Ac 1:5
2043:17-18			24:49		
2043:33-47				20:27-29	
2043:49-50	26:32 28:7,10	14:28 16:7		20:17	
2044:31				17:18	
2044:34-35				16:13	
2044:35-36	24:32 28:19-20	13:10 16:15	24:27	20:21	Ac 1:8

PAPER 192: Appearances in Galilee

2045: 8-10	28:12-15				
2045:17	–	–			Ac 1:26
2045:31-33				21:1	
2045:34-35	(Same as 2035:38-39, above.				
2046: 2- 7	–	–		21:4	
2046:13-26				21:5-8	
2046:37-41	–	–		21:9-10	

The URANTIA Book Page:Line	MATTHEW Chap:Verse	MARK Chap:Verse	LUKE Chap:Verse	JOHN Chap:Verse	Other BOOKS Chap:Verse
2046:45-46	—	—		21:11	
2047: 1- 7				21:12-13	
2047: 9-10	—	—		21:14	
2047:33-35				21:15	
2047:37	—	—		—	2Ch 19:7 Jb 34:19
					Ac 10:34 Ro 2:11
					Ga 2:6 Ep 6:9
	—	—			
2047:40-42				21:16	
2047:46-2048:3		—		21:17	
2048: 6				21:19	
2048: 7-12	—	—		21:20-22	
2048:13-15				21:23	
2048:34-35	—	—		—	2Co 9:6 Jb 4:8
					Ga 6:7
2048:36-37	—	—		—	Ac 12:1-2
2049:12-13					Ac 8:5
2049:13-14	—	—		—	1Sa 15:22
					Pv 21:3 Ho 6:6
2050: 4-20	28:16-17				
2050:33-44					1Co 15:6

PAPER 193: Final Appearances and Ascention

The URANTIA Book Page:Line	MATTHEW Chap:Verse	MARK Chap:Verse	LUKE Chap:Verse	JOHN Chap:Verse	Other BOOKS Chap:Verse
2052:12-40			24:44-48		
2052:14-16				16: 5-16	
2052:16-18	16:21	8:31	9:22		
	17:23	9:31			
	20:19	10:34	18:33		
2052:39-40	24:14	13:10	24:47	20:21	Ac 1:8
	28:19-20	16:15			
2053: 6- 8				10:17-18	
2053: 9-10	27:52-53				
2053:14				1:12	Is 56:5
	—	—		—	Ro 8:14-17
					Ga 3:26; 4:6
					1Jo 3:1-2
2053:14-16	24:14	13:10	24:47	20:21	Ac 1:8
	28:19-20	16:15			

The URANTIA Book Page:Line	MATTHEW Chap:Verse	MARK Chap:Verse	LUKE Chap:Verse	JOHN Chap:Verse	Other BOOKS Chap:Verse
2053:16				13:34;15:12	1Jo 4:11
2053:17	10:8				
2053:17-19	(Same as 2035:38-39, above.)				
2053:19	28:20				
2053:34-35				11:25	
2053:35-36	—	—		3:3-6	
2053:36-37				3:15-16	1Jo 5:11-12
	—	—		5:24-25,39-40	
				6:40,47;10:10	
	—	—		11:25-26	
2053:38					1Jo 3:1-2
2053:38-40	24:14 28:19-20	13:10 16:15	24:47	20:21	Ac 1:8
2053:40-41				4:23-24	
2053:42-43	—	16:16			
2053:44-45					Ga 5:22-23 Ep 5:9
2054: 5- 6	28:19-20 24:14	16:15 13:10	24:47	20:21	Ac 1:8
2054:18-19				3:3-6	
2054:19-21	5:6 26:26 —	14:22 —	6:21 22:29	4:10-14 6:35,48 6:51,58 7:37-38	Is 55:1-2 Re 7:16-17
2054:25-27	28:19-20 24:14	16:15 13:10	24:47	20:21	Ac 1:8
2054:29-33	—	—	—		Ga 5:22-23 Ep 5:9
2054:33-34					Ja 2:17
2054:33-39	3:8-10 7:16-20 12:33		3:8-9 6:43-44 13:6-9	15:2,5-8 15:16	Ga 5:22-23 Ep 5:9
2054:39-41	—	—	—		1Co 3:1-2 Ep 4:14-15 1Pe 2:2 2Pe 3:18
2054:41-42	28:19-20 24:14	16:15 13:10	24:47	20:21	Ac 1:8
2054:42-43	—	—	24:49	14:16-18 14:26;25,26 16:7;13-14	Ek 11:19 36:26-27 Ek 36:26-27 Ac 1:4;2:2-4
	—	—			Ac 2:16-18 Jl 2:28

The URANTIA Book Page:Line	MATTHEW Chap:Verse	MARK Chap:Verse	LUKE Chap:Verse	JOHN Chap:Verse	Other BOOKS Chap:Verse
2054:43			2:14	14:27;16:33	Pp 4:7
2055: 6-11	3:11	1:18	3:16,24,49	1:33	Ac 1:4-8
2055: 9-11			24:49	14:16-18	Ek 11:19 36:26-27
	—	—		14:26;25,26	Ek 36:26-27
				16:7;13-14	Ac 1:4;2:2-4
	—	—			Ac 2:16-18 Jl 2:28
2055:12-13					Ac 1:6
2055:16-18	28:19-20 24:14	16:15 13:10	24:47	20:21	Ac 1:8
2055:18-19	—	—		13:34-35 15:12,17	
2055:21	—	—		—	Ge 2:18
2055:21-22					Ro 14:7
2055:22-23	—				Pv 18:24
2055:23-24		6:7	10:1	9:1-2	
2055:30	—	—		14:12,28;20:17 16:10,15-16,28	
2057:14-31			24:50-51		
2057:21-22	(Same as 2054:42-43, above.)				
2057:24-25	28:19-20 24:14	16:15 13:10	24:47	20:21	Ac 1:8
2057:29-30	28:20				
2057:31			24:51		
2057:31-34					Ac 1:9-11
2057:35-42	22:24	12:36 16:19	20:42		Ps 110:1 Ro 8:34 Cl 3:1 He 10:12 1Pe 3:22
		—		—	
2057:45-2058: 8					Ac 1:12-14
2058: 9-16	—	—		—	Ac 1:15-23
2058:17-20					Ac 1:26

PAPER 194:   Bestowal of The Spirit of Truth

2059: 3-12					Ac 2:1-2
2059:35-38	—	—		—	Ac 2:4
2060: 2- 4					Ac 2:5
2060: 9-11	—	—		—	Ac 2:14-40
2060:15-19					Ac 2:6-12

The URANTIA Book Page:Line	MATTHEW Chap:Verse	MARK Chap:Verse	LUKE Chap:Verse	JOHN Chap:Verse	Other BOOKS Chap:Verse
2060:16-19	—	—		—	Ac 2:4
2060:22-25					Ac 2:41
2061: 3	—	—			Ek 11:19;36:26-27
2061:10-13			24:49	15:26	Ek 11:19;36:26-27
	—	—		14:16-18,26	Ac 2:2-4,16-18
				16:7,13-14	Ac 1:4 Jl 2:28
2061:20-21	(Same as 2061:10-13, above.)				
2061:43-46	3:11	1:8	3:16	1:33	Ac 1:5;11:16
2061:47-2062:2	28:19				Ac 2:33 1Co 12:4-6
	—	—		—	1Jo 5:7
2062:22					Re 2:17
2062:39	—	—		—	Ek 11:19;36:26-27
2062:40					Ga 5:22 Ep 5:9
2062:43	(Same as 2061:10-13, above)				
2063: 5- 6	27:41-43	15:36			
	27:49				
2063:28-29	—	—		—	2Co 3:17
2063:34-40					Ek 11:19;36:26-27
2064: 7	—	—	24:49	15:26	Ek 11:19;36:26-27
				14:16-18,26	Ac 1:4;2:1-42
	—	—		16:7,13-14	Jl 2:28
2064:27-37					Ep 6:11-17
2064:31	—	—		—	Ro 12:21
2064:35-36					1Sa 1:3,11+
2064:36-37	—	—		—	Ro 15:6
					2Co 1:3;11:31
	—	—		—	Ep 1:3 Cl 1:3
					1Pe 1:3
2065:16	—	—		—	2Co 3:17
2065:32-33					Ac 4:32
2065:40-43	—	—		—	Ek 11:19;36:26-27
2066:11-12			24:19		
2066:24-26					Ac 2:46-47
2066:26-30	—	—		—	Ac 4:31-32
2066:35-37					Ac 2:22-23
2066:37-38	—	—		—	Ac 3:18
2066:38-41					Ac 2:32-33
2066:39	—	—		—	Ac 2:36
2066:41-44					Ac 3:19-21

The URANTIA Book Page:Line	MATTHEW Chap:Verse	MARK Chap:Verse	LUKE Chap:Verse	JOHN Chap:Verse	Other BOOKS Chap:Verse
2067: 7- 8	—	—		—	2Co 1:3
					Ep 1:3 Cl 1:3
2067:19-21	—	—		—	Ac 2:41-42
2067:22					Ro 16:16 1Co 16:20
2067:22	—	—		—	Ro 15:26 Ga 2:10
2067:22-24					Ac 2:44
2067:31-32					Ac 2:45
2067:34-35		—		—	Ac 11:29-30
2067:40	28:19			—	Ac 2:33 1Jo 5:7
	—	—		—	1Co 12:4-6
2067:46					Ac 5:17-18
2067:47-2068:3		—		—	Ac 5:34,38-39
2068: 3					Ac 5:40
2068:15:17	—	—		—	Ac 7:51-58
2068:26					Ac 8:1
2068:27-28	—	—		—	Ac 11:26

PAPER 195: After Pentecost

The URANTIA Book Page:Line	MATTHEW Chap:Verse	MARK Chap:Verse	LUKE Chap:Verse	JOHN Chap:Verse	Other BOOKS Chap:Verse
2069:10-11					Ac 4:10-12
	—	—		—	Ac 5:29-32
					Ac 13:26-39
	—	—		—	1Co 2:2
2071: 2- 4					Ac 17:22-23
2071: 4- 6	—	—		—	Ac 17:24-31
2071:20					1Co 2:2
2075:27	6:33		12:31		
2077:25					Ac 4:13
2077:26-27					Ac 17:6
2078:8	6:10;7:21	3:35	8:21	4:34;5:30	
	12:50	14:36-39	11:2	6:38;7:17	
	26:39		22:42	14:23-24	
	26:42,44			15:10,14;17:4	
2083:33-35					Ac 14:27
2084: 8- 9	—	—		3:14-15	Je 31:3
				6:48;8:28	
				12:32	
2084: 9	—	—			Ro 8:37

The URANTIA Book Page:Line	MATTHEW Chap:Verse	MARK Chap:Verse	LUKE Chap:Verse	JOHN Chap:Verse	Other BOOKS Chap:Verse
2084:24	—		— 17:21		
2084:25-26				4:24	
2084:27-31	5:38-41				
2085:20	12:25	3:24-25	11:17		

PAPER 196: The Faith of Jesus

2087:11-12	5:16,45,48	11:25-26	10:21		
	6:1,9;7:11				
	11:25;16:17				
	18:35;23:9				
	(See also 2078:8, above.)				
2087:12					Ps 71:22 Is 1:4
2088:28	6:33		12:31		
2088:30-31	6:10;7:21	3:35	8:21	4:34;5:30	
	12:50	14:36-39	11:2	6:38;7:17	
	26:39		22:42	14:23-24	
	26:42,44			15:10,14;17:4	
2088:42-43	19:16-17	10:17-18	18:18-19		
2089:12-14	(Same as 2078:8, above.)				
2089:41-42	18:3	10:15	18:17		
2089:50	16:24	8:34	9:59	12:26	
2090: 1	(See also 2078:8, above)			6:38	
2090:28	—			—	Pp 3:12
2090:45		12:37			
2091:28-29					He 12:2
2091:32-34	—	—		—	Ac 9:1-20
2091:41-42					1Pe 2:21-23
2092: 2	—	—		1:1;5:18	
				10:30,38	
	—	—		14:9-11,20	
				17:11,21-22	
2092:10-12	19:17	10:18	18:19		
2092:13				8:46	
2092:30	—	—		14:6	He 10:20
2092:40-42					Ac 2:29-36;17:2-3
	—	—		—	Ro 8:34 Cl 2:12
					1Co 15:11-22

The URANTIA Book Page:Line	MATTHEW Chap:Verse	MARK Chap:Verse	LUKE Chap:Verse	JOHN Chap:Verse	Other BOOKS Chap:Verse
2092:42-43	16:27 24:30 25:31	8:38 13:26	9:26 21:27		
2093:16 .	5:3		6:20		
2093:16-17	19:23-24	10:24-25	18:24-25		
2095:18					1Co 13:13
2097:18-20	—	—		—	1Jo 5:11-12

SECTION THREE

The LIFE and TEACHINGS of JESUS
From The Four Gospels
(MATTHEW, MARK, LUKE and JOHN)
Cross Referenced to *The URANTIA Book*

* * * * *

A: The Gospel According to MATTHEW

MATTHEW Chap:Verse	The URANTIA Book Page:Line	MARK Chap:Verse	LUKE Chap:Verse	JOHN Chap:Verse	Other BOOKS Chap:Verse
1: 1	1341:43				Mt 1:6,17
1: 1-16	1344:26-33	_	3:23-38		
1: 2-16	1348: 7-11		3:23-37		
1: 6	1341:43	_			Mt 1:1,17
	1347:37-42		1:27,31		
1:14-16	1347:39-42	_	2:4;3:23-24		
1:17	1341:43				Mt 1:1,6
1:18-21	(Mary's Pregnancy:)				
	1346: 7- 8				
	1347:17-18				
	(Joseph and Mary:)				
	1345:15-20		1:27;2:4-5		Mt 1:24-25
	1349:20-23	_	1:27;2:4-5		Mt 1:24-25
	1350:22		1:27;2:4-5		Mt 1:24-25
1:20	(Joseph's Dream)				
	0407:17-18	_	1:11		Ge 16:7
	1347:21-29				
1:21	1346:35-36	_	1:31		
	2035:35				

133

Matthew 1:22 to 3:2

MATTHEW Chap:Verse	The URANTIA Book Page:Line	MARK Chap:Verse	LUKE Chap:Verse	JOHN Chap:Verse	Other BOOKS Chap:Verse
1:22-23	1341:43				Is 7:14
	(Use of Prophesy in Matthew:)				
	1341:41-43				Mt 2:5-6,15,17-18,23
					Mt 4:14-16;8:17;12:17-25
					Mt 13:25;27:8-10,35;21:4-5
	1347:43-1348:13 (Same as 1341:41-43, above)				
1:23	1348: 6- 7				Is 7:14
1:24-25	(Joseph and Mary. See Matthew 1:18-21, above.)				
1:25	1351:29-34		2:6-7		
2: 1- 2	0584: 9-10	_	2:7-11	1:14	
2: 1-10	1680:34-36				
2: 1-11	1317:19-26				
2: 1-12	1352: 9-19				
2: 2	0988:22-25				
	1352:22	_	_		Mt 2:7,9-10
2: 3- 8	1353:45-1354: 7				
2: 5- 6	1341:41-43				Mi 5:2
2: 7	1352:22	_	_		Mt 2:2,9-10
2: 9-10	1352:22				Mt 2:2,7
2:11	1352:19-21				
2:12	1354: 7				
2:13-15	1354:29-38				
2:14	1047:16-17				
2:15	1341:41-43	_	_		Ho 11:1
2:16	1354:20-24				
2:17-18	1341:41-43	_	_		Je 31:15
2:19-21	1354:37-38				
	1356: 1- 2				
2:22-23	1356:14-20				
2:23	1341:41-43				Is 11:1
3: 1	1497:30-33	_	3:2		
	1501:37-42		3:3		
3: 1- 2	1858:28-29				
3: 2	(Repent, Kingdom of Heaven is at Hand:)				
	1501:27-28	1:15			Mt 4:17;10:7
	1502: 3	1:15	_		Mt 4:17;10:7
	1503: 3- 4	1:15			Mt 4:17;10:7
	1510:26-27	1:15	_		Mt 4:17;10:7

(Matthew 3:2 Continued on next page.)

134

MATTHEW Chap:Verse	The URANTIA Book Page:Line	MARK Chap:Verse	LUKE Chap:Verse	JOHN Chap:Verse	Other BOOKS Chap:Verse
3: 2	1510:46	1:15			Mt 4:17;10:7
	1536: 8-1537:23	1:15	_		Mt 4:17;10:7
	1537:11-12	1:15			Mt 4:17;10:7
	1588:25-28	1:15	_		Mt 4:17;10:7
	1681:41-42	1:15			Mt 4:17;10:7
	1801: 6	1:15	_		Mt 4:17;10:7
	1858:23-31	1:15			Mt 4;17;10:7
	1866: 7- 8	1:15	_		Mt 4:17;10:7
3: 3	1501:29-35	1:2-3	3:4-6	1:23	Is 40:3-5
	1502:25-33	1:3	3:4-6	1:22-23	Is 40:3-5
3: 4	1497: 5-11	1:6	1:80;3:4		
3: 5	1501:37-42	1:5	3:3		
3: 6	(Baptism:)				
	0947: 1- 2	1:4-5,8	3:7,16	1:25-33	Mt 3:11
	0964:37	1:4-5,8	3:7,16	1:25-33	Mt 3:11
	1502:13	1:4-5,8	3:7,16	1:25-33	Mt 3:11
	1593:11-13	1:4-5,8	3:7,16	1:25-33	Mt 3:11
	(Baptism to Repentance, See Matthew 3:11, below.)				
3: 7	1501:35		3:7		
	1545:39	_	3:7		
3: 7- 9	1502:34-42		3:7-9		Mt 23:33
3: 8-10	(Requirement to Bring Forth Good Fruit:)				
	1502:42-44		3:8-9	15:2,5-8,16	
			6:43-44		Mt 7:16-20;12:33
			13:6-9		Ga 5:22-23 Ep 5:9
	1569: 6- 8	(Same as 1502:42-44, above)			
	1571:32-37	(Same as 1502:42-44, above)			
	1572:27	(Same as 1502:42-44, above)			
	1582:33-34	(Same as 1502:42-44, above)			
	1596:26-27	(Same as 1502:42-44, above)			
	1601: 8-10	(Same as 1502:42-44, above)			
	1714:36-38	(Same as 1502:42-44, above)			
	1830:39-45	(Same as 1502:42-44, above)			
	1917:30-32	(Same as 1502:42-44, above)			
	1945:40-47	(Same as 1502:42-44, above)			
	1946:21-26	(Same as 1502:42-44, above)			
	2054:33-39	(Same as 1502:42-44, above)			
	(For Fruits of the Spirit, See Ga 5:22-23 Ep 5:9)				

Matthew 3:11 to 4:4

MATTHEW Chap:Verse	The URANTIA Book Page:Line	MARK Chap:Verse	LUKE Chap:Verse	JOHN Chap:Verse	Other BOOKS Chap:Verse
3:11	(Baptism, See Matthew 3:6, above.)				
	(Baptism of Repentence:)				
	1502:12-17	1:4,8	3:3,16	1:25-28,33	
	1503:31	1:4,8	3:3,16	1:25-28,33	
	1510:26-27	1:4,8	3:3,16	1:25-28,33	
	1536:34-36	1:4,8	3:3,16	1:25-28,33	
	1584:31-32	1:4,8	3:3,16	1:25-28,33	
	1625:30-35	1:4,8	3:3,16	1:25-28,33	
3:11-12	1503:24-28	1:7-8	3:16-17	1:27	
3:13-17	(The Baptism of Jesus:)				
	1504:11-42	1:9-11	3:21-22		
	1510:45-46	1:9-11	3:21-22		
3:16	(The Descending Spirit:)				
	1506: 6	1:10	3:22		
	1511:37-38	1:10	3:22		
	1511:42-43	1:10	3:22		
	1511:48	1:10	3:21		
3:17	(Voice, Beloved Son/Well Pleased:)				
	0538:10-11	1:11	3:22		
	1506: 7- 8	1:11	3:22		
	1511: 8-42	1:11	3:22		
	1512: 5- 7	1:11	3:22		
	1545:21-22	1:11	3:22		
4: 1	1492:33-36		4:1		
	1515:25-26	1:12-13	4:1-2		
4: 1- 2	1504:44	1:12-13	4:2		
4: 1-11	(The Temptation:)				
	1493:33-1494: 6	1:12-13	4:1-13		
	1512:30-34	1:12-13	4:1-13		
	1514:38-39	1:12-13	4:1-13		
4: 2- 4	(Hunger/Fasting:)				
	1493:14-15		4:2-4		
	1514:24-28	_	4:2-4		
	1517:46-48		4:2-4		
	1518:26-28		4:2-4		
4: 4	(Man Cannot Live by Bread, Alone:)				
	1518:23-28		4:3-4		De 8:3
	1777:21		4:3-4		De 8:3

MATTHEW Chap:Verse	The URANTIA Book Page:Line	MARK Chap:Verse	LUKE Chap:Verse	JOHN Chap:Verse	Other BOOKS Chap:Verse
4: 5- 7	(Personal Safety:)				
	1519:23-43	_	4:9-11		Ps 91:10-12
	1521: 2- 5		4:9-11		
4: 8-10	(Earthly Kingdom:)				
	1522: 1-18		4:5-8		De 6:13-14;10:20
	1522:33-34	_	4:5-8		
4:10	(Satan:)				
	0602: 1- 2	1:13	4:8		1Ch 21:1
	0609:44-45		4:8		
4:11	1841:27-28	1:13			
4:12	1506:11-12	1:14			
	1506:38-42	1:14			
	1535:31-37	1:14			
4:14-16	1341:41-43				Is 9:1-2
4:16	(Jesus as Light:)				
	0447:38-39		1:79	1:4-9;5:35	Is 9:2
		_	2:32	8:12 9:5	1Jo 2:8
				12:35-36,46	
	0513:31	(Same as 0447:38-39, above)			
	0590:33	(Same as 0447:38-39, above)			
	1104:14-15	(Same as 0447:38-39, above)			
	1181: 7- 8	(Same as 0447:38-39, above)			
	1353:38-39	(Same as 0447:38-39, above)			
	1458:33-35	(Same as 0447:38-39, above)			
	1671:10-11	(Same as 0447:38-39, above)			
	1795: 1	(Same as 0447:38-39, above)			
	1965:31	(Same as 0447:38-39, above)			
	2035:28-29	(Same as 0447:38-39, above)			
4:17	1535:31-37	1:15			
	(Repent, Kingdom at hand, See Matthew 3:2, above.)				
4:18-20	(Call of Simon Peter and Andrew:)				
	1524: 9-1525:2	1:16-18	6:14	1:40-42	Mt 10:2
		3:16,18			Ac 1:13
	1548:34-35	1:16	5:10		
	1628:27-1629:11		5:1-11		
	(Andrew:)				
	1548:28-1550:22 (Same as 1524:9-1525:2, above.)				

(Matthew 4:18-20 Continued on next page.)

MATTHEW Chap:Verse	The URANTIA Book Page:Line	MARK Chap:Verse	LUKE Chap:Verse	JOHN Chap:Verse	Other BOOKS Chap:Verse
4:18-20	(Simon Peter:)				
	1549:10-12				
	1550:23-1552:20 (Same as 1524:9-1525:2, above.)				
4:19	1544:47	1:17	5:10		
4:21-22	(Call of James and John)				
	1525: 7-46	1:19-20	6:14		Ac 1:13
		3:17			
	1628:27-1629:11		5:1-11		
	(James:)				
	1552:21-1553:38 (Same as 1525:7-46, above)				
	(John:)				
	1553:39-1556:4 (Same as 1525:7-46, above)				
4:23	1637: 2				
	1858:30				
	2035:40-41				
4:24	0863:42-44				
5: 1	1568: 3-13				
5: 2	1570: 8-26				
5: 3	Blessed are Poor in Spirit:)				
	1570:27-28		6:20		
	1573:42	_	6:20		
	2093:16		6:20		
5:3-7:23	1859:41-42	_	6:20-38		
5: 4	(Blessed are They that Mourn:)				
	1570:35-36		6:21		
	1575: 3	_	6:21		
	1776:41		6:21		
5: 5	(Blessed are the Meek:)				
	1570:31				Zp 2:3
	1574:19				Zp 2:3
5: 5- 6	2035:36-37				
5: 6	(Blessed, who Hunger & Thirst after Righteousness:)				
	1206:35-37	_	6:21		Is 55:1-3
	1570:29-30		6:21		
	1574: 6-16	_	6:21		
	1739:20		6:21		
	1861:12	_	6:21	7:37-38	

(Matthew 5:6 Continued on next page.)

MATTHEW Chap:Verse	The URANTIA Book Page:Line	MARK Chap:Verse	LUKE Chap:Verse	JOHN Chap:Verse	Other BOOKS Chap:Verse
5: 6	1865:14-16		6:21		
	2054:19-20		6:21	4:10-14;6:35	

(Jesus as The Bread & Water of Life:)

MATTHEW	URANTIA	MARK	LUKE	JOHN	Other
	1711: 3- 5				
	1712: 8-17			6:35	
	2054:19-20			6:35	

(Jesus as The Bread of Life:)

MATTHEW	URANTIA	MARK	LUKE	JOHN	Other
	1711:14-16	14:22	22:19	6:35,48,51,58	Mt 26:26
	1711:38-43	14:22	22:19	6:35,48,51,58	Mt 26:26
	1942: 9-16	14:22	22:19	6:35,48,51,58	Mt 26:26
	1965:29	14:22	22:19	6:35,48,51,58	Mt 26:26

(Jesus as The Water of Life:)

MATTHEW	URANTIA	MARK	LUKE	JOHN	Other
	0381: 5- 9			4:10,13-14	Is 55:1
				6:35;7:37-38	Re 7:16-17
	1613: 3- 5	(Same as 0381:5-9, above)			
	1954: 3- 6	(Same as 0381:5-9, above)			
	1965:30	(Same as 0381:5-9, above)			
	2035:39-40	(Same as 0381:5-9, above)			
	2054:19-21	(Same as 0381:5-9, above)			

MATTHEW	URANTIA	MARK	LUKE	JOHN	Other
5: 7	(Blessed are the Merciful:)				
	1570:37				
	1575:16				
5: 8	(Blessed are the Pure in Heart:)				
	1570:32				
	1574:25				
5: 9	(Blessed are the Peacemakers:)				
	1570:38				
	1575:23				
	1861:29		20:36		
5:10-12	(Blessed, those Persecuted for Righteousness:)				
	1570:39-42	_	6:22-23		
	1575:34-37		6:22-23		
	1860: 3- 5	_	6:22-23		Mt 6:19-20
	(Value System, See Matthew 6:19-21, below.)				
5:12	1103: 4				
5:13	(Salt of the Earth:)				
	1570:43-45	9:50	14:34-35		
	1572: 7- 9	9:50	14:34-35		
	1870:17-20	9:50	14:34-35		

Matthew 5:14 to 5:42

MATTHEW Chap:Verse	The URANTIA Book Page:Line	MARK Chap:Verse	LUKE Chap:Verse	JOHN Chap:Verse	Other BOOKS Chap:Verse
5:14-16	(You are Light of the World:)				
	1570:46-1571: 2	4:21	8:16;11:33		
	1572:13-16	4:21	8:16;11:33		
	(Children of Light:)				
	1327:26-27		16:8	12:36	Ep 5:8 1Th 5:5
	1655:37-38	—	16:8	12:36	Ep 5:8 1Th 5:5
	1854:11-12		16:8	12:36	Ep 5:8 1Th 5:5
	1904:24-28	—	16:8	12:36	Ep 5:8 1Th 5:5
	1953:33		16:8	12:36	Ep 5:8 1Th 5:5
	2042: 2		16:8	12:36	Ep 5:8 1Th 5:5
5:15	1692: 8-10	4:21	8:16;11:33		
5:16	(Let Your Light Shine:)				
	1571: 1- 2	4:21	8:16;11:33		
	1572:15-16	4:21	8:16;11:33		
	(Father in Heaven, See Matthew 6:9, below.)				
5:17	1576:18-21				
5:17-20	1653:26-37				
5:20	1576:22-25				
	1861:37-40				
5:21-22	1576:27-32	—	—		De 5:17 Ex 20:13
5:27-28	1576:34-36				De 5:18 Ex 20:14
5:31-32	1576:39-1577:2	10:2-12	16:18		Mt 19:3-9
5:38-40	1770:29-34		6:29		De 19:21 Ex 21:24
					Le 24:20
5:38-41	2084:27-31				
5:38-42	1577:16-21	—	—		De 19:21 Ex 21:24
					Le 24:20
5:38-45	1454:20-21	—	6:27-31		
5:38-48	1771: 2- 3		6:27-38		Mt 7:12 To 4:15
5:39	(Resist Not Evil, Turn other Cheek:)				
	1571: 5- 7		6:29		
	1590:20				
	1770: 8-12	—	6:29		
	2018:18				
5:41	1770:41-46				

140

MATTHEW Chap:Verse	The URANTIA Book Page:Line	MARK Chap:Verse	LUKE Chap:Verse	JOHN Chap:Verse	Other BOOKS Chap:Verse
5:43-44	(Love Your Enemies:)				
	1206:40-42	—	6:27,35		
	1454:44		6:27,35		
	<u>1571:10-11</u>		6:27,35		
	1580: 7	—	6:27,35		
	1897:16-17		6:27,35		
5:44	(Pray for Adversaries, Abusers:)				
	1640: 1- 2		6:28		
	1932:20-21		6:28		
5:45	(Children of the Heavenly Father:)				
	1454:47				
	2087:12				
	(Sun Shines on Just and Unjust:)				
	0039: 1- 2				
	<u>1571:13-14</u>				
	1671:35-38				
	1830:23-24				
5:46	1739:37-38				
5:48	(Be You Perfect:)				
	0021:30-31	Ge 17:1	Le 19:2 De 18:13	2Co 13:11	Ja 1:4
	0022:15-16	Ge 17:1	Le 19:2 De 18:13	2Co 13:11	Ja 1:4
	0086: 3	Ge 17:1	Le 19:2 De 18:13	2Co 13:11	Ja 1:4
	0086:11-12	Ge 17:1	Le 19:2 De 18:13	2Co 13:11	Ja 1:4
	0149: 3- 4	Ge 17:1	Le 19:2 De 18:13	2Co 13:11	Ja 1:4
	0290:20	Ge 17:1	Le 19:2 De 18:13	2Co 13:11	Ja 1:4
	0295:10-11	Ge 17:1	Le 19:2 De 18:13	2Co 13:11	Ja 1:4
	0297: 5- 6	Ge 17:1	Le 19:2 De 18:13	2Co 13:11	Ja 1:4
	0348:21	Ge 17:1	Le 19:2 De 18:13	2Co 13:11	Ja 1:4
	0411: 5	Ge 17:1	Le 19:2 De 18:13	2Co 13:11	Ja 1:4
	0449:14	Ge 17:1	Le 19:2 De 18:13	2Co 13:11	Ja 1:4
	0637: 8- 9	Ge 17:1	Le 19:2 De 18:13	2Co 13:11	Ja 1:4
	1091: 9-10	Ge 17:1	Le 19:2 De 18:13	2Co 13:11	Ja 1:4
	1165:24-25	Ge 17:1	Le 19:2 De 18:13	2Co 13:11	Ja 1:4
	1176:17	Ge 17:1	Le 19:2 De 18:13	2Co 13:11	Ja 1:4
	1444:42-43	Ge 17:1	Le 19:2 De 18:13	2Co 13:11	Ja 1:4
	1537: 2	Ge 17:1	Le 19:2 De 18:13	2Co 13:11	Ja 1:4
	<u>1571:16-17</u>	Ge 17:1	Le 19:2 De 18:13	2Co 13:11	Ja 1:4
	1573: 6- 7	Ge 17:1	Le 19:2 De 18:13	2Co 13:11	Ja 1:4

(Matthew 5:48 Continued on next page.)

Matthew 5:48 to 6:9

MATTHEW Chap:Verse	The URANTIA Book Page:Line	MARK Chap:Verse	LUKE Chap:Verse	JOHN Chap:Verse	Other BOOKS Chap:Verse
5: 48	1573:19-21	Ge 17:1 Le 19:2 De 18:13 2Co 13:11 Ja 1:4			
	1574:45	Ge 17:1 Le 19:2 De 18:13 2Co 13:11 Ja 1:4			
	1583:38	Ge 17:1 Le 19:2 De 18:13 2Co 13:11 Ja 1:4			
	1584:28-29	Ge 17:1 Le 19:2 De 18:13 2Co 13:11 Ja 1:4			
	1604:35-36	Ge 17:1 Le 19:2 De 18:13 2Co 13:11 Ja 1:4			
	1784:43-44	Ge 17:1 Le 19:2 De 18:13 2Co 13:11 Ja 1:4			
	1953:34-35	Ge 17:1 Le 19:2 De 18:13 2Co 13L11 Ja 1:4			
	1961:33-34	Ge 17:1 Le 19:2 De 18:13 2Co 13:11 Ja 1:4			
	(Father in Heaven, See Matthew 6:9, below.)				
6: 1	1577:29-30				
	(Father in Heaven, See Matthew 6:9, below.)				
6: 1- 3	1583: 2- 4				
6: 1- 4	1577:29-30				
6: 1- 6	1454:42-43				
6: 5-13	(Prayer:)				
	0096:37-38	11:24	11:2-4		Mt 26:39,42
		14:35-36	18:1-14		Ro 8:26-27
			22:41		
	1001:12-1002:41 (Same as 0096:37-38, above)				
	1511:46-48 (Same as 0096:37-38, above)				
	1618:35-1624:10 (Same as 0096:37-38, above)				
	1638:10-1641: 9 (Same as 0096:37-38, above)				
	1848:16-1849:23 (Same as 0096:37-38, above)				
	1968:11-15 (Same as 0096:37-38, above)				
	1968:22-24 (Same as 0096:37-38, above)				
	1968:31-34 (Same as 0096:37-38, above)				
6: 6- 8	1577:30-32	—	—		Mt 6:32
	1620:21-23				
6: 7	1640:32-34				
6: 8	0049:16-17		—		Is 65:24
6: 9	(Father in Heaven:)				
	0023:24	11:25-26	10:21		Mt 5:16,48;6:1
			11:2		Mt 7:11,21;11:25
					Mt 16:17;18:35
					Mt 23:9
	1053:41-42 (Same as 0023:24, above)				
	1103:19 (Same as 0023:24, above)				
	1569:10 (Same as 0023:24, above)				

(Matthew 6:9 Continued on next page.)

MATTHEW Chap:Verse	The URANTIA Book Page:Line	MARK Chap:Verse	LUKE Chap:Verse	JOHN Chap:Verse	Other BOOKS Chap:Verse
6: 9	1571: 2	(Same as 0023:24, above)			
	1571:16-17	(Same as 0023:24, above)			
	1619:23	(Same as 0023:24, above)			
	1620: 1	(Same as 0023:24, above)			
	1638:35	(Same as 0023:24, above)			
	1764: 2	(Same as 0023:24, above)			
	1807:18-19	(Same as 0023:24, above)			
	1907:16	(Same as 0023:24, above)			
	1923:12	(Same as 0023:24, above)			
	2087:11-12	(Same as 0023:24, above)			
6: 9-10	1619:46-1620:10		11:2-4		
6:10	1860:23-24		11:2		

(Doing the Father's Will:)

	The URANTIA Book	MARK	LUKE	JOHN	Other BOOKS
	0008:42	3:35	8:21	4:34;5:30	Mt 7:21
		14:36	11:2	6:38;7:17	Mt 12:50
		14:39	22:42	14:23-24	Mt 26:39,42
				15:10,14	Mt 26:44
	0052: 1- 4	(Same as 0008,42, above)			
	1200:41	(Same as 0008:42, above)			
	1221:33-34	(Same as 0008:42, above)			
	1303: 7	(Same as 0008:42, above)			
	1318:29-30	(Same as 0008:42, above)			
	1324:21-22	(Same as 0008:42, above)			
	1327:10	(Same as 0008:42, above)			
	1328:38-41	(Same as 0008:42, above)			
	1331: 9-10	(Same as 0008:42, above)			
	1417: 5- 7	(Same as 0008:42, above)			
	1453:43-44	(Same as 0008:42, above)			
	1500:27	(Same as 0008:42, above)			
	1511:47-48	(Same as 0008:42, above)			
	1514:35	(Same as 0008:42, above)			
	1569: 8-10	(Same as 0008:42, above)			
	1574:21	(Same as 0008:42, above)			
	1582: 8	(Same as 0008:42, above)			
	1594:33-34	(Same as 0008:42, above)			
	1608: 1	(Same as 0008:42, above)			
	1769:42-44	(Same as 0008:42, above)			Ja 1:22-25
					Ja 2:17 1Jo 3:18

(Matthew 6:10 continued on next page.)

143

MATTHEW Chap:Verse	The URANTIA Book Page:Line	MARK Chap:Verse	LUKE Chap:Verse	JOHN Chap:Verse	Other BOOKS Chap:Verse
6:10	1774:28	(Same as 0008:42, above)			
	1947:50-1948:1	(Same as 0008:42, above)			
	1968:21-24	(Same as 0008:42, above)			
	1972: 5- 7	(Same as 0008:42, above)			
	2078: 8	(Same as 0008:42, above)			
	2087:11	(Same as 0008:42, above)			
	2088:30-31	(Same as 0008:42, above)			
	2089:12-14	(Same as 0008:42, above)			
	2090: 1	(Same as 0008:42, above)			
6:11	1001:36		11:3		
6:12	(Forgiveness:)				
	1475: 4- 7	11:25-26	11:4		Mt 6:14-15
			6:37		Mt 18:21-35
	1638:36-41	(Same as 1475: 4- 7, above)			
	1763:23-1764:4	(Same as 1475: 4- 7, above)			
	1862: 5- 6	(Same as 1475: 4- 7, above)			
	2017:44-45	(Same as 1475: 4- 7, above)			
6:13	(Temptation:)				
	1738:25		11:4		
6:14-15	(Forgiveness, See Matthew 6:12, above.)				
6:16	1577:32-33				
6:19-21	(Value System, "Treasures" in Heaven & on Earth:)				
	1474:37-42		6:35;12:33-34		Mt 5:10-12
	1577:33-36		6:35;12:33-34		Mt 5:10-12
	1821:40-1822:11		6:35;12:33-34		Mt 5:10-12
	1823:44-48		6:35;12:33-34		Mt 5:10-12
	1853:26-34		6:35;12:33-34		Mt 5:10-12
	1860: 3- 5		6:35;12:33-34		Mt 5:10-12
6:21	1571:37-39		12:34		
6:22-23	0955:19-20	—	11:34		
	1577:37-40		11:34		
6:24	(No Man can Serve Two Masters:)				
	1199:33-34	—	16:13		
	1577:44-46		16:13		
	1803: 6- 8	—	16:13		
	1854:25-27		16:13		
6:25-26	1577:47-50	—	12:22-23		Mt 6:31
	1578: 1- 4		12:22-23		Mt 6:32-34

MATTHEW Chap:Verse	The URANTIA Book Page:Line	MARK Chap:Verse	LUKE Chap:Verse	JOHN Chap:Verse	Other BOOKS Chap:Verse
6:25-27	1823:15-25	—	12:22-26		
6:25-34	1096:20-21		12:22-34		
	1580:10-11	—	12:22-34		
6:28-30	1823:26-30		12:27-28		
6:31	1577:47-50	—	12:22-23		Mt 6:25-26
	1823:15-17				
6:31-32	1823:36-39	—	12:29-30		
6:32	1577:30-32				Mt 6:6-8
6:32-34	1578: 1- 4	—	12:22-23		Mt 6:25-26
6:33	(Priorities--Seek First the Kingdom of God:)				
	1206:35-37		12:31		
	1536:24-26	—	12:31		
	1569:11-13		12:31		
	1897:33-34	—	12:31		
	2075:27		12:31		
	2088:28	—	12:31		
6:33-34	1823:39-43		12:31		
7: 1- 2	(Judge Not:)				
	1454:43	—	6:37		
	1474:44-1475: 7		6:36-38		
	1571:18-20	—	6:36-37		
	1580:42		6:37		
	1639: 8-10	—	6:36-37		
7: 3- 5	1571:20-23		6:37,41-42		
7: 6	(Cast Not Pearls before Swine:)				
	1571:29-30				
	1585:11-12				
	1999:12-13				
7: 7- 8	(Ask, Seek, Knock:)				
	1619:13-15		11:9-10		
	(Ask, Seek:)1838:41-42				
	(Ask:)1454:22-23			14:13-14	
				15:7,16	
				16:23-24	
	1639:18-23	(Same as 1454:22-23, above)			
	1639:39-42	(Same as 1454:22-23, above)			
	1849:19-20	(Same as 1454:22-23, above)			
	1945:37-44	(Same as 1454:22-23, above)			

(Matthew 7:7-8 Continued on next page.)

MATTHEW Chap:Verse	The URANTIA Book Page:Line	MARK Chap:Verse	LUKE Chap:Verse	JOHN Chap:Verse	Other BOOKS Chap:Verse
7: 7- 8	(Seek:)				
	1440:22-23				Je 28:13
	1445:33				Je 28:33
7: 8	1102:38-39	_	11:10		
7: 9-11	1619:16-24		11:11-13		
7:11	1454: 2- 5		11:13		
	(Father in Heaven, See Matthew 6:9, above.)				
7:12	(Golden Rule, Do Unto Others etc.:)				
	1445:47-48		6:31		To 4:15
	1454:35-36		6:31		To 4:15
	1464:37-38		6:31		To 4:15
	1571:11-12		6:31		To 4:15
	1585:29-32		6:31		To 4:15
	1650:15-1651:21		6:31		To 4:15
	1771: 2- 3		6:31		To 4:15
	1931:23-24		6:31		To 4:15
	1949:43-1950:28		6:31		To 4:15
	(Compare: Love Neighbor as Self:)				
	1445:47	12:31,33	10:27-28		Mt 19:19;22:39
					Le 19:18 Ro 13:9
					Ga 5:14 Ja 2:8
	1446:11	(Same as 1445:47, above)			
	1453:37	(Same as 1445:47, above)			
	1600: 1- 3	(Same as 1445:47, above)			
	1600:33-36	(Same as 1445:47, above)			
	1769:26	(Same as 1445:47, above)			
	1770: 4- 8	(Same as 1445:47, above)			
	1805:10-11	(Same as 1445:47, above)			
	1809:25-28	(Same as 1445:47, above)			
	1862: 8	(Same as 1445:47, above)			
	1901:17-20	(Same as 1445:47, above)			
	1950:17-18	(Same as 1445:47, above)			
	(The New Standard, Act & Love as Jesus Does:)				
	1206:40-42		6:31		
	1571:10-11		6:31		To 4:15 Ga 5:14
	1944:23-31	(Same as 1453:37, above)			
7:13-14	1828:36-42				
7:15	1571:31-32				
	1585:11				

MATTHEW Chap:Verse	The URANTIA Book Page:Line	MARK Chap:Verse	LUKE Chap:Verse	JOHN Chap:Verse	Other BOOKS Chap:Verse
7:16-20	(Need for Good Fruit, See Matthew 3:8-10, above.)				
7:20	0065: 5		6:44		
7:21	(Father in Heaven, See Matthew 6:9, above.)				
	(Do The Father's Will, See Matthew 6:10, above.)				
7:22-23	1571:40-43				
	1829:14-23				
7:24-27	1571:43-46	_	6:47-49		
	1738: 9-14		6:47-49		
7:28-29	1571:47-48	1:22			
	1630:42-44	1:22	4:31-32		
8: 1	1643:27-29				
8: 2- 3	(Faith Makes Whole:)				
	1643:29-41	1:40-41	5:12-13		Mt 8:13
		2:5;5:34	8:48,50		Mt 9:2,22,29
		10:52	17:19;18:42		Mt 15:28
	1648: 7-13	(Same as 1643:29-40, above)			
	1667:12	(Same as 1643:29-40, above)			
	1698:33-1699:6	(Same as 1643:29-40, above)			
	1735:21-25	(Same as 1643:29-40, above)			
	1828:10-11	(Same as 1643:29-40, above)			
	1873:28-29	(Same as 1643:29-40, above)			
	1875:13-14	(Same as 1643:29-40, above)			
	1905:23-24	(Same as 1643:29-40, above)			
8: 4	1643:42-45	1:43-45	5:12-15		
	(Tell No Man:)				
	1520:20-21	1:44;5:43	5:14		Mt 9:30
		7:36;8:26	8:56		
	1669:14-16	(Same as 1520:20-21, above)			
	1699:32-33	(Same as 1520:20-21, above)			
8: 5- 6	1647:27-36		7:1-5		
8: 5-13	1420:27-32	_	7:1-10		
8: 7- 9	1647:37-1648:6		7:6-8		
8:10	1648: 7- 9	_	7:9		
8:11	1829:26-31		13:28-30		
8:11-12	1568:30-34		13:28-30		
8:13	(Faith Makes Whole, See Matthew 8:2-3, above.)				
8:14-15	1631:22-27	1:29-31	4:38-39		
8:16	1632: 1-1633:15	1:32-34	4:40-41		
8:17	1341:41-43				Is 53:4

Matthew 8:18 to 9:14

MATTHEW Chap:Verse	The URANTIA Book Page:Line	MARK Chap:Verse	LUKE Chap:Verse	JOHN Chap:Verse	Other BOOKS Chap:Verse
8:18	1694:21-25	4:35	8:22		
8:19-22	1801:31-39		9:57-60		
	1723:35-37		9:58		
	1750:27-29	–	9:58		
8:20+	(Son of Man:)				
	1390: 4- 5	2:10+	5:24+	1:51+	En 46:1-71:17
	1390:24-31	2:10+	5:24+	1:51+	En 46:1-71:17
	1407:27	2:10+	5:24+	1:51+	+ = 78 times
8:21-22	1672: 3- 5		9:59-60		
8:23-24	1694:26-43	4:36-38	8:22-23		
8:25-27	1695: 3-27	4:38-41	8:24-25		
8:28	1695:35-48	5:1-4	8:26-27,29		
8:28-32	1765: 8-12	5:1-13	8:26-33		
8:29	1696: 9-11	5:6-7	8:28		
8:30-33	1696:15-28	5:8,11-15	8:29,32-25		
8:34	1696:42-1697: 3	5:16-19	8:36-37		
9: 2	1102:29	6:50		16:33	Mt 14:27
	(Faith Makes Whole, See Matthew 8:2-3, above.)				
9: 2- 3	1666:39-1667:12	2:3-5	5:18-20		
9: 3- 8	1667:13-27	2:6-12	5:21-26		
9: 9	(Call of Matthew Levi:)				
	1540:16-21	2:14	5:27-28		Mt 10:3
		3:18	6:15		Ac 1:13
	1559:20-1560:49	2:14	5:27-28		
	1957:43-44	2:14	5:27-28		
9:10-11	(Friend of Publicans & Sinners:)				
	1342:17-18	2:15-16	5:29-30		Mt 11:19
			7:34;15:2		
	1627:26-27	(Same as 1342:17-18, above)			
	1850:18-19	(Same as 1342:17-18, above)			
	1851: 7- 8	(Same as 1342:17-18, above)			
9:10-13	1540:31-1541:14	2:15-17	5:29-32		Mt 11:19
9:13	(Came to Call Sinners to Repentance:)				
	1537:17-19	2:17	5:32		
	1750:10-11	2:17	5:32		
9:14-15	(Fasting)				
	0976:16-17	2:18-22	5:33		2Sa 12:16;21:23
					Ps 35:13 Is 58:3-6

(Matthew 9:14-15 Continued on next page.)

MATTHEW Chap:Verse	The URANTIA Book Page:Line	MARK Chap:Verse	LUKE Chap:Verse	JOHN Chap:Verse	Other BOOKS Chap:Verse
9:14-15	1609:24-25	2:18-22	5:33		
	1655:28-47	2:18-22	5:33-38		
9:18-19	1698: 8-16	5:22-24	8:41-42		
9:20-22	1698:16-37	5:25-34	8:43-48		
9:22	(Faith Made Whole, See Matthew 8:2-3, above.)				
9:23-25	1699:13-22	5:35-42	8:49-55		
9:26	1699:35-36				
9:27	1699:34-35				
9:27-30	1873: 1				
9:29	(Faith Made Whole, See Matthew 8:2-3, above.)				
9:30	(Tell no Man:)				
	1520:20-21	1:44;5:43	5:14		Mt 8:4
		7:36;8:26	8:56		
	1643:42-45	(Same as 1520:20-21, above)			
	1669:14-16	(Same as 1520:20-21, above)			
9:32-33	1713:40-48		11:14		Mt 12:22
9:34	(Devils, See Matthew 10:25, below.)				
9:35	2035:40-41				
9:37-38	1681:29-32	_	10:2		
	1800:30-32		10:2		
10: 1- 4	(The Commission:)				
	1584: 1- 6	3:13-14	9:1-2		Mt 10:7-8
	1590:44-45	3:15	9:2;10:9		Mt 10:8
	1681:28:38	3:13	9:1-2		Mt 10:7-8
	(The 12 Apostles:)				
	1548: 2-1567:47	3:16-19	6:13-16		Ac 1:13
	1568: 2-1571:46	3:14			Mt 5:1-7:27
	1681:35-38	3:16-19	6:13-16		
10: 2	(The Call of Simon:)				
	1524:25-1525:2	1:16-18		1:41-42	Mt 4:18-20
		3:16	6:14		Ac 1:13
	1549:10-12			1:40-42	
	1550:23-1552:20	(Same as 1524:25-1525: 2, above)			
	1628:27-1629:11		5:1-11		
	(Simon is called Peter or Cephas:)				
	1524:36-1525:2	3:16	6:14	1:42	Mt 16:18
	1550:29-32	3:16	6:14	1:42	Mt 16:18
	1897:13-14	3:16	6:14	1:42	Mt 16:18

(Matthew 10:2 Continued on next page.)

Matthew 10:2 to 10:6

MATTHEW Chap:Verse	The URANTIA Book Page:Line	MARK Chap:Verse	LUKE Chap:Verse	JOHN Chap:Verse	Other BOOKS Chap:Verse
10: 2	(Call of Andrew:)				
	1524: 9-20	1:16-18		1:40	Mt 4:18-20
		3:18	6:14		Ac 1:13
	1548:28-1520:22 (Same as 1524: 9-20, above)				
	1628:27-1629:11		5:1-11		
	(Call of James and John Bar-Zebedee:)				
	1525: 7-46	1:19-20	6:14		Mt 4:21-22
		3:17			Ac 1:13
	1628:27-1629:11		5:1-11		
	1955:37				
	(James Zebedee:)				
	1552:21-1553:38 (Same as 1525: 7-46, above)				
	(John Zebedee:)				
	1553:39-1556: 4 (Same as 1525: 7-46, above)				
10: 3	(Call of Philip)				
	1526:21-44	3:18	6:14	1:43-44	Ac 1:13
	1556: 5-1558: 6	3:18	6:14	1:43-44	Ac 1:13
	(Call of Nathaniel Bar-Tholomew:)				
	1526:45-1527:13	3:18	6:14	1:45-49	Ac 1:13
	1558: 7-1559:19	3:18	6:14	1:45-49	Ac 1:13
	(Call of Thomas Didymus:)				
	1542: 4- 9	3:18	6:15	11:16	Ac 1:13
	1561: 1-1563:13	3:18	6:15	11:16	Ac 1:13
	(Call of Matthew Levi:)				
	1540:16-21	2:14	5:27-28		Mt 9:9
		3:18	6:15		Ac 1:13
	1559:20-1560:49 (Same as 1540:16-21, above)				
	(Call of James and Judas Bar-Alphaeus; AKA James the Lesser, Thaddeus and Lebbeus:)				
	1541:26-31	3:18	6:15-16		Ac 1:13
	1563:14-1564:32	3:18	6:15-16		Ac 1:13
10: 4	(Call of Simon the Zealot or Cananite:)				
	1540:27-30	3:18	6:15		Ac 1:13
	1564:33-1565:40	3:18	6:15		Ac 1:13
	(Call of Judas Iscariot, the Betrayer:)				
	1542: 4-11	3:19	6:16	12:4	
	1565:41-1567:47	3:19	6:16	12:4	
10: 5	2055:23-24	6:7	9:1-2;10:1		
10: 5- 6	1681:39-41				

MATTHEW Chap:Verse	The URANTIA Book Page:Line	MARK Chap:Verse	LUKE Chap:Verse	JOHN Chap:Verse	Other BOOKS Chap:Verse
10: 7	(Kingdom of Heaven is at Hand:)				
	1501:27-28	1:15			Mt 3:2;4:17
	1502: 3	1:15			Mt 3:2;4:17
	1503: 3- 4	1:15			Mt 3:2;4:17
	1510:26-27	1:15			Mt 3:2;4:17
	1510:46	1:15			Mt 3:2;4:17
	1536: 8-1537:23	1:15			Mt 3:2;4:17
	1537:11-12	1:15			Mt 3:2;4:17
	1588:25-28	1:15			Mt 3:2;4:17
	1681:41-42	1:15			Mt 3:2;4:17
	1801: 6	1:15			Mt 3:2;4:17
	1858:23-31	1:15			Mt 3:2;4:17
	1866: 7- 8	1:15			Mt 3:2;4:17
10: 7- 8	1584: 4- 6	16:15			Mt 28:19
	1801: 6- 8		10:9		
10: 8	1590:44-45		9:2;10:9		Mt 10:1
	(Freely Received, Freely Give:)				
	1102:36-37				
	1740:37-38				
	1764: 6- 7				
	1918:20-21				
	2042:11-12				
	2053:17				
10: 9-10	1584: 7- 8	6:8-9	9:3;10:4		
	1800:34-35	6:8-9	9:3;10:4		
10:11-13	1800:36-38	6:10	10:5-7		
10:14-15	1801: 9-13	6:11	9:5		
10:16	1580:47				
	1800:33-34	_	10:3		
	1930:33-34				
10:16-22	1584: 8-17		10:3		
10:17-20	1912:33-1913:1	13:5-13	21:8-17		Mt 24:9-13
10:21	1951:29-30	13:12	21:16		
10:21-22	1913: 1- 6	13:12-13	21:16-18		
10:24-26	1681:43-47		6:40	13:16;15:20	
10:25	(Devils:)				
	0602:11	3:22,30	11:15		Mt 9:34;12:24
	0863:27	3:22,30	11:15		Mt 9:34;12:24

(Matthew 10:25 Continued on next page.)

151

MATTHEW Chap:Verse	The URANTIA Book Page:Line	MARK Chap:Verse	LUKE Chap:Verse	JOHN Chap:Verse	Other BOOKS Chap:Verse
10:25	1714: 7-13	3:22,30	11:15		Mt 9:34;12:24
	1850:24-25	3:22,30	11:15		Mt 9:34;12:24
	1924:45-46	3:22,30	11:15		Mt 9:34;12:24
10:26-27	(Covered Revealed; Hear in Dark, Speak in Light:)				
	1682: 1- 3	4:22	8:17;12:2-3		
	1692:10-13	4:22	8:17;12:2-3		
	1820: 7-12	4:22	8:17;12:2-3		
10:26-28	1681:47-1682:7	4:22	8:17;12:2-5		
10:28	1820:14-15		12:4-5		
10:29	0048:47-0049: 1		12:6		
10:29-31	(Human Value:)				
	1682: 8-11	—	12:6-7		
	1820:19-24		12:6-7		
10:30	(Hairs are Numbered:				
	0049: 1- 2		12:7		
	0419:25	—	12:7		
10:31	(Fear Not:)				
	1103:14		5:10;8:50		
			12:7,32		
	1582:19-20	(Same as 1103:14, above)			
10:32-33	1820:25-28		12:8-9		
10:34	0597:21-22	—	12:51		
	1782:10-11		12:51		
10:34-36	1682:11-18	—	12:51-53		
10:36	1722:45		12:52-53		
10:37	(Priority, God Before Family:)				
	1682:19-20		14:26		
	1869:34-40		14:26		
10:38	(Priority, Assume Responsibilities & Follow Jesus:)				
	1750: 5- 6	8:34;10:21	9:23;14:27		Mt 16:24
	1760:17-19	(Same as 1750:5-6, above)			
	1770:22-23	(Same as 1750:5-6, above)			
	1869:37-41	(Same as 1750:5-6, above)			
10:39	(Priority, Spiritual Life over Physical Life:)				
	1134:28-29	8:35	9:24;17:33	12:25	Mt 16:25
	1575:32-33	8:35	9:24;17:33	12:25	Mt 16:25
	1760:19-20	8:35	9:24;17:33	12:25	Mt 16:25
	1782: 9-10	8:35	9:24;17:33	12:25	Mt 16:25
	1903:39-41	8:35	9:24;17:33	12:25	Mt 16:25

MATTHEW Chap:Verse	The URANTIA Book Page:Line	MARK Chap:Verse	LUKE Chap:Verse	JOHN Chap:Verse	Other BOOKS Chap:Verse
10:40	1761:19-20	9:37	9:48;10:16	13:20	Mt 18:5
	1801:13-14	9:37	9:48;10:16	13:20	Mt 18:5
10:42	1764:38-40	9:41			
11: 2- 3	1626:38-42		7:19-20		
11: 2- 6	1507:36-45	—	7:18-23		
11: 4- 5	1626:43-45		7:21-22		
11: 5	(Gospel for ALL, Beginning with Needy and Oppressed:)				
	1594:12-13		4:18;7:22		Is 61:1
			14:13		
	1608:15-24	(Same as 1594:12-13, above)			
	1859:39-40	(Same as 1594:12-13, above)			
11: 7-10	1626:45-1627: 8		7:24-27	1:6-8	Ml 3:1
11:11	1509:10-13		7:28		
	1627: 9-12	—	7:28		
11:13	1731: 4- 6				
11:14	1754:25-27	9:11-13			Mt 17:11-12
					Ml 4:5-6
11:16-19	1627:20-27		7:31-35		
11:19	(Friend of Publicans and Sinners, See Matthew 9:10-11, above.)				
11:20-23	1807:34-43		10:13-15		
11:21	1726:32-40	—	10:13		
11:25	1453:38		10:21		
	(Father in Heaven, See Matthew 6:9, above.)				
11:25-26	1627:28-31				
	1807:16-27		10:21-22		
11:27	(Son Reveals the Father:)				
	0028:14-15		10:22	1:18;6:45-46	
				8:26;12:49-50	
				14:7-9,20	
				17:6,25-26	
	0093:46	(Same as 0028:14-15, above)			
	0109:28-33	(Same as 0028:14-15, above)			
	0196:10	(Same as 0028:14-15, above)			
	0232:42-44	(Same as 0028:14-15, above)			
	0233: 4- 5	(Same as 0028:14-15, above)			
	1324:23-32	(Same as 0028:14-15, above)			
	1328:38-41	(Same as 0028:14-15, above)			

(Matthew 11:27 Continued on next page.)

MATTHEW Chap:Verse	The URANTIA Book Page:Line	MARK Chap:Verse	LUKE Chap:Verse	JOHN Chap:Verse	Other BOOKS Chap:Verse
11:27	1331:21-22	(Same as 0028:14-15, above)			
	1608: 1- 2	(Same as 0028:14-15, above)			
	1710:15-16	(Same as 0028:14-15, above)			
	1750:14-15	(Same as 0028:14-15, above)			
	1855:46-47	(Same as 0028:14-15, above)			
	1947:42-47	(Same as 0028:14-15, above)			
	1965: 8-12	(Same as 0028:14-15, above)			
11:28-29	(Those Who Labor for Me Will Find Rest for Souls:)				
	1590:13-14				
	1627:31-33				
	1808: 9-11				
11:30	1766:14				
12: 1-14	(Conduct on the Sabbath:)				
	1649:47-1650:5	2:23-28	6:1-10	5:5,9	Mt 15:1-9
		3:1-5	11:37-41	5:16-18	Ex 20:8-11
		7:1-7	13:10-17	9:14	De 5:12-15
			14:1-6		
	1654:29-1655:12	(Same as 1649:47-1650:5, above)			
	1665: 7-35	(Same as 1649:47-1650:5, above)			
	1712:21-42	(Same as 1649:47-1650:5, above)			
	1813:13-16	(Same as 1649:47-1650:5, above)			
	1834: 6-32	(Same as 1649:47-1650:5, above)			
	1835:40-1836:26	(Same as 1649:47-1650:5, above)			
	1850:22-23	(Same as 1649:47-1650:5, above)			
12:17-21	1341:41-43				Is 42:1-4
					Ho 6:9-10
	(Prophecy in Matthew, See Matthew 1:22-23, above.)				
12:22	(Demon Posession:)				
	1713:40-1714: 6		11:14		Mt 9:32-33
12:23	1714: 7	3:22	11:15		Mt 9:34
12:24	(Devils, See Matthew 10:25, above.)				
12:25	2085:20	3:24-25	11:17		
12:25-30	1714:14-25	3:23-27	11:17-23		
12:30	1764:42		11:23		
12:31-32	1714:26-32	3:28-29			

MATTHEW Chap:Verse	The URANTIA Book Page:Line	MARK Chap:Verse	LUKE Chap:Verse	JOHN Chap:Verse	Other BOOKS Chap:Verse
12:33	(Requirement to Bring Forth Good Fruit:)				
	1502:42-44		3:8-9 15:2,8,16		
			6:43-44		Mt 3:10;7:16-20
			13:6-9		Ep 5:9 Ga 5:22-23
	1569: 6- 8	(Same as 1502:42-44, above)			
	1571:32-37	(Same as 1502:42-44, above)			
	1572:27-30	(Same as 1502:42-44, above)			
	1582:33-34	(Same as 1502:42-44, above)			
	1596:26-27	(Same as 1502:42-44, above)			
	1601: 8-10	(Same as 1502:42-44, above)			
	1714:36-38	(Same as 1502:42-44, above)			
	1830:39-45	(Same as 1502:42-44, above)			
	1917:30-32	(Same as 1502:42-44, above)			
	1945:40-47	(Same as 1502:42-44, above)			
	1946:21-26	(Same as 1502:42-44, above)			
	2054:33-39	(Same as 1502:42-44, above)			
12:33-36	1714:33-40		6:43-44		Mt 7:17-20
12:34-37	1713: 1-14	7:15			Mt 15:11
12:38	(Show us a Sign:)				
	1520:21-23	8:11	11:16	2:18;6:30	Mt 16:1
	1714:41-43	8:11	11:16	2:18;6:30	Mt 16:1
	1744:40-45	8:11	11:16	2:18;6:30	Mt 16:1
	1895:30-34	8:11	11:16	2:18;6:30	Mt 16:1
12:39	(The only "sign:")				
	1714:44-47	8:12	11:29		Mt 16:4
	1744:46-1745:4	8:12	11:29		Mt 16:4
	1895:34-36	8:12	11:29		Mt 16:4
	1982:39-40	14:58			Mt 26:60-61
	1983:11-12	14:58			Mt 26:60-61
12:46-47	(Jesus' "Family," Mother, Brothers.)				
	1721: 4- 6	3:31	8:19		
	1721:42-48	3:31-32	8:19-20		
12:48-50	1722:14-19	3:35	8:21		
12:50	(Do Will of Father in Heaven:)				
	0008:42	3:35	8:21	4:34;5:30	Mt 6:10
		14:36	11:2	6:38;7:17	Mt 7:21
		14:39	22:42	14:23-24	Mt 26:39,42
				15:10,14	Mt 26:44

(Matthew 12:50 Continued on next page.)

155

Matthew 12:50 to 13:10

MATTHEW Chap:Verse	The URANTIA Book Page:Line	MARK Chap:Verse	LUKE Chap:Verse	JOHN Chap:Verse	Other BOOKS Chap:Verse
12:50	0052: 1- 4	(Same as 0008:42, above)			
	1200:41	(Same as 0008:42, above)			
	1221:33-34	(Same as 0008:42, above)			
	1303: 7	(Same as 0008:42, above)			
	1318:29-30	(Same as 0008:42, above)			
	1324:21-22	(Same as 0008:42, above)			
	1327:10	(Same as 0008:42, above)			
	1328:38-41	(Same as 0008:42, above)			
	1331: 9-10	(Same as 0008:42, above)			
	1417: 5- 7	(Same as 0008:42, above)			
	1453:43-44	(Same as 0008:42, above)			
	1500:27	(Same as 0008:42, above)			
	1511:47-48	(Same as 0008:42, above)			
	1514:35	(Same as 0008:42, above)			
	1569: 8-10	(Same as 0008:42, above)			
	1574:21	(Same as 0008:42, above)			
	1582: 8	(Same as 0008:42, above)			
	1594:33-34	(Same as 0008:42, above)			
	1608: 1	(Same as 0008:42, above)			
	1769:42-44	(Same as 0008:42, above)			Ja 1:22-25 Ja 2:17 1Jo 3:18
	1774:28	(Same as 0008:42, above)			
	1947:50-1948:1	(Same as 0008:42, above)			
	1968:21-24	(Same as 0008:42, above)			
	1972: 5- 7	(Same as 0008:42, above)			
	2078: 8	(Same as 0008:42, above)			
	2087:11	(Same as 0008:42, above)			
	2088:30-31	(Same as 0008:42, above)			
	2089:12-14	(Same as 0008:42, above)			
	2090: 1	(Same as 0008:42, above)			
	(The Family of God:)				
	1454:40-41	3:35	8:21		
	1861:27	3:35	8:21		Ep 3:14-15
	1865:45-46	3:35	8:21		
13: 1- 3	1688:21-36	4:1-2			
13: 3- 9	(Parable of Sower:)				
	1688:37-1689:8	4:3-9	8:5-8		
13: 8	1536:43-44	4:8,20	8:8		Mt 13:23
13:10	1689: 9-13	4:10	8:9		

MATTHEW Chap:Verse	The URANTIA Book Page:Line	MARK Chap:Verse	LUKE Chap:Verse	JOHN Chap:Verse	Other BOOKS Chap:Verse
13:11-15	1689:14-31	4:11-12	8:10-11		
13:12	(To Him Who Hath is Given, Hath Not is Taken Away:)				
	1199: 1- 3	4:25	8:18;19:26		Mt 25:29
	1689:23-24	4:25	8:18;19:26		Mt 25:29
	1692:15-16	4:25	8:18;19:26		Mt 25:29
	1917:27-28	4:25	8:18;19:26		Mt 25:29
13:16-17	1807:28-33		10:23-24		
13:18-23	(More about Parable of Sower:)				
	1689:37-45	4:13	8:11-15		
	1689:37-45	4:13	8:11-15		
	1689:46-1690:17	4:14-20	8:11-15		
13:23	1536:43-44	4:8,20	8:8		Mt 13:8
13:24-30	(Parable of the Wheat & Tares:)				
	1429:21-23				
	1693:31-43				
13:31-32	(Parable of Mustard Seed:)				
	1583:10-11	4:31-32	13:19		
	1693:44-1694:2	4:30-32	13:19		
	1860:37-39	4:30-32	13:19		
	1931:43-44	4:31-32	13:19		
13:33	(Parable of the Leaven:)				
	1694: 3- 5		13:21		
	1931:43-44	—	13:21		
13:35	1341:41-43				
13:44	(Parable of Hidden Treasure:)				
	1694: 6- 8				
13:45-46	1583:14-15				
	1694: 9-11				
13:47-48	1694:12-15				
13:54	1684:37-38	6:2	4:16		
	1686:15-16	6:2	4:22		
13:55-56	(Jesus' Family:)				
	1686:28-31	6:3	4:22	6:42	
	1711:22-24	6:3	4:22	6:42	
	(Joseph the Carpenter's Son:)				
	1051:11	6:3	4:22	1:45;6:42	
	1686:30-31	6:3	4:22	1:45;6:42	

(Matthew 13:55-56 Continued on next page.)

MATTHEW Chap:Verse	The URANTIA Book Page:Line	MARK Chap:Verse	LUKE Chap:Verse	JOHN Chap:Verse	Other BOOKS Chap:Verse
13:55-56	(Brother James:)				
	1357: 5- 6	6:3			Mt 27:56 Ga 1:19
	(Sister Miriam:)				
	1357:47-48	6:3			
	(Brother Joseph:)				
	1362: 1- 2	6:3			Mt 27:56
	(Brother Simon:)				
	1365: 9-10	6:3			
	(Sister Martha:)				
	1367:18	6:3			
	(Brother Jude:)				
	1370:11	6:3			
	(Sister Ruth:)				
	1389:21-22	6:3			
13:55-57	1686:28-35	6:3-4	4:22-24	4:44;6:42	
13:57	1538:19	6:4	4:24	4:44	
13:58	1686:40-44	6:5			
14: 1- 2	1717:17-23	6:14-16	9:7-9		
14: 3	1506:36-40	6:17			
14: 3- 4	1506:27-29	6:18	3:19		
14: 3- 5	1508: 7-15	6:19-20			
14: 6-12	1508:23-45	6:19-29			
14: 9-12	1627:35-40	6:26-29			
14:13-14	1700:20-32	6:31-34	9:10-11	6:1-3	
14:15-17	1701:14-35	6:35-38	9:12-13	6:5-9	
14:18-21	1701:36-49	6:39-44	9:14-17	6:10-13	
14:22-23	1702:44-1073: 7	6:45-46		6:15	
14:24-33	1703:11-38	6:47-51		6:17-21	
14:25	1519:46	6:48		6:19	
14:27	1102:29	6:50		16:33	Mt 9:2
14:34	1703:40-41	6:53			
15: 1- 9	1712:21-42	7:1-13	11:37-41		De 5:16 Ex 20:12
					Is 29:13
	(Conduct on Sabbath, See Matthew 12:1-14, above.)				
15:10-20	1712:43-1713:14	7:14-23			Mt 12:34-37
15:14	(Blind Leading Blind)				
	1571:25-26	6:39			Mt 23:16
	1771: 9-10		6:39		
	1907:38-40		6:39		Mt 23:16

MATTHEW Chap:Verse	The URANTIA Book Page:Line	MARK Chap:Verse	LUKE Chap:Verse	JOHN Chap:Verse	Other BOOKS Chap:Verse
15:16-20	1671:42-43	7:14-23			
15:21	1734: 3- 5	7:24			
15:22	1734:17-28	7:24-26			
15:23	1734:30-1735: 4				
15:24-27	1735: 5-14	7:27-28			
	1809:35	7:27-28			
15:28	(Faith makes Whole:)				
	1643:29-41	1:40-41	5:12-13		Mt 8:2-3,13
		2:5;5:34	8:48,50		Mt 9:2,22,29
		10:52	17:19;18:42		
	1648: 7-13	(Same as 1643:29-41, above)			
	1667:12	(Same as 1643:29-41, above)			
	1698:33-1699:6	(Same as 1643:29-41, above)			
	1735:21-25	(Same as 1643:29-41, above)			
	1828:10-11	(Same as 1643:29-41, above)			
	1873:28-29	(Same as 1643:29-41, above)			
	1875:13-14	(Same as 1643:29-41, above)			
	1905:23-24	(Same as 1643:29-41, above)			
15:32-39	(Feeding a Multitude, See Matthew 14:14-22, above.)				
16: 1- 4	1744:37-1745: 4	8:11	11:16	2:18;6:30	Mt 12:38-39
	(Show us a Sign, See Matthew 12:38, above.)				
16: 4	1714:44-47	8:11-12	11:29		Mt 12:38-39
	(The Only Sign, See Matthew 12:39, above.)				
16: 6-12	(Beware of the Leaven of The Pharisees & Sadducees:)				
	1745:10-11	8:15	12:1		
	1751:25	8:15	12:1		
	1820: 2- 5	8:15	12:1		
16:13	1745:29-30	8:27	9:18		
	1745:45-47	8:27	9:18		
16:14	1746:10-14	8:28	9:19		
		6:14,15			
16:15	1746:14-17	8:29	9:20		
16:16	(Peter: You are the Christ, Son of the Living God:)				
	0031: 2- 3			6:57	
	1746:17-21	8:29	9:20		
	1748: 2- 3	8:29	9:20		
	1939: 1- 3	8:29	9:20		

MATTHEW Chap:Verse	The URANTIA Book Page:Line	MARK Chap:Verse	LUKE Chap:Verse	JOHN Chap:Verse	Other BOOKS Chap:Verse
16:17	1746:22-23				
	(Father in Heaven:)				
	0023:24	11:25-26	10:21		Mt 5:16,48;6:1
			11:2		Mt 7:11,21;11:25
					Mt 16:17;18:35;23:9
	1053:41-42	(Same as 0023:24, above)			
	1103:19	(Same as 0023:24, above)			
	1511:46	(Same as 0023:24, above)			
	1569:10	(Same as 0023:24, above)			
	1571: 2	(Same as 0023:24, above)			
	1571:16-17	(Same as 0023:24, above)			
	1619:23	(Same as 0023:24, above)			
	1620: 1	(Same as 0023:24, above)			
	1638:35	(Same as 0023:24, above)			
	1764: 2	(Same as 0023:24, above)			
	1807:18-19	(Same as 0023:24, above)			
	1907:16	(Same as 0023:24, above)			
	1923:12	(Same as 0023:24, above)			
	2087:11-12	(Same as 0023:24, above)			
16:17-18	("Rock" Foundation for Church:)				
	1524:38-1525: 2			1:42	
	1550:31-32	—	—	1:42	
	1747:19-28				
	1748: 8-12				
	1897:13-14				
16:19	(The Keys of the Kingdom:)				
	0435:45-46				
	0992:43				
	1747:28-32				
	1756:26-27				
16:20	1746:24-25	8:30	9:21		
	1747:32-33	8:30	9:21		
16:21	(Jesus Foretells the End:)				
	1759:10-15	8:31;9:31	9:22,44		Mt 17:22-23
		10:32-34	18:31-33		Mt 20:18-19
		14:41	24:6-8,46		Mt 26:2
	1759:39-46	(Same as 1759:10-15, above)			
	1871:29-41	(Same as 1759:10-15, above)			

(Matthew 16:21 Continued on next page.)

MATTHEW Chap:Verse	The URANTIA Book Page:Line	MARK Chap:Verse	LUKE Chap:Verse	JOHN Chap:Verse	Other BOOKS Chap:Verse
16:21	1872:38-43	(Same as 1759:10915, above)			
	1952:16-17	(Same as 1759:10-15, above)			
	1962:32	(Same as 1759:10-15, above)			
	2001:14	(Same as 1759:10-15, above)			
	2035:18-19	(Same as 1759:10-15, above)			
	2052:16-18	(Same as 1759:10-15, above)			
16:22	1760: 1- 4	8:32			
16:23	0609:44-45	8:33	4:8		
	1760:10-15	8:33			
16:24	(Take up Cross, deny Self, "follow Me":)				
	1750: 5- 6	8:34;10:21	9:23;14:27		Mt 10:38
	1760:17-19	8:34;10:21	9:23;14:27		Mt 10:38
	1770:22-23	8:34;10:21	9:23;14:27		Mt 10:38
	1869:37-41	8:34;10:21	9:23;14:27		Mt 10:38
	2089:50	8:34	9:59	12:26	
16:24-25	(Whosoever Will may come:)				
	0039: 7	8:34-35	9:23-24	3:15-16	Re 22:17
	1102:18-19	8:34-35	9:23-24	3:15-16	Re 22:17
	1205: 1- 2	8:34-35	9:23-24	3:15-16	Re 22:17
	1567: 3- 5	8:34-35	9:23-24	3:15-16	Re 22:17
	1750:16-17	8:34-35	9:23-24	3:15-16	Re 22:17
	1820:44-45	8:34-35	9:23-24	3:15-16	Re 22:17
	1829:44-45	8:34-35	9:23-24	3:15-16	Re 22:17
16:25	(Saving or Losing Life for Jesus' Sake:)				
	1134:28-29	8:35	9:24;17:33	12:25	Mt 10:39
	1575:32-33	8:35	9:24;17:33	12:25	Mt 10:39
	1760:19-20	8:35	9:24;17:33	12:25	Mt 10:39
	1782: 9-10	8:35	9:24;17:33	12:25	Mt 10:39
	1903:39-41	8:35	9:24;17:33	12:25	Mt 10:39
16:26	(Value of Soul:)				
	1581:28-29	8:36	9:25		
	1760:20-21	8:36	9:25		
	1822:37-38	8:36	9:25		
16:27	(Jesus' Promise to Return:)				
	0596:38	8:38;13:26	9:26;21:27		Mt 24:30;25:31
	1591:16-17	8:38;13:26	9:26;21:27		Mt 24:30;25:31
	1860:16-17	8:38;13:26	9:26;21:27		Mt 24:30;25:31
	1915: 1- 4	8:38;13:26	9:26;21:27		Mt 24:30;25:31
	2092:42-43	8:38;13:26	9:26;21:27		Mt 24:30;25:31

Matthew 16:28 to 18:4

MATTHEW Chap:Verse	The URANTIA Book Page:Line	MARK Chap:Verse	LUKE Chap:Verse	JOHN Chap:Verse	Other BOOKS Chap:Verse
16:28	1569:24-25	9:1	9:27		
	1760:25-26	9:1	9:27		
17: 1	1752:16-21	9:2	9:28		
17: 2- 3	1753:31-38	9:2-4	9:29-32		
17: 4	1753:41-48	9:5-6	9:33		
17: 5- 8 (The Voice on the Mountain)					
	1753:49-1754: 7	9:7-8	9:34-36		
	1755:18-19	9:7	9:35		
17: 9	1754: 9-12	9:9			
17:10-13	1754:21-29	9:11-13			Mt 11:14 Ml 4:5-6
17:14-16	1757: 8-18	9:22	9:38-40		
17:17	1757:19-25	9:19	9:41		
17:18	1757:38-44	9:25-27	9:42-43		
17:19	1758: 9-15	9:28			
17:20	1619:36-38				1Co 13:2
	1758:16-27	9:29			
17:22-23 (Jesus Foretells the End, See Matthew 16:21, above.)					
17:24-25	1743:27-36				
17:25-27	1744: 2-28				
18: 1	1761: 9-13	9:33-34	9:46		
18: 2	1761:13-15	9:36	9:47		
18: 2-10	1761:13-29	9:35-37	9:42-48;17:2		Mt 10:40
18: 3- 4 (Become as a child:)					
	1118:35-36	10:15	18:17		
	1536:26-28	10:15	18:17		
	1576:14-16	10:15	18:17		
	1585: 9-23	10:15	18:17		
	1621: 5-11	10:15	18:17		
	1676:48-1677:2	10:15	18:17		
	1733: 3- 8	10:15	18:17		
	1761:13-19	10:15	18:17		
	1840: 1- 4	10:15	18:17		
	1861: 7-11	10:15	18:17		
	1861:41-42	10:15	18:17		
	1960:37-38	10:15	18:17		
	2089:41-42	10:15	18:17		
(Suffer children to come:)					
	1840: 1- 2	10:14	18:16		Mt 19:14

162

MATTHEW Chap:Verse	The URANTIA Book Page:Line	MARK Chap:Verse	LUKE Chap:Verse	JOHN Chap:Verse	Other BOOKS Chap:Verse
18: 5	(Receive Child in My Name:)				
	1761:19-20	9:37	9:48;10:16	13:20	Mt 10:40
	1801:13-14	9:37	9:48;10:16	13:20	Mt 10:40
18: 6-10	(Woe to Offenders:)				
	1241:20-22	9:42-47	17:2		
	1761:21-29	9:42-47	17:2		
18:11	(Jesus Came to Save the Lost)				
	1750:12-13	–	19:10		
	1770:48-1771:1		19:10		
	1851:14		19:10		
	1874:23-24		19:10		
	2035:36		19:10		
18:12-14	(Parable of Lost Sheep:)				
	1762:21-32	–	15:3-7		
	1770:47-1771: 1		15:3-10		
	1850:34-1851: 5		15:3-7		
	1853: 6- 7		15:3-7		
18:14	1454: 6				2Pe 3:9
18:15-17	1762:33-1763: 5				
18:18-20	1763: 5-19				
18:21-22	(Forgive Seventy Times Seven:)				
	0449:40		17:3-4		
	1551: 4- 6		17:3-4		
	1763:20-23		17:3-4		
18:21-35	(Forgiveness Essential to Being Forgiven:)				
	1638:34-41	11:25-26	6:37;11:4		Mt 6:12,14-15
	1763:23-1764:3	11:25-26	6:37;11:4		Mt 6:12,14-15
	1862: 5- 6	11:25-26	6:37;11:4		Mt 6:12,14-15
	2017:44-45	11:25-26	6:37;11:4		Mt 6:12,14-15
18:35	(Father in Heaven, See Matthew 16:17, above.)				
19: 3	1838:29-32	10:2			
19: 3- 9	1576:39-1577: 2	–		–	Mt 5:31-32
19: 4- 5	1839:29-34	10:6-8			Ge 1:27;2:24
19: 4-12	1838:43-1839:11	10:3-5			
19:13	1839:40-48	10:13	18:15		
19:14	1840: 1- 2	10:14	18:16		Mt 18:3-4
19:15	1840: 5- 7	10:16			
19:16-17	2088:42-43	10:17-18	18:18-19		
19:16-20	1801:46-1802:15	10:17-20	18:18-21		De 5:7-21 Ex 20:3-17

163

Matthew 19:17 to 19:25

MATTHEW Chap:Verse	The URANTIA Book Page:Line	MARK Chap:Verse	LUKE Chap:Verse	JOHN Chap:Verse	Other BOOKS Chap:Verse
19:17	2092:10-12	10:18	18:19		
19:19	(Love Neighbor as Self:)				
	1206:40-42	12:31,33	10:27-28		Mt 22:39
					Le 19:18 Ro 13:9
					Ga 5:14 Ja 2:8
	1445:47	(Same as 1206:40-42, above)			
	1453:37	(Same as 1206:40-42, above)			
	1769:26	(Same as 1206:40-42, above)			
	1770: 4- 8	(Same as 1206:40-42, above)			
	1862: 8	(Same as 1206:40-42, above)			
	1950:17-18	(Same as 1206:40-42, above)			
	(The Second of Two Great Commandments:)				
	1600: 1- 3	(Same as 1206:40-42, above)			
	1600:33-36	(Same as 1206:40-42, above)			
	1805:10-11	(Same as 1206:40-42, above)			
	1809:25-28	(Same as 1206:40-42, above)			
	1901:17-20	(Same as 1206:40-42, above)			
	(For The New Standard, Act & Love as Jesus Does, see John 13:34, below.)				
	(Compare: Golden Rule, Do Unto Others etc.:)				
	1454:35-36		6:31		Mt 7:12 To 4:15
	1464:37-38		6:31		Mt 7:12 To 4:15
	1571:11-12		6:31		Mt 7:12 To 4:15
	1585:29-32		6:31		Mt 7:12 To 4:15
	1650:15-1651:21		6:31		Mt 7:12 To 4:15
	1771: 2- 3		6:31		Mt 7:12 To 4:15
	1931:23-24		6:31		Mt 7:12 To 4:15
	1949:43-1950:28		6:31		Mt 7:12 To 4:15
19:20-22	(The Price of Discipleship:)				
	1564:13-15	10:21-22	18:22-23		
	1672: 3- 5	10:21-22	18:22-23		
	1802:16-26	10:21-22	18:22-23		
19:23-24	1803:26-33	10:23-25	18:24-25		
	2093:16-17	10:24-25	18:24-25		
19:24	1803: 5- 8	10:25	18:25		
	1821:43-46	10:25	18:25		
19:25-26	1803:34-40	10:26-27	18:26-27		

164

MATTHEW Chap:Verse	The URANTIA Book Page:Line	MARK Chap:Verse	LUKE Chap:Verse	JOHN Chap:Verse	Other BOOKS Chap:Verse
19:26	(With God, All Things Possible:)				
	0034:13-14	10:27	1:37		
		14:36	18:27		
	0046:42	(Same as 0034:13-14, above)			
	0291:26-27	(Same as 0034:13-14, above)			
	1453:41	(Same as 0034:13-14, above)			
	1757:34-35	(Same as 0034:13-14, above)			
	1803:38-40	(Same as 0034:13-14, above)			
19:27	1804: 5- 6	10:28	18:28		
19:29	1537:6-9	10:29-30	18:29-30		
19:29-30	1804: 6-11	10:29-31	18:29-30		Mt 20:16
19:30	(Least--Greatest, First--Last:)				
	0316:40	9:35	9:48;14:11		Mt 20:16,26-27
		10:31,43-44	18:14;13:30		Mt 23:11
			22:26		
	0466:33-34	(Same as 0316:40, above)			
	0647:31-32	(Same as 0316:40, above)			
	1536:38-39	(Same as 0316:40, above)			
	1569:18-20	(Same as 0316:40, above)			
	1758:33-35	(Same as 0316:40, above)			
	1761:20-21	(Same as 0316:40, above)			
	1804:10-11	(Same as 0316:40, above)			
	1829:31-32	(Same as 0316:40, above)			
	1834:42-44	(Same as 0316:40, above)			
	1838:27-28	(Same as 0316:40, above)			
	1862:13-14	(Same as 0316:40, above)			
	1907:12-14	(Same as 0316:40, above)			
	1940:13-15	(Same as 0316:40, above)			
20: 1- 7	1804:14-24				
20: 8-12	1804:25-34				
20:13-15	1804:35-39				
20:16	(First--Last, See Matthew 19:30, above.)				
20:17-19	1871:29-41	10:32-34	18:31-33		
20:18-19	(Jesus Foretells the End, See Matthew 16:21, above.)				
20:19	1872:38-43	10:34	18:33		
20:20-23	(Request for Personal Honors in Heaven:)				
	1553:21-30	10:35-39			
	1867:23-1868:5	10:35-40			
	1958:19-22	10:35-39			

MATTHEW Chap:Verse	The URANTIA Book Page:Line	MARK Chap:Verse	LUKE Chap:Verse	JOHN Chap:Verse	Other BOOKS Chap:Verse
20:22-23	(Drinking the Cup:)				
	0229:46	10:38-39	22:42		Mt 26:39,42,44
		14:36,39			
	1867:37-1868:4	(Same as 0229:46, above)			
	1955:30-32	(Same as 0229:46, above)			
	1968:11-15	(Same as 0229:46, above)			
	1968:22-24	(Same as 0229:46, above)			
	1968:33-34	(Same as 0229:46, above)			
	1972: 5- 7	(Same as 0229:46, above)			
20:23	1958:25-26	10:39			Ac 12:1-2
20:24	1958:24-25	10:41			
20:24-28	1868: 6-17	10:41-45			
20:26-27	(Great--Minister, See Matthew 19:30, above.)				
20:28	1750:11	10:45			
20:29	1873: 2- 3	10:46	18:35-36		
20:29-34	1905:23-24	10:46-52	18:35-43		
20:30-31	1873:16-20	10:47-48	18:36-39		
20:32-34	1873:21-31	10:49-52	18:40-43		
21: 1- 3	1881:27-32	11:1-3	19:28-31		
21: 4	1341:41-43				
21: 4- 5	(King Arrives Riding an Ass:)				
	1881:12-18			12:14-15	Zc 9:9
	1884:49-50	—		12:14-15	Zc 9:9
	1885:38-39			12:14-15	Zc 9:9
21: 6- 7	1881:33-38	11:4-7	19:32-35		
21: 7- 9	1882: 6-13	11:7-10	19:35-38	12:12-14	
21: 8- 9	1403:33-35	11:8-10	19:36-38	12:12-13	
21:10-11	1883: 9-11				
21:12	1888:17-18	11:15	19:45		
21:12-13	(Casting Out the Money Changers:)				
	1378:27-29	11:15-17	19:45-46	2:14-16	
	1890:11-25	11:15-17	19:45-46	2:15-16	
	1911: 6- 7	11:15-17	19:45-46	2:13-16	
21:15-16	1890:26-32				Ps 8:2
21:17	1895:42-44	11:19			
21:23	1891:28-32	11:27-28	20: 1- 2		
21:24-25	1892: 6- 9	11:29-30	20: 3- 4		
21:25-27	1892:10-24	11:31-33	20: 5- 8		
21:28-32	1893: 5-20				

Matthew 21:33 to 22:38

MATTHEW Chap:Verse	The URANTIA Book Page:Line	MARK Chap:Verse	LUKE Chap:Verse	JOHN Chap:Verse	Other BOOKS Chap:Verse
21:33-40	1893:35-1894:10	12:1-9	20:9-15		
21:41	1894:11-13	12:9	20:16		
21:42-44	1894:18-30	12:10	20:17-18		
21:45-46	1894:31-33	12:12	20:19		
22: 1-13	(Parable of The Spurned Marriage Feast:)				
	1894:38-1895:27		14:16-24		
	1835: 7-27				
22:14	1895:28-29				
22:15	1899: 2-10	12:13	20:20		
22:16-21	1899:13-26	12:14-17	20:21-25		
22:21	(Render Proper Dues to both Caesar & God:)				
	1114:25-26	12:17	20:25		
	1474:14-19	12:17	20:25		
	1580:16-17	12:17	20:25		
	1740:19-20	12:17	20:25		
	1929:33-35	12:17	20:25		
	1957: 4- 5	12:17	20:25		
22:22	1899:27-30	12:17	20:26		
22:23-28	1900: 2-12	12:18-23	20:27-33		
22:24	0926:12-14	12:19	20:28		De 25:5-6
22:29-32	1900:17-29	12:23-27	20:34-38		
22:30	(Resurrected Do Not Marry:)				
	0419:12-13	12:25	20:35		
	0495:32	12:25	20:36		
22:33	1900:34-35				
22:34	1901: 2- 9				
22:34-40	1809:21-28	12:28-31	10:25-28		
22:35-40	1901:10-20	12:28-31	10:25-28		De 6:4-5
22:37	(First Commandment: Love God:)				
	1206:38-39	12:30	10:27-28		De 6:4-5
	1444: 7- 9	12:30	10:27-28		De 6:4-5
	1453:36-37	12:30	10:27-28		De 6:4-5
22:37-40	(The Two Great Commandments:)				
	1446:11-12	12:29-31	10:27-28		De 6:5 Le 19:18
	1600: 1- 3	12:29-31	10:27-28		De 6:5 Le 19:18
	1600:33-36	12:29-31	10:27-28		De 6:5 Le 19:18
	1805: 9-11	12:30-31	10:27-28		De 6:5 Le 19:18
	1809:25-27	12:30-31	10:27-28		De 6:5 Le 19:18
	1901:13-20	12:30-31	10:27-28		De 6:5 Le 19:18

167

MATTHEW Chap:Verse	The URANTIA Book Page:Line	MARK Chap:Verse	LUKE Chap:Verse	JOHN Chap:Verse	Other BOOKS Chap:Verse
22:39	(Love Neighbor as Self, See Matthew 19:19, above.)				
	(For New Standards, See John 13:34, below.)				
22:41-46	(Jesus Denies that He is a Son of David:)				
	1348: 5- 6	12:35-37	20:41-44		
	1901:40-1902:6	12:35-37	20:41-44		Ps 110:1
22:43-44	(The Lord Said to My Lord:)				
	1902: 2- 3	12:35-36	20:42-44		Ps 110:1
	(Right Hand of the Father:)				
	0064:33	12:35-36	20:42-44		Ps 110:1 Ro 8:34
					Cl 3:1 He 10:12 1Pe 3:22
	0239:45-46	(Same as 0064:33, above)			
	0418: 6- 7	(Same as 0064:33, above)			
23: 1	1905: 3- 6				
23: 1-39	1911:20-22		11:39-53		
23: 2	1924:17				
23: 2- 4	1906:38-49		11:46		Da 4:17,25,32;5:21
23: 5- 7	1907: 1- 5	12:38-39	20:46;11:43		
23: 6- 7	1826:22-24	12:38-39	11:43		
23: 9	1907: 9-11				
	(Father in Heaven, See Matthew 16:17, above.)				
23:11-12	1907:12-14				
	(Greatest--Servant, See Matthew 19:30, above.)				
23:13	1826:40-41		11:52		
	1907:24-27		11:52		
23:14	1907: 5- 8	12:40	20:47		
	1907:34-37				
23:15	1907:30-33				
23:16	1907:38	—	6:39		Mt 15:14
23:16-19	1907:41-50				
23:23	1826:18-19		11:42		
23:23-24	1908: 1- 5	—	11:42		
23:24	1736:41-42				
23:25	1826: 8- 9		11:39		
23:25-26	1908: 6-10	—	11:39-40		
23:27	1826:44-46				
23:27-28	1908:14-18				
23:28	1826: 9-12		11:42		
23:29-31	1826:32-36	—	11:47-50		
23:29-32	1908:19-26		11:47:50		

MATTHEW Chap:Verse	The URANTIA Book Page:Line	MARK Chap:Verse	LUKE Chap:Verse	JOHN Chap:Verse	Other BOOKS Chap:Verse
23:33	1502:37-38				Mt 3:7-10
	1908:27-29				
23:34-36	1908:30-41		11:49-51		
23:35-36	1826:36-38	—	11:50-51		
23:37-39	1872:25-30		13:34-35		
	1908:42-49	—	13:34-35		
23:38	1924:12-13		13:35		
24: 1	1908:50				
24: 1- 2	(Jesus Foretells the Destruction of Jerusalem:)				
	1414: 8- 9	13:1-2	21:5-6		
	1912: 3-14	13:1-2	21:5-6		
	1934:31-32	13:1-2	21:5-6		
24: 3	1912:21-24	13:3-4	21:7		
	1913:48-49				
24: 4-14	(Jesus Discusses Future Difficulties of Believers:)				
	1912:29-1913:6	13:5-13	21:8-17		Mt 10:17-22
24: 6- 7	0597:20-21	13:7-8	21:9-10		
	1490:30-32	13:7-8	21:9-10		
24: 9-13	1584:10-17	13:9-13	21:12-17		
24:14	(The Great Commission:)				
	1051: 8	13:10;16:15	24:47	20:21	Mt 28:19-20 Ac 1:8
	1584: 4- 6	(Same as 1051:8, above)			
	1608:22	(Same as 1051:8, above)			
	1824:43-44	(Same as 1051:8, above)			
	1934:28-30	(Same as 1051:8, above)			
	1957:35-37	(Same as 1051:8, above)			
	1961:49	(Same as 1051:8, above)			
	2033:17-18	(Same as 1051:8, above)			
	2034: 2- 3	(Same as 1051:8, above)			
	2042: 8- 9	(Same as 1051:8, above)			
	2043: 4- 5	(Same as 1051:8, above)			
	2044:35-36	(Same as 1051:8, above)			
	2052:39-40	(Same as 1051:8, above)			
	2053:14-16	(Same as 1051:8, above)			
	2053:38-40	(Same as 1051:8, above)			
	2054: 5- 6	(Same as 1051:8, above)			
	2054:25-27	(Same as 1051:8, above)			

(Matthew 24:14 Continued on next page.)

MATTHEW Chap:Verse	The URANTIA Book Page:Line	MARK Chap:Verse	LUKE Chap:Verse	JOHN Chap:Verse	Other BOOKS Chap:Verse
24:14	2054:41-42	(Same as 1051:8, above)			
	2055:16-18	(Same as 1051:8, above)			
	2057:24-25	(Same as 1051:8, above)			
24:15-18	1913:26-31	13:14-16	21:20-21		Da 11:31;12:11
24:15-21	1934:32-33	13:14-19	21:20-24		
24:15-51	1915:30-40				
24:21	1913:31-32	13:19	21:20-22		
24:23	1536:29-30	13:21			
24:23-25	1913:35-38	13:21-23			
24:26-27	1569:15-17		17:20-21		
24:27-37	(Jesus' Promised Return to Earth:)				
	0227:18-27	13:32-33		14:3	Mt 24:42;25:13
	0409:10	13:32-33		14:3	Mt 24:42;25:13
	1319: 6- 8	13:32-33		14:3	Mt 24:42;25:13
	1915: 5- 6	13:32-33		14:3	Mt 24:42;25:13
	1915: 13-15	13:32-33		14:3	Mt 24:42;25:13
	1915:20-24	13:32-33		14:3	Mt 24:42;25:13
	1916:25-27	13:32-33		14:3	Mt 24:42;25:13
	1918:47-48	13:32-33		14:3	Mt 24:42;25:13
24:29-31	(Expectations About the Kingdom:)				
	1860:39-40	13:24-27	21:25-28		
	1863:43-47	13:24-27	21:25-28		
24:30	(Coming in Power and Glory:)				
	0596:38	8:38;13:26	9:26;21:27		Mt 16:27;25:31
	1569:13-15				
	1591:16-17	8:38;13:26	9:26;21:27		Mt 16:27;25:31
	1860:16-17	8:38;13:26	9:26;21:27		Mt 16:27;25:31
	1915: 1- 4	8:38;13:26	9:26;21:27		Mt 16:27;25:31
	2092:42-43	8:38;13:26	9:26;21:27		Mt 16:27;25:31
24:31	0568:45-0569:1	13:27			
	1247:32-33	13:27			
24:32-33	1915:15-19	13:28-29	21:29-31		
24:34	1915:11-12	13:30	21:32		
24:35	1736:20-21	13:31	21:33		
	1914: 2	13:31	21:33		2Pe 3:10
24:42	(The Second Coming, See Matthew 24:27-37, above.)				
24:43-44	1824:11-14		12:39-40		
24:45-47	1824:20-27	—	12:42-44		
24:48-51	1824:28-31		12:45-46		

MATTHEW Chap:Verse	The URANTIA Book Page:Line	MARK Chap:Verse	LUKE Chap:Verse	JOHN Chap:Verse	Other BOOKS Chap:Verse
25: 1-13	1915:40-42				
25:13	(Jesus' Second Coming, See Matthew 24:27-37, above.)				
25:14-23	(Parable of the Talents:)				
	1916:37-1917:14				
25:14-28	0315:24		19:12-26		
25:21,23	0274:33-35	_	19:17		
	1917:49				
25:24-26	1918: 2- 8				
25:24-28	1917:14-26				
25:29	1917:27-28				
	(To Him Who Hath is Given, From Hath Not is Taken Away, See Matt. 13:12, above.)				
25:31	(Coming in Glory, See Matthew 24:30, above.)				
25:40	(Do to Least, Do to Me:)				
	1727:29-30				
	1917:32-34				
26: 2	(Jesus Foretells the Crucifixion & Resurrection:)				
	1759:10-15	8:31;9:31	9:22,44		Mt 16:21
		10:32,34	18:31-33		Mt 17:22-23
		14:41	24:6-8,46		Mt 20:18-19
	1759:39-46	(Same as 1759:10-15, above)			
	1871:29-41	(Same as 1759:10-15, above)			
	1872:38-43	(Same as 1759:10-15, above)			
	1952:16-17	(Same as 1759:10-15, above)			
	1962:32	(Same as 1759:10-15, above)			
	2001:14	(Same as 1759:10-15, above)			
	2035:18-19	(Same as 1759:10-15, above)			
	2052:16-18	(Same as 1759:10-15, above)			
26: 3- 4	(The Plot To Kill Jesus:)				
	1911:23-27				
	1924:28-34	14:1	22:2		
26: 5	1925:43-46	14:2	22:2		
26: 6	1878:34-36	14:3		12:1-2	
26: 7-13	(The Alabaster Box of Ointment:)				
	1567:18-21	14:3-5		12:3-5	
	1879:10-37	14:3-9		11:2;12:3-5	
	1879:38-39	14:6-9		12:7-8	
	1879:42-44	14:3		12:3	

Matthew 26:14 to 26:38

MATTHEW Chap:Verse	The URANTIA Book Page:Line	MARK Chap:Verse	LUKE Chap:Verse	JOHN Chap:Verse	Other BOOKS Chap:Verse
26:14-15	(Judas Agrees to Betray Jesus:)				
	1567:21-27	14:10	22:4		
	1924:24-28	14:10	22:4		
	1925:47-1926:6	14:10	22:4		
	1998:11-13	14:10	22:4		Mt 27:3
26:16	1926: 3-12	14:11	22:4-6		
26:17	1933:12-14	14:12	22:8-9		
26:18	1933:22-28	14:13-15	22:10-12		
26:19	1933:29-32	14:16	22:13		
26:20	1937:35-38	14:17	22:14		
26:21	1940:28-35	14:18		13:21	
26:22	1940:36-39	14:19		13:22	
26:23	1940:44-45	14:18,20			
26:24	1940:40-44	14:21	22:21-22		
26:25	1940:47-1941: 1				
26:26-29	(The Remembrance Supper--Eucharist:)				
	1941:40-1943:14	14:22-25	22:19-20		1Co 11:23-25
26:26	(Jesus as The Bread of Life:)				
	1711:14-16	14:22	22:19	6:35,48,51,58	Mt 5:6
	1711:38-43	14:22	22:19	6:35,48,51,58	Mt 5:6
	1942: 9-16	14:22	22:19	6:35,48,51,58	Mt 5:6
	1965:29	14:22	22:19	6:35,48,51,58	Mt 5:6
26:27-29	1941:41-47	14:23-25	22:20		1Co 11:25-26
26:29	1938: 8-11	14:25	22:18,20		
26:30	1943:12-14	14:26			
26:31	1962:15-16	14:27		_	Zc 13:7
	1976:34	14:27			Zc 13:7
26:32	(Jesus Foretells His Resurrection Appearances:)				
	1952: 5-25	14:28		14:28;16:16-22	
	1954:11-13	14:28		14:28;16:16-22	
	1962:13-19	14:28		14:28;16:16-22	
26:33	1962:20-22	14:29	22:33	13:37	Mt 26:35
26:34	1962:24-27	14:30	22:34	13:38	
26:35	1962:20-22	14:29	22:33	13:37	Mt 26:33
26:36-39	1968: 5-14				
	(See Matthew 26:39, below, all entries)				
26:38	1968:16-20	14:34,37			Mt 26:40

MATTHEW Chap:Verse	The URANTIA Book Page:Line	MARK Chap:Verse	LUKE Chap:Verse	JOHN Chap:Verse	Other BOOKS Chap:Verse
26:39	(Drink Cup:)				
	0229:46	10:38-39	22:42		Mt 20:22-23
		14:36,39			Mt 26:42,44
	1867:37-39	(Same as 0229:46, above)			
	1955:30-32	(Same as 0229:46, above)			
	1968:11-34	(Same as 0229:46, above)			
	1972: 5- 7	(Same as 0229:46, above)			
	(Do Father's Will:)				
	0008:42	3:35	8:21	4:34;5:30	Mt 6:10
		14:36	11:2	6:38;7:17	Mt 7:21
		14:39	22:42	14:23-24	Mt 12:50
				15:10,14	Mt 26:42,44
	0052: 1- 4	(Same as 0008:42, above)			
	1200:41	(Same as 0008:42, above)			
	1221:33-34	(Same as 0008:42, above)			
	1303: 7	(Same as 0008:42, above)			
	1318:29-30	(Same as 0008:42, above)			
	1324:21-22	(Same as 0008:42, above)			
	1327:10	(Same as 0008:42, above)			
	1328:38-41	(Same as 0008:42, above)			
	1331: 9-10	(Same as 0008:42, above)			
	1417: 5- 7	(Same as 0008:42, above)			
	1453:43-44	(Same as 0008:42, above)			
	1500:27	(Same as 0008:42, above)			
	1511:47-48	(Same as 0008:42, above)			
	1514:35	(Same as 0008:42, above)			
	1569: 8-10	(Same as 0008:42, above)			
	1574:21	(Same as 0008:42, above)			
	1582: 8	(Same as 0008:42, above)			
	1594:33-34	(Same as 0008:42, above)			
	1608: 1	(Same as 0008:42, above)			
	1769:42-44	(Same as 0008:42, above)			Ja 1:22-25
	1774:28	(Same as 0008:42, above)			
	1947:50-1948:1	(Same as 0008:42, above)			
	1968:21-24	(Same as 0008:42, above)			
	1972: 5- 7	(Same as 0008:42, above)			
	2078: 8	(Same as 0008:42, above)			
	2087:11	(Same as 0008:42, above)			

Matthew 26:39 Continued on next page.)

MATTHEW Chap:Verse	The URANTIA Book Page:Line	MARK Chap:Verse	LUKE Chap:Verse	JOHN Chap:Verse	Other BOOKS Chap:Verse
26:39	2088:30-31	(Same as 0008:42, above)			
	2089:12-14	(Same as 0008:42, above)			
	2091: 1	(Same as 0008:42, above)			
	(Prayer:)				
	0096:37-38	11:24	11:2-4		Mt 6:5-13
		14:35-36	18:1-14		Mt 26:42,44
			22:41		Ro 8:26-27
	1001:12-1002:41	(Same as 0096:37-38, above)			
	1511:46-48	(Same as 0096:37-38, above)			
	1618:35-1624:10	(Same as 0096:37-38, above)			
	1638:10-1641: 9	(Same as 0096:37-38, above)			
	1848:16-1849:23	(Same as 0096:37-38, above)			
	1968:11-15	(Same as 0096:37-38, above)			
	1968:22-24	(Same as 0096:37-38, above)			
	1968:31-34	(Same as 0096:37-38, above)			
26:40	1968:16-20	14:34,37			Mt 26:38
26:41	1968:27-30	14:38,40	22:40,45-46		Mt 26:43
	1968:32-33	14:38	22:40		
26:42	1968:21-24	14:39			
	(Drink Cup, See Matthew 26:39, above.)				
	(Submit to Father's Will, See Matthew 26:39, above.)				
	(Prayer, See Matthew 26:39, above.)				
26:43	1968:27-30	14:38,40	22:40,45-46		Mt 26:41
26:44	(Drink Cup, See Matthew 26:39, above.)				
	(Submit to Father's Will, See Matthew 26:39, above.)				
	(Prayer, See Matthew 26:39, above.)				
26:44-46	1968:31-41	14:38,41-42			Mt 26:41
26:47	1973:29-36	14:43	22:47	18:3	
26:48	1974: 4- 6	14:44			
26:49-50	1974:30-32	14:45	22:47-48		
26:50-52	1974:41-1975:1	14:46-47	22:49-51	18:10-11	
26:52	1957:21				
26:53	(Legions of Angels:)				
	0421:36-37				
	1516: 5				
	1934:41-42				
	1969:20-23				
	1975: 1- 3				
26:55	1975: 7-10	14:48-49	22:52-53		

174

MATTHEW Chap:Verse	The URANTIA Book Page:Line	MARK Chap:Verse	LUKE Chap:Verse	JOHN Chap:Verse	Other BOOKS Chap:Verse
26:56	1975:11-14	14:50			
26:57	1980: 1- 5	14:53		18:24	
26:58	(Peter Follows Afar Off:)				
	1551:32	14:54	22:54	18:15	
	1975:32	14:54	22:54	18:15	
	1980: 7-18	14:54	22:54-55	18:15-16,18	
26:59-60	1982:27-33	14:55-56			
26:60-61	1982:37-40	14:57-59		2:19	
26:60-62	1999: 5- 6	14:56-61			
26:62-63	1982:43-45	14:60-61			
26:63-64	(Jesus Response to the High Priests:)				
	1979:44-50	14:61-62	22:70		
	1983:20-27	14:61-62	22:67,70		
	1999: 6- 9	14:61-62	22:67,70		
26:65-66	1983:28-32	14:63-64	22:71		
26:67	1983:45-49	14:65	22:63		
26:67-68	1984:16-22	14:65	22:63-65	18:22	
	2000:12-14	14:65	22:63-65	18:22	
26:69-70	1980:31-38	14:66-68	22:56-57	18:17	
26:69-72	1551:15-17	14:66-70	22:56-57	18:16-17	
26:69-75	1551: 6- 8	14:66-72	22:55-62	18:15-18,25-27	
26:71-72	1980:44-1981:2	14:68-71			
26:73-74	1981: 3- 8	14:70	22:59-60	18:25	
26:74-75	1981:13-15	14:72	22:60-61	18:27	
26:75	1981:24-25	14:72	22:62		
27: 1	1985:22-46	15:1			
27: 2	1986:12-14	15:1	23:1	18:28	
27: 3- 5	(Judas' Remorse and Suicide;)				
	1567:35-44				
	1997:38-1998:36				Mt 26:15
	1998:43-50				
27: 9-10	1341:41-43				
27:11	(Jesus Before Pilate:)				
	1991:13-14	15:2	23:3	18:33-35	
	1991:30-32	15:2	23:3	18:37	
	1999:10-12	15:2	23:3	18:33-37	
27:12-14	1990:25-44	15:3-5	23:2		
27:15	1993:17-19	15:6	23:17	18:39	
27:16	1993:25-29	15:7	23:19	18:40	

MATTHEW Chap:Verse	The URANTIA Book Page:Line	MARK Chap:Verse	LUKE Chap:Verse	JOHN Chap:Verse	Other BOOKS Chap:Verse
27:17	1993:30-34	15:9		18:39	
27:18	1993:45-47	15:10			
27:19	1994:13-20				
27:20	1994:22-24	15:11			
27:21	1994:35-38				
27:22	1994:25-28	15:12-13	23:20-21		
27:23	1994:31-34	15:14	23:22		
27:24	2001:27				
27:24-25	1996:40-47	15:15	23:23-25	19:6	
27:26	1995: 4- 6	15:15	23:16	19:1	
	2001:29-31	15:15	23:24-25		
27:27-31	1995: 8-18	15:16-20		19:2-3	
27:31	2001:31-34	15:20			
	2001:37-38	15:20			
27:32	1438:34-38	15:21	23:26		
	2006:14-20	15:21	23:26		
27:33	2006:32-33	15:22	23:33		
27:34	2007: 7-11	15:23			
27:35	(The Crucifixion:)				
	2006:36-46	15:24	23:33	19:18	
	(Casting Lots for Garments:)				
	1341:41-43	15:24	23:34	19:23-24	Ps 22:18
	2007:44-49	15:24	23:34	19:23-24	Ps 22:18
27:36	2008:30-33				
27:37	(Sign: King of Jews:)				
	2005: 7- 9	15:24	23:38	19:19-20	
	2007:22-24	15:26	23:38	19:19-20	
27:38	2007:15-16	15:27	23:33-34	19:18	
27:39-44	1520: 6- 7	15:29-32	23:35		
	2008:20-28	15:29-32	23:35,37		
27:41-43	2063: 5- 6	15:36	23:35,37		
27:42	1518:31-32	15:31	23:35,37		
27:43	1102:20				
27:45	2010: 9-13	15:33	23:44-45		
	2011:34	15:33	23:44-45		
27:46	2010:21-38	15:34			Ps 20:6;21:8;22:1
27:48	2010:39-42	15:36		19:28-29	
27:49	2063: 5- 6				
27:50	2011: 3- 5	15:37	23:46	19:30	

MATTHEW Chap:Verse	The URANTIA Book Page:Line	MARK Chap:Verse	LUKE Chap:Verse	JOHN Chap:Verse	Other BOOKS Chap:Verse
27:52	0568:35-37				
27:52-53	(The Dispensational Resurrection:)				
	1328: 3- 4	_	_	5:25-29	
	2024:13-43				
	2053: 9-10				
27:54	1590: 4	15:39	23:47		
	2011: 5- 7	15:39	23:47		
27:55-56	(Faithful Women's Corps:)				
	1403:36-36	15:40-41	8:2-3 23:27,49 24:10	19:25	Ac 1:14
	1671:20-26	(Same as 1403:35-36, above)			
	1678:28-1679:15	(Same as 1403:35-36, above)			
	1680:21-24	(Same as 1403:35-36, above)			
	1680:28-29	(Same as 1403:35-36, above)			
	2005:33-45	(Same as 1403:35-36, above)			
	2008:14-17	(Same as 1403:35-36, above)			
27:56	(Mary, Jesus' Mother, Watched:)				
	1357: 5- 6	6:3;15:40	_		Ga 1:19 Mt 13:55
	1362: 1- 2	6:3;15:40			Ga 1:19 Mt 13:55
	2007:37-38				
27:57-58	2012:18-26	15:42-45	23:50-52	19:38	
27:59-60	2013:17-33	15:46	23:53	19:39-41	
27:61	2013:38-47	15:47	23:55-56		
27:62-64	2014: 5-18				
27:63	2001:14	8:31;10:34	9:22;24:7		Mt 16:21;17:23
27:65-66	2014:19-27				
28: 1	2025:30-39	16:1-2	24:1	20:1	
28: 2	0407:17-18		1:11		Ex 3:2+
28: 2- 4	2023:15-24				
28: 5- 6	2026:32-49	16:5-6,9	24:4-8	20:11-16	Mt 28:9
28: 7	(Go Tell Disciples:)				
	2027: 4- 7	16:7		20:17	Mt 28:10
	2027:46-2028:1	16:7		20:17	Mt 28:10
	2037:35	16:7		20:17	Mt 28:10
	2039:30-31	16:7		20:17	Mt 28:10

(Matthew 28:7 Continued on next page.)

MATTHEW Chap:Verse	The URANTIA Book Page:Line	MARK Chap:Verse	LUKE Chap:Verse	JOHN Chap:Verse	Other BOOKS Chap:Verse
28: 7	(Go To Galilee:)				
	1962:18-19	14:28;16:7		20:17	Mt 26:32;28:10
	2028: 1- 2	14:28;16:7		20:17	Mt 26:32;28:10
	2043:49-50	14:28;16:7		20:17	Mt 26:32;28:10
28: 8	2027: 8-10	16:8	24:9-10	20:2	
28: 9	2026:32-49	16:5-6,9	24:4-8	20:11-16	Mt 28:5-6
28:10	(Go Tell Disciples, See Matthew 28:7, above.0)				
	(Go to Galilee, See Matthew 28:7, above.)				
28:11-15	2023:24-36				
28:12-15	2045: 8-10				
28:16-17	2050: 4-20				
28:18	(All Power is Given To Me:)				
	0240:14				
	0367:22				
	0368:45-46				
	0375:28-29				
	0605:34				
	1918:45				
28:19	(The Trinity:)				
	0108:10-15				Ac 2:33 1Jo 5:7
					1Co 12:4-6
	0115:15-18	(Same as 0108:10-15, above)			
	0640:33-35	(Same as 0108:10-15, above)			
	1144:43-45	(Same as 0108:10-15, above)			
	1144:48-1145:2	(Same as 0108:10-15, above)			
	2061:47-2062:2	(Same as 0108:10-15, above)			
	2067:40	(Same as 0108:10-15, above)			
28:19-20	(The Great Commission, See Matthew 24:14, above.)				
28:20	(I Am With You to the End:)				
	1957:14-15				
	2033:20				
	2042:12-13				
	2053:19				
	2057:29-30				

B: The Gospel According to MARK

MARK Chap:Verse	The URANTIA Book Page:Line	MATTHEW Chap:Verse	LUKE Chap:Verse	JOHN Chap:Verse	Other BOOKS Chap:Verse
1: 1	(Jesus is the Son of God:)				
	1317: 9-13	16:16		1:34;3:16-18	
	1746:17-21	16:16		1:34;3:16-18	
	1748: 2- 3	16:16		1:34;3:16-18	
1: 2- 3	1501:29-35	3:3	3:4-6	1:23	Is 40:3-5
1: 3	1502:25-33	3:3	3:4-6	1:22-23	Is 40:3-5
1: 4- 5	(Baptism:)				
	0947: 1- 2	3:6,11	3:7,16	1:25-33	Mk 1:8
	0964:37	3:6,11	3:7,16	1:25-33	Mk 1:8
	1502:13	3:6,11	3:7,16	1:25-33	Mk 1:8
	1593:11-13	3:6,11	3:7,16	1:25-33	Mk 1:8
	(Baptism of Repentance:)				
	1502:11-20	3:6,11	3:3	1:25-33	Ac 13:24
	1503:31	3:6,11	3:3	1:25-33	Ac 13:24
	1510:26-27	3:6,11	3:3	1:25-33	Ac 13:24
	1536:34-36	3:6,11	3:3	1:25-33	Ac 13:24
	1584:31-32	3:2,11	3:3	1:25-33	Ac 13:24
	1625:30-35	3:6,11	3:3	1:25-33	Ac 13:24
1: 6	1497: 5-11	3:4	1:80		
1: 7	1506: 2- 3			1:15,30	
1: 7- 8	1503:24-28	3:11-12	3:16-17	1:27	
1: 8	(Baptism, See Mark 1:4-5, above.)				
	(Baptism of Repentance, See Mark 1:4-5, above.)				
1: 9-11	(Jesus' Baptism:)				
	1504:11-42	3:13-17	3:21-22	1:28	
	1510:45-46	3:13-17	3:21-22		
1:10	(The Descending Spirit:)				
	1511:37-38	3:16	3:22		
	1511:42-43	3:16	3:22	1:32	
	1511:48	3:16	3:21		
1:11	(The Voice From Heaven:)				
	0538:10-11	3:17	3:22		
	1506: 7- 8	3:17	3:22		
	1511:39-41	3:17	3:22		
	1512: 5	3:17	3:22		
	1545:21	3:17	3:22		

Mark 1:12 to 1:16

MARK Chap:Verse	The URANTIA Book Page:Line	MATTHEW Chap:Verse	LUKE Chap:Verse	JOHN Chap:Verse	Other BOOKS Chap:Verse
1:12-13	(Forty Days in The Wilderness:)				
	1504:42-44	4:1-2	4:2		
	1512:30-34	4:1-11	4:1-13		
	1514:27-28	4:3	4:2		
	1514:38-39	4:1-11	4:1-13		
	1515:25-26	4:1	4:1-2		
	1841:27-28	4:11			
1:13	(Overcoming Satan:)				
	0602: 1- 2	4:3-11	4:3-11		1Ch 21:1 Is 14:12
	0609:35-0610: 3	4:3-11	4:8;10:18		
	1493:33-1494:6	4:3-11	4:3-13		
1:14	(Jesus Begins His Ministry:)				
	1506:11-12	4:12			
	1506:38-42	4:12	3:20		
	1535:31-37	4:12			
1:15	(Kingdom of Heaven is at hand:)				
	1501:27-28	3:2;4:17 10:7			
	1502: 3	(Same as 1501:27-28, above)			
	1503: 3- 4	(Same as 1501:27-28, above)			
	1510:26-27	(Same as 1501:27-28, above)			
	1510:46	(Same as 1501:27-28, above)			
	1536:8-1537:23	(Same as 1501:27-28, above)			
	1537:11-12	(Same as 1501:27-28, above)			
	1588:25-28	(Same as 1501:27-28, above)			
	1681:41-42	(Same as 1501:27-28, above)			
	1801: 6	(Same as 1501:27-28, above)			
	1858:23-31	(Same as 1501:27-28, above)			
	1866: 7- 8	(Same as 1501:27-28, above)			
1:16-18	(The Call of Simon and Andrew:)				
	1524: 9-1525:2	4:18-20 10:2	6:14	1:40-42	Mk 3:16,18 Ac 1:13
	1548:34-35	4:18-19	5:10		
	1628:27-1629:11		5:1-11		
	(Simon Peter:)				
	1549:10-12				
	1550:23-1552:20	(Same as 1524:9-1525:2, above)			
	(Andrew:)				
	1548:28-1550:22	(Same as 1524:9-1525:2, bove)			

MARK Chap:Verse	The URANTIA Book Page:Line	MATTHEW Chap:Verse	LUKE Chap:Verse	JOHN Chap:Verse	Other BOOKS Chap:Verse
1:17	1544:47	4:19	5:10		
1:19-20	(The Call of James and John Bar-Zebedee:)				
	1525: 7-46	4:21-22	5:10;6:14		Mk 3:17 Ac 1:13
	1628:27-1629:11		5:1-11		
	(James Bar-Zebedee:)				
	1552:21-1553:28	4:21-22	5:10;6:14		Mk 3:17 Ac 1:13
	(John:)				
	1553:39-1556:4	4:21-22	5:10;6:14		Mk 3:17 Ac 1:13
1:21	1628: 3- 4		4:31		
	1629:18-19	_	4:31		
	1687:16-17		4:31		
1:22	1571:47-48	7:28-29	4:31-32		
	1630:42-44	7:28-29	4:31-32		
1:23-26	1630:45-1631: 2		4:33-35		
1:27-28	1631:14-19		4:36-37		
1:29-31	1631:22-27	8:14-15	4:38-39		
1:32-34	1632: 1-1633:15	8:16	4:40-41		
1:34	1634:18-19				
1:35	1634:42-45	_	4:42		
1:36-37	1635: 8-11				
1:37	1635:25-26		4:42		
1:38	1635:41-1636: 3		4:43		
1:39	1636: 9-10	_	4:44		
	1643:17-18		4:44		
1:40-41	(Faith Makes Whole:)				
	1643:27-40	8:2-3,13	5:12-13		Mk 2:5
		9:2,22,29	8:48,50		Mk 5:34
		15:28	17:19;18:42		Mk 10:52
	1648: 7-13	(Same as 1643:27-40, above)			
	1667:12	(Same as 1643:27-40, above)			
	1698:33-1699:6	(Same as 1643:27-40, above)			
	1735:21-25	(Same as 1643:27-40, above)			
	1828:10-11	(Same as 1643:27-40, above)			
	1873:28-29	(Same as 1643:27-40, above)			
	1875:13-14	(Same as 1643:27-40, above)			
	1905:23-24	(Same as 1643:27-40, above)			
1:42-45	1643:41-1644:3	8:1-4	5:12-15		

Mark 1:44 to 2:23

MARK Chap:Verse	The URANTIA Book Page:Line	MATTHEW Chap:Verse	LUKE Chap:Verse	JOHN Chap:Verse	Other BOOKS Chap:Verse
1:44	(Tell No Man:)				
	1520:22-21	8:4;9:30	5:14;8:56		Mk 5:43;7:36;8:26
	1643:42-43	8:4;9:30	5:14;8:56		Mk 5:43;7:36;8:26
	1669:14-16	8:4;9:30	5:14;8:56		Mk 5:43;7:36;8:26
	1699:32-33	8:4;9:30	5:14;8:56		Mk 5:43;7:36;8:26
2: 1- 2	1666:30-38		5:17		
2: 3- 5	1666:39-1667:12	9:2-3	5:18-20		
2: 5	(Reward of Faith, See Mark 1:40-41, above.)				
2: 6-12	1667:13-27	9:3-8	5:21-26		
2:10	1407:27	8:20	5:24	1:51+	He 2:14
2:14	(The Call of Matthew Levi:)				
	1540:16-21	9:9	5:27-28		Mk 3:18
		10:3	6:15		Ac 1:13
	1559:20-1560:49 (Same as 1540:16-20, above)				
	1957:43-44	9:9	5:27-28		
2:15-16	(Friend of Publicans and Sinners,)				
	1342:17-18	9:10-11	5:29-30		
		11:19	7:34;15:2		
	1540:31-1541:3 (Same as 1342:17-18, above)				
	1850:18-19 (Same as 1342:17-18, above)				
	1851: 7- 8 (Same as 1342:17-18, above)				
2:17	(Jesus Came to Call Sinners to Repentance:)				
	1537:17-19	9:12-13	5:31-32		
	1541: 3-14	9:12-13	5:31-32		
	1750:10-11	9:12-13	5:31-32		
2:18-22	(Fasting:)				
	0976:16-20	9:14	5:33		2Sa 12:16;21:23
					Is 58:3-6 Ps 35:13
	1609:24-25	9:14	5:33		
	1655:28-47	9:14-17	5:33-38		
2:23-28	(Use of The Sabbath:)				
	1649:47-1650:5	12:1-8	6:1-10	5:5-9	Mk 3:1-5
		12:9-14	11:37-41	5:16-18	Mk 7:1-13
		15:1-9	13:10-17	9:14	Ex 20:8-11
			14:1-6		De 5:12-15
	1654:29-1655:12 (Same as 1649:47-1650:5, above.)				
	1665: 7-35 (Same as 1649:47-1650:5, above)				
	1712:21-42 (Same as 1649:47-1650:5, above)				

(Mark 2:23-28 Continued on next page.)

MARK Chap:Verse	The URANTIA Book Page:Line	MATTHEW Chap:Verse	LUKE Chap:Verse	JOHN Chap:Verse	Other BOOKS Chap:Verse
2:23-28	1813:13-16	(Same as 1649:47-1650:5, above)			
	1835:40-1836:26	(Same as 1649:47-1650:5, above)			
	1850:22-23	(Same as 1649:47-1650:5, above)			
2:25-28	(Sabbath Made for Man:)				
	1654:49-1655:12	12:3-8	6:3-5		
3: 1- 5	1665: 7-35	12:9-14	6:6-10		
	(Use of Sabbath, See Mark 2:23-28, above.)				
3: 7- 8	1669:10-14				
3:13-14	(The Ordination of the Twelve on The Mountain:)				
	1568:2	10:1	6:13		
	(The Ordination Sermon:)				
	1570: 8-1571:46	5:3-7:27			
3:16-19	(The 12 Apostles Listed:)				
	1548: 2	10:2-4	6:13-16		Ac 1:13
3:16	(Simon Peter:)				
	1524:25-1525:2	4:18-20	6:14	1:41	Mk 1:16-18
		10:2			Ac 1:13
	1549:10-12	(Same as 1524:25-1525:2, above)			
	1550:23-1552:20	(Same as 1524:25-1525:2, above)			
	1628:27-1628:11		5:1-11		
3:17	(James and John:)				
	1525: 7-46	4:21-22	1:10-11		Mk 1:19-20
		10:2	6:14		Ac 1:13
	1552:21-1556:4	10:2	6:14		Mk 1:19-20 Ac 1:13
	1955:37				
3:18	(Andrew:)				
	1524: 9-20	10:2	6:14	1:40	Mk 1:16-18 Ac 1:13
	1548:28-1550:22	(Same as 1524: 9-20, above)			
	(Phillip:)				
	1526:21-44	10:3	6:14	1:43-44	Ac 1:13
	1556: 5-1558:6	10:3	6:14	1:43-44	Ac 1:13
	(Nathaniel, Son of Bartholomew:)				
	1526:45-1527:13	10:3	6:14	1:45-49	Ac 1:13
	1557:21-23				
	1558: 7-1559:19	10:3	6:14	1:45-49	Ac 1:13
3:18	(Matthew Levi:)				
	1540:16-21	9:9;10:3	5:27-28;6:15		Mk 2:14 Ac 1:13
	1559:20-1560:49	9:9	5:27-28		Mk 2:14 Ac 1:13
		10:3	6:15		

Mark 3:18 to 3:35

MARK Chap:Verse	The URANTIA Book Page:Line	MATTHEW Chap:Verse	LUKE Chap:Verse	JOHN Chap:Verse	Other BOOKS Chap:Verse
3:18	(Thomas Didymus:)				
	1542: 4- 9	10:3	6:15	11:16	Ac 1:13
	1561: 1-1563:13	10:3	6:15	11:16	Ac 1:13
	(The Alpheus Twins: James the Lesser, also called				
	Thaddeus; and Judas, also called Lebbeus:)				
	1541:26-31	10:3	6:15-16		Ac 1:13
	1563:14-1564:32	10:3	6:15-16		Ac 1:13
	(Simon the Zealot:)				
	1540:27-30	10:4	6:15		Ac 1:13
	1564:33-1565:40	10:4	6:15		Ac 1:13
3:19	(Judas Iscariot:)				
	1542:4-11	10:4	6:16	12:4	
	1565:41-1567:47	10:4	6:16	12:4	
3:21	1537:29-30				
	1546:37-38				
	1594:14-16				
3:22	(Devils:)				
	0602:11	9:34;10:25	11:15		Mk 3:30
		12:24			
	0863:27	(Same as 0602:11, above)			
	1714: 7-13	(Same as 0602:11, above)			
	1850:24-25	(Same as 0602:11, above)			
	1924:45-46	(Same as 0602:11, above)			
3:23-27	1714:14-19	12:25-29	11:17-22		
3:24-25	2085:20	12:25	11:17		
3:28-29	1714:28-32	12:31-32			
3:30	(Unclean Spirit, See Mark 3:22, above)				
3:31-32	(Jesus' Family--Mother & Brothers:)				
	1721: 4- 6	12:46-47	8:19-20		
	1721:42-48	12:46-47	8:19-20		
3:33-35	1722:14-19	12:48-50	8:21		
3:35	(Doing the Father's Will:)				
	0008:42	6:10;7:21	8:21	4:34;5:30	Mk 14:36,39
		12:50;26:39	11:2	6:38;7:17	
		26:42,44	22:42	14:23-24	
				15:10,14	
	0052: 1- 4	(Same as 0008:42, above)			
	1200:41	(Same as 0008:42, above)			

(Mark 3:35 Continued on next page.)

MARK Chap:Verse	The URANTIA Book Page:Line	MATTHEW Chap:Verse	LUKE Chap:Verse	JOHN Chap:Verse	Other BOOKS Chap:Verse
3:35	1221:33-34	(Same as 0008:42, above)			
	1303: 7	(Same as 0008:42, above)			
	1318:29-30	(Same as 0008:42, above)			
	1324:21-22	(Same as 0008:42, above)			
	1327:10	(Same as 0008:42, above)			
	1328:38-41	(Same as 0008:42, above)			
	1331: 9-10	(Same as 0008:42, above)			
	1417: 5- 7	(Same as 0008:42, above)			
	1453:43-44	(Same as 0008:42, above)			
	1500:27	(Same as 0008:42, above)			
	1511:47-48	(Same as 0008:42, above)			
	1514:35	(Same as 0008:42, above)			
	1569:8-9	(Same as 0008:42, above)			
	1574:21	(Same as 0008:42, above)			
	1582: 8	(Same as 0008:42, above)			
	1594:33-34	(Same as 0008:42, above)			
	1608: 1	(Same as 0008:42, above)			
	1769:42-44	(Same as 0008:42, above)			
	1774:28	(Same as 0008:42, above)			
	1947:50-1948:1	(Same as 0008:42, above)			
	1968:21-24	(Same as 0008:42, above)			
	1968:33-32	(Same as 0008:42, above)			
	1972: 5- 7	(Same as 0008:42, above)			
	2078: 8	(Same as 0008:42, above)			
	2087:11	(Same as 0008:42, above)			
	2088:30-31	(Same as 0008:42, above)			
	2089:12-14	(Same as 0008:42, above)			
	2090: 1	(Same as 0008:42, above)			
	(Brotherhood Through Jesus:)				
	1454:40-41	12:50	8:21		
	1865:45-46	12:50	8:21		
4: 1- 2	1688:21-36	13:1-3	8:4		
4: 3- 9	(Parable of Sower:)				
	1688:37-1689:8	13:3-9	8:5-8		
4: 8	1536:43-44	13:8,23	8:8		Mk 4:20
4:10	1689: 9-13	13:10	8:9		
4:11-12	1689:14-31	13:11-15	8:10-11		Is 6:9-10
		25:9	19:26		Ac 28:25-27
4:13	1689:37-45	13:18-23			

185

MARK Chap:Verse	The URANTIA Book Page:Line	MATTHEW Chap:Verse	LUKE Chap:Verse	JOHN Chap:Verse	Other BOOKS Chap:Verse
4:14-20	1689:46-1690:17	13:18-23	8:11-15		
4:20	1536:43-44	13:8,23	4:8		Mk 4:8
4:21	(Let Light Shine:)				
	1570:46-1571:2	5:15	8:16;11:33		
	1572:13-16	5:15	8:16;11:33		
	1692: 8-10	5:15	8:16;11:33		
4:22	(Hidden Made Known, Secrets Revealed:)				
	1681:47-1682:4	10:26-27	8:17;12:2-3		
	1692:10-13	10:26-27	8:17;12:2-3		
	1820: 7-12	10:26-27	8:17;12:2-3		
4:23-25	1692:13-16	13:12	19:26		
		25:29			
4:25	(To Him Who Hath is Given, Hath Not is Taken Away.)				
	1199: 1- 3	13:12	8:18		
		25:29	19:26		
	1689:23-24	(Same as 1119: 1- 3, above)			
	1692:15-16	(Same as 1199: 1- 3, above)			
	1917:27-28	(Same as 1199: 1- 3, above)			
4:26-29	1693:20-27				
4:30-32	(Parable of the Mustard Seed:)				
	1583:10-11	13:31,33	13:19		
	1693:44-1694:2	13:31-32	13:18-19		
	1860:37-39	13:31-33	13:18-21		
	1931:43-44	13:31,33	13:19		
4:33-34	1694:16-19				
4:35	1694:21-25	8:18	8:22		
4:36-38	1694:26-43	8:23-24	8:22-23		
4:38-41	1695: 3-27	8:25-27	8:24-25		
5: 1	1695:35-39	8:28	8:26		
5: 1-13	(Healing the Gadarene of "Unclean Spirits":)				
	1765: 8-12	8:28-32	8:26-33		
5: 2- 4	1695:40-48	8:28	8:27,29		
5: 5	1696: 1- 8				
5: 6- 7	1696: 9-11	8:29	8:28		
5: 7	0488:15				Ge 14:18-22+
5: 8	1696:15-18	8:31-32	8:29		
5: 9-14	1696:26-35	8:32-33	8:30-34		
5:11-14	1696:26-28	8:32-33	8:32-33		
5:15	1696:18-25		8:35		

MARK Chap:Verse	The URANTIA Book Page:Line	MATTHEW Chap:Verse	LUKE Chap:Verse	JOHN Chap:Verse	Other BOOKS Chap:Verse
5:16-19	1696:42-1697:3	8:34	8:36-37		
5:18-20	1697: 5-12		8:38-39		
5:21-24	1698: 4-16	9:19-19	8:40-42		
5:25-33	(Healing Woman with Issue of Blood:)				
	1698:16-31	9:20-22	8:43-48		
	1875:13-14	9:20-22	8:43-48		
5:30	1669:20		8:46		
5:34	1698:32-1699:6				
	(Faith Makes Whole, See Mark 1:40-41, above.)				
5:35-42	1699: 9-22	9:23-25	8:49-55		
5:43	1699:23-24		8:55		
	(Tell no man:)				
	1520:20-21	8:4;9:30	5:14;8:56		Mk 1:44;7:36;8:26
	1643:42-45	8:4;9:30	5:14;8:56		Mk 1:44;7:36;8:26
	1669:14-16	8:4;9:30	5:14;8:56		Mk 1:44;7:36;8:26
	1699:32-33	8:4;9:30	5:14;8:56		Mk 1:44;7:36;8:26
6: 1	1683:36-43		4:16		
6: 2	1684:37-38	13:54	4:16		
	1686:15-16	13:54	4:22		
6: 3	(Jesus' Family:)				
	1686:28-31	13:55-56	4:22	6:42	
	1711:22-24	13:55-56	4:22	6:42	
	(Joseph the Carpenter's Son:)				
	1051:11	13:55	4:22	1:45;6:42	
	1686:30-31	13:55	4:22	1:45;6:42	
	(Brother James:)				
	1357: 5- 6	13:55;27:56			Ga 1:19
	(Sister Miriam:)				
	1357:47-48	13:56			
	(Brother Joseph:)				
	1362: 1- 2	13:55;27:56			
	(Brother Simon:)				
	1365: 9-10	13:55			
	(Sister Martha:)				
	1367:18	13:56			
	(Brother Jude:)				
	1370:11	13:55			
	(Sister Ruth:)				
	1389:21-22	13:56			

187

MARK Chap:Verse	The URANTIA Book Page:Line	MATTHEW Chap:Verse	LUKE Chap:Verse	JOHN Chap:Verse	Other BOOKS Chap:Verse
6: 4	(Prophet Without Honor in Own Country:)				
	1538:19	13:57	4:24	4:44	
	1686:31-35	13:55-57	4:22-24	4:44	
6: 5	1686:40-44	13:58			
6: 7	1681:32-35	10:1	9:1-2		
	2055:23-24	10:1	9:1-2;10:1		
6: 8- 9	1584: 7- 8	10:9-10	9:3;10:4		
	1800:34-35	10:9-10	9:3;10:4		
6:10	1800:37-1801: 3		9:4		
6:11	1801: 9-13	10:14-15	9:5		
			10:10-12		
6:12-13	1682:21-23		9:6		
6:13	1678: 9				
6:14	1717: 9-16		9:7		
6:14-15	1746:12-13	14:1-2	9:7-9		
6:14-16	1717:17-23	14:1-2	9:7-9		
6:17	1506:36-40	14:3	3:19-20		
6:18	1506:27-29	14:3-4	3:19		
6:19	1508:14-15				Mk 6:20
	1508:25-27				Mk 6:21-29
6:20	1508: 7-18	14:5			Mk 6:19
6:21-29	(Death of John The Baptist:)				
	1508:23-45	14:6-12			Mk 6:19
6:26-29	1627:35-40	14:9-12			
6:31-34	1700:20-32	14:13-14	9:10-11	6:1-3	
6:35-44	(Feeding of the Five Thousand:)				
6:35-38	1701:14-35	14:15-17	9:12-13	6:5-9	
6:39-44	1701:36-49	14:18-21	9:14-17	6:10-13	
6:45-46	1702:44-1073:7	14:22-23		6:15-17	
6:47-51	1703:11-38	14:24-33		6:17-21	
6:48	1519:46	14:25		6:19	
6:50	1102:29	9:12;14:27		16:33	
6:53	1703:40-41	14:34			
7: 1-13	(Use of Sabbath, See Mark 2:23-28, above.)				
7: 5-13	1712:21-42	15:1-9		De 5:16 Ex 20:12 Is 29:13	
7:14-23	(Cleanliness of Heart over Hands and Food:)				
	1671:42-43	12:33-37			
		15:10-20			
	1712:43-1713:14	(Same as 1671:42-43, above)			

MARK Chap:Verse	The URANTIA Book Page:Line	MATTHEW Chap:Verse	LUKE Chap:Verse	JOHN Chap:Verse	Other BOOKS Chap:Verse
7:24	1734: 3- 5	15:21			
	1734:22-26	15:21			
7:25-26	1734:17-21	15:22			
7:25-30	1905:23-24	15:22-28			
7:27-28	1735: 5-14	15:24-27			
	1809:35	15:26-27			
7:29-30	1735:21-25	15:28			
7:36	(Tell No Man, See Mark 8:26, below.)				
8: 1-12	(COMPARE)	14:14-22	9:11-17		Mk 6:34-44
8:11	(Show Us a Sign:)				
	1520:21-23	12:38;16:1	11:16	2:18;6:30	
	1714:41-43	12:38;16:1	11:16	2:18;6:30	
	1744:40-45	12:38;16:1	11:16	2:18;6:30	
	1895:30-34	12:38;16:1	11:16	2:18;6:30	
8:12	(The only "sign:")				
	1714:44-47	12:39;16:4	11:29		
	1744:46-1745:4	12:39;16:4	11:29		
	1895:34-36	12:39;16:4	11:29		
	1982:39-40	26:60-61			Mk 14:58
	1983:11-12	26:60-61			Mk 14:58
8:15	(Beware of the Leaven of The Pharisees & of Herod:)				
	1745:10-11	16:6-12	12:1		
	1751:25	16:6-12	12:1		
	1820: 4- 5	16:6-12	12:1		
8:18	1745:16-17				
8:22-25	1811:16				
8:26	(Tell No Man:)				
	1520:20-21	8:4;9:30	5:14;8:56		Mk 1:44;5:43;7:36
	1643:42-45	8:4;9:30	5:14;8:56		Mk 1:44;5:43;7:36
	1669:14-16	8:4;9:30	5:14;8:56		Mk 1:44;5:43;7:36
	1699:23-33	8:4;9:30	5:14;8:56		Mk 1:44;5:43;7:36
8:27	1745:29-30	16:13			
	1745:45-47	16:13	9:18		
8:28	1746:10-14	16:14	9:19		Mk 6:14-15
8:29	(Peter Acknowledges Jesus as The Messiah:)				
	1746:14-20	16:15-16	9:20		
	1748: 2- 3	16:16	9:20		
	1939: 1- 3	16:15-16	9:20		
8:30	1746:24-25	16:20	9:21		

MARK Chap:Verse	The URANTIA Book Page:Line	MATTHEW Chap:Verse	LUKE Chap:Verse	JOHN Chap:Verse	Other BOOKS Chap:Verse
8:31	(Jesus Foretells His Crucifixion & Resurrection:)				
	1759:10-15	16:21;26:2	9:22,44		Mk 9:31
		17:22-23	18:31-33		Mk 10:32-34
		20:18-19	24:6-8,46		Mk 14:41
	1759:39-46	(Same as 1759:10-15, above)			
	1871:29-41	(Same as 1759:10-15, above)			
	1872:38-43	(Same as 1759:10-15, above)			
	1952:16-17	(Same as 1759:10-15, above)			
	1962:32	(Same as 1759:10-15, above)			
	2001:14	(Same as 1759:10-15, above)			
	2035:18-19	(Same as 1759:10-15, above)			
	2052:16-18	(Same as 1759:10-15, above)			
8:32	1760: 1- 4	16:22			
8:33	0609:44-45	4:10;16:23	4:8		
	1760:10-15	16:23			
8:34	(Take up Cross, Deny Self, "Follow Me:")				
	1750: 5- 6	10:38;16:24	9:23;14:27		Mk 10:21
	1760:17-19	10:38;16:24	9:23;14:27		Mk 10:21
	1770:22-23	10:38;16:24	9:23;14:27		Mk 10:21
	1869:37-41	10:38;16:24	9:23;14:27		Mk 10:21
8:34-35	(Whosoever Will may Come:)				
	0039: 7	16:24-25	9:23-24	3:15-16	Re 22:17
	1102:18-19	16:24-25	9:23-24	3:15-16	Re 22:17
	1205:16-17	16:24-25	9:23-24	3:15-16	Re 22:17
	1567: 4	16:24-25	9:23-24	3:15-16	Re 22:17
	1750:16-17	16:24-25	9:23-24	3:15-16	Re 22:17
	1820:44-45	16:24-25	9:23-24	3:15-16	Re 22:17
	1829:44-45	16:24-25	9:23-24	3:15-16	Re 22:17
8:35	(Valuing Life, Lose It--Save It:)				
	1134:28-29	16:25	9:24	12:25	
		10:39	17:33		
	1575:32-33	(Same as 1134:28-29, above)			
	1760:19-20	(same as 1134:28-29, above)			
	1782: 9-10	(Same as 1134:28-29, above)			
	1903:39-41	(Same as 1134:28-29, above)			
8:36	(Value of Soul:)				
	1581:28-29	16:26	9:25		
	1760:20-21	16:26	9:25		
	1822:37-38	16:26	9:25		

MARK Chap:Verse	The URANTIA Book Page:Line	MATTHEW Chap:Verse	LUKE Chap:Verse	JOHN Chap:Verse	Other BOOKS Chap:Verse
8:36-38	1760:20-26	16:26-28 10:38-39	9:25-27 14:27		Mk 9:1
8:38	(Jesus' Return in Glory:)				
	0596:38	24:30 16:27;25:31	21:27 9:26		Mk 13:26
	1591:16-17	(Same as 0596:38, above)			
	1860:16-17	(Same as 0596:38, above)			
	1915: 1- 4	(Same as 0596:38, above)			
	2092:42-43	(Same as 0596:38, above)			
9: 1	1569:24-25	16:28	9:27		Mk 8:34-35
	1760:25-26	16:28	9:27		
9: 2-13	(The Transfiguration:)				
9: 2	1752:16-21	17:1	9:28		
9: 2- 4	1753:31-38	17:2-3	9:29-32		
9: 5- 6	1753:41-48	17:4	9:33		
9: 7- 8	(The Voice on the Mountain:)				
	1753:49-1754:7	17:5-8	9:34-36		
	1755:18-19	17:5	9:35		
	(For Voice at Baptism, See Mark 1:11, above.)				
9: 9	1754: 9-12	17:9			
9:10	1754:33-35		9:36		
9:11-13	1754:21-29	11:14;17:10-13			Ml 4:5-6
9:14	1755:29-35		9:37		
9:15-19	1757: 2-25	17:14-17	9:38-41		
9:20-24	1757:25-37		9:42		
9:22	1757:11-13	17:15	9:39		
9:25-27	1757:38-44	17:18	9:42-43		
9:28	1758: 9-15	17:19			
9:29	1758:17-27	17:20			
9:30	1759:19-31				
9:31	(Jesus Foretells Death & Resurrection, See Mark 8:31.)				
9:32	1759:15-17		9:45		
9:33-34	1761: 6-13	18:1	9:46		
9:35	(First Shall be Last and Servant of All:)				
	0316:40	19:30 20:16,26-27 23:11	9:48 13:30;14:11 8:14;22:26		Mk 10:31,43-44
	0466:33-34	(Same as 0316:40, above)			

(Mark 9:35 Continued on next page.)

191

Mark 9:35 to 10:15

MARK Chap:Verse	The URANTIA Book Page:Line	MATTHEW Chap:Verse	LUKE Chap:Verse	JOHN Chap:Verse	Other BOOKS Chap:Verse
9:35	0647:31-32	(Same as 0316:40, above)			
	1536:38-39	(Same as 0316:40, above)			
	1569:18-20	(Same as 0316:40, above)			
	1758:33-35	(Same as 0316:40, above)			
	1761:20-21	(Same as 0316:40, above)			
	1804:10-11	(Same as 0316:40, above)			
	1829:31-32	(Same as 0316:40, above)			
	1834:42-44	(Same as 0316:40, above)			
	1838:27-28	(Same as 0316:40, above)			
	1862:13-14	(Same as 0316:40, above)			
	1907:12-14	(Same as 0316:40, above)			
	1940:11-17	(Same as 0316:40, above)			
9:36-37	1761:13-20	10:40;18:2-6	9:47-48		
9:38	1555: 4- 5		9:49		
9:38-40	1764:24-36		9:50		
9:41	1764:38-40	10:42			
9:42-47	1761:21-29	18:6-10	17:2		
9:50	(Salt Which Lost its Saltiness:)				
	1570:44-45	5:13	14:34-35		
	1572: 7- 9	5:13	14:34-35		
	1870:17-20	5:13	14:34		
10: 2	1838:29-32	19:3			
10: 2-12	(On Divorce:)				
	1576:39-1577:2	5:31-32	16:18		
		19:3-9			
10: 3- 5	1838:43-1839:11	19:4-12			
10: 6- 8	1839:29-34	19:4-5	_		Ge 1:27;2:24
10:10	1839:23-25				
10:13	1726:32-40	11:21			
	1839:40-48	19:13	18:15		
10:14	1840: 1- 2	19:14	18:16		
10:15	(Receive Kingdom As a Little Child:)				
	1118:35-36	18:3-4	18:17		
	1536:26-28	18:3-4	18:17		
	1576:14-16	18:3-4	18:17		
	1585: 9-23	18:3-4	18:17		
	1621: 5-11	18:2-5	18:17		
	1676:48-1677:2	18:3-4	18:17		

Mark 10:15 Continued on next page.)

MARK Chap:Verse	The URANTIA Book Page:Line	MATTHEW Chap:Verse	LUKE Chap:Verse	JOHN Chap:Verse	Other BOOKS Chap:Verse
10:15	1733: 3- 8	18:3-4	18:17		
	1761:13-19	18:3-4	18:17		
	1840: 2- 4	18:3-4	18:17		
	1861: 7-11	18:3-4	18:17		
	1861:41-42	18:3-4	18:17		
	1960:37-38	18:3-4	18:17		
	2089:41-42	18:3-4	18:17		
10:16	1840: 5- 7	19:15			
10:17-22	(The Rich Young Ruler:)				
	1802: 5-24	19:16-22	18:18-24		De 5:7-21 Ex 20:3-17
	1564:13-15	19:16-22	18:18-24		
10:18	2088:42-43	19:16-17	18:18-19		
	2092:10-12	19:17	18:19		
10:21	1802:17-24	19:20-21	18:22		
	(Deny Self, Take up Cross, "Follow Me:")				
	1750: 5- 6	10:38;16:24	9:23;14:27		Mk 8:34
	1760:17-19	10:38;16:24	9:23;14:27		Mk 8:34
	1770:22-23	10:38;16:24	9:23;14:27		Mk 8:34
	1869:37-41	10:38;16:24	9:23;14:27		Mk 8:34
10:21-22	1672: 3- 5	19:21-22	18:22-23		
		8:21-22	9:59-62		
10:22	1802:25-26	19:22	18:23		
10:23-25	1803:26-33	19:23-24	18:24-25		
10:24-25	2093:16-17	19:23-24	18:24-25		
10:25	1803: 5- 8	19:24	18:25		
	1821:43-46	19:24	18:25		
10:26-27	1803:34-40	19:25-26	18:26-27		
10:27	(With God, All Things are Possible:)				
	0034:13-14	19:26	1:37;18:27		Mk 14:36
	0046:42	19:26	1:37;18:27		Mk 14:36
	0291:26-27	19:26	1:37;18:27		Mk 14:36
	1453:41	19:26	1:37;18:27		Mk 14:36
	1757:34-35	19:26	1:37;18:27		Mk 14:36
10:28-30	1804: 5-10	19:29			
10:31	1804:10-11	19:30;20:16	13:30		
	(First Last & Last First, See Mark 9:35, above.)				
10:32-34	(Jesus Foretells His Crucifixion & Resurrection, See Mark 8:31, above.)				

Mark 10:35 to 11:10

MARK Chap:Verse	The URANTIA Book Page:Line	MATTHEW Chap:Verse	LUKE Chap:Verse	JOHN Chap:Verse	Other BOOKS Chap:Verse
10:35-40	(Request for Honors in Heaven:)				
	1553:21-32	20:21-22			Ac 12:1-2
	1867:23-1868:5	20:20-23			
	1958:19-22	20:20-22			
10:38-39	(Drinking the Cup:)				
	0229:46	20:22123	22:42		Mk 14:36,39
		26:39,42,44			
	1867:37-39	(Same as 0229:46, above)			
	1955:30-32	(Same as 0229:46, above)			
	1968:11-14	(Same as 0229:46, above)			
	1968:21-24	(Same as 0229:46, above)			
	1968:32-34	(Same as 0229:46, above)			
	1972: 5- 7	(Same as 0229:46, above)			
10:38-40	1867:32-1868:5	20:22-23			
10:39	1958:25-26	20:23			Ac 12:1-2
10:41	1958:24-25	20:24			
10:41-45	1868: 6-17	20:24-28			
10:43-44	(Great Minister, Chief Serve, See Mark 9:35, above.)				
10:45	1750:11	20:28			
10:46	1873: 2- 5	20:29	18:35		
10:47-48	1873:16-20	20:30-31	18:36-39		
10:49-51	1873:21-27	20:32-34	18:40-43		
10:52	(Faith Makes Whole:)				
	1643:27-40	8:2-3,13	5:12-13		Mk 1:40-41
		9:2,22,29	8:48,50		Mk 2:5
		15:28	17:19;18:42		Mk 5:34
	1648: 7-13	(Same as 1643:27-40, above)			
	1667:12	(Same as 1643:27-40, above)			
	1698:33-1699:6	(Same as 1643:27-40, above)			
	1735:21-25	(Same as 1643:27-40, above)			
	1828:10-11	(Same as 1643:27-40, above)			
	1873:28-29	(Same as 1643:27-40, above)			
	1875:13-14	(Same as 1643:27-40, above)			
	1905:23-24	(Same as 1643:27-40, above)			
11: 1- 3	1881:27-32	21:1-3	19:28-31		
11: 4- 7	1881:33-38	21:6-7	19:32-35		
11: 7-10	1882: 6-13	27:7-9	19:35-38	12:12-14	Ps 118:26
11: 8-10	1403:33-35	21:8-9	19:36-38	12:12-13	

MARK Chap:Verse	The URANTIA Book Page:Line	MATTHEW Chap:Verse	LUKE Chap:Verse	JOHN Chap:Verse	Other BOOKS Chap:Verse
11:11	1883:13-15				
	1883:35-40				
11:12	1888: 4- 5			2:13	
11:15	1888:17-18	21:12	19:45		
11:15-17	(Cleansing the Temple:)				
	1378:27-29	21:12-13	19:45-46	2:14-16	
	1890:11-25	21:12-13	19:45-46	2:14-15	Is 56:7
					Je 7:11
	1911: 6- 7	21:12-13	19:45-46	2:13-16	
11:18	1890:36-42		19:47-48		
11:19	1895:42-44	21:17			
11:24	(Prayer:)				
	0096:37-38	6:5-13	11:2-4	14:13-14	Mk 14:35-36
		26:39-42	18:1-14		Ro 8:26-27
			22:42		
	1001:12-1002:41 (Same as 0096:37-38, above)				
	1511:46-48 (Same as 0096:37-38, above)				
	1618:35-1624:10 (Same as 0096:37-38, above)				
	1638:10-1641: 9 (Same as 0096:37-38, above)				
	1848:16-1849:23 (Same as 0096:37-38, above)				
	1968:11-15 (Same as 0096:37-38, above)				
	1968:22-24 (Same as 0096:37-38, above)				
	1968:31-34 (Same as 0096:37-38, above)				
11:25-26	(Forgive if You Expect Forgiveness:)				
	1475: 4- 7	6:12,14-15	6:37;11:4		
			18:21-25		
	1638:34-41 (Same as 1475:4-7, above)				
	1763:23-1764:4 (Same as 1475:4-7, above)				
	1862: 5- 6 (Same as 1475:4-7, above)				
	2017:44-45 (Same as 1475:4-7, above)				
	(Forgive Seventy Times Seven:)				
	0449:40				
	1551: 4- 6				
	1763:20-23				
11:25-26	(Father in Heaven:)				
	0023:24	5:16,48;6:1,9	10:21		
		7:11,21;11:25	11:2		
		16:17;18:35;23:9			

(Mark 11:25-26 Continued on next page.)

Mark 11:25 to 12:27

MARK Chap:Verse	The URANTIA Book Page:Line	MATTHEW Chap:Verse	LUKE Chap:Verse	JOHN Chap:Verse	Other BOOKS Chap:Verse
11:25-26	1053:41-42	(Same as 0023:24, above)			
	1103:19	(Same as 0023:24, above)			
	1511:46	(Same as 0023:24, above)			
	1569:10	(Same as 0023:24, above)			
	1571: 2	(Same as 0023:24, above)			
	1571:16-17	(Same as 0023:24, above)			
	1619:23	(Same as 0023:24, above)			
	1620: 1	(Same as 0023:24, above)			
	1638:35	(Same as 0023:24, above)			
	1764: 2	(Same as 0023:24, above)			
	1807:18-19	(Same as 0023:24, above)			
	1907:16	(Same as 0023:24, above)			
	1923:12	(Same as 0023:24, above)			
	2087:11-12	(Same as 0023:24, above)			
11:27-28	1891:28-32	21:23	20:1-2	2:18	
11:29-30	1892: 6- 9	21:24-25	20:3-4		
11:31-33	1892:10-24	21:25-27	20:5-8		
12: 1- 9	(Parable of The Vineyard:)				
	1893:35-1894:10	21:33-40	20:9-15		
12: 9	1894:11-13	21:41	20:16		
12:10	1894:18-24	21:42	20:17		
12:12	1894:31-35	21:45-46	20:19		
12:13	1899: 2-10	22:15	20:20		
12:14-17	1899:13-26	22:16-21	20:21-25		
12:17	1899:27-30	22:22	20:26		
	(Render Proper Dues to Caesar and God:)				
	1114:25-26	22:21	20:35		
	1474:14-15	22:21	20:25		
	1580:16-17	22:21	20:25		
	1740:19-20	22:21	20:25		
	1929:33-35	22:21	20:25		
	1957: 4- 5	22:21	20:25		
12:18-23	1900: 2-12	22:23-28	20:27-33		De 25:5-6
12:19	0926:12-14	22:24	20:28		Ge 38:6-10 De 25:5-6
12:23-27	1900:17-29	22:29-32	20:34-38		Ex 3:6 Ac 7:32
12:25	(Resurrected Do Not Marry:)				
	0419:12-13	22:30	20:35-36		
	0495:32	22:30	20;35-36		

MARK Chap:Verse	The URANTIA Book Page:Line	MATTHEW Chap:Verse	LUKE Chap:Verse	JOHN Chap:Verse	Other BOOKS Chap:Verse
12:28-31	1809:21-28	22:34-40	10:25-28		De 6:4-5 Le 19:18
	1901:10-20	22:35-40	10:25-28		De 6:4-5 Le 19:18
12:29	(The Shema, One God:)				
	0031:36		Mk 12:32 De 4:35,39 De 6:4 Ro 3:30		
			1Co 8:4-6 Ga 3:20 Ep 4:6 Ja 2:19		
	0115:16	(Same as 0031:36, above)			
	0513:41	(Same as 0031:36, above)			
	0640:19-22	(Same as 0031:36, above)			
	1009:32-33	(Same as 0031:36, above)			
	1058:27-28	(Same as 0031:36, above)			
	1453:36	(Same as 0031:36, above)			
	1901:13-16	(Same as 0031:36, above)			
12:30	(The First Commandment, Love God:)				
	1206:38-39	22:37	10:27-28		De 6:5
	1444: 7- 9	22:37	10:27-28		De 6:5
	1453:36-37	22:37	10:27-28		De 6:5
12:30-31	(The Two Greatest Commandments:)				
	1446:11-12	22:37-40	10:27-28		De 6:5 Le 19:18
	1600: 1- 3	22:37-40	10:27-28		De 6:5 Le 19:18
	1600:33-36	22:37-40	10:27-28		De 6:5 Le 19:18
	1805:10-11	22:37-40	10:27-28		De 6:5 Le 19:18
	1809:25-27	22:37-40	10:27-28		De 6:5 Le 19:18
	1901:15-20	22:37-40	10:27-28		De 6:5 Le 19:18
12:31	(The Second Commandment, Love Neighbor as Self:)				
	1445:47	19:19	10:27-28	Mk 12:33 Le 19:18	
		22:39		Ro 13:9 Ga 5:14 Ja 2:8	
	1453:37	(Same as 1445:47, above)			
	1769:26	(Same as 1445:47, above)			
	1770: 4- 8	(Same as 1445:47, above)			
	1862: 8	(Same as 1445:47, above)			
	1950:17-18	(Same as 1445:47, above)			
	(COMPARE: The New Standard, Act & Love as Jesus Does:)				
	1206:40-42		13:34;15:12		
	1571:11-12		13:34;15:12		
	1944:23-31		13:34;15;12		
	(COMPARE: The Golden Rule: Do Unto Others, etc.:)				
	1445:47-48	6:31		Mt 7:12 To 4:15	
	1454:35-36	6:31		Mt 7:12 To 4:15	

(Mark 12:31 Continued on next page.)

Mark 12:31 to 13:10

MARK Chap:Verse	The URANTIA Book Page:Line	MATTHEW Chap:Verse	LUKE Chap:Verse	JOHN Chap:Verse	Other BOOKS Chap:Verse
12:31	1464:37-38	6:31			Mt 7:12 To 4:15
	1585:29-32	6:31			Mt 7:12 To 4:15
	1650:15-1651:21	6:31			Mt 7:12 To 4:15
	1771: 2- 3	6:31			Mt 7:12 To 4:15
	1931:23-24	6:31			Mt 7:12 To 4:15
	1949:43-1950:28	6:31			Mt 7:12 To 4:15
12:32	(One God, See Mark 12:29, above.)				
12:32-34	1901:24-31		10:27		
12:33	(Love God, See Mark 12:30, above.)				
	(Love Neighbor as Self, See Mark 12:31, above.)				
12:35-37	(Jesus' Relationship to David:)				
	1348: 5- 6	22:41-46	20:41-44		
	1901:40-1902:6	22:41-46	20:41-44		Ps 110:1
12:37	1902:15-16				
	2090:45				
12:38-40	(Woe to Those Seeking Self-Honor:)				
	1826:22-24	23:6-7	11:43		
		23:14	20:46-47		
	1907: 1- 8	(Same as 1826:22-24, above)			
12:41-44	(The Widow's Mite:)				
	1883:26-34		21:1-4		
13: 1- 2	(Jesus Foretells Destruction of Temple:)				
	1414: 8- 9	24:1-2	21:5-6;19:44		
	1912: 3-10	24:1-2	21:5-6;19:44		
	1934:31-32	24:1-2	21:5-6;19:44		
13: 3- 4	1912:21-24	24:3	21:7		
13: 5-13	(Jesus Foretells Confusion and Persecution:)				
	1912:29-1913:6	24:4-14	21:8-17		
			10:17-22		
13: 7	0597:20	24:6			
13: 7-8	1490:30-32	24:6-7	21;9-10		
13: 8	0597:20-21	24:7	21:10		
13: 9-13	1584:10-17	24:9	21:12-17		
			12:11-12		
13:10	(The Great Commission;)				
	1051: 8	24:14	24:47	20:21	Ac 1:8
		28:19-20			Mk 16:15
	1584: 4- 6	(Same as 1051: 8, above)			

(Mark 13:10 Continued on next page.)

MARK Chap:Verse	The URANTIA Book Page:Line	MATTHEW Chap:Verse	LUKE Chap:Verse	JOHN Chap:Verse	Other BOOKS Chap:Verse
13:10	1608:22	(Same as 1051: 8, above)			
	1824:43-44	(Same as 1051: 8, above)			
	1934:28-30	(Same as 1051: 8, above)			
	1957:35-37	(Same as 1051: 8, above)			
	1961:49	(Same as 1051: 8, above)			
	2033:15-18	(Same as 1051: 8, above)			
	2034: 2- 3	(Same as 1051: 8, above)			
	2042: 8- 9	(Same as 1051: 8, above)			
	2043: 3- 6	(Same as 1051: 8, above)			
	2044:35-36	(Same as 1051: 8, above)			
	2052:39-40	(Same as 1051: 8, above)			
	2053:14-16	(Same as 1051: 8, above)			
	2053:38-40	(Same as 1051: 8, above)			
	2054: 5- 6	(Same as 1051: 8, above)			
	2054:25-27	(Same as 1051: 8, above)			
	2054:41-42	(Same as 1051: 8, above)			
	2055:16-18	(Same as 1051: 8, above)			
	2057:24-25	(Same as 1051: 8, above)			
13:12	1951:29-30	10:21	21:16		
13:14-16	1913:26-31	24:15-18	21:20-21		
13:14-19	1934:32-33	24:15-21	21:20-24		
13:19	1913:31-32	24:21	21:22		
13:21	1536:29-30	24:23			
13:21-23	1913:35-38	24:23-25			
13:24-27	(Conceptions about the Coming Kingdom:)				
	1860:39-40	24:29-31	21:25-28		
	1863:43-47	24:29-31	21:25-28		
13:26	(Jesus'Return in Power & Glory, See Mark 8:38, above.)				
	0596:38	24:30	21:27		Mk 8:38
		16:27;25:31	9:26		
	1591:16-17	24:30	21:27		Ac 1:8
	1860:16-17	(Same as 0596:38, above)			
	1915: 1- 4	(Same as 0596:38, above)			
	2092:42-43	(Same as 0596:38, above)			
13:27	0568:45-0569:1	24:31			
	1247:32-33	24:31			
13:28-29	1915:15-19	24:32-33	21:29-31		
13:30	1915:11-12	24:34	21:32		

Mark 13:31 to 14:22

MARK Chap:Verse	The URANTIA Book Page:Line	MATTHEW Chap:Verse	LUKE Chap:Verse	JOHN Chap:Verse	Other BOOKS Chap:Verse
13:31	1736:20-21	24:35	21:33		
	1914: 2	24:35	21:33		2Pe 3:10
13:32-33	(Jesus' Return to Earth:)				
	0227:18-27	24:27-37		14:3	
		24:42;25:13			
	0409:10	(Same as 0227:18-27, above)			
	1319: 6- 8	(Same as 0227:18-27, above)			
	1915: 5- 6	(Same as 0227:18-27, above)			
	1915:20-24	(Same as 0227:18-27, above)			
	1916:25-27	(Same as 0227:18-27, above)			
	1918:47-48	(Same as 0227:18-27, above)			
13:33-37	1915:30-42		21:20-36		
14: 1	1924:28-34	26:3-4	22:2		
14: 2	1925:43-46	26:5	22:2		
14: 3	1878:34-36	26:6		12:1-2	
	1879:42-44	26:7		12:3	
14: 3- 5	1879:10-21	26:7-8		11:2;12:3-5	
14: 6- 9	1879:22-37	26:10-13		12:7-8	
	1879:38-39	26:10-13		12:7-8	
14:10	(Judas Agrees to Betray Jesus:)				
	1567:21-27	26:14-16	22:4-5		
	1924:24-28	26:14-16	22:4-5		
	1925:47-1926:6	26:14-16	22:4-5		
	1998:11-13	26:14-16	22:4-5		Mt 27:3
14:11	1926: 9-12	26:16	22:6		
14:12	1933:12-14	26:17	22:8-9		
14:13-15	1933:22-28	26:18	22:10-12		
14:16	1933:29-32	26:19	22:13		
14:17	1937:35-38	26:20	22:14		
14:18	1940:28-35	26:21		13:21	
	1940:44-45	26:23			Mk 14:20
14:19	1940:36-39	26:22		13:22	
14:20	1940:44-45	26:23			Mk 14:18
14:21	1940:40-44	26:24	22:21-22		
14:22-25	(The Remembrance Supper--Eucharist:)				
	1941:40-1943:14	26:26-29	22:19-20		1Co 11:23-25

MARK Chap:Verse	The URANTIA Book Page:Line	MATTHEW Chap:Verse	LUKE Chap:Verse	JOHN Chap:Verse	Other BOOKS Chap:Verse
14:22	1942: 9-14	26:26	22:19	6:35,48	1Co 11:23-24
	(Jesus as the Bread of Life:)				
	1711:14-16	5:6;26:26	22:19	6:35,48,51,58	
	1711:38-43	5:6;26:26	22:19	6:35,48,51,58	
	1942: 9-16	5:6;26:26	22:19	6:35,48,51,58	
	1965:29	5:6;26:26	22:19	6:35,48,51,58	
14:23-25	1941:41-47	26:27-29	22:20		1Co 11:25-26
14:25	1938: 8-11	26:29	22:18		
14:26	1943:12-14	26:30			
	1962:37-38				
14:27	1962:13-18	26:31			Zc 13:7
	1976:34	26:31			Zc 13:7
14:28	(Jesus Foretells His Resurrection Appearances:)				
	1952: 5-25	26:32		14:28;16:16-22	
	1954:11-13	26:32		14:28;16:16-22	
	1962:17-19	26:32		14:28;16:16-22	
14:29	1962:20-22	26:33,35	22:33	13:37	
14:30	1962:24-27	26:34	22:34	13:38	
14:32-33	1968: 5-11	26:36-37	22:39-41		
14:34	1968:18-20	26:38,40			Mk 14:37
14:35	1968: 9-14	26:39	22:41-42		
14:35-36	(Prayer, See Mark 11:24, above.)				
14:36	(With God, all things possible;)				
	0034:13-14	19:26	1:37;18:27		Mk 10:27
	0046:42	19:26	1:37;18:27		Mk 10:27
	0291:26-27	19:26	1:37;18:27		Mk 10:27
	1453:41	19:26	1:37;18:27		Mk 10:27
	1757:34-35	19:26	1:37;18:27		Mk 10:27
	1803:38-40	19:26	1:37;10:27		Mk 10:27
	(Drinking the Cup:)				
	0229:46	20:22-23	22:42		Mk 10:38-39
		26:39,42,44			Mk 14:39
	1867:37-39	(Same as 0229:46, above)			
	1955:30-32	(Same as 0229:46, above)			
	1968:11-14	(Same as 0229:46, above)			
	1968:21-24	(Same as 0229:46, above)			
	1968:32-34	(Same as 0229:46, above)			
	1972: 5- 7	(Same as 0229:46, above)			

(Mark 14:36 Continued on next page.)

Mark 14:36 to 14:39

MARK Chap:Verse	The URANTIA Book Page:Line	MATTHEW Chap:Verse	LUKE Chap:Verse	JOHN Chap:Verse	Other BOOKS Chap:Verse
14:36	(Doing the Father's Will:)				
	0008:42	6:10;7:21	8:21	4:34;5:30	Mk 3:35
		12:50;26:39	11:2	6:38;7:17	Mk 14:39
		26:42,44	22:42	14:23-24	
				15:10,14	
	0052: 1- 4	(Same as 0008:42, above)			
	1200:41	(Same as 0008:42, above)			
	1221:33-34	(Same as 0008:42, above)			
	1303: 7	(Same as 0008:42, above)			
	1318:29-30	(Same as 0008:42, above)			
	1324:21-22	(Same as 0008:42, above)			
	1327:10	(Same as 0008:42, above)			
	1328:38-41	(Same as 0008:42, above)			
	1331: 9-10	(Same as 0008:42, above)			
	1417: 5- 7	(Same as 0008:42, above)			
	1453:43-44	(Same as 0008:42, above)			
	1500:27	(Same as 0008:42, above)			
	1511:47-48	(Same as 0008:42, above)			
	1514:35	(Same as 0008:42, above)			
	1569:8-9	(Same as 0008:42, above)			
	1574:21	(Same as 0008:42, above)			
	1582: 8	(Same as 0008:42, above)			
	1594:33-34	(Same as 0008:42, above)			
	1608: 1	(Same as 0008:42, above)			
	1769:42-44	(Same as 0008:42, above)			
	1774:28	(Same as 0008:42, above)			
	1947:50-1948:1	(Same as 0008:42, above)			
	1968:21-24	(Same as 0008:42, above)			
	1968:33-34	(Same as 0008:42, above)			
	1972: 5- 7	(Same as 0008:42, above)			
	2078: 8	(Same as 0008:42, above)			
	2087:11	(Same as 0008:42, above)			
	2088:30-31	(Same as 0008:42, above)			
	2089:12-14	(Same as 0008:42, above)			
	2090: 1	(Same as 0008:42, above)			
14:37	1968:16-20	26:40			Mk 14:34
14:38	1968:27-30	26:41,43	22:40,45-46		Mk 14:40
	1968:32-33	26:41			
14:39	(See Mark 14:36, above, all entries.)				

202

MARK Chap:Verse	The URANTIA Book Page:Line	MATTHEW Chap:Verse	LUKE Chap:Verse	JOHN Chap:Verse	Other BOOKS Chap:Verse
14:40	1968:27-30	26:41,43	22:40,45-46		Mk 14:38
14:41	(Jesus Foretells Betrayal, See Mark 8:31, above.)				
14:41-42	1968:31-41	26:44-46			
14:43	1973:29-36	26:47	22:47	18:3	
14:44	1974: 4- 6	26:48			
14:45	1974:30-32	26:49-50	22:47-48		
14:46-47	1974:41-50	26:50-51	22:49-51	18:10	
14:48-49	1975: 7-10	26:55	22:52-53		
14:50	1975:11-14	26:56			
14:51-52	(John Mark's Embarassment:)				
	1975:14-22				
	1975:32-34				
14:53	1980: 1- 5	26:57		18:24	
14:54	(Peter Follows Afar Off:)				
	1551:32	26:58	22:54		
	1975:32	26:58	22:54		
	1980: 7-18	26:58	22:54-55	18:15-16,18	
14:55-56	1982:27-33	26:59-60			
14:56-61	1999: 5- 6	26:60-62			
14:57-59	1982:37-40	26:60-61		2:19	
14:60-61	1982:43-45	26:62-63			
14:61-62	(Jesus Response To High Priests:)				
	1979:44-50	26:63-64	22:70		
	1983:20-27	26:63-64	22:66		
	1999: 6- 9	26:63-64	22:67-70		
14:63-64	1983:28-32	26:65-66	22:71		
14:65	(Physical Abuse of Jesus:)				
	1983:45-49	26:67	22:63		
	1984:16-22	26:67-68	22:63-65		
	2000:12-14	26:67-68	22:63-65		
14:66-68	1980:31-38	26:69-70	22:56-57	18:17	
14:66-70	1551:15-17	26:69-72	22:56-57	18:16-17	
14:66-72	1551: 6- 8	26:69-75	22:55-62	18:15-18	
14:68-70	1980:44-48	26:71-72			
14:70	1981: 3- 8	26:73-74	22:59-60	18:25	
14:71	1980:48-1981:2	26:72			
14:72	1981:13-15	26:74-75	22:60-61	18:27	
	1981:24-25	26:75	22:62		

Mark 15:1 to 15:28

MARK Chap:Verse	The URANTIA Book Page:Line	MATTHEW Chap:Verse	LUKE Chap:Verse	JOHN Chap:Verse	Other BOOKS Chap:Verse
15: 1	1985:22-46	27:1			
	1986:12-14	27:2	23:1	18:28	
15: 2	(Jesus' Response to Pilate:)				
	1991:13-14	27:11	23:3	18:33-34	
	1991:30-32	27:11	23:3	18:37-38	
	1999:10-12	27:11	23:3	18:33-37	
15: 3- 5	1990:25-44	27:12-14			
15: 6	1993:17-19	27:15	23:17	18:39	
15: 7	1993:25-29	27:16	23:19	18:40	
15: 8	1993:15-16				
15: 9	1993:32-34	27:17		18:39	
15:10	1993:45-47	27:18			
15:11	1993:34-38		23:18	18:40	
	1994:22-24	27:20			
15:12-13	1994:25-28	27:22	23:20-21		
15:14	1994:31-34	27:23	23:22		
15:15	(Release Barabbas; Scourge & Crucify Jesus;)				
	1995: 4- 6	27:26	23:23-25	19:1,16	
	1996:40-43	27:24-25	23:23-25	19:6	
	2001:29-31	27:26	23:24-25	19:16	
15:16-20	1995: 8-18	27:27-31		19:2-3	
15:20	2001:31-34	27:31			
	2001:37-38	27:31			
15:21	(Simon of Cyrenia Carries the Cross:)				
	1438:34-38	27:32	23:26		
	2006:14-20	27:32	23:26		
	2006:28-29				
15:22	2006:32-33	27:33	23:33		
15:23	2007: 7-11	27:34			
15:24	(The Crucifixion:)				
	2006:36-46	27:35	23:33	19:18	
	(Casting Lots for Garments:)				
	1341:41-43	27:35	23:34	19:23-24	Ps 22:18
	2007:44-49	27:35	23:34	19:23-24	Ps 22:18
15:25	2008: 8- 9	27:35	23:33	19:18	
15:26	(Superscription, King of the Jews:)				
	2005: 7- 9	27:37	23:38	19:19	
	2007:22-24	27:37	23:38	19:19	
15:27	2007:15-16	27:38	23:33	19:18	

MARK Chap:Verse	The URANTIA Book Page:Line	MATTHEW Chap:Verse	LUKE Chap:Verse	JOHN Chap:Verse	Other BOOKS Chap:Verse
15:29-32	1520: 6- 7	27:39-44	23:35		
	2008:20-28	27:39-44	23:35-37		
15:31	1518:31-32	27:42			
15:33	2010: 9-13	27:45	23:44-45		
	2011:34	27:45	23:44-45		
15:34	2010:21-38	27:46			Ps 20:6;21:8;22:1
15:36	2010:39-42	27:48		19:28-29	
	2063: 5- 6	27:41-43,49			
15:37	2011: 3- 5	27:50	23:46	19:30	
15:39	1590: 4	27:54	23:47		
	2011: 5- 7	27:54	23:47		
15:40	1357: 5- 6	13:55;27:56			Ga 1:19
	1362: 1- 2	13:55;27:56			
15:40-41	(Faithful Women's Corps:)				
	1403:35-36	27:55-56	8:2-3 23:27,49 24:10	19:25	Ac 1:14
	1671:20-26	(Same as 1403:35-36, above)			
	1678:28-1679:15	(Same as 1403:35-36, above)			
	1680:21-22	(Same as 1403:35-36, above)			
15:40	1680:28-29	(Same as 1403:35-36, above)			
	2005:33-45	(Same as 1403:35-36, above)			
	2008:14-17	(Same as 1403:35-36, above)			
15:41	1403:35-36	27:55-56	24:10	19:25;23:27-40	
15:42	2011:19		23:54	19:31,42	
15:42-45	2012:18-26	27:57-58	23:50-52	19:38	
15:46	2013:17-33	27:59-60	23:53	19:39-41	
15:47	2013:38-47	27:61	23:55-56		
16: 1- 2	2025:30-39	28:1	24:1	20:1	
16: 3- 4	2025:45-47		24:2	20:1	
16: 5- 6	2026:32-49	28:5-6,9	24:4-8	20:11-16	Mk 16:9
16: 7	(Go Tell Disciples:)				
	2027:46-2028:1	28:7		20:17	
	(---And Peter:)				
	2027: 4- 7	28:7		20:17	
	2037:35				
	2039:30-31				

(Mark 16:7 Continued on next page.)

205

MARK Chap:Verse	The URANTIA Book Page:Line	MATTHEW Chap:Verse	LUKE Chap:Verse	JOHN Chap:Verse	Other BOOKS Chap:Verse
16: 7	(Go To Galilee:)				
	1962:18-19	28:7,10			
	2028: 1- 2	28:7,10			
	2043:49-50	28:7,10			
16: 8	2027: 8-10	28:8	24:9	20:18	
16: 9	2026:32-49	28:9	24:4-8	20:12-16	Mk 16:5-6
16:10-11	2027: 8-11	28:8	24:9	20:18	
16:12	2034:27-37		24:13-16		
16:13	2036: 6-13		24:33-35		
16:14	2040:18-29		24:36-38	20:19	1Co 15:5
			24:44-46		
16:15	(The Great Commission:)				
	1051: 8	24:14	24:47	20:21	Ac 1:8
		28:19-20			Mk 13:10
	1584: 4- 6	(Same as 1051: 8, above)			
	1608:22	(Same as 1051: 8, above)			
	1824:43-44	(Same as 1051: 8, above)			
	1934:28-30	(Same as 1051: 8, above)			
	1957:35-37	(Same as 1051: 8, above)			
	2033:17-18	(Same as 1051: 8, above)			
	2034: 2- 3	(Same as 1051: 8, above)			
	2042: 8- 9	(Same as 1051: 8, above)			
	2043: 3- 6	(Same as 1051: 8, above)			
	2044:35-36	(Same as 1051: 8, above)			
	2052:39-40	(Same as 1051: 8, above)			
	2053:14-16	(Same as 1051: 8, above)			
	2053:38-40	(Same as 1051: 8, above)			
	2054: 5- 6	(Same as 1051: 8, above)			
	2054:25-27	(Same as 1051: 8, above)			
	2054:41-42	(Same as 1051: 8, above)			
	2055:16-18	(Same as 1051: 8, above)			
	2057:24-25	(Same as 1051: 8, above)			
16:16	2053:42-43				
16:19	(Right Hand of The Father:)				
	0064:33	22:44	20:42		Ps 110:1 Ro 8:34
					Cl 3:1 He 10:12 1Pe 3:22
	0239:45-46	(Same as 0064:33, above)			
	0418: 6- 7	(Same as 0064:33, above)			
	2057:35-42	(Same as 0064:33, above)			

C: The Gospel According to LUKE

LUKE Chap:Verse	The URANTIA Book Page:Line	MATTHEW Chap:Verse	MARK Chap:Verse	JOHN Chap:Verse	Other BOOKS Chap:Verse
1: 5	1334:27-30				
	1496:18-20				
1: 5- 7	1345:22-26				
1: 8-10	1345:30-31				
1:11	0407:17-18	1:20			Ge 16:7
1:11-17	1345:27-38				
1:11-24	1496: 3- 9				
1:15	1496:28-36				
1:17	1502: 7- 8				
1:18-21	1345:44-1346: 5				
1:24	1345:43-44				
	1345:47				
1:26-27	1346: 6- 7	1:18-21			
1:26-38	(The Annunciation to Mary:)				
	1346: 6- 7				
	1346:31-44				
	1347:17-19				
1:27	(Joseph & Mary:)				
	1345:15-20	1:18-21,25			Lk 2:4-5
	1349:20-23	1:18-21,25			Lk 2:4-5
	1350:22	1:18-21,25			Lk 2:4-5
	(The Lineage of Joseph:)				
	1344:26-33	1:6-16			Lk 2:4-5;3:23-31
	1347:37-42	1:6-16			Lk 2:4-5;3:23-31
1:32-33	1347:32-36				
1:33	1568:28-30				
1:37	(With God All Things are Possible:)				
	0034:13-14	19:26	10:27;14:36		Lk 18:27
	0046:42	19:26	10:27;14:36		Lk 18:27
	0291:26-27	19:26	10:27;14:36		Lk 18:27
	1453:41	19:26	10:27;14:36		Lk 18:27
	1757:34-35	19:26	10:27;14:36		Lk 18:27
	1803:38-40	19:26	10:27;14:36		Lk 18:27
1:39-40	1346: 7-16				
1:56	1346:12-13				
1:57	1496: 3- 4				
1:57-66	1346:17-20				

LUKE Chap:Verse	The URANTIA Book Page:Line	MATTHEW Chap:Verse	MARK Chap:Verse	JOHN Chap:Verse	Other BOOKS Chap:Verse
1:59-80	1496:10				
1:67	1353:12-14				Lk 2:27-28
1:68	1864:25-27	—	—		Ga 3:13
1:68-79	1353:15-34				
1:79	(Jesus is Light:)				
	0447:38-39	4:16		1:4;8:12 Lk 2:32 Is 9:2	
				9:5;12:46 1Jo 2:8	
	0513:31	(Same as 0447:38-39, above)			
	0590:33	(Same as 0447:38-39, above)			
	1104:14-15	(Same as 0447:38-39, above)			
	1181: 7- 8	(Same as 0447:38-39, above)			
	1353:38-39	(Same as 0447:38-39, above)			
	1458:33-39	(Same as 0447:38-39, above)			
	1671:10-11	(Same as 0447:38-39, above)			
	1795: 1	(Same as 0447:38-39, above)			
	1965:31	(Same as 0447:38-39, above)			
	2035:28-29	(Same as 0447:38-39, above)			
	(Children of Light, See Luke 16:8, below.)				
1:80	(John The Baptist's Youth:)				
	1346:24-29				
	1496:10-23				
	1497: 5-11	3:4	1:6		
2: 1	1350:22-30				
2: 4	1347:38-42	1:14-16			Lk 3:23-24
2: 4- 5	(Joseph and Mary, See Luke 1:27, above.)				
	(The Lineage of Joseph, See Like 1:27, above.)				
	1350:31-41				
2: 6- 7	1351:29-34	1:25			
2: 7	1351:16-20				
2: 7-11	0584: 9-10	2:1-2		1:14	
2: 8-18	1352: 7-12				
2: 9-14	1316:42-44				
2:14	(Peace on Earth, Good Will Among Men:)				
	0437:32-33				
	0437:38				
	0597:14				
	1491:32-34				
	1565:11				

(Luke 2:14 Continued on next page.)

LUKE Chap:Verse	The URANTIA Book Page:Line	MATTHEW Chap:Verse	MARK Chap:Verse	JOHN Chap:Verse	Other BOOKS Chap:Verse
2:14	1569: 1				
	1777:15				
	1801: 3- 4				
	(The Peace of Jesus, Beyond all Understanding)				
	0066:46-47			14:27	Pp 4:7
				16:33	
	1101:6-8	(Same as 0066:46-47, above)			
	1627:32-33	(Same as 0066:46-47, above)			
	1663:13-14	(Same as 0066:46-47, above)			
	1954: 7- 9	(Same as 0066:46-47, above)			
	1954:28-47	(Same as 0066:46-47, above)			Is 53:3
	1955: 7- 9	(Same as 0066:46-47, above)			
	2042:13-14	(Same as 0066:46-47, above)			
	2054:43	(Same as 0066:46-47, above)			
2:20	1352: 7-12				
2:21	1351:35-37				
2:22-24	0935:36-38				Le 12:2-8
	1352:37-47	_	_		Le 12:2-8
2:25	1502: 1				
2:25-26	1353: 1- 5				
2:27-28	1353: 8-14	_	_		Lk 1:67
2:29-32	1353:35-39				
2:32	(Jesus as Light, See Luke 1:79, above.)				
2:33	1353:40-43	_	_		Lk 2:38
2:36	1353: 1- 5				
2:38	1353:41-42	_	_		Lk 2:33
2:39	1356:22-24				
	1356:32-33				
2:40	1342:16-17	_	_		Ac 15:11
	1356:39-40				
2:42	1374: 4-1375:35				
2:43-44	1381: 5-27				
2:45	1381:41-42				
2:46-48	1383:46-1384: 7				
2:49	("My Father's Business":)				
	1102:48				
	1316:16				
	1384:21-24				

(Luke 2:49 Continued on next page.)

LUKE Chap:Verse	The URANTIA Book Page:Line	MATTHEW Chap:Verse	MARK Chap:Verse	JOHN Chap:Verse	Other BOOKS Chap:Verse
2:49	1389:46-47				
	1390:45				
	1403:15				
2:50-51	1384:37-39				
2:52	1387:46-47				
3: 1	1512:23-29				
3: 2	1497:30-33	3:1			
	1499:15-48	3:1			
3: 3	1501:37-42	3:1-6	1:4		
	1502:11-13	3:1-6	1:4		
	(Baptism:)				
	0947: 1- 2	3:6,11	1:4,8	1:25-28,33	Lk 3:16
	0964:37	3:6,11	1:4,8	1:25-28,33	Lk 3:16
	1502:13	3:6,11	1:4,8	1:25-28,33	Lk 3:16
	1593:11-13	3:6,11	1:4,8	1:25-28,33	Lk 3:16
	(Baptism of Repentance:)				
	1502:11-20	3:6,11	1:4,8	1:25-28,33	Ac 13:24
	1503:31	3:6,11	1:4,8	1:25-28,33	Ac 13:24
	1510:26-27	3:6,11	1:4,8	1:25-28,33	Ac 13:24
	1536:34-36	3:6,11	1:4,8	1:25-28,33	Ac 13:24
	1584:31-32	3:6,11	1:4,8	1:25-28,33	Ac 13:24
	1625:30-35	3:6,11	1:4,8	1:25-28,33	Ac 13:24
3: 4- 6	1501:29-35	3:3	1:2-3		
	1502:25-33	3:3	1:3	1:22-23	
3: 7	1545:39	3:7			
	(Baptism, See Luke 3:3, above.)				
	(Baptism of Repentance, See Luke 3:3, above.)				
3: 7	1502:34-38	3:7			
3: 8- 9	(Requirement for Good Fruit:)				
	1502:38-44	3:8-9		15:2,8,16	
		7:16-20			Lk 6:43-44;13:6-9
		12:33			Ga 5:22-23 Ep 5:9
	1569: 6- 8	(Same as 1502:38-44, above)			
	1571:32-37	(Same as 1502:38-44, above)			
	1572:27-30	(Same as 1502:38-44, above)			
	1582:33-34	(Same as 1502:38-44, above)			
	1596:26-27	(Same as 1502:38-44, above)			
	1601: 8-10	(Same as 1502:38-44, above)			

(Luke 3:8-9 Continued on next page.)

LUKE Chap:Verse	The URANTIA Book Page:Line	MATTHEW Chap:Verse	MARK Chap:Verse	JOHN Chap:Verse	Other BOOKS Chap:Verse
3: 8- 9	1714:36-38	(Same as 1502 38-44, above)			
	1830:39-45	(Same as 1502:38-44, above)			
	1917:30-32	(Same as 1502:38-44, above)			
	1945:40-47	(Same as 1502:38-44, above)			
	1946:21-26	(Same as 1502:38-44, above)			
	2054:33-39	(Same as 1502:38-44, above)			
	(For Fruits of the Spirit, See Ga 5:22-23, Ep 5:9.)				
3:10-14	1502:47-1503: 2				
3:15	1334: 4- 8				
	1509: 3- 5				
3:15-18	1503:20-28	3:11-12	1:7-8	1:27	
3:16	(Baptism, See Luke 3:3, above.)				
3:19-20	1506:31-40	14:2-3	6:17		
3:21	1511:48	3:16	1:10		
3:21-22	(The Baptism of Jesus:)				
	1504:11-42	3:13-17	1:9-11		
	1510:45-46	3:13-17	1:9-11		
3:22	(The Descending Spirit:)				
	1506: 6	3:16	1:10		
	1511:37-38	3:16	1:10		
	1511:42-43	3:16	1:10		
	(Voice, Beloved Son/Well Pleased:)				
	0538:10-11	3:17	1:11		
	1506: 7- 8	3:17	1:11		
	1511:38-42	3:17	1:11		
	1512: 5- 7	3:17	1:11		
	1545:21-22	3:17	1:11		
	(For Voice on Mountain, See Luke 9:35, below.)				
3:23-31	1347:37	1:6-16			Lk 1:27;2:4-5
3:23	1512:22				
3:23-24	1347:39-42	1:14-16			Lk 2:4
3:23-37	1348: 7-11	1:2-16			
3:23-38	1344:26-33	1:1-16			
4: 1	1492:33-36	4:1			
4: 1- 2	1515:25-26	4:1	1:12-13		
4: 1-13	(The Temptation:)				
	1493:33-1494: 6	4:1-11	1:12-13		
	1512:30-34	4:1-11	1:12-13		
	1514:38-39	4:1-11	1:12-13		

Luke 4:2 to 4:27

LUKE Chap:Verse	The URANTIA Book Page:Line	MATTHEW Chap:Verse	MARK Chap:Verse	JOHN Chap:Verse	Other BOOKS Chap:Verse
4: 2	1504:42-44	4:2	1:12-13		
4: 2-4	(Hunger/Fasting:)				
	1493:14-15	4:2	1:13		
	1514:24-28	4:2	1:13		
4: 3- 4	(Easy Food, Man Cannot live on Bread Alone:)				
	1517:46-48	4:2-4			
	1518:23-28	4:2-4			De 8:3
	1777:21	4:4			De 8:3
4: 5- 8	1522: 1-18	4:8-10			De 6:13-14;10:20
	1522:33-34	4:8-10			
4: 8	(Satan:)				
	0602: 1- 2	4:10	1:13		1Ch 21:1
	0609:44-45	4:10	1:13		
		16:23	8:33		
	(Worship/Serve Only God:)				
	1522:17-18	4:10			De 6:13-14
4: 9-11	(Personal Safety:)				
	1519:27-33	4:5-6			
	1521: 2- 5	4:5-6			
4:16	1683:36-43		6:1		
	1684:37-38	13:54	6:2		
4:17	1685:45-49				
4:17-19	1686: 7-11				Is 61:1-2
4:18	(Freeing Spiritual Captives:)				
	1328:14-15	—	—		Is 61:1
	1570:23-24				Is 61:1
	(Gospel for All, Beginning With Needy and Oppressed:)				
	1594:12-13	11:5			Lk 7:22;14:13
	1608:18-20	11:5			Lk 7:22;14:13
	1859:39-40	11:5			Lk 7:22;14:13
4:20-21	1686:12-16	13:54	6:2		
4:22	(Joseph' Son:)				
	1051:11	13:55	6:3	1:45;6:42	
	1686:28-31	13:55	6:3	1:45;6:42	
	1711:22-24	13:55-56	6:3	1:45;6:42	
4:23	1686:30-33	13:55	6:3		
4:24	1538:19	13:57	6:4	4:44	
	1686:30-33	13:57	6:4	4:44	
4:25-27	1686:41-44				

LUKE Chap:Verse	The URANTIA Book Page:Line	MATTHEW Chap:Verse	MARK Chap:Verse	JOHN Chap:Verse	Other BOOKS Chap:Verse
4:25-27	1686:41-44				
4:28-30	1686:45-1687:14				Pv 15:1
4:31	(At Capernaum:)				
	1628: 3- 4		1:21		
	1629:18-19		1:21		
	1687:16-17		1:21		
4:31-32	1630:42-44	7:28-29	1:22		
4:33-35	1630:45-1631: 2		1:23-26		
4:36-37	1631:14-19		1:27-28		
4:38-39	1631:22-27	8:14-15	1:29-31		
4:40-41	1632: 1-1633:15	8:16	1:32-34		
4:42	1634:42-45		1:35		
	1635:20-28		1:37		
4:43	1635:41-1636: 3		1:38		
4:44	1636: 9-10		1:39		
5: 1- 3	1628:27-35	4:18	1:16		
5: 1- 9	1524: 9-1525:2	4:18-20	1:16-18		
5: 4-11	1628:36-1629:11	4:19-22	1:17-20		
5: 4- 9	(The Call of Simon Peter and Andrew:				
	1524: 9-1525:2	4:18-20	1:16-18	1:40-42	
	1548:29-35				
	1550:24-27				
5:10	(Fear Not:)				
	1103:14	10:31			Lk 8:50;12:7,22
	1582:19-20	10:31			Lk 8:50;12:7,32
	(Fishing Partners:)				
	1548:34-35	4:18	1:16		
	1550:26-27	4:18	1:16		
	(Fishers of Men:)				
	1544:47	4:19	1:17		
5:10-11	(The Call of James and John:)				
	1525: 7-46	4:21-22	1:19-20		
	1552:22-28	4:21-22	1:19-20		
	1553:40-43	4:21-22	1:19-20		
5:12-13	(Faith Makes Whole:)				
	1643:27-41	8:2-3,13	1:40-41		Lk 8:48,50
		9:2,22,29	2:5;5:34		Lk 17:19
		15:28	10:52		Lk 18:42

(Luke 5:12-13 Continuewd on next page.)

LUKE Chap:Verse	The URANTIA Book Page:Line	MATTHEW Chap:Verse	MARK Chap:Verse	JOHN Chap:Verse	Other BOOKS Chap:Verse
5:12-13	1648: 7-13	(Same as 1643:27-41, above)			
	1667:12	(Same as 1643:27-41, above)			
	1698:33-1699:6	(Same as 1643:27-41, above)			
	1735:21-25	(Same as 1643:27-41, above)			
	1828:10-11	(Same as 1643:27-41, above)			
	1873:28-29	(Same as 1643:27-41, above)			
	1875:13-14	(Same as 1643:27-41, above)			
	1905:23-24	(Same as 1643:27-41, above)			
5:12-15	1643:42-1644:3	8:4	1:43-45		
5:14	(Tell no man:)				
	1520:20-21	8:4	1:44;5:43		Lk 8:56
		9:30	7:36;8:26		
	1643:42-43	(Same as 1520:20-21, above)			
	1669:14-16	(Same as 1520:20-21, above)			
	1699:32-33	(Same as 1520:20-21, above)			
5:17	1666:30-38		2:1-2		
5:18-20	1666:39-1667:12	9:2-3	2:3-5		
	1905:23-24	9:2	2:3-5		
5:21-26	1667:13-27	9:3-8	2:6-12		
5:24	1407:27	8:20	2:10	1:51	
5:27-28	(The Call of Matthew Levi:)				
	1540:16-21	9:9;10:3	2:14;3:18		Lk 6:15 Ac 1:13
	1559:20-1560:49	9:9;10:3	2:14;3:18		Lk 6:15 Ac 1:13
	1957:43-44	9:9;10:3	2:14;3:18		Lk 6:15 Ac 1:13
5:29-30	(Friend of Publicans and Sinners:)				
	1342:17-18	9:10-11;11:19	2:15-16		Lk 7:34; 15:2
	1540:31-1541:3	(Same as 1342:17-18, above)			
	1627:26-27	(Same as 1342:17-18, above)			
	1850:18-19	(Same as 1342:17-18, above)			
	1851: 7- 8	(Same as 1342:17-18, above)			
5:31-32	(Jesus Calls Sinners to Repentance:)				
	1537:17-19	9:12-13	2:17		
	1541: 3-14	9:12-13	2:17		
	1750:10-11	9:12-13	2:17		
5:33-35	(Fasting:)				
	0976:16-17	9:14-15	2:18-20		2Sa 12:16;21:23 Is 58:3-6 Ps 35:13
	1609:24-25	9:14-15	2:18-20		
	1635:28-37	9:14-15	2:18-20		

LUKE Chap:Verse	The URANTIA Book Page:Line	MATTHEW Chap:Verse	MARK Chap:Verse	JOHN Chap:Verse	Other BOOKS Chap:Verse
5:37-38	1655:38-47	9:16-17	2:21-22		
5:39	1656: 3- 9				
6: 1-10	(Use of The Sabbath:)				
	1649:47-1650:5	12:1-8	2:23-28	5:5-9	Lk 11:37-41
		12:9-14	3:1-5	5:16-18	Lk 13:10-17
		15:1-9	7:1-13	9:14	Lk 14:1-6
				De 5:12-15	Ex 20:8-11
	1654:29-1655:12	(Same as 1649:47-1650:5, above.)			
	1665: 7-35	(Same as 1649:47-1650:5, above.)			
	1712:21-42	(Same as 1649:47-1650:5, above.)			
	1813:13-16	(Same as 1649:47-1650:5, above.)			
	1834: 6-32	(Same as 1649:47-1650:5, above.)			
	1835:40-1836:26	(Same as 1649:47-1650:5, above.)			
	1850:22-23	(Same as 1649:47-1650:5, above.)			
6: 3- 4	1655: 2- 5	12:3-4	2:25-26		1Sa 21:3-6
6: 6-11	1665: 7-35	12:9-14	3:1-6		
	1850:22-23	12:9-14	3:1-6		
6:11-12	(The Ordination of the Twelve on The Mountain:)				
	1568:2	10:1	6:13		
	(The Ordination Sermon:)				
	1570: 8-1571:46	5:3-7:27			
	(The Commission:)				
	1584: 1- 6	10:1,7-8	3:13-15		Lk 10:9
	1590:44-45	10:1,7-9	3:13-15		LK 10:9
6:14-16	(The 12 Apostles Listed:)				
	1548: 2-1567:47	10:2-4	3:16-19		Ac 1:13
6:14	(Simon Peter:)				
	1524:25-1525:2	4:18-20	1:16-18	1:41	Ac 1:13
		10:2	3:16		
	1549:10-12	(Same as 1524:25-1525:2, above)			
	1550:23-1552:20	(Same as 1524:25-1525:2, above)			
	1628:27-1628:11		5:1-11		
	(Andrew:)				
	1524: 9-20	10:2;3:18	1:16-18	1:40	Ac 1:13
	1548:28-1550:22	10:2;3:18	1:16-18	1:40	Ac 1:13
	1628:27-1628:11		5:1-11		

(Luke 6:14 Continued on next page.)

215

LUKE Chap:Verse	The URANTIA Book Page:Line	MATTHEW Chap:Verse	MARK Chap:Verse	JOHN Chap:Verse	Other BOOKS Chap:Verse
6:14	(James and John:)				
	1525: 7-46	4:21-22	1:19-20		Ac 1:13
	10:2	3:17		Ac 1:13	
	1552:21-1556:4	10:2	6:14	Mk 1:19-20	Ac 1:13
	1628:27-1628:11		5:1-11		
	1955:37				
	(Phillip:)				
	1526:21-44	10:3	3:18	1:43-44	Ac 1:13
	1556: 5-1558:6	10:3	3:18	1:43-44	Ac 1:13
	(Nathaniel, Son of Bartholomew:)				
	1526:45-1527:13	10:3	3:18	1:45-49	Ac 1:13
	1557:21-23				
	1558: 7-1559:19	10:3	3:18	1:45-49	Ac 1:13
6:15	(Matthew Levi, See Luke 5:27-28, above)				
	(Thomas Didymus:)				
	1542: 4- 9	10:3	3:18	11:16	Ac 1:13
	1561: 1-1563:13	10:3	3:18	11:16	Ac 1:13
	(Simon the Zealot:)				
	1540:27-30	10:4	3:18		Ac 1:13
	1564:33-1565:40	10:4	3:18		Ac 1:13
6:15-16	(The Alpheus Twins: James the Lesser, also called Thaddeus; and Judas, also called Lebbeus:)				
	1541:26-31	10:3	3:18		Ac 1:13
	1563:14-1564:32	10:3	3:18		Ac 1:13
6:16	(Judas Iscariot:)				
	1542:4-11	10:4	3:19	12:4	
	1565:41-1567:47	10:4	3:19	12:4	
6:19	1669:20-22				
6:20	(Blessed are Poor:)				
	1570:27-28	5:3			
	1573:42	5:3			
	2093:16	5:3			
6:20-38	1859:41-42	5:3-48			
6:21	(Blessed, those who Hunger;)				
	1570:29-30	5:6			
	1574: 6- 7	5:6			
	1739:20	5:6			
	1861:12-13	5:6			

(Luke 6:21 Continued on next page.)

LUKE Chap:Verse	The URANTIA Book Page:Line	MATTHEW Chap:Verse	MARK Chap:Verse	JOHN Chap:Verse	Other BOOKS Chap:Verse
6:21	1865:14-16	5:6			
	2054:19-20	5:6			
	(Blessed, those who Weep:)				
	1570:35-36	5:4			
	1575: 3	5:4			
	1776:41	5:4			
6:22-23	(Blessed, the Hated and Reproached:)				
	1570:39-42	5:10-12			
	1575:34-37	5:10-12			
	1860: 3- 5	5:10-12			
6:27-28	(Love Your Enemies:)				
	1206:40-42	5:43-44			Lk 6:35
	1454:44	5:43-44			Lk 6:35
	1571:10-11	5:43-44			Lk 6:35
	1580: 7	5:43-44			Lk 6:35
	1860: 3- 5	5:43-44			Lk 6:35
	1897:16-17	5:43-44			Lk 6:35
6:27-31	1454:20-21	5:38-45			
6:27-38	1771: 2- 3	5:38-48			
6:28	(Seek Good for Adversaries:)				
	1640: 1- 2	5:44			
	1932:20-21	5:43-44			Lk 6:35
6:29-30	(Turn Cheek, Let Go, Don't Strive:)				
	1571: 5- 7	5:39			
	1770: 8-12	5:39			
	1770:29-30	5:40			
6:31	(Golden Rule:)				
	1445:47-48	7:12			To 4:15 Ga 5:14
	1454:35-36	7:12			To 4:15 Ga 5:14
	1464:37-38	7:12			To 4:15 Ga 5:14
	1571:11-12	7:12			To 4:15 Ga 5:14
	1585:30	7:12			To 4:15 Ga 5:14
	1650:15-1651:21	7:12			To 4:15 Ga 5:14
	1771: 2- 3	7:12			To 4:15 Ga 5:14
	1931:23-24	7:12			To 4:15 Ga 5:14
	1949:43-1950:28	7:12			To 4:15 Ga 5:14
6:35	(Love Your Enemies, See Luke 6:27-28, above.)				
	(For Rewards, See Luke 12:33-34, below.)				
6:36	1571:15-16				

LUKE Chap:Verse	The URANTIA Book Page:Line	MATTHEW Chap:Verse	MARK Chap:Verse	JOHN Chap:Verse	Other BOOKS Chap:Verse
6:36-37	1639: 8-10	7:1-2			
6:36-38	1475: 4- 7	6:12,14-15	11:25-26		Lk 11:4
		7:2;18:21-35			
6:37	(Judge Not:)				
	1454:43	7:1-2			
	1474:44-1475:7	7:1-2			
	1571:18-20	7:1-2			
	1580:42	7:1			
	1639: 8-10	7:1-2			
	(Forgive and be Forgiven:)				
	1475: 4- 7	6:12,14-15	11:25-26		Lk 11:4
		18:21-35			
	1638:34-41	(Same as 1475: 4- 7, above)			
	1763:23-1764:4	(Same as 1475: 4- 7, above)			
	1862: 5- 6	(Same as 1475: 4- 7, above)			
	2017:44-45	(Same as 1475: 4- 7, above)			
	(Forgive Seventy Times seven:)				
	0449:40	18:21-22			Lk 17:3-4
	1551: 4- 6	18:21-22	—		Lk 17:3-4
	1763:20-23	18:21-22			Lk 17:3-4
6:38	1474:44-45	7:2			
6:39	(Blind Lead the Blind:)				
	1571:25-26	15:14			
	1771: 9-10	15:14			
	1907:38-40	15:14;23:16			
6:40	1681:43-45			13:16	
6:41-42	1571:20-23	7:3-5			
6:43-44	(Tree known by Fruit:)				
	1502:38-44	3:8-10		15:2,8,16	Ga 5:22-23
		7:16-20			Lk 3:8-9;13:6-9
		12:33			Ep 5:9
	1569: 6- 8	(Same as 1502:38-44, above)			
	1571:32-35	(Same as 1502:38-44, above)			
	1572:27-30	(Same as 1502:38-44, above)			
	1582:33-34	(Same as 1502:38-44, above)			
	1596:26-27	(Same as 1502:38-44, above)			
	1601: 8-10	(Same as 1502:38-44, above)			
	1714:36-38	(Same as 1502:38-44, above)			

(Luke 6:43-44 Continued on next page.)

LUKE Chap:Verse	The URANTIA Book Page:Line	MATTHEW Chap:Verse	MARK Chap:Verse	JOHN Chap:Verse	Other BOOKS Chap:Verse
6:43-44	1830:39-45	(Same as 1502:38-44, above)			
	1917:30-32	(Same as 1502:38-44, above)			
	1945:40-47	(Same as 1502:38-44, above)			
	1946:21-26	(Same as 1502:38-44, above)			
	2054:33-39	(Same as 1502:38-44, above)			
6:45	1571:37-39	6:21			
6:47-49	1571:43-46	7:24-27			
	1738: 9-14	7:24-27			
7: 1-10	(Healing the Centurian's Servant:)				
	1420:26-32	8:5-13			
	1905:23-24	8:5-13			
7: 2- 5	1647:27-36	8:5-6			
7: 6- 8	1647:37-1648:6	8:7-9			
7: 9-10	1648: 7-13	8:10,13			
7:11-15	1645:19-36				
7:16	1645:39-42				
7:17	1646: 1- 3				
7:18-23	1507:36-45	11:2-6			
7:19-20	1626:38-42	11:2-3			
7:21-22	1626:43-45	11:4-5			
7:22	(Gospel for All, Beginning With Needy and Oppressed:)				
	1594:12-13	11:5			Lk 4:18;14:13 Is 61:1
	1608:18-19	11:5	—		Lk 4:18;14:13 Is 61:1
	1859:39-40	11:5			Lk 4:18;14:13 Is 61:1
7:24-27	1626:45-1627:8	11:7-10			
7:28	1509:10-13	11:11			
	1627: 9-12	11:11			
7:29	1627:13-14				
7:31-35	1627:20-27	11:16-19			
7:34	(Friend, Publicans/Sinners, See Luke 5:29-30, above:)				
7:36	1651:29-33				
7:36-38	1651:43-1652: 9				
7:39-43	1652:10-19				
7:44-48	1652:19-31				
7:49-50	1652:32-36				
8: 1	1678:19-25				
	(Glad Tidings:)				
	1509:17				
	1535:18				

Luke 8:2 to 8:21

LUKE Chap:Verse	The URANTIA Book Page:Line	MATTHEW Chap:Verse	MARK Chap:Verse	JOHN Chap:Verse	Other BOOKS Chap:Verse
8: 2- 3	(The Women's Corps:)				
	1403:35-36	27:55-56	15:40-41	19:25	Ac 1:14
					Lk 23:27,49;24:10
	1671:20-26	(Same as 1403:35-36, above)			
	1678:28-1679:15	(Same as 1403:35-36, above)			
	1680:21-24	(Same as 1403:35-36, above)			
	1680:28-29	(Same as 1403:35-36, above)			
	2005:33-45	(Same as 1403:35-36, above)			
	2008:14-19	(Same as 1403:35-36, above)			
8: 4	1688:26-29	13:1-2	4:1		
8: 5- 8	(Parable of Sower:)				
	1688:37-1689:8	13:3-9	4:3-9		
8: 8	1536:43-44	13:8	4:8		
8: 9	1689: 9-13	13:10	4:10		
8:10-11	1689:14-31	13:11-15	4:11-12		
8:11-15	1689:46-1690:17	13:18-23	4:14-20		
8:16	(Let Light Shine:)				
	1570:46-1571:2	5:15-16	4:21		Lk 11:33
	1572:13-16	5:15-16	4:21		Lk 11:33
	1692: 8-10	5:15-16	4:21		Lk 11:33
8:17	(Secrets Revealed:)				
	1682: 1- 3	10:26-27	4:22		Lk 12:2-3
	1692:10-13	10:25-27	4:22		Lk 12:2-3
	1820: 7-12	10:26-27	4:22		Lk 12:2-3
8:18	(To Whom Hath is Given, Hath Not is Taken Away:)				
	1199: 1- 3	13:12;25:29	4:25		Lk 19:26
	1689:23-24	13:12;25:29	4:25		Lk 19:26
	1692:14-16	13:12;25:29	4:25		Lk 19:26
	1876:34-36	13:12;25:29	4:25		Lk 19:26
	1917:27-28	13:12;25:29	4:25		Lk 19:26
8:19	1721: 4- 6	12:46	3:31		
8:19-20	(Jesus' Family, Mother & Brothers:)				
	1721: 4- 6	12:46-47	3:31-32		
	1721:42-48	12:46-47	3:31-32		
8:21	(Brotherhood of Man:)				
	1454:40-41	12:50	3:35		
	1722:17-19	12:50	3:35	7:17	
	1865:45-46	12:50	3:35		

(Luke 8:21 Continued on next page.)

LUKE Chap:Verse	The URANTIA Book Page:Line	MATTHEW Chap:Verse	MARK Chap:Verse	JOHN Chap:Verse	Other BOOKS Chap:Verse
8:21	(Doing the Father's Will:)				
	0008:42	6:10;7:21	3:35	4:34;5:30	Lk 11:2
		12:50;26:39	14:36	6:38;7:17	Lk 22:42
		26:42,44	14:39	14:23-24	
				15:10,14	
	0052: 1- 4	(Same as 0008:42, above)			
	1200:41	(Same as 0008:42, above)			
	1221:33-34	(Same as 0008:42, above)			
	1303: 7	(Same as 0008:42, above)			
	1318:29-30	(Same as 0008:42, above)			
	1324:21-22	(Same as 0008:42, above)			
	1327:10	(Same as 0008:42, above)			
	1328:38-41	(Same as 0008:42, above)			
	1331: 9-10	(Same as 0008:42, above)			
	1417: 5- 7	(Same as 0008:42, above)			
	1453:43-44	(Same as 0008:42, above)			
	1500:27	(Same as 0008:42, above)			
	1511:47-48	(Same as 0008:42, above)			
	1514:35	(Same as 0008:42, above)			
	1569:8-9	(Same as 0008:42, above)			
	1574:21	(Same as 0008:42, above)			
	1582: 8	(Same as 0008:42, above)			
	1594:33-34	(Same as 0008:42, above)			
	1608: 1	(Same as 0008:42, above)			
	1615:22-23	(Same as 0008:42, above)			
	1769:42-44	(Same as 0008:42, above)			
	1774:28	(Same as 0008:42, above)			
	1947:50-1948:1	(Same as 0008:42, above)			
	1968:21-24	(Same as 0008:42, above)			
	1968:33-34	(Same as 0008:42, above)			
	1972: 5- 7	(Same as 0008:42, above)			
	2078: 8	(Same as 0008:42, above)			
	2087:11	(Same as 0008:42, above)			
	2088:30-31	(Same as 0008:42, above)			
	2089:12-14	(Same as 0008:42, above)			
	2090: 1	(Same as 0008:42, above)			
8:22	1694:21-25	8:18	4:35		
8:22-23	1694:26-43	8:23-24	4:36-38		
8:24-25	1695: 3-27	8:25-27	4:38-41		

221

LUKE Chap:Verse	The URANTIA Book Page:Line	MATTHEW Chap:Verse	MARK Chap:Verse	JOHN Chap:Verse	Other BOOKS Chap:Verse
8:26	1695:35-39	8:28	5:1		
8:26-33	(Healing the Gadarene of "Unclean Spirits":)				
	1765: 8-12	8:28-32	5:1-13		
8:27	1695:40-48	8:28	5:2-4		
8:28	1696: 9-11	8:29	5 6-7		
8:29	1695:44-48	8:29			
	1696:15-18	8:30-32	5:8		
8:30-34	1696:26-35		5:9-14		
8:32-33	1696:26-28	8:33	5:11-14		
8:35	1696:18-25		5:15		
8:36-37	1696:42-1697:3	8:34	5:16-19		
8:38-39	1697: 5-12		5:18-20		
8:40-42	1698: 4-16	9:18-19	5:21-24		
8:43-48	(The Woman With the Issue of Blood:)				
	1698:16-37	9:20-22	5:25-34		
	1875:13-14	9:20-22	5:25-34		
8:46	1669:20		5:30		
8:48	(Faith Makes Whole, See Luke 5:12-13, above.)				
8:49-55	(Healing of Jairus' Daughter:)				
	1699: 9-22	9:23-25	5:35-42		
8:50	(Fear Not:)				
	1103:14	10:31			Lk 5:10;12:7,32
	1582:19-20	10:31			Lk 5:10;12:7,32
	(Faith Makes Whole, See Luke 5:12-13, above.)				
8:55	1699:23-24		5:43		
8:56	1699:32-33				
	(Tell No Man, See Luke 5:14, above.)				
9: 1- 2	1681:28-38	10:1	6:7		
	2055:23-24	10:1	6:7		Lk 10:1
	(Call Apostles Together, See Luke 6:11-12, above.)				
9: 2	1590:44-45	10:1			
	1858:30	4:17	1:15		
9: 3	1584: 7- 8	10:9-10	6:8-9		
	1800:34-35	10:9-10	6:8-9		Lk 10:4
9: 4	1800:38-39	10:11-13	6:10		Lk 10:5-7
9: 5	1801: 9-13	10:14-15	6:11		
9: 6	1682:21-23		6:12-13		
9: 7	1717: 9-16		6:14		
9: 7- 9	1717:17-23	14:1-2	6:14-16		

LUKE Chap:Verse	The URANTIA Book Page:Line	MATTHEW Chap:Verse	MARK Chap:Verse	JOHN Chap:Verse	Other BOOKS Chap:Verse
9:10-11	1700:20-32	14:13-14	6:31-34	6:1-3	
9:12-13	1701:14-35	14:15-17	6:35-38	6:5-9	
9:14-17	1701:36-49	14:18-21	6:39-44	6:10-13	
9:18	1745:45-47	16:13	8:27		
9:19	1746:10-14	16:14	8:28		
8:20	(Peter' Recognition of Jesus as Christ of God:)				
	1746:14-20	16:15-16	8:29		
	1748: 2- 3	16:16	8:29		
	1939: 1- 3	16:15-16	8:29		
9:21	1746:24-25	16:20	8:30		
9:22	(Jesus Foretells His Death and Resurrection:)				
	1759:10-15	16:21;26:2	8:31;9:31		Lk 9:44
		17:22-23	10:32-34		Lk 18:31-33
		20:18-19	14:41		Lk 24:6-8,46
	1759:43-46	(Same as 1759:10-15, above)			
	1871:29-41	(Same as 1759:10-15, above)			
	1872:38-43	(Same as 1759:10-15, above)			
	1952:16-17	(Same as 1759:10-15, above)			
	1962:32	(Same as 1759:10-15, above)			
	2001:14	(Same as 1759:10-15, above)			
	2035:18-19	(Same as 1759:10-15, above)			
	2052:16-18	(Same as 1759:10-15, above)			
9:23	(Deny Self, Take up Cross, and "Follow Me:")				
	1750: 5- 6	10:38;16:24	8:34;10:21		Lk 14:27
	1760:17-19	10:38;16:24	8:34;10:21		Lk 14:27
	1770:22-23	10:38;16:24	8:34;10:21		Lk 14:27
	1869:37-41	10:38;16:24	8:34;10:21		Lk 14:27
9:23-24	(Whosoever Will May Come:)				
	0039: 7	16:24-25	8:34-35	3:15-16	Re 22:17
	1102:18-19	16:24-25	8:34-35	3:15-16	Re 22:17
	1205:16-17	16:24-25	8:34-35	3:15-16	Re 22:17
	1567: 4	16:24-25	8:34-35	3:15-16	Re 22:17
	1750:16-17	16:24-25	8:34-35	3:15-16	Re 22:17
	1820:44-45	16:24-25	8:34-35	3:15-16	Re 22:17
	1829:44-45	16:24-25	8:34-35	3:15-16	Re 22:17
9:24	1760:19-20	16:25	8:35		
	(Value of Life, Lose it--Save it:)				
	1134:28-29	10:39;16:25	8:35	12:25	Lk 17:33

(Luke 9:24 Continued on next page.)

Luke 9:24 to 9:47

LUKE Chap:Verse	The URANTIA Book Page:Line	MATTHEW Chap:Verse	MARK Chap:Verse	JOHN Chap:Verse	Other BOOKS Chap:Verse
9:24	1575:32-33	10:39;16:25	8:35	12:25	Lk 17:33
	1760:19-20	10:39;16:25	8:35	12:25	Lk 17:33
	1782: 9-10	10:39;16:25	8:35	12:25	Lk 17:33
	1903:39-41	10:39;16:25	8:35	12:25	Lk 17:33
9:25	(What Price the Soul?)				
	1581:28-29	16:26	8:36		
	1760:20-22	16:26	8:36		
	1822:37-38	16:26	8:36		
9:26	(Fate of Those Ashamed of Jesus:)				
	1760:22-25	16:27	8:38		
	(Jesus' return in Glory:)				
	0596:38	16:27;24:30	8:38		Lk 21:27
		25:31	13:26		
	1591:16-17	(Same as 0596:38, above)			
	1860:16-17	(Same as 0596:38, above)			
	1915: 1- 4	(Same as 0596:38, above)			
	2092:42-43	(Same as 0596:38, above)			
9:27	(Jesus Foretells Pentecost:)				
	1569:24-25	16:28	9:1		
	1760:25-26	16:28	9:1		
9:28-36	(The Transfiguration:)				
	1752:18-1754:7	17:1-9	9:2-9		
9:28	1752:16-21	17:1	9:2		
9:29-32	1753:31-38	17:2-3	9:2-4		
9:33-34	1753:41-50	17:4-5	9:5-7		
9:35	(The Voice on The Mountain:)				
	1754:1-3	17:5	9:7		
	1755:18-19	17:5	9:7		
	(The Voice at Baptism, See Luke 3:22, above.)				
9:36	1754: 3-12	17:6-9	9:8-9		
9:37	1755:29-35		9:14		
9:38-40	1757: 8-18	17:14-16			
9:41	1757:19-25	17:17	9:19		
9:42	1757:26-30		9:20-24		
9:42-43	1757:38-44	17:18	9:25-27		
9:43-44	1759:10-15	17:22-23	9:31		
9:44	(Jesus Fortetells Death, See Luke 9:22, above.)				
9:45	1759:15-17		9:32		
9:46-48	1761: 9-20	18:1-10	9:33-37		

224

LUKE Chap:Verse	The URANTIA Book Page:Line	MATTHEW Chap:Verse	MARK Chap:Verse	JOHN Chap:Verse	Other BOOKS Chap:Verse
9:48	(Receive Child in My Name:)				
	1761:19-20	10:40;18:5	9:37	13:20	Lk 10:16
	1801:13-14	10:40;18:5	9:37	13:20	Lk 10:16
	(Least Greatest, Greatest Least:)				
	0316:40	19:30;20:16	9:35		Lk 13:30;14:11
		20:26-27	10:31		Lk 18:14;22:26
		23:11	10:43-44		
	0466:33-34	(Same as 0316:40, above)			
	0647:31-32	(Same as 0316:40, above)			
	1536:38-39	(Same as 0316:40, above)			
	1569:18-20	(Same as 0316:40, above)			
	1758:33-35	(Same as 0316:40, above)			
	1761:20-21	(Same as 0316:40, above)			
	1804:10:11	(Same as 0316:40, above)			
	1829:31-32	(Same as 0316:40, above)			
	1834:42-44	(Same as 0316:40, above)			
	1838:27-28	(Same as 0316:40, above)			
	1862:13-14	(Same as 0316:40, above)			
	1907:12-14	(Same as 0316:40, above)			
	1940:13-15	(Same as 0316:40, above)			
9:49-50	(In Religion, Who is Not Against Us is For Us:)				
	1555: 4- 5		9:38		
	1764:24-36		9:38-40		
9:51-53	1788: 3-15				
9:54-56	(Disciples Seek Revenge & are Rebuked:)				
	1553: 9-11				
	1555: 3- 4				
	1788:16-23				
	1955:38-40				
9:55	(What Manner of Spirit:)				
	0311:12				
	0313:31				
9:57-60	1801:31-39	8:19-22			
9:58	(Jesus Had No Home:)				
	1723:35-37	8:20			
	1750:27-29	8:20			
9:59	2089:50	16:24	8:34	12:26	
9:59-60	1672: 3- 5	8:21-22			
9:61-62	1801:40-45				

LUKE Chap:Verse	The URANTIA Book Page:Line	MATTHEW Chap:Verse	MARK Chap:Verse	JOHN Chap:Verse	Other BOOKS Chap:Verse
10: 1	(Sending Out Seventy "Two by Two":)				
	1800: 8-11				
	1801:18-20				
	2055:23-24				
10: 2	1681:28-32	9:37-38			
	1800:29-32	9:37-38			
10: 3	1584: 8- 9				
	1800:32-33	10:16			
10: 4	1800:34-35	10:9-10	6:8-9		Lk 9:3
	1805:33				
10: 4-7	1584: 7- 8				
10: 5-7	1800:36-1801:3	10:12-14	6:10-11		Lk 9:4
10: 8-9	1801: 6- 9	10:11			
10: 9	1590:44-45	10:8			
10:10-11	1801:10-11	10:14	6:11		
10:13-15	1807:34-43	11:20-23			
10:16	1801:13-15	10:40		13:20	
10:17	1806:38-46				
10:17-18	1807: 4- 9				
10:18	(Satan's Fall:)				
	0490:28				
	0609:38-39				
	1807: 7- 9				
10:20	1807: 9-15				
10:21	(Father in Heaven:)				
	0023:24	5:16,48	11:25-26		Lk 11:2
		6:1,9;7:11,21			
		11:25;16:17			
		18:35;23:9			
	1053:41-42	(Same as 0023:24, above)			
	1103:19	(Same as 0023:24, above)			
	1511:46	(Same as 0023:24, above)			
	1569:10	(Same as 0023:24, above)			
	1571: 2	(Same as 0023:24, above)			
	1571:16-17	(Same as 0023:24, above)			
	1619:23	(Same as 0023:24, above)			
	1620: 1	(Same as 0023:24, above)			
	1638:35	(Same as 0023:24, above)			

(Luke 10:21 Continued on next page.)

LUKE Chap:Verse	The URANTIA Book Page:Line	MATTHEW Chap:Verse	MARK Chap:Verse	JOHN Chap:Verse	Other BOOKS Chap:Verse
10:21	1764: 2	(Same as 0023:24, above)			
	1807:18-19	(Same as 0023:24, above)			
	1907:16	(Same as 0023:24, above)			
	1923:12	(Same as 0023:24, above)			
	2087:11-12	(Same as 0023:24, above)			
10:21-22	1807:16-27	11:25-26			
10:22	(Son Reveals the Father:)				
	0028:14-15	11:27		1:18;6:45-46	
				8:26;12:49-50	
				14:7-9,20	
				17:6,25-26	
	0093:46	(Same as 0028:14-15, above)			
	0109:28-33	(Same as 0028:14-15, above)			
	0196:10	(Same as 0028:14-15, above)			
	0232:42-44	(Same as 0028:14-15, above)			
	0233: 4- 5	(same as 0028:14-15, above)			
	1324:23-32	(Same as 0028:14-15, above)			
	1328:38-41	(Same as 0028:14-15, above)			
	1331:21-22	(Same as 0028:14-15, above)			
	1608: 1- 2	(Same as 0028:14-15, above)			
	1710:15-16	(Same as 0028:14-15, above)			
	1750:14-15	(Same as 0028:14-15, above)			
	1855:46-47	(Same as 0028:14-15, above)			
	1947:42-47	(Same as 0028:14-15, above)			
	1965: 8-12	(Same as 0028:14-15, above)			
10:23-24	1807:28-33	13:16-17			
10:25-28	1809:21-28	22:34-40	12:28-31		
	1901:10-20	22:35-40	12:28-31		
10:27-28	(First Commandment, Love God:)				
	1206:38-39	22:37	12:30		De 6:4-5
	1444: 7- 9	22:37	12:30		De 6:4-5
	1453:36-37	22:37	12:30		De 6:4-5
	(The Two Greatest Commandments:)				
	1446:11-12	22:37-40	12:30-31		De 6:4-5 Le 19:18
	1600: 1- 3	22:37-40	12:30-31		De 6:4-5 Le 19:18
	1600:33-36	22:37-40	12:30-31		De 6:4-5 Le 19:18
	1805: 9-11	22:37-40	12:30-31		De 6:4-5 Le 19:18
	1809:25-27	22:37-40	12:30-31		De 6:4-5 Le 19:18
	1901:13-20	22:37-40	12:30-31		De 6:4-5 Le 19:18

Luke 10:27 to 11:4

10:27-28 (Second Commandment, Love Neighbor as Thyself:)
        1206:40-42   19:19   12:31   Le 19:18 Ro 13:9
                      22:39   Ga 5:14 Ja 2:8
        1445:47   (Same as 1206:40-42, above)
        1453:37   (Same as 1206:40-42, above)
        1769:26   (Same as 1206:40-42, above)
        1770: 4- 5   (Same as 1206:40-42, above)
        1862: 8   (Same as 1206:40-42, above)
        1950:17-18   (Same as 1206:40-42, above)
10:29-37 (Who Is My Neighbor?)
        1580:29-32
        1809:29-32
        1810: 3-19
        1810:22
10:38-42 1797:41-1798:15
11: 1   (Teach us to Pray:)
        1618:21-32
        1619:40-45
        1620:12
11: 2   1860:23-24   6:10
        (Father in Heaven, See Luke 10:21, above)
        (Doing the Father's Will, See Luke 8:21, above.)
11: 2- 4 (The Lord's Prayer:)
        1619:46-1620:10 6:9-13
11: 2- 4 (Prayer;)
        0096:37-38   6:5-13 11:24   Lk 18:1-14
                       26:39,42 14:35-36   Lk 22:41
        1001:12-1002:41 (Same as 0096:37-38, above)
        1511:46-48   (Same as 0096:37-38, above)
        1618:35-1621:40 (Same as 0096:37-38, above)
        1638:10-1641:9 (Same as 0096:37-38, above)
        1848:16-1849:23 (Same as 0096:37-38, above)
        1968:11-34   (Same as 0096:37-38, above)
11: 4   1738:25   6:13
        (Forgive Us as We Forgive Others:)
        1475: 4- 7 6:12,14-15 11:25-26   Lk 6:37
                  18:21-35
        1638:36-41   (Same as 1475:4-7, above)
(Luke 11:4 Continued on next page.)

LUKE Chap:Verse	The URANTIA Book Page:Line	MATTHEW Chap:Verse	MARK Chap:Verse	JOHN Chap:Verse	Other BOOKS Chap:Verse
11: 4	1763:23-1764:4	(Same as 1475:4-7, above)			
	1862: 5- 6	(Same as 1475:4-7, above)			
	2017:44-45	(Same as 1475:4-7, above)			
11: 5- 8	1619: 2-10				
11: 9-10	(Ask, Seek:)				
	1454:22-23	7:7-8		14:13-14	
				15:7,16	
				16:23-24	
	1619:12-15	(Same as 1454:22-23, above)			
	1639:18-23	(Same as 1454:22-23, above)			
	1639:39-42	(Same as 1454:22-23, above)			
	1838:41-42	(Same as 1454:22-23, above)			
	1849:19-20	(Same as 1454:22-23, above)			
	1945:37-44	(Same as 1454:22-23, above)			
11:10	1102:38-39	7:8			
11:11-13	1619:16-24	7:9-11			
11:13	1454: 2- 5	7:11			
11:14	1713:40-48	12:22			
		9:32-33			
11:15	(Devils:)				
	0602:11	9:34;10:25	3:22,30		
		12:24			
	0863:27	(Same as 0602:11, above)			
	1714: 7-13	(Same as 0602:11, above)			
	1850:24-25	(Same as 0602:11, above)			
	1924:45-46	(Same as 0602:11, above)			
11:16	(Show Us a Sign from Heaven:)				
	1520:21-23	12:38;16:1	8:11	2:18;6:30	
	1714:41-43	12:38;16:1	8:11	2:18;6:30	
	1744:40-45	12:38;16:1	8:11	2:18;6:30	
	1895:30-34	12:38;16:1	8:11	2:18;6:30	
11:17	2085:20	12:25	3:24-25		
11:17-23	1714:14-25	12:25-32	3:23-29		
11:23	1764:42	12:30			
11:27-28	1722:31-35				
11:29	1714:44-47	16:4	8:11-12		
11:33	(Let Light Shine, See Luke 8:16, above.)				
11:34	0955:19-20	6:22-23			
	1577:37-40	6:22-23			

LUKE Chap:Verse	The URANTIA Book Page:Line	MATTHEW Chap:Verse	MARK Chap:Verse	JOHN Chap:Verse	Other BOOKS Chap:Verse
11:37-38	1825:17-30				
11:37-41	(Ceremony over Substance, See Luke 6:1-10, above.)				
11:39	1826: 8-12	23:25,28			
11:39-40	1908: 6-10	23:25-26			
11:39-53	1911:20-22	23:1-39			
11:40-41	1826:13-17				
11:42	1826:17-21	23:23			
	1908: 1- 5	23:23-24			
11:43	1826:22-24	23:6-7	12:38-39		
	1907: 3- 5	23:6-7	12:38-39		Lk 20:46
11:45	1826:25-28				
11:46	1826:28-32				
	1906:47-49	23:4			
11:47-48	1908:19-26				
11:47-51	1826:32-38	23:29-31			
11:49-51	1908:30-41	23:34-36			
11:52	1826:38-41	23:13			
	1907:24-27	23:13			
11:53-54	1826:47-1827: 4				
12: 1	1819:47-48				
	(Beware of Hypocracy:)				
	1745:10-11	16:6-12	8:15		
	1751:25	16:6-12	8:15		
	1820: 2-6	16:6-12	8:15		
12: 2- 3	(Covered Revealed, Spoken in Dark--Heard in light:)				
	1682: 1- 3	10:26-27	4:22	Lk 8:17	
	1692:10-13	10:26-27	4:22	Lk 8:17	
	1820: 7-12	10:26-27	4:22	Lk 8:17	
12: 4- 5	1682: 4- 7	10:28			
	1820:13-18	10:28			
12: 6	0048:47-0049:1	10:29			
12: 6- 7	(Human Worth:)				
	1682: 8-11	10:29-31			
	1820:19-24	10:29-31			
12: 7	(Fear Not:)				
	1582:19-20	10:31		Lk 5:10;8:50;12:32	
	(Hairs are Numbered:)				
	0049: 1- 2	10:30			
	0419:25	10:30			

LUKE Chap:Verse	The URANTIA Book Page:Line	MATTHEW Chap:Verse	MARK Chap:Verse	JOHN Chap:Verse	Other BOOKS Chap:Verse
12: 8- 9	1820:25-28	10:32-33			
12:10	1820:29-32				
12:11-12	1584:10-17				
	1820:33-37				
12:13-15	1821: 3-12				
12:15	1581:26-27				
12:16-19	1821:18-25				
12:20-21	1821:26-34				
12:22-26	1823:15-25	6:25-27,31			
12:22-31	1577:47-1578:4				
12:22-34	1580:10-11	6:25-34			
12:27-28	1823:26-30	6:28-30			
12:29-30	1823:36-39	6:31-32			
12:31	(Priorities; Seek First Kingdom of God:)				
	1206:35-37	6:33			
	1536:24-26	6:33			
	1569:11-13	6:33			
	1823:39-43	6:33-34			
	1897:33-34	6:33			
	2075:27	6:33			
	2088:28	6:33			
12:32	1861:27			6:38-40	
	(Fear Not:)				
	1103:14	10:31			Lk 5:10;8:50;12:7
	1582:19-20	10:31			Lk 5:10;8:50;12:7
12:33-34	(Value System; "Treasures" in Heaven & on Earth:)				
	1474:37-42		5:10-12		Lk 6:35
			6:19-21		
	1577:33-36	(Same as 1474:37-42, above)			
	1821:40-1822:11	(Same as 1474:37-42, above)			
	1823:44-48	(Same as 1474:37-42, above)			
	1853:26-34	(Same as 1474:37-42, above)			
	1860: 3- 5	(Same as 1474:37-42, above)			
12:34	1822: 1	6:21			
12:35-38	1824: 3-10				
12:39-40	1824:11-14	24:43-44			
12:41	1824:18-19				
12:42-44	1824:20-27	24:45-47			
12:45-46	1824:28-31	24:48-51			

LUKE Chap:Verse	The URANTIA Book Page:Line	MATTHEW Chap:Verse	MARK Chap:Verse	JOHN Chap:Verse	Other BOOKS Chap:Verse
12:48	1570:16-17				
12:48-53	1824:33-40				
12:51	0597:21-22	10:34			
	1782:10-11	10:34			
12:51-53	1682:11-18	10:34-36			
12:52-53	1722:45	10:36			
12:54-57	1744:48-1745:2	16:2-3			

13: 1- 5 (Accidents Happen to Just and Unjust:)

	0039: 1- 2	5:45			
	1571:13-14	5:45			
	1671:35-38	5:45			
	1830:24-30	5:45			

13: 6- 9 (Produce Good Fruit or Die:)

	1502:38-44	3:8-10		15:2,8,16	Lk 3:8-9
		7:16-20			Lk 6:43-44
		12:33			Ga 5:22-23 Ep 5:9
	1571:32-37	(Same as 1502:38-44, above)			
	1572:27-30	(Same as 1502:38-44, above)			
	1582:33-34	(Same as 1502:38-44, above)			
	1601: 8-10	(Same as 1502:38-44, above)			
	1714:36-38	(Same as 1502 38-44, above)			
	1830:39-45	(Same as 1502 38-44, above)			
	1945:40-47	(Same as 1502:38-44, above)			
	1946:21-26	(Same as 1502:38-44, above)			
	2054:36-39	(Same as 1502:38-44, above)			
	1830:39-45				

13:10-17 (The Use of the Sabbath:)

	1649:47-1650:5	12:1-8	2:23-28	5:5-9	Lk 6:1-10
		12:9-14	3:1-5	5:16-18	Lk 11:37-41
		15:1-9	7:1-13	9:14	Lk 14:1-6
					De 5:12-15 Ex 20:8-11
	1654:29-1655:12	(Same as 1649:47-1650:5, above)			
	1665: 7- 35	(Same as 1649:47-1650:5, above)			
	1712:21-42	(Same as 1649:47-1650:5, above)			
	1813:13-16	(Same as 1649:47-1650:5, above)			
	1834: 6-32	(Same as 1649:47-1650:5, above)			
	1835:40-1836:26	(Same as 1649:47-1650:5, above)			
	1850:22-23	(Same as 1649:47-1650:5, above)			

LUKE Chap:Verse	The URANTIA Book Page:Line	MATTHEW Chap:Verse	MARK Chap:Verse	JOHN Chap:Verse	Other BOOKS Chap:Verse
13:19	(Parable of the Mustard Seed:)				
	1583:10-11	13:31-32	4:31-32		
	1693:44-1694:2	13:31-32	4:31-32		
	1860:37-39	13:31-32	4:31-32		
	1931:43-44	13:31	4:31		
13:21	(Parable of the Leaven:)				
	1694: 3- 5	13:33			
	1931:43-44	13:33			
13:22-23	1828:27-29				
13:24	1828:43-46				
13:25-27	1829: 5-23	8:21-23			
13:28-29	1568:30-34	8:11-12			
	1829:26-30	8:11-12			
13:30	(Last First/First Last, See Luke 9:48, above.)				
13:31	1872: 5- 8				
13:32	1393:23				
	1872:18-21				
13:33-35	1872:22-30	23:37-39			
13:34-35	1908:42-49	23:37-39			
13:35	1924:12-13	23:38			
14: 1	1833:26-28				
	1834: 3- 4				
14: 1- 6	1834: 6-32				
	(Use of The Sabbath, See Luke 13:10-17, above.)				
14: 7	1833:33-39				
14: 7-11	1834:33-44				Lk 18:14
14:11	(Exalted Abased--Humble Exalted, See Luke 9:48, above.)				
14:12-14	1580:37-39				
	1834:44-49				
14:13	1594:12-13	11:5	—		Lk 4:18;7:22
14:15	1835: 2- 4				
14:16-20	1894:40-44				
14:16-24	1835: 7-26	22:1-10			
14:21-24	1895:13-21				
14:25	1869:29-33				
14:26	(Priority, God Before Family:)				
	1682:19-20	10:37			
	1869:34-40	10:37			

233

Luke 14:27 to 15:32

LUKE Chap:Verse	The URANTIA Book Page:Line	MATTHEW Chap:Verse	MARK Chap:Verse	JOHN Chap:Verse	Other BOOKS Chap:Verse
14:27	(Assume Responsibilities and Follow Jesus:)				
	1750: 5- 6	10:38;16:24	8:34;10:21		Lk 9:23
	1760:17-19	10:38;16:24	8:34;10:21		Lk 9:23
	1770:22-23	10:38;16:24	8:34;10:21		Lk 9:23
	1869:41	10:38;16:24	8:34;10:21		Lk 9:23
14:28-30	1869:42-1870: 1				
14:31-32	1870: 1- 6				
14:33	1870:10-12				
14:34-35	(Salt that Loses its Savor:)				
	1570:44-45	5:13	9:50		
	1572: 7- 9	5:13	9:50		
	1870:16-24	5:13	9:50		
15: 2	(Friend of Publicans and Sinners:)				
	1342:17-18	9:10-11;11:19	2:15-16		Lk 5:29-30;7:34
	1540:31-1541:3	(Same as 1342:17-18, above)			
	1627:26-27	(Same as 1342:17-18, above)			
	1850:15-19	(Same as 1342:17-18, above)			
	1851: 7- 8	(Same as 1342:17-18, above)			
15: 3- 7	(Parable of the Lost Sheep:)				
	1762:21-32	18:12-14			
	1850:34-1851:5	18:12-13			
	1853: 6- 7	18:12-13			
15: 3-10	1770:48-1771:1	18:11-14			
15: 7	1841:30-32				
15: 8-10	(Parable of the Lost Coin:)				
	1851:15-22				
	1853: 9-10				
15:10	1841:32-33				
15:11-32	(Parable of The Prodigal Son:)				
	0616: 5				
	1853:12-13				
15:11-12	1851:35-47				
15:13-16	1851:48-1852: 6				
15:17-19	1852: 7-13				
15:20-22	1852:16-24				
15:23-24	1852:25-29				
15:25-27	1852:30-36				
15:28-30	1852:37-45				
15:31-32	1852:47-1853: 2				

LUKE Chap:Verse	The URANTIA Book Page:Line	MATTHEW Chap:Verse	MARK Chap:Verse	JOHN Chap:Verse	Other BOOKS Chap:Verse
16: 1-13	(The Unfaithful Steward:)				
16: 1- 2	1853:35-41				
16: 3- 8	1853:42-1854:10				
16: 8	(Children of Light:)				
	1327:26-27	5:14-16		12:36	Is 14:12
	1655:37-38	5:14-16		12:36	Ep 5:8 1Th 5:5
	1854:11-12	5:14-16		12:36	Ep 5:8 1Th 5:5
	1904:24-28	5:14-16		12:36	Ep 5:8 1Th 5:5
	1953:33	5:14-16		12:26	Ep 5:8 1Th 5:5
	2042: 2	5;14-16		12:36	Ep 5:8 1Th 5:5
	(Jesus is Light, See Like 1:79, above.)				
16: 9	1853:22-24				
	1854:12-17				
16:10-12	1854:18-24				
16:13	(No Man can Serve Two Masters:)				
	1199:33-34	6:24			
	1577:44-46	6:24			
	1803: 7- 8	6:24			
	1854:25-27	6:24			
16:14	1854:28-29				
16:15	1854:29-31				
16:18	1576:39-1577:2	5:31-32	10: 2-12		
16:19-31	0953:41-42				
	1854:46-1855:22				
17: 2	1761:21-29	18:6-10	9:42-47		
17: 3-4	(Forgive Seven Times Daily:)				
	0449:40	18:21-22			
	1551: 4- 6	18:21-22			
	1763:20-23	18:21-22			
17:11-13	1827:15-28				
17:14-16	1827:45-1828: 4				
17:17-18	1828: 7-10				
17:19	(Faith Makes Whole:)				
	1643:27-41	8:2-3,13	1:40-42		Lk 5:12-13
		9:2,22,29	2:5;5:34		Lk 8:48,50
		15:28	10:52		Lk 18:42
	1648: 7-13	(Same as 1643:27-41, above)			
	1667:12	(Same as 1643:27-41, above)			

(Luke 17:19 Continued on next page.)

LUKE Chap:Verse	The URANTIA Book Page:Line	MATTHEW Chap:Verse	MARK Chap:Verse	JOHN Chap:Verse	Other BOOKS Chap:Verse
17:19	1698:33-1699:6	(Same as 1643:27-41, above)			
	1735:21-25	(Same as 1643:27-41, above)			
	1828:10-11	(Same as 1643:27-41, above)			
	1873:28-29	(Same as 1643:27-41, above)			
	1875:13-14	(Same as 1643:27-41, above)			
	1905:23-24	(Same as 1643:27-41, above)			
17:20-21	(The Coming Kingdom is Already Here:)				
	1533:23-25				
	1569:15-17	24:26-27			
	1588:26-28	10:7;4:17			
17:21	(The Kingdom of God is Within You:)				
	1193: 5- 6				
	1306:39				
	1856:21-24				
	1859:10-11				
	1859:18				
	1861:24-25				
	1862:30				
	1864:34-35				
	1867:15-16				
	2084:24				
17:33	(Value of Life, Lose It--Save It:)				
	1134:28-29	10:39;16:25	8:35	12:25	Lk 9:24
	1575:32-33	10:39;16:25	8:35	12:25	Lk 9:24
	1760:19-20	10:39;16:25	8:35	12:25	Lk 9:24
	1782: 9-10	10:39;16:25	8:35	12:25	Lk 9:24
	1903:39-41	10:39;16:25	8:35	12:25	Lk 9:24
18: 1-14	0096:37-38				
	1619:24				
	(Prayer:)				
	1001:12-1002:41	6:5-13	11:24		Lk 11:2-4
		26:39,42	14:35-36		Lk 22:41-42
	1511:46-48	(Same as 1001:12-1002:41, above)			
	1618:35-1621:40	(Same as 1001:12-1002:41, above)			
	1638:10-1641:9	(Same as 1001:12-1002:41, above)			
	1848:16-1849:23	(Same as 1001:12-1002:41, above)			
	1968:11-15	(Same as 1001:12-1002:41, above)			
	1968:22-24	(Same as 1001:12-1002:41, above)			
	1968:31-34	(Same as 1001:12-1002:41, above)			

LUKE Chap:Verse	The URANTIA Book Page:Line	MATTHEW Chap:Verse	MARK Chap:Verse	JOHN Chap:Verse	Other BOOKS Chap:Verse
18: 2- 5	1619:25-35				
18: 9	1838:10-13				
18:10-14	1573:46-47				
	1838:19-28				
18:14	(Exalted Abased--Humble Exalted:)				
	0316:40	19:30;20:16	9:35		Lk 9:48;13:30
		20:26-27	10:31		Lk 14:11;22:26
		23:11	10:43-44		
	0466:33-34	(Same as 0316:40, above)			
	0647:31-32	(Same as 0316:40, above)			
	1536:38-39	(Same as 0316:40, above)			
	1569:18-20	(Same as 0316:40, above)			
	1758:33-35	(Same as 0316:40, above)			
	1761:20-21	(Same as 0316:40, above)			
	1804:10:11	(Same as 0316:40, above)			
	1829:31-32	(Same as 0316:40, above)			
	1834:42-44	(Same as 0316:40, above)			
	1838:27-28	(Same as 0316:40, above)			
	1862:13-14	(Same as 0316:40, above)			
	1907:12-14	(Same as 0316:40, above)			
	1940:13-15	(Same as 0316:40, above)			
18:15	1839:40-48	19:13	10:13		
18:16	1840: 1- 2	19:14	10:14		
18:17	(Receive Kingdom As a Little Child:)				
	1118:35-36	18:3-4	10:15		
	1536:26-28	18:3-4	10:15		
	1576:14-16	18:3-4	10:15		
	1585:13-15	18:3-4	10:15		
	1621: 5-11	18:3-4	10:15		
	1676:48-1677:2	18:3-4	10:15		
	1733: 3- 6	18:3-4	10:15		
	1761:13-19	18:3-4	10:15		
	1840: 2- 4	18:3-4	10:15		
	1861: 7-11	18:3-4	10:15		
	1861:41-42	18:3-4	10:15		
	1960:37-38	18:3-4	10:15		
	2089:41-42	18:3-4	10:15		
18:18-19	2088:42-43	19:16-17	10:17-18		
18:18-21	1802: 5-15	19:16-20	10:17-20		Ex 20:3-17 De 5:7-21

237

LUKE Chap:Verse	The URANTIA Book Page:Line	MATTHEW Chap:Verse	MARK Chap:Verse	JOHN Chap:Verse	Other BOOKS Chap:Verse
18:19	2092:10-12	19:17	10:18		
18:22-23	(The Cost of Discipleship:)				
	1564:13-15	19:20-22	10:21-22		
	1672: 3- 5	19:20-22	10:21-22		
	1802:17-26	19:20-22	10:21-22		
	(Difficult for Rich to Enter Kingdom:)				
	1803: 5- 8	19:24	10:25		
	1803:26-33	19:23-24	10:23-25		
18:24-25	1821:43-46	19:24	10:25		
	2093:16-17	19:23-24	10:24-25		
18:26-27	1803:34-40	19:25-26	10:26-27		
18:27	(Impossible With Men, Possible With God:)				
	0034:13-14	19:26	10:27;14:36		Lk 1:37
	0046:42	19:26	10:27;14:36		Lk 1:37
	0291:26-27	19:26	10:27;14:36		Lk 1:37
	1453:41	19:26	10:27;14:36		Lk 1:37
	1757:34-35	19:26	10:27;14:36		Lk 1:37
	1803:38-40	19:26	10:27;14:36		Lk 1:37
18:28-30	1804: 5-10	19:27,29	10:28-30		
18:30	1957:21-23	19:29	10:30		
18:31-33	(Jesus Foretells His Crucifixion & Resurrection:)				
	1759:10-15	16:21;26:2	8:31;9:31		Lk 9:22,44
		17:22-23	10:32-34		Lk 24:6-8,46
		20:18-19	14:41		
	1759:43-46	(Same as 1759:10-15, above)			
	1871:29-41	(Same as 1759:10-15, above)			
	1872:38-43	(Same as 1759:10-15, above)			
	1952:16-17	(Same as 1759:10-15, above)			
	1962:32	(Same as 1759:10-15, above)			
	2001:14	(Same as 1759:10-15, above)			
	2035:18-19	(Same as 1759:10-15, above)			
	2052:16-18	(Same as 1759:10-15, above)			
18:34	1871:43-48				
18:35	1873: 2- 5	20:29	10:46		
18:36-39	1873:16-20	20:30-31	10:47-48		
18:40-43	1873:21-31	20:32-34	10:49-52		
18:42	(Faith and Healing, See Luke 17:19, above.)				
19: 1- 4	1873:34-46				
19: 5- 6	1874: 1- 6				

LUKE Chap:Verse	The URANTIA Book Page:Line	MATTHEW Chap:Verse	MARK Chap:Verse	JOHN Chap:Verse	Other BOOKS Chap:Verse
19: 7- 8	1874: 7-17				
19: 9	1874:20-23				
19:10	(Jesus Came to Seek & to Save Those Who are Lost.)				
	1750:12-13	18:11			
	1770:48-1771:1	18:11			
	1851:14	18:11			
	1874:23-24	18:11			
	2035:36	18:11			
19:11	1875:27-31				
	1875:40-41				
19:12-26	(Parable of the Talents:)				
	0315:24				
19:12	1875:41-43				
19:13	1876: 7-12				
19:14	1875:43-45				
19:15	1876:13-15				
19:15-23	1876:16-31	25:19-27			
19:17	0274:33-35	25:21			
19:24-25	1876:32-34	25:28			
19:26	(To Whom Hath is Given; Hath Not, Taken Away:)				
	1199: 1- 3	13:12;25:29	4:25		Lk 8:18
	1689:23-24	13:12;25:29	4:25		Lk 8:18
	1692:15-16	13:12;25:29	4:25		Lk 8:18
	1876:34-36	13:12;25:29	4:25		Lk 8:18
	1917:27-28	13:12;25:29	4:25		Lk 8:18
19:28	1877: 9-10				
19:28-31	1881:27-32	21:1-3	11:1-3		
19:32-35	1881:33-38	21:6-7	11:4-7		
19:35-38	1882: 6-13	21:7-9	11:7-10	12:12-14	Ps 118:26
19:36-38	1403:33-35	21:8-9	11:8-10	12:12-13	
19:39-40	1882:40-45				
19:41-44	1882:16-27				
19:44	1414: 8- 9				
19:45	1888:17-18	21:12	11:15		
19:45-46	(Cleansing The Temple:)				
	1378:27-29	21:12-13	11:15-17	2:14-16	
	1890:11-25	21:12-13	11:15-17	2:15-16	
	1911: 6- 7	21:12-13	11:15-17	2:13-16	
19:47-48	1890:36-42		11:18		

Luke 20:1 to 20:47

LUKE Chap:Verse	The URANTIA Book Page:Line	MATTHEW Chap:Verse	MARK Chap:Verse	JOHN Chap:Verse	Other BOOKS Chap:Verse
20: 1- 2	1891:28-32	21:23	11:27-28	2:18	
20: 3- 4	1892: 6- 9	21:24-25	11:29-30		
20: 5- 8	1892:10-24	21:25-27	11:31-33		
20: 9-15	1893:35-1894:10	21:33-40	12:1-9		
20:16	1894:11-17	21:41	12:9		
20:17-18	1894:18-30	21:42-44	12:10		Ps 118:22
20:19	1894:31-33	21:45-46	12:12		
20:20	1899: 2-10	22:15	12:13		
20:21-24	1899:13-25	22:16-21	12:14-17		
20:25	(Render to Both Caesar & God Their Proper Dues:)				
	1114:25-26	22:21	12:17		
	1474:14-15	22:21	12:17		
	1580:16-17	22:21	12:17		
	1740:19-20	22:21	12:17		
	1899:25-26	22:21	12:17		
	1929:33-35	22:21	12:17		
	1957: 4- 5	22:21	12:17		
20:26	1899:27-30	22:22	12:17		
20:27-33	1900: 2-12	22:23-28	12:18-23		De 25:5-6
20:28	0926:12-14	22:24	12:19		De 25:5-6
20:34-38	1900:17-29	22:29-32	12:23-27		Ex 3:6
20:35-36	(Resurrected Do Not Marry:)				
	0419:13-15	22:30	12:25		
20:36	(----But are "as the Angels":				
	0495:32	22:30	12:25		
	(Children of God:)				
	1453:39	5:9			Ro 8:16+
	1861:29	5:9			Ro 8:16+
20:39-40	1900:31-35	22:33			
20:41-44	1348: 5- 6	22:41-46	12:35-37		
	1901:45-1902:3	22:41-46	12:35-37		Ps 110:1
20:42	(Right Hand of the Father:)				
	0064:33	24:44	16:19		Ps 110:1 Ro 8:34 Cl 3:1 He 10:12 1Pe 3:22
	0239:45-46	(Same as 0064:33, above)			
	0418: 6- 7	(Same as 0064:33, above)			
	2057:35-42	(Same as 0064:33, above)			
20:46-47	1907: 1- 8	23:5-7,14	12:38-40		Lk 11:43

LUKE Chap:Verse	The URANTIA Book Page:Line	MATTHEW Chap:Verse	MARK Chap:Verse	JOHN Chap:Verse	Other BOOKS Chap:Verse
21: 1- 4	(The Widow's Mite:)				
	1883:26-34		12:41-44		
21: 5- 6	(Jesus Foretells the Destruction of The Temple:)				
	1414: 8- 9	24:1-2	13:1-2		Lk 21:20
	1912: 3-10	24:1-2	13:1-2		Lk 21:20
	1934:31-32	24:1-2	13:1-2		Lk 21:20
21: 7	1912:22-24	24:3	13:3-4		
21: 8-17	(Jesus Foretells Confusion and Persecution:)				
	1912:29-1913:6	24:4-14	13:5-13		
			10:17-22		
21: 9-10	1490:30-32	24:6-7	13:7-8		
21:10	0597:20-21	24:7	13:8		
21:12-17	1584:10-17	24:9	13:9-13		
21:16	1951:29-30	10:21	13:12		
21:19	1958:26-27				
21:20	(Jesus Foretells Destruction of The Temple,				
	See Luke 21:5-6, above.)				
21:20-21	1913:26-31	24:15-18	13:14-16		
21:20-24	1934:32-33	24:15-21	13:14-19		
21:20-36	1915:39-40		13:33-37		
21:22-24	1913:31-35				
21:25-28	(Ideas About the Coming Kingdom:)				
	1860:39-40	24:29-31	13:24-27		
	1863:43-47	24:29-31	13:24-27		
21:27	(Jesus' Return in Power & Glory:)				
	0596:38	16:27;24:30	8:38		Lk 9:26
		25:31	13:26		
	1591:16-17	(Same as 0596:38, above)			
	1760:23-25	(Same as 0596:38, above)			
	1860:16-17	(Same as 0596:38, above)			
	1915: 1- 4	(Same as 0596:38, above)			
	2092:42-43	(Same as 0596:38, above)			
21:29-31	1915:15-19	24:32-33	13:28-29		
21:31	1537:11-12	4:17	1:15		
21:32	1915:11-12	24:34	13:30		
21:33	1736:20-21	24:35	13:31		
	1914: 2	24:35	13:31		2Pe 3:10
22: 2	1924:28-34	26:3-4	14:1		
	1925:43-46	26:5	14:2		

241

Luke 22:4 to 22:42

LUKE Chap:Verse	The URANTIA Book Page:Line	MATTHEW Chap:Verse	MARK Chap:Verse	JOHN Chap:Verse	Other BOOKS Chap:Verse
22: 4- 5	1567:21-27	26:14-15	14:10		
	1924:24-28	26:14-15	14:10		
	1925:47-1926:6	26:14-15	14:10		
	1998:11-13	26:14-15	14:10		
22: 6	1926: 9-12	26:16	14:11		
22: 8- 9	1933:12-14	26:17	14:12		
22:10-12	1933:22-28	26:18	14:13-15		
22:13	1933:29-32	26:19	14:16		
22:14	1937:35-38	26:20	14:17		
22:15-16	1937:45-1938:5				
22:17-18	1938: 6-11	26:29	14:25		Lk 22:20
22:19	1942: 9-14	26:26	14:22	6:35,48	1Co 11:23-24
	1942:44-46				1Co 11:24-26
22:20	1938: 8-11	26:29	14:25		Lk 22:17-18
	1941:41-47	26:27-29	14:23-25		1Co 11:25-26
22:21-22	1940:40-44	26:24	14:21		
22:23	1940:46	26:22	14:19		
22:24	1937: 9-23				
	1940: 3- 5				
22:25-27	1940:11-17 (Same as 03016:40, below)				
22:26	(Greatest Be as Younger, Chief as Server,				
	See Luke 18:14, above.)				
22:28-30	1536:39-42				
	1940:17-19				
22:31-32	1971:32-33				
	2039:35-36				
22:32	1962:28-29				
	1962:33-35				
22:33	1962:20-22	26:33	14:29	13:37	
22:34	1962:24-27	26:34	14:30	13:38	
22:35-36	1944: 5-11				
22:40	1968:27-30	26:43	14:40		
22:41	(Prayer, See Luke 18:1-14, above.)				
22:41-42	1968:21-24	26:42	14:36		
22:42	(Drinking the Cup:)				
	0229:46	20:22-23	10:38-39		
		26:39,42,42	14:36,39		
	1867:37-39	(Same as 0229:46, above)			

(Luke 22:42 Continued on next page.)

LUKE Chap:Verse	The URANTIA Book Page:Line	MATTHEW Chap:Verse	MARK Chap:Verse	JOHN Chap:Verse	Other BOOKS Chap:Verse
22:42	1955:30-32	(Same as 0229:46, above)			
	1968:11-15	(Same as 0229:46, above)			
	1968:22-24	(Same as 0229:46, above)			
	1968:33-34	(Same as 0229:46, above)			
	1972: 5- 7	(Same as 0229:46, above)			

(Doing the Father's Will:)

	0008:42	6:10;7:21	3:35	4:34;5:30	Lk 8:21
		12:50;26:39	14:36	6:38;7:17	Lk 11:2
		26:42;44	14:39	14:23-24;15:10,14	

	0052: 1- 4	(Same as 0008:42, above)			
	1200:41	(Same as 0008:42, above)			
	1221:33-34	(Same as 0008:42, above)			
	1303: 7	(Same as 0008:42, above)			
	1318:29-30	(Same as 0008:42, above)			
	1324:21-22	(Same as 0008:42, above)			
	1327:10	(Same as 0008:42, above)			
	1328:38-41	(Same as 0008:42, above)			
	1331: 9-10	(Same as 0008:42, above)			
	1417: 5- 7	(Same as 0008:42, above)			
	1453:43-44	(Same as 0008:42, above)			
	1500:27	(Same as 0008:42, above)			
	1511:47-48	(Same as 0008:42, above)			
	1514:35	(Same as 0008:42, above)			
	1569:8-9	(Same as 0008:42, above)			
	1574:21	(Same as 0008:42, above)			
	1582: 8	(Same as 0008:42, above)			
	1594:33-34	(Same as 0008:42, above)			
	1608: 1	(Same as 0008:42, above)			
	1769:42-44	(Same as 0008:42, above)			
	1774:28	(Same as 0008:42, above)			
	1947:50-1948:1	(Same as 0008:42, above)			
	1968:21-24	(Same as 0008:42, above)			
	1968:33-34	(Same as 0008:42, above)			
	1972: 5- 7	(Same as 0008:42, above)			
	2078: 8	(Same as 0008:42, above)			
	2087:11	(Same as 0008:42, above)			
	2088:30-31	(Same as 0008:42, above)			
	2089:12-14	(Same as 0008:42, above)			
	2090: 1	(Same as 0008:42, above)			

Luke 22:43 to 23:7

LUKE Chap:Verse	The URANTIA Book Page:Line	MATTHEW Chap:Verse	MARK Chap:Verse	JOHN Chap:Verse	Other BOOKS Chap:Verse
22:43	1968:25-26				
22:44	1969:13-16				
22:45-46	1968:27-30	26:41	14:38		
22:47	1973:33-36	26:47	14:43	18:3	
22:47-48	1974:28-32	26:49-50	14:45		
22:49-51	1974:41-50	26:50-52	14:46-47	18:10-11	
22:52-53	1975: 7-10	26:55	14:48-49		
22:54	(Peter Follows Afar Off:)				
	1551:32	26:58	14:54	18:15	
	1975:32	26:58	14:54	18:15	
	1980: 7-18	26:58	14:54	18:15-16,18	
22:55-62	1551: 6- 8	26:69-75	14:66-72	18:15-18	
22:56-57	1551:15-17	26:69-72	14:66-70	18:16-17	
	1980:31-38	26:69-70	14:66-68	18:17	
22:58	1980:39-43			18:26-27	
22:59-60	1981: 3- 8	26:73-74	14:70	18:25	
22:60	1981:13-14	26:74	14:72	18:27	
22:61	1981:14-20				
22:62	1981:24-25	26:75	14:72		
22:63	1983:45-49	26:67	14:65		
22:63-65	1984:16-22	26:67-68	14:65		
	2000:12-14	26:67-68	14:65		
22:66	1982: 5- 7				
	1982:23-24				
22:67-68	1986:10-11				
22:67-70	(Jesus' Response to High Priests:)				
	1979:44-50	26:63-64	14:61-62		
	1983:20-27	26:63-64	14:61-62		
	1999: 6- 9	26:63-64	14:61-62		
22:71	1983:28-30	26:65	14:63		
23: 1	1986:12-14	27:2	15:1	18:28	
23: 2	1990:25-33	27:12	15:3		
23: 3	(Jesus Before Pilate:)				
	1991:13-14	27:11	15:2	18:33-35	
	1991:30-32	27:11	15:2	18:37	
	1999:10-12	27:11	15:2	18:33-37	
23: 4	1991:47-1992: 2			18:38	
23: 5	1992: 2- 7				
23: 6- 7	1992: 8-17				

LUKE Chap:Verse	The URANTIA Book Page:Line	MATTHEW Chap:Verse	MARK Chap:Verse	JOHN Chap:Verse	Other BOOKS Chap:Verse
23: 8	1992:29-32				
23: 9	1992:33-37				
	1999: 9-10				
23:10-11	1992:38-42				
23:12	1992:12-13				
23:13-16	1993: 4-13				
23:16	1995: 4- 6	26:27	15:15	19:1	
23:17	1993:17-19	27:15	15:6	18:39	
23:18	1993:34-38	27:20	15:11	18:40	
23:19	1993:25-29	27:16	15:7	18:40	
23:20-21	1994:25-28	27:22	15:12-13		
23:22	1994:31-32	27:23	15:14		
	1995:19-21			19:4-6	
23:23	1995:29-31			19:6	
23:23-25	1996:40-43	27:24-26	15:15		
23:25	1997:26-28			19:14	
23:26	(Simon, a Cyrenian, Carries the Cross:)				
	1438:34-38	27:32	15:21		
	2006:14-20	27:32	15:21		
	2006:28-29				
23:27	2004:22-25				
	2005:33-37				
	(The Faithful Women's Corps, See Luke 23:49, below.)				
23:28-30	2005:37-45				
23:32	2001:47-2002: 3				
	2004:12-14				
23:33	2006:32-46	27:35	15:24	19:18	
23:33-34	2007:15-18	27:38	15:27	19:18	
23:34	2018:43				
	(Casting Lots for Rament:)				
	1341:43	27:35	15:24	19:23-24	Ps 22:18
	2007:44-49	27:35	15:24	19:23-24	Ps 22:18
23:35	1520: 6- 7	27:39-44	15:29-32		
	2008:20-25	27:39-42	15:29-31		Lk 23:37
23:36	2008:33-40				
23:37	2008:20-25	27:39-42	15:29-31		Lk 23:35
23:38	(Superscription, "King of The Jews":)				
	2005: 7- 9	27:37	15:24		
	2007:22-24	27:37	15:26		

245

Luke 23:39 to 24:43

LUKE Chap:Verse	The URANTIA Book Page:Line	MATTHEW Chap:Verse	MARK Chap:Verse	JOHN Chap:Verse	Other BOOKS Chap:Verse
23:39-43	2008:45-2009: 9				
23:44-45	2010: 9-13	27:45	15:33		
	2011:34	27:45	15:33		
23:46	2011: 3- 5	27:50	15:37	19:30	
	2015: 3				
23:47	1590: 4	27:54	15:39		
	2011: 5- 7	27:54	15:39		
23:49	2010:46-2011:2				
	(The Faithful Women's Corps:)				
	1403:35-36	27:55-56	15:40-41	19:25	Ac 1:14
					Lk 23:27;24:10
	1671:20-26	(Same as 1403:35-36, above)			
	1678:28-1679:15	(Same as 1403:35-36, above)			
	1680:21-24	(Same as 1403:35-36, above)			
	1680:28-29	(Same as 1403:35-36, above)			
	2005:33-45	(Same as 1403:35-36, above)			
	2008:14-19	(Same as 1403:35-36, above)			
23:50-52	2012:18-26	27:57-58	15:42-45	19:38	
23:53	2013:10-28	27:59-60	15:46	19:39-41	
23:54	2011:19		15:42	19:42	
23:55-56	2013:38-44	27:61	15:47		
24: 1	2025:30-35	28:1	16:1-2	20:1	
24: 2	2025:45-47		16:3-4	20:1	
24: 3	2026:10-23				
24: 4- 8	2026:32-49	28:5-6	16:5-6	20:11-16	
24: 6- 8	(Recalling Jesus Foretelling Death Resurrection, See Luke 18:31-33, above.)				
24: 9-12	2027: 8-17	28:8	16:8,10-11	20:2,1	
24:10	1403:35-36		15:41	19:25	Lk 23:27,49
	(Faithful Women's Corps: See Luke 23:49, above.)				
24:12	2027:29-34			20:4-9	
24:13-16	2034:27-37		16:12		
24:17-24	2034:38-2035: 7				
24:19	2066:11-12				
24:21	1864:25-27				Ga 4:4-5
24:25-27	2035: 8-42				
24:28-32	2035:43-2036: 5				
24:33-35	2036: 6-13		16:13		
24:36-38	2040:18-23		16:14	20:19	1Co 15:5

LUKE Chap:Verse	The URANTIA Book Page:Line	MATTHEW Chap:Verse	MARK Chap:Verse	JOHN Chap:Verse	Other BOOKS Chap:Verse
24:44-46	2040:24-27		16:14		
24:44-48	2052:12-40				
24:46	(Jesus Foretells His Suffering and Resurrection, See Luke 18:31-33, above.)				
24:47	(The Great Commission:)				
	1051: 8	24:14 28:19-20	13:10 16:15	20:21	Ac 1:8
	1584: 4- 6	(Same as 1051:8, above)			
	1608:22	(Same as 1051:8, above)			
	1824:43-44	(Same as 1051:8, above)			
	1934:28-30	(Same as 1051:8, above)			
	1957:35-37	(Same as 1051:8, above)			
	1961:49	(Same as 1051:8, above)			
	2033:17-18	(Same as 1051:8, above)			
	2034: 2- 3	(Same as 1051:8, above)			
	2042: 8- 9	(Same as 1051:8, above)			
	2043: 3- 6	(Same as 1051:8, above)			
	2044:35-36	(Same as 1051:8, above)			
	2052:39-40	(Same as 1051:8, above)			
	2053:14-16	(Same as 1051:8, above)			
	2053:38-40	(Same as 1051:8, above)			
	2054: 5- 6	(Same as 1051:8, above)			
	2054:25-27	(Same as 1051:8, above)			
	2054:41-42	(Same as 1051:8, above)			
	2055:16-18	(Same as 1051:8, above)			
	2057:24-25	(Same as 1051:8, above)			
24:47-48	2043: 3- 6		16:15	20:21	
24:49	(Wait in Jerusalem for The Spirit of Truth:)				
	2053:17-19				Ac 1:4
	2055: 9-11				Ac 1:4
	2057:21-22				Ac 1:4
24:49	(The Comforter, the "Spirit of Truth," The "New Teacher," Poured Out "On all Flesh":)				
	0241:41-42			14:16-18,26 14:26;15:26 16:7,13-14 Ek 11:19;36:26-27	Ac 2:2-4 Ac 2:16-18 Jl 2:28
	0365:32-33	(Same as 0241:41-42, above)			

(Luke 24:49 Continued on next page.)

LUKE Chap:Verse	The URANTIA Book Page:Line	MATTHEW Chap:Verse	MARK Chap:Verse	JOHN Chap:Verse	Other BOOKS Chap:Verse
24:49	0379:36	(Same as 0241:41-42, above)			
	0382:10-14	(Same as 0241:41-42, above)			
	0596:31-32	(Same as 0241:41-42, above)			
	1328: 4- 5	(Same as 0241:41-42, above)			
	1328:22-25	(Same as 0241:41-42, above)			
	1340:24-27	(Same as 0241:41-42, above)			
	1591:15-16	(Same as 0241:41-42, above)			
	1594: 3- 4	(Same as 0241:41-42, above)			
	1642:18-24	(Same as 0241:41-42, above)			
	1897:33	(Same as 0241:41-42, above)			
	1918:45-47	(Same as 0241:41-42, above)			
	1947:14-17	(Same as 0241:41-42, above)			
	1948: 9-24	(Same as 0241:41-42, above)			
	1948:34-36	(Same as 0241:41-42, above)			
	1951:45-48	(Same as 0241:41-42, above)			
	1953:22-26	(Same as 0241:41-42, above)			
	1954: 2	(Same as 0241:41-42, above)			
	1958: 7- 9	(Same as 0241:41-42, above)			
	1959:22-24	(Same as 0241:41-42, above)			
	1961:24-27	(Same as 0241:41-42, above)			
	2035:38-39	(Same as 0241:41-42, above)			
	2044:34-35	(Same as 0241:41-42, above)			
	2053:17-19	(Same as 0241:41-42, above)			
	2054:42-43	(Same as 0241:41-42, above)			
	2055: 9-11	(Same as 0241:41-42, above)			
	2057:21-22	(Same as 0241:41-42, above)			
	2061:10-13	(Same as 0241:41-42, above)			
	2061:20-21	(Same as 0241:41-42, above)			
	2062:43	(Same as 0241:41-42, above)			
	2064: 7	(Same as 0241:41-42, above)			
	(COMPARE: Tarry in Judea & Galilee a While:)				
	2043:17-18				
24:50-51	2057:14-31				
24:51	2057:31				

D: The Gospel According to JOHN

John 1:4 to 1:13

JOHN Chap:Verse	The URANTIA Book Page:Line	MATTHEW Chap:Verse	MARK Chap:Verse	LUKE Chap:Verse	Other BOOKS Chap:Verse
1: 4- 9	(Jesus as Light:)				
	0447:38-39	4:16		1:79;2:32	Is 9:2 Jn 5:35
					Jn 8:12;9:5;12:46
					Jn 12:35-36 1Jo 2:8
	0513:31	(Same as 0447:38-39, above)			
	0590:33	(Same as 0447:38-39, above)			
	1104:14-15	(Same as 0447:38-39, above)			
	1181: 7- 8	(Same as 0447:38-39, above)			
	1353:38-39	(Same as 0447:38-39, above)			
	1458:33-35	(Same as 0447:38-39, above)			
	1671:10-11	(Same as 0447:38-39, above)			
	1795: 1	(Same as 0447:38-39, above)			
	1965:31	(Same as 0447:38-39, above)			
	2035:28-29	(Same as 0447:38-39, above)			
	(Children of Light, See John 12:36, below.)				
1: 6- 7	1627: 6- 8	11:10		7:27	Ml 3:1 Jn 5:32-35
1: 6- 8	0514:24-25				
1:10-13	1954: 1- 4				Jl 2:28-29 Ac 2:17
1:12	(Power to become Sons of God:)				
	0039:18-19				Is 56:5 Ro 8:14-17
					Ga 3:26;4:6
					1Jo 3:1-2
	0067:32-33	(Same as 0039:18-19, above)			
	0447:40-0448:35	(Same as 0039:18-19, above)			
	1112:41-42	(Same as 0039:18-19, above)			
	1191:16-17	(Same as 0039:18-19, above)			
	1454:37	(Same as 0039:18-19, above)			
	1603:37-40	(Same as 0039:18-19, above)			
	1610: 2-20	(Same as 0039:18-19, above)			
	1725:28	(Same as 0039:18-19, above)			
	1861:29-30	(Same as 0039:18-19, above)			
	1945:21	(Same as 0039:18-19, above)			
	1957:36-37	(Same as 0039:18-19, above)			
	1958:17	(Same as 0039:18-19, above)			
	2053:14,38	(Same as 0039:18-19, above)			
1:12-13	1601:18-37				Is 32:15-17
		—	—		Ro 8:9-16 1Jo 5:4
	1860: 6- 8				Ga 4:4-7

250

JOHN Chap:Verse	The URANTIA Book Page:Line	MATTHEW Chap:Verse	MARK Chap:Verse	LUKE Chap:Verse	Other BOOKS Chap:Verse
1:14	1874:29-30				

(The Only Begotten Son of the Father:)

	0073:37				Jn 1:18;3:16,18
					Ps 2:7 Ac 13:33
					He 1:5;5:5 1Jo 4:9
	0109:22	(Same as 0073:37, above)			
	0232:33-35	(Same as 0073:37, above)			
	0234: 7	(Same as 0073:37, above)			
	0235: 6	(Same as 0073:37, above)			
	0366:15	(Same as 0073:37, above)			
	1522:43-47	(Same as 0073:37, above)			

(Incarnation of Deity, the "Word" made Flesh:)

	0094:12				
	0227:33				
	0584: 9-10	2:1-2		2:7-11	
	1407:30-32				
	1510:41-43	_	_		Jn 1:1-5
	1594: 2- 3				
	1594:47-48				
	1712:10-11				Jn 6:53-58
1:15	1505:45-1506: 3		1:7		Jn 1:29-30
1:18					

(Father is Revealed by/through the Son:)

	0028:14-15	11:27		10:22	Jn 6:45-46;8:26
					Jn 12:49-50;14:7-9
					Jn 14:20:17:6,25-26
	0093:46	(Same as 0028:14-15, above)			
	0109:28-33	(Same as 0028:14-15, above)			
	0196:10	(Same as 0028:14-15, above)			
	0232:42-0233:6	(Same as 0028:14-15, above)			
	1324:23-32	(Same as 0028:14-15, above)			
	1328:38-41	(Same as 0028:14-15, above)			
	1331:21-22	(Same as 0028:14-15, above)			
	1608: 1- 2	(Same as 0028:14-15, above)			
	1710:15-16	(Same as 0028:14-15, above)			
	1750:14-15	(Same as 0028:14-15, above)			
	1855:46-47	(Same as 0028:14-15, above)			
	1947:42-47	(Same as 0028:14-15, above)			
	1965: 8-12	(Same as 0028:14-15, above)			

(John 1:18 Continued on next page.)

John 1:18 to 1:41

JOHN Chap:Verse	The URANTIA Book Page:Line	MATTHEW Chap:Verse	MARK Chap:Verse	LUKE Chap:Verse	Other BOOKS Chap:Verse
1:18	(Bosom of the Father:)				
	0064:34				
	0144:30-31				
	0148:45-46				
	0227: 8- 9				
	(Only Begotten Son: see John 1:14, above.)				
1:19-21	1505:21-25				
1:22-23	1502:25-33	3:3	1:3	3:4-6	Is 40:3-5
1:24-26	1505:25-30				
1:26	0964:37	3:6,11	1:4,8	3:7,16	Jn 1:28
1:27	1503:24-28	3:11-12	1:7-8	3:16	
1:28	(Baptism:)				
	0964:37	3:6,11	1:4,8	3:7,16	Jn 1:26
	1502:21-22	3:5-6	1:4-5		
	1503:35-36				
	1504:11-17		1:9-11		
	1869:30				
1:29-32	1505:45-1506:8	3:17	1:7,11	3:17	Jn 1:15
1:31	1503: 6-19				
1:32	1511:42-43	3:16	1:10	3:22	
1:32-34	1504:45-48				
1:33	1593:12-13	3:11	1:8	3:16	Ac 1:5
1:34	(The "Son of God:")				
	1317: 9-13		1:1		
	1505: 4- 7				
	1511:39-40	3:17	1:11	3:22	
	1746:19-20				
	1786:28-29				
	(Only Begotten Son, See John 1:14, above.)				
1:35-37	1526: 8-10				
1:38	1534: 9		—		Jn 1:49;3:2;6:25
1:40	(The Call of Andrew:)				
	1524: 9-20	4:18-20	1:16-18		
		10:2	3:18	6:14	Ac 1:13
	1548:28-1550:22 (Same as 1524: 9-20, above)				
1:41-42	(The Call of Simon Bar-Jona:)				
	1524:25-1525:2	4:18-20	1:16-18		
		10:2	3:16	6:14	Ac 1:13

(John 1:41-42 Continued on next page.)

252

JOHN Chap:Verse	The URANTIA Book Page:Line	MATTHEW Chap:Verse	MARK Chap:Verse	LUKE Chap:Verse	Other BOOKS Chap:Verse
1:41-42	1549:10-12	(Same as 1524:25-1525:2, above)			
	1550:23-1552:20	(Same as 1524:25-1525:2, above)			
	1628:27-1629:11			5:1-9	
1:42	1548:31				Jn 21:15-17
	(Simon is called Cephas or Peter:)				
	1524:36-1525:2	10:2;16:18	3:16	6:14	
	1550:31-32	10:2;16:18	3:16	6:14	
	1897:13-14	10:2;16:18	3:16	6:14	
1:43	1506:14-16				
	1526: 4- 6				
1:43-44	(The Call of Philip:)				
	1526:21-44	10:3	3:18	6:14	Ac 1:13
	1556: 5-1558:6	10:3	3:18	6:14	Ac 1:13
1:45-49	(The Call of Nathaniel, Son of Bartholomew:)				
	1526:45-1527:13	10:3	3:18	6:14	Ac 1:13
	1557:21-23				
	1558: 7-1559:19	10:3	3:18	6:14	Ac 1:13
1:46	1363: 2				
	1558:25-26				
1:47	1558:19-20				
1:49	1534: 9				Jn 1:38;3:2;6:25
1:51	(Son of Man:)				
	1390: 3- 5	8:20+	2:10+	5:24+	He 2:14
					En 46:1-6;48:1-7
					En 62:1-5;63:11
					En 69:27-29;71:14,17
	1390:24-31	(Same as 1390:3-5, above)			
	1407:27	(Same as 1390:3-5, above)			
	1501:22-28	(Same as 1390:3-5, above)			
	(Spiritual Vision:)				
	1841:16-17				Ge 28:12
2: 1	1528:31-32				
2: 1-11	1545:24				
2: 2	1527:26-27				
2: 3- 4	1529:31-1530: 5				
2: 4	1103: 8				
	1417:23-24				
2: 5	1530: 6-16				
2: 6- 8	1530:25-30				

John 2:9 to 3:3

JOHN Chap:Verse	The URANTIA Book Page:Line	MATTHEW Chap:Verse	MARK Chap:Verse	LUKE Chap:Verse	Other BOOKS Chap:Verse
2: 9-10	1531: 4- 8				
2:11	1531: 9-17				
2:12	1531:24-27				
	1532:34-35				
2:13	1888: 3- 5		11:12		
2:14	1888:23-25				
	1888:33-35				
	1889:10-13				
2:14-16	(Cleansing of the Temple:)				
	1378:27-29	21:12-13	11:15-17	19:45-46	
	1890:11-25	21:12-13	11:15-17	19:45-46	Is 56:7
					Je 7:11
	1911: 6- 7	21:12-13	11:15-17	19:45-46	
2:18	(Show us a Sign:)				
	1520:21-23	12:38;16:1	8:11	11:16	Jn 6:30
	1714:41-43	12:38;16:1	8:11	11:16	Jn 6:30
	1744:40-45	12:38;16:1	8:11	11:16	Jn 6:30
	1895:30-34	12:38;16:1	8:11	11:16	Jn 6:30
2:19	(The only "sign:")				
	1714:44-47	12:39;16:4	8:12	11:29	
	1744:46-1745:4	12:39	8:12	11:29	
		14:4			
	1895:34-36	12:39;16:4	8:12	11:29	
	1982:39-40	26:60-61	14:58		
	1983:11-12	26:60-61	14:58		
2:20-22	1895:36-41				
2:23	1595:38				
	1596:28-29				
3: 1- 2	1601:45-1602: 9				
3: 2	(Jesus as Rabbi, or Teacher:)				
	0513:38				
	1534: 9				Jn 1:38,49;6:25
	1594:23-24				
	1602:16-19				
3: 3	(Requirement for a New Birth:)				
	0380:33				
	1130:43-44				
	1234: 8-11				

(John 3:3 Continued on next page.)

JOHN Chap:Verse	The URANTIA Book Page:Line	MATTHEW Chap:Verse	MARK Chap:Verse	LUKE Chap:Verse	Other BOOKS Chap:Verse
3:3	1545:35-37				
	1576:14-16	18:3	9:37;10:15	18:17	
	1592:46				
	1660: 2- 4				
	1602:20-21				
	1829:36-37				
	1859:44-45				
	2053:35-36				
	2054:18-19				
3: 4	1602:21-23				
3: 5- 8	1602:24-30				
	(New Birth, See John 3:3, above.)				
3: 9-13	1602:31-37				
3:14	0946:23				Ex 4:3-4;7:9-12
					Nu 21:8-9 2Ki 18:4
3:14-15	(Spirit Gravity; Son "lifted up" will "draw" men:)				
	0026:29				Je 31:3 Jn 6:44
					Jn 8:28;12:32
	0082:24-29	(Same as 0026:29, above)			
	0084:12-20	(Same as 0026:29, above)			
	0139:43-44	(Same as 0026:29, above)			
	0224:22-23	(Same as 0026:29, above)			
	1067:40-41	(Same as 0026:29, above)			
	1190:17-18	(Same as 0026:29, above)			
	1750:15	(Same as 0026:29, above)			
	1904:20-21	(Same as 0026:29, above)			
	2019:19-25	(Same as 0026:29, above)			
	2084: 8- 9	(Same as 0026:29, above)			
3:15-16	(Whosoever Will may Come;)				
	0039: 7	16:24-25	8:34-35	9:23-24	Re 22:17
	1102:18-19	16:24-25	8:34-35	9:23-24	Re 22:17
	1205: 1- 2	16:24-25	8:34-35	9:23-24	Re 22:17
	1567: 3- 5	16:24-25	8:34-35	9:23-24	Re 3:8;22:17
	1750:16-17	16:24-25	8:34-35	9:23-24	Re 22:17
	1820:44-45	16:24-25	8:34-35	9:23-24	Re 22:17
	1829:44-45	16:24-25	8:34-35	9:23-24	Re 22:17

(John 3:15-16 Continued on next page.)

JOHN Chap:Verse	The URANTIA Book Page:Line	MATTHEW Chap:Verse	MARK Chap:Verse	LUKE Chap:Verse	Other BOOKS Chap:Verse
3:15-16	(Eternal/Everlasting Life:)				
	0044: 5- 6				Jn 5:24-25,39-40;6:40,47
					Jn 10:10;11:25-26
					1Tm 6:12 1Jo 5:11-12
	1113: 7- 8	(Same as 0044:5-6, above)			
	1567: 3- 5	(Same as 0044:5-6, above)			
	1649:39-43	(Same as 0044:5-6, above)			
	1711:12-13	(Same as 0044:5-6, above)			
	1750:16-17	(Same as 0044:5-6, above)			
	1792: 4- 5	(Same as 0044:5-6, above)			
	1829:44-45	(Same as 0044:5-6, above)			
	1843: 9-10	(Same as 0044:5-6, above)			
	1861:23	(Same as 0044:5-6, above)			
	1965:33-34	(Same as 0044:5-6, above)			
	2035:38	(Same as 0044:5-6, above)			
	2053:36-37	(Same as 0044:5-6, above)			
3:16	0028: 5- 6				
	0228:24-29				Ro 5:6-21 1Jo 4:9
					2Co 5:14-21
					He 9:11-28;13:12
3:18	(Only Begotten Son: See John 1:14, above.)				
3:22	1605:29-31				
	1615:33-34				Jn 3:26;4:39-41
	1625:18-34	—	—		Jn 3:26
3:25-26	1507: 9-13				
3:26	1615:33-34				Jn 3:22;4:39-41
	1625:18-34	—	—		Jn 3:22
3:27-30	1507:13-19				
3:31-36	1507:19-25				
3:32	0644: 8- 9	—	—		Jn 5:19;8:38
4: 1- 3	1606:19-21				
4: 2	1625:23-26				
4: 3	1611:46-48				
4: 4- 6	1612:30-37	—	—		Jn 4:8
4: 7	1612:40-42				
4: 8	1612:31-34	—	—		Jn 4:6
4: 9	1535: 8- 9				
	1612:42-1613: 3				

JOHN Chap:Verse	The URANTIA Book Page:Line	MATTHEW Chap:Verse	MARK Chap:Verse	LUKE Chap:Verse	Other BOOKS Chap:Verse
4:10	(Living Water--The Water of Life:)				
	0381: 5- 9	5:6			Jn 4:13-14;6:35
					Jn 7:37-38
					Is 55:1 Re 7:16-17
	1613: 3- 5	(Same as 0381:5-9, above)			
	1795:34-1796:18	(Same as 0381:5-9, above)			
	1861:12	(Same as 0381:5-9, above)			
	1954: 3- 6	(Same as 0381:5-9, above)			
	1965:30	(Same as 0381:5-9, above)			
	2035:39-40	(Same as 0381:5-9, above)			
	2054:19-21	(Same as 0381:5-9, above)			
4:11-12	1613: 5- 8				
4:13-14	1613: 9-12				
	(Living Water, See John 4:10, above.)				
4:15	1613:12-14				
4:16-18	1613:19-29				
4:18	1615: 2- 3				
4:19-20	1613:34-43				
4:20-21	0945:24-27	_	_		Is 2:2;8:18
4:21-24	1613:47-1614:8				
4:23-24	(Worship God in Spirit and in Truth:)				
	1454:17-19				
	1640:28-31				
	1849: 2	_	_		Ep 6:18
	2053:40-41				
4:24	(God is Spirit:)				
	0025: 2				
	0026:17				
	0030:40				
	0074: 4				
	0096:11-14				
	0139:26				
	0140:44				
	0513:33-34				
	1486:40-42				
	1487:11				
	1782:21-22				
	1856: 2- 3				

(John 4:24 Cointinued on nest page.)

John 4:24 to 4:34

JOHN Chap:Verse	The URANTIA Book Page:Line	MATTHEW Chap:Verse	MARK Chap:Verse	LUKE Chap:Verse	Other BOOKS Chap:Verse
4:24	1856:24-25				
	1857:24				
	2084:25-26				
4:25	1509:27				
4:25-26	1614: 9-15				
4:27	1614:25-29				
4:28-30	1614:31-37				
4:29	1615: 1				
4:31-32	1615:12-18				
4:32	0286:40				
4:33-38	1615:18-30				
4:34	(Jesus' "Work:")				
	1615:22-23			Jn 5:17,36;9:4;17:4;19:30	
	1649:30-31			Jn 5:17,36;9:4;17:4;19:30	
	1812: 8-11			Jn 5:17,36;9:4;17:4;19:30	
	1897:26			Jn 5:17,36;9:4;17:4;19:30	
	1955:30-32			Jn 5:17,36;9:4;17:4;19:30	
	1963:37-39			Jn 5:17,36;9:4;17:4;19:30	
	2011: 3- 4			Jn 5:17,36;9:4;17:4;19:30	
	(Doing the Father's Will:)				
	0008:42	6:10;7:21	3:35	8:21	Jn 5:30;6:38
		12:50;26:39	14:36	11:2	Jn 7:17;14:23-24
		26:42,44	14:39	22:42	Jn 15:10,14
	0052: 1- 4	(Same as 0008:42, above)			
	1200:41	(Same as 0008:42, above)			
	1221:33-34	(Same as 0008:42, above)			
	1303: 7	(Same as 0008:42, above)			
	1318:29-30	(Same as 0008:42, above)			
	1324:21-22	(Same as 0008:42, above)			
	1327:10	(Same as 0008:42, above)			
	1328:38-41	(Same as 0008:42, above)			
	1331: 9-10	(Same as 0008:42, above)			
	1417: 5- 7	(Same as 0008:42, above)			
	1453:43-44	(Same as 0008:42, above)			
	1500:27	(Same as 0008:42, above)			
	1511:47-48	(Same as 0008:42, above)			
	1514:35	(Same as 0008:42, above)			
	1569: 8- 9	(Same as 0008:42, above)			

(John 4:34 Continued on next page.)

JOHN Chap:Verse	The URANTIA Book Page:Line	MATTHEW Chap:Verse	MARK Chap:Verse	LUKE Chap:Verse	Other BOOKS Chap:Verse
4:34	1574:21	(Same as 0008:42, above)			
	1582: 8	(Same as 0008:42, above)			
	1594:33-34	(Same as 0008:42, above)			
	1608: 1	(Same as 0008:42, above)			
	1615:22-23	(Same as 0008:42, above)			
	1769:42-44	(Same as 0008:42, above)			Ja 1:22-25
					Ja 2:17 1Jo 3:18
	1774:28	(Same as 0008:42, above)			
	1947:50-1948:1	(Same as 0008:42, above)			
	1968:21-34	(Same as 0008:42, above)			
	1972: 5- 7	(Same as 0008:42, above)			
	2078: 8	(Same as 0008:42, above)			
	2087:11	(Same as 0008:42, above)			
	2088:30	(Same as 0008:42, above)			
	2089:12-14	(Same as 0008:42, above)			
	2090: 1	(Same as 0008:42, above)			
4:39-41	1615:31-34				Jn 3:22,26
4:43	1644:24				
4:44	1538:19	13:57	6:4	4:24	
	1686:33-35	13:57	6:4	4:24	
4:45-53	1644:25-45				
4:54	1644:47-48				
5: 1- 4	1649: 2-12				
5: 2- 4	0947: 2- 3				
5: 5- 9	(Conduct on the Sabbath:)				
	1649:47-1650:5	12:1-14	2:23-28	6:1-10	Jn 5:16-18
		15:1-9	3:1-5	11:37-41	Jn 9:14
			7:1-7	13:10-17	
				14:1-6	
	1654:29-1655:12	(Same as 1649:47-1650:5, above)			
	1665: 7-35	(Same as 1649:47-1650:5, above)			
	1712:21-42	(Same as 1649:47-1650:5, above)			
	1813:13-16	(Same as 1649:47-1650:5, above)			
	1835:40-1836:26	(Same as 1649:47-1650:5, above)			
	1850:22-23	(Same as 1649:47-1650:5, above)			
5:10-15	1650: 6-11				
5:16-18	(Conduct on Sabbath, See John 5:5-9, above.)				
5:17	1649:30-31				
	(Jesus' "Work," See John 4:34, above.)				

JOHN Chap:Verse	The URANTIA Book Page:Line	MATTHEW Chap:Verse	MARK Chap:Verse	LUKE Chap:Verse	Other BOOKS Chap:Verse
5:18	(Jesus & the Father are One, See John 1:1, above.)				
5:19	0644: 8- 9				Jn 3:32;8:38
5:24	1642: 7- 8				
5:24-25	1649:39-43				
	(Eternal/Everlasting Life, see John 3:15-16, above.)				
5:25-29	1328: 3- 4	27:52-53			
5:26	0035:36				
	1642: 3				
5:30	(Doing the Father's Will, See John 4:34, above.)				
5:32-35	1627: 6- 8	11:10		7:27	Ml 3:1 Jn 1:6-7
5:35	(Jesus as Light: See John 1:4-9, above.)				
5:36	(Jesus' "Work," See John 4:34, above.)				
5:39-40	2029: 9 (Everlasting Life: See John 3:15-16, above.)				
6: 1- 3	1700:20-32	14:13-14	6:31-34	9:10-11	
6: 4	1700:15-17				
6: 5- 7	1960:24				
6: 5- 9	1701:14-35	14:15-17	6:35-38	9:12-13	
6: 8	1549:35	10:2		6:14	Jn 1:40
6:10-13	1701:36-49	14:18-21	6:39-44	9:14-17	
6:14	1702:20-25				
6:15-17	1703: 1- 7				
6:17-21	1703:11-38	14:24-33	6:47-51		
6:19	1519:46	14:25	6:48		
6:22	1703:43-45				
6:23-24	1710:27-29				
6:25	1534: 9	—	—		Jn 1:38,49;3:2
6:26	1702:34-36				
6:26-27	1710:29-43				
6:27	1860: 1				
6:28-29	1710:43-45				
6:30	(Show Us a Sign, See John 2:18, above.)				
6:30-33	1710:46-1711: 2				Ex 16:14-15
6:32-35	0513:43				Ge 1:1 Jn 1:1-4
6:34	1711: 3				
6:35	(The Bread & Water of Life:)				
	1711: 3- 5				
	2054:19-20	5:6			
	1712: 8-17				

(John 6:35 Continued on next page.)

JOHN Chap:Verse	The URANTIA Book Page:Line	MATTHEW Chap:Verse	MARK Chap:Verse	LUKE Chap:Verse	Other BOOKS Chap:Verse
6:35	(The Bread of Life:)				
	1711:14-16	5:6;26:26	14:22	22:19	Jn 6:48,51,58
	1711:38-43	5:6;26:26	14:22	22:19	Jn 6:48,51,58
	1942: 9-14	5:6;26:26	14:22	22:19	Jn 6:48,51,58
	1965:29	5:6;26:26	14:22	22:19	Jn 6:48,51,58
	(The Water of Life:)				
	0381: 5- 9	5:6			Jn 4:10,13-14;7:37-38
					Is 55:1 Re 7:17
	1613: 3- 5	(Same as 0381:5-9, above)			
	2054:19-21	(Same as 0381:5-9, above)			
	1954: 3- 6	(Same as 0381:5-9, above)			
	1965:30	(Same as 0381:5-9, above)			
	2035:39-40	(Same as 0381:5-9, above)			
6:38	(Doing the Father's Will, See John 4:34, above.)				
6:38-40	1861:27			12:32	
6:39	1191:32-33				
6:39-40	(Resurrection of Believers:)				
	0532:39-0533:11			Jn 11:24-26;13:36;14:3;17:24	
	0568:21			Jn 11:24-26;13:36;14:3;17:24	
	1944:16-20			Jn 11:24-26;13:36;14:3;17:24	
	1947:26-34			Jn 11:24-26;13:36;14:3;17:24	
	1965: 2- 8			Jn 11:24-26;13:36;14:3;17:24	
	2029: 9-12			Jn 11:24-26;13:36;14:3;17:24	
6:40	(Everlasting/Eternal Life: See John 3:15-16, above.)				
6:41-42	1711:17-25	13:55-56	6:3	4:22	
6:42	(Jesus' Human Family:)				
	1686:28-31	13:55-56	6:3		
	1711:22-24	13:55-56	6:3		
	(Father, Joseph the Carpenter:)				
	1051:11	13:55	6:3	4:22	Jn 1:45
	(Brother James:)				
	1357: 5- 6	13:55	6:3		Ga 1:19
	(Sister Miriam:)				
	1357:47-48	13:56	6:3		
	(Brother Joseph:)				
	1362: 1- 2	13:55	6:3		
	(Brother Simon:)				
	1365: 9-10	13:55	6:3		

(John 6:42 Continued on next page.)

John 6:42 to 6:60

JOHN Chap:Verse	The URANTIA Book Page:Line	MATTHEW Chap:Verse	MARK Chap:Verse	LUKE Chap:Verse	Other BOOKS Chap:Verse
6:42	(Sister Martha:)				
	1367:18	13:56	6:3		
	(Brother Jude:)				
	1370:11	13:55	6:3		
	(Sister Ruth:)				
	1389:21-22	13:56	6:3		
6:43-47	1711:26-37				Is 54:13
6:44	(Jesus' "Drawing Power," See John 3:14-15, above.)				
6:45	1331:9-10				
6:45-46	(The Son Reveals the Father:)				
	0028:14-15	11:27		10:22	Jn 1:18;8:26
					Jn 12:49-50;14:7-9
					Jn 14:20;17:6,25-26
	0093:46	(Same as 0028:14-15, above)			
	0109:28-33	(Same as 0028:14-15, above)			
	0196:10	(Same as 0028:14-15, above)			
	0232:42-44	(Same as 0028:14-15, above)			
	0233: 4- 5	(Same as 0028:14-15, above)			
	1324:23-32	(Same as 0028:14-15, above)			
	1328:38-41	(Same as 0028:14-15, above)			
	1331:21-22	(Same as 0028:14-15, above)			
	1608: 1- 2	(Same as 0028:14-15, above)			
	1710:15-16	(Same as 0028:14-15, above)			
	1750:14-15	(Same as 0028:14-15, above)			
	1855:46-47	(Same as 0028:14-15, above)			
	1947:42-47	(Same as 0028:14-15, above)			
	1965: 8-12	(Same as 0028:14-15, above)			
6:47	(Everlasting Life, See John 3:15-16, above.)				
6:48	(The Bread of Life, See John 6:35, above.)				
6:48-51	1711:38-44				Jn 6:58
6:51	1965:29	—	—		Jn 6:35,48
6:52	1711:46-48				
	1712: 5- 8				
6:53-58	1712: 8-20		—		Jn 1:14
6:57	0031: 2- 3	16:16-17			
6:58	1711:38-40		—		Jn 6:48-51
6:59	1707:26-28				
6:60	1715: 4-24				
6:60-69	1577:21-26				

262

JOHN Chap:Verse	The URANTIA Book Page:Line	MATTHEW Chap:Verse	MARK Chap:Verse	LUKE Chap:Verse	Other BOOKS Chap:Verse
6:61-62	1715:25-36	—	—		Re 3:16
6:63	0380:39-40				
6:63-70	1715:37-1716: 1				
7: 1	1789:14-16				
7: 2- 4	1788:37-40				
7: 6	1789: 4- 5				
7: 8-10	1789:49-1790: 2				
7:11	1790: 4- 6				
7:12-13	1790:10-16				
7:14-15	1790:25-29				
7:15	1790:16-18				
7:16	1855:47-48	—	—		Jn 7:29;8:42;12:49
7:16-19	1790:30-39				De 5:17 Ex 20:13
7:17	(Doing the Father's Will, See John 4:34, above.)				
7:20-26	1790:40-1791:14				
7:24	1897:18				
7:25	1791:15				
7:27-29	1791:15-26				
7:29	1855:47-48	—	—		Jn 7:16;8:42;12:49
7:30	1791:47				
7:30-32	1791:27-44				
7:33-34	1792: 6-10				Jn 8:21
7:33-36	1795:17-18	—	—		Jn 8:21
7:35-36	1792:11-14				Jn 8:22
7:37-38	(Thirst for Living Water, See John 4:10, above.)				
7:40-44	1796:19-23				
7:45-52	1792:15-36				
7:53	1792:37-38				
8: 1	1792:37-38				
8: 2- 5	1793: 1- 6				
8: 3- 9	1792:40-48				
8: 6	1793: 7-12				
8: 6-11	1793:25-37				
8:12	(Jesus Is Light:)				
	0447:38	4:16		1:79	Is 9:2 Jn 1:4-9
				2:32	Jn 9:5;12:35-36
					Jn 12:46 1Jo 2:8
	0513:31	(Same as 0447:38, above)			

(John 8:12 Continued on next page.)

JOHN Chap:Verse	The URANTIA Book Page:Line	MATTHEW Chap:Verse	MARK Chap:Verse	LUKE Chap:Verse	Other BOOKS Chap:Verse
8:12	0590:33	(Same as 0447:38, above)			
	1104:14-15	(Same as 0447:38, above)			
	1181: 7- 8	(Same as 0447:38, above)			
	1353:38-39	(Same as 0447:38, above)			
	1458:33-35	(Same as 0447:38, above)			
	1671:10-11	(Same as 0447:38, above)			
	1795: 1	(Same as 0447:38, above)			
	1965:31	(Same as 0447:38, above)			
	2035:28-29	(Same as 0447:38, above)			
8:12-19	1795: 1-16	(Same as 0447:38, above)			
8:20	1795:32-33				
8:21	1792: 7- 9				Jn 7:33-34
	1795:17-18	—	—		Jn 7:33-34
8:22	1792:11-14				Jn 7:35-36
8:23-26	1795:18-27				
8:26	(Son Reveals the Father, See John 6:45-46, above.)				
8:28	(Lifted Up, See John 3:14-15, above.)				
8:28-30	1795:28-32				
8:31-36	1796:27-38				
8:32	(Knowing Truth makes You Free:)				
	1112:43-44				
	1594: 1- 2				
	1859:36-38				
	1796:30-31				
	(Jesus as Truth, See John 14:6, below.)				
8:37-41	1796:39-1797:1				
8:38	0644: 8- 9				Jn 3:22;5:19
8:42	1855:47-48	—	—		Jn 7:16,29;12:49
8:42-45	1797: 1- 9				
8:44	0754:22-24				
8:46	1103:23				
	2092:13				
8:46-50	1797:10-18				
8:51-59	1797:19-38				
8:58	1750:21	—	—		Jn 16:28
	1786:35-36				
9: 1	1811:18-20				
	1874:46-47				
	1875:20				

JOHN Chap:Verse	The URANTIA Book Page:Line	MATTHEW Chap:Verse	MARK Chap:Verse	LUKE Chap:Verse	Other BOOKS Chap:Verse
9: 2	1811:26-28				
9: 3- 5	1812: 5-12				
9: 4	(Jesus' "Work", See John 4:34, above.)				
9: 5	(Jesus as Light, See John 8:12, above.)				
9: 6	1044:42-46				
9: 6- 7	1812:16-21				
9: 8- 9	1812:24-27				
9:10-12	1812:28-35				
9:13-15	1813:32-40				
9:14	(Conduct on the Sabbath:)				
	1649:47-1650:5	12:1-14	2:23-28	6:1-10	Jn 5:5-9
		15:1-9	3:1-5	11:37-41	Jn 5:16-18
			7:1-7	13:10-17	
				14:1-6	
	1654:29-1655:12 (Same as 1649:47-1650:5, above)				
	1665: 7-35 (Same as 1649:47-1650:5, above)				
	1712:21-42 (Same as 1649:47-1650:5, above)				
	1813:13-16 (Same as 1649:47-1650:5, above)				
	1835:40-1836:26 (Same as 1649:47-1650:5, above)				
	1850:22-23 (Same as 1649:47-1650:5, above)				
9:16	1813:41-1814: 5				
9:17-18	1814: 7-12				
9:19-23	1814:13-24				
9:24	1814:25-34				
9:25-26	1814:35-40				
9:27-29	1814:41-48				
9:30-33	1814:49-1815:9				
9:34	1815: 9-13				
9:35-38	1816:12-18				
9:39	1112:45				
9:41	1818:31-33				
10: 1- 5	1818:34-43				Jn 10:8
10: 3- 4	1815:37	—	—		Jn 10:27
10: 6- 7	1819: 7- 9				
10: 7	(Jesus as the Door:)				
	1829:43-45				Jn 10:9;14:6
	1965:33	—	—		Jn 3:16;10:9
10: 7-16	1861:29				

John 10:8 to 10:30

JOHN Chap:Verse	The URANTIA Book Page:Line	MATTHEW Chap:Verse	MARK Chap:Verse	LUKE Chap:Verse	Other BOOKS Chap:Verse
10: 8	1818:36-37	—	—		Jn 10:1-5
	1818:47-48				
	1819: 9-10				
10: 9	1819:10-13				
	1829:43-45	—	—		Jn 10:7;14:6
	1965:33				Jn 3:16;10:7
10:10	(More Abundant Life:)				
	1558:42-43				
	1749: 8- 9				
	1792: 4- 5				
	(Everlasting Life, See John 11:25-26, below.)				
10:10-12	1819:14-19				
10:11	1965:35				Jn 10:14
10:14	0028:28-31	—	—		1Jo 4:19
	1965:35				Jn 10:11
10:14-15	1819:19-23				
10:16	(Other Sheep--Not of This Fold:)				
	1577:13-14				
	1625: 3- 4				
	1819:24-28				
	1841:18-19				
	1959:42				
10:17-18	(Power to Lay Down & Take up Own Life:)				
	1819:29-37				
	2004:15-20				
	2020:11-12				
	2020:29-31				
	2053: 6- 8				
10:19-21	1819:38-43				
10:22-31	1815:28-43	—	—		Jn 10:3-4
10:29	0051:10-11				
10:30	("I and My Father are One":)				
	0028:20				Jn 1:1;5:18;10:38
					Jn 14:9-11,20
					Jn 17:11,21-22
	0074:10-11	(Same as 0028:20, above)			
	0080: 3- 5	(Same as 0028:20, above)			
	0227:29-34	(Same as 0028:20, above)			

(John 10:30 Continued on next page.)

266

JOHN Chap:Verse	The URANTIA Book Page:Line	MATTHEW Chap:Verse	MARK Chap:Verse	LUKE Chap:Verse	Other BOOKS Chap:Verse
10:30	0361:17-18	(Same as 0028:20, above)			
	0367: 5- 6	(Same as 0028:20, above)			
	1331:18-20	(Same as 0028:20, above)			
	1750:30	(Same as 0028:20, above)			
	1784:27	(Same as 0028:20, above)			
	1786:33	(Same as 0028:20, above)			
	1786:38-39	(Same as 0028:20, above)			
	1815:41	(Same as 0028:20, above)			
	1855:44	(Same as 0028:20, above)			
	1947:45-1948:3	(Same as 0028:20, above)			
	1985: 9-12	(Same as 0028:20, above)			
	2092: 2	(Same as 0028:20, above)			
10:30-39	1850:20-21	(Same as 0028:20, above)			Jn 5:18
10:32-33	1815:44-48				
10:34-35	1474:27				
10:36-39	1815:48-1816: 8				
10:38	(Jesus & the Father are One, See John 10:30, above.)				
10:40	1816:26-27				
	1818:10-11				
10:41	1817:33-34				
10:42	1819:44-45				
	1820:46-47				
11: 1- 3	1836:39-41				
11: 2	1879:11-15	26:7	14:3		Jn 12:3-5
11: 4	(Lazarus' Sickness "Not Unto Death":)				
	1836:45-47				
	1842:20-21				
	1844:28				
	1848:12				
11: 5	1837: 1- 2				
11: 6	1837:21-22				
11: 7	1837:23-24				
11: 8	1837:28-31				
11: 9-10	1837:32-35				
11:11	1837:39-40				
11:12-15	1837:41-46				
11:15-16	1838: 1- 6				
11:16	1562:23-24				
11:17	1842: 3- 6				

John 11:18 to 11:39

JOHN Chap:Verse	The URANTIA Book Page:Line	MATTHEW Chap:Verse	MARK Chap:Verse	LUKE Chap:Verse	Other BOOKS Chap:Verse
11:18-19	1842:23-24				
11:20	1842: 3				
11:20-24	1842:32-1843: 7				
11:24-26	(Resurrection of Believers:)				
	0532:39-40			Jn 6:39-40;13:36;14:3;17:24	
	0533: 3-11			Jn 6:39-40;13:36;14:3;17:24	
	0568:21			Jn 6:39-40;13:36;14:3;17:24	
	1944:16-20			Jn 6:39-40;13:36;14:3;17:24	
	1947:26-34			Jn 6:39-40;13:36;14:3;17:24	
	1965: 2- 8			Jn 6:39-40;13:36;14:3;17:24	
	2029: 9-12			Jn 6:39-40;13:36;14:3;17:24	
11:25	("I am the Resurrection and the Life":)				
	1843: 8- 9				
	1845:43				
	1846:34				
	1871:15-16				
	1965:37				
	2053:34-35				
11:25-26	(Eternal/Everlasting Life--"Never Die":)				
	1113: 7- 8			Jn 3:15-16;5:24-25,39-40	
				Jn 6:40,47;10:10 1Jo 5:11-12	
	1567: 3- 5	(Same as 1113: 7- 8, above)			
	1649:39-43	(Same as 1113: 7- 8, above)			
	1711:12-13	(Same as 1113: 7- 8, above)			
	1750:16-17	(Same as 1113: 7- 8, above)			
	1792: 4- 5	(Same as 1113: 7- 8, above)			
	1829:44-45	(Same as 1113: 7- 8, above)			
	1843: 9-11	(Same as 1113: 7- 8, above)			
	1861:23	(Same as 1113: 7- 8, above)			
	1965:33-34	(Same as 1113: 7- 8, above)			
	2035:38	(Same as 1113: 7- 8, above)			
	2053:36-37	(Same as 1113: 7- 8, above)			
11:27-31	1843:11-20				
11:32-33	1843:29-32				
11:34	1843:47-48				
	1844:29				
11:35	1844: 6-23				
11:35-38	1844: 1- 5				
11:39	1845: 9				

JOHN Chap:Verse	The URANTIA Book Page:Line	MATTHEW Chap:Verse	MARK Chap:Verse	LUKE Chap:Verse	Other BOOKS Chap:Verse
11:39-40	1845:20-28				
11:41	1845:30-32				
11:41-43	1846: 4- 9				
11:41-44	1905:22-23				
11:44	1846:11-15				
11:45-47	1846:44-1847: 2				
11:47	1847: 8- 9				
11:48	1847:34-38				
11:49-50	1847:39-41	—	—		Jn 18:14
11:53-54	1847:42-47				
11:55-56	1878:27-28				
11:57	1878:16-18				
12: 1- 2	1878:34-39	16:6	14:3		
12: 3	1879:42-44	26:7	14:3		
12: 3- 5	1879:10-21	26:7-8	14:3-5		Jn 11:2
12: 6	1547:33				Jn 13:29
12: 7- 8	1879:22-29	26:10-13	14:6-9		
12: 7- 8	1879:38-39	26:10-13	14:6-9		
12: 9	1878:23-25				
12:10-11	1880: 3- 7				
12:12-13	1403:33-35	21:8-9	11:8-10	19:36-38	
12:12-14	1882: 6-13	21:7-9	11:7-10	19:35-38	Ps 118:26
12:14-15	(King Arrives Riding an Ass:)				
	1881:12-18	21:4-5			Zc 9:9
	1884:49-1887:16	21:4-5			Zc 9:9
12:16	1883:41				
12:17-18	1881:39-46				
12:19	1882:46-50				
12:20-22	1557:30-36				
12:20-22	1902:18-35				
12:21	1557: 2	—	—		Jn 1:44
12:23-24	1903:36-39				
12:25	(Valuing Life to Lose or Save It:)				
	1134:28-29	10:39;16:25	8:35	9:24;17:33	
	1575:32-33	10:39;16:25	8:35	9:24;17:33	
	1760:19-20	10:39;16:25	8:35	9:24;17:33	
	1782: 9-10	10:39;16:25	8:35	9:24;17:33	
	1903:39-41	10:39;16:25	8:35	9:24;17:33	
	(Life Eternal: See John 11,25-26, above.)				

JOHN Chap:Verse	The URANTIA Book Page:Line	MATTHEW Chap:Verse	MARK Chap:Verse	LUKE Chap:Verse	Other BOOKS Chap:Verse
12:26	1861:29-30				
	(Follow Me:)				
	1903:41-43	16:24	8:34	9:59	
	2089:50	16:24	8:34	9:59	
12:27-28	1903:46-1904: 2				
12:28-30	1904: 3-14				
12:31	(The "Prince of this World:")				
	0602: 5- 6				Jn 14:30;16:11
	0610: 4- 5	—	—		Jn 14:30;16:11
	0610: 7- 8				Jn 14:30;16:11
	1904:17-18	—	—		Jn 14:30;16:11
12:32	(Jesus' Drawing Power:)				
	0026:29				Je 31:3 Jn 3:14-15 Jn 6:44;8:28
	0082:24-29	(Same as 0026:29, above)			
	0084:12-20	(Same as 0026:29, above)			
	0139:43-44	(Same as 0026:29, above)			
	0224:22-23	(Same as 0026:29, above)			
	1067:40-41	(Same as 0026:29, above)			
	1190:17-18	(Same as 0026:29, above)			
	1750:15	(Same as 0026:29, above)			
	1904:20-21	(Same as 0026:29, above)			
	2019:19-25	(Same as 0026:29, above)			
	2084: 8- 9	(Same as 0026:29, above)			
12:34-36	1904:21-28				
12:35-36	(Jesus is Light, See John 12:46, below.				
12:36	(Children of Light:)				
	1327:26-27	5:14-16		16:8	Ep 5:8 1Th 5:5
	1655:37-38	5:14-16		16:8	Ep 5:8 1Th 5:5
	1854:11-12	5:14-16		16:8	Ep 5:8 1Th 5:5
	1904:32-35	5:14-15		16:8	Ep 5:8 1Th 5:5
	1953:33	5:14-16		16:8	Ep 5:8 1Th 5:5
	2042: 2	5:14-16		16:8	Ep 5:8 1Th 5:5
12:37	1902:15-16				
12:37-43	1902:38-1903:8	—	—		Is 6:10;53:1
12:42	1910:42-46				
12:44-48	1861:28				
12:44-50	1903:21-35				

JOHN Chap:Verse	The URANTIA Book Page:Line	MATTHEW Chap:Verse	MARK Chap:Verse	LUKE Chap:Verse	Other BOOKS Chap:Verse
12:46	(Jesus is Light:)				
	0447:38	4:16		2:32	Is 9:2 Jn 1:4-9
					Jn 9:5;12:35-36
					Jn 8:12 1Jo 2:8
	0513:31	(Same as 0447:38, above)			
	0590:33	(Same as 0447:38, above)			
	1104:14-15	(Same as 0447:38, above)			
	1181: 7- 8	(Same as 0447:38, above)			
	1353:38-39	(Same as 0447:38, above)			
	1458:33-35	(Same as 0447:38, above)			
	1671:10-11	(Same as 0447:38, above)			
	1795: 1	(Same as 0447:38, above)			
	1965:31	(Same as 0447:38, above)			
	(Children of Light, See John 12:36, above.)				
12:49	1855:47-48				Jn 7:16,29;8:42
12:49-50	(Son Reveals Father;)				
	0028:14-15	11:27		10:22	Jn 1:18;6:45-46
					Jn 8:26;14:7-9,20
					Jn 17:6,25-26
	0093:46	(Same as 0028:14-15, above)			
	0109:28-33	(Same as 0028:14-15, above)			
	0196:10	(Same as 0028:14-15, above)			
	0232:42-44	(Same as 0028:14-15, above)			
	0233: 4- 5	(Same as 0028:14-15, above)			
	1324:23-32	(Same as 0028:14-15, above)			
	1328:38-41	(Same as 0028:14-15, above)			
	1331:21-22	(Same as 0028:14-15, above)			
	1608: 1- 2	(Same as 0028:14-15, above)			
	1710:15-16	(Same as 0028:14-15, above)			
	1750:14-15	(Same as 0028:14-15, above)			
	1855:46-47	(Same as 0028:14-15, above)			
	1947:42-47	(Same as 0028:14-15, above)			
	1965: 8-12	(Same as 0028:14-15, above)			
13: 1- 3	1938:12-21				Ep 6:12
13: 4- 6	1938:33-42				
13: 6- 8	1939: 9-13				
13: 8- 9	1551: 9-11				
	1939:21-31				
13:10	1939:32-34				

JOHN Chap:Verse	The URANTIA Book Page:Line	MATTHEW Chap:Verse	MARK Chap:Verse	LUKE Chap:Verse	Other BOOKS Chap:Verse
13:11	1939:34				
13:12	1939:38-40				
13:12-17	1939:42-49				
13:16	1681:43-45	10:24-25		6:40	Jn 15:20
13:19	1941:16-21				
13:20	1801:13-14	10:40		10:16	
13:21	1940:28-35	26:21	14:18		
13:22	1940:36-39	26:22	14:19		
13:23	(Disciple Whom Jesus Loved:)				
	1554: 1				Jn 19:26;20:2;21:7,20
	1554:22				Jn 19:26;20:2;21:7,20
13:23-24	1941:10-12				
13:25-26	1941: 1- 4				
13:27-30	1941:22-28				
13:29	1547:33	—	—		Jn 12:6
13:31	1944:13-14				
13:33	1944:14-16				
13:34	(Love One Another)				
	1206:38-42				Jn 15:12,17
	1601:36-37				Jn 15:12,17
	1932:19	—	—		Jn 15:12,17
	1944:25-26				Jn 15:17
	2055:18-19				Jn 15:12,17
	(New Commandment, Love "as I Love You":)				
	1125:20				Jn 15:12
	1571:10-12				Jn 15:12
	1573:10-18	—	—		Jn 15:12
	1944:23-45				Jn 15:12
	1946:27-28	—	—		Jn 15:12
	1949: 6- 9				Jn 15:12
	1951:23-24	—	—		Jn 15:12
	1955:41-42				Jn 15:12
	1961:45	—	—		Jn 15:12
	1962:36				Jn 15:12
	1964:44-47	—	—		Jn 15:12
	2041:41				Jn 15:12
	2053:16				Jn 15:12

JOHN Chap:Verse	The URANTIA Book Page:Line	MATTHEW Chap:Verse	MARK Chap:Verse	LUKE Chap:Verse	Other BOOKS Chap:Verse
13:35	(Known as Disciples by Your Love:)				
	1125:20				
	1609:27-29				
	1944:30-31				
	1945:42-44				
	1964:44-47				
	2042: 6- 7				
13:36	(Resurrection of Believers, See John 11:24-26, above.)				
13:37	1962:20-22	26:33	14:29	22:33	
13:38	1962:24-27	26:34	14:30	22:34	
14: 1	(Let Not your Heart be Troubled:)				
	1575:26-27				Jn 14:27
	1947:18-19				Jn 14:27
	1954: 9-10	—	—		Jn 14:27
	1955: 4				Jn 14:27
14: 2	1102:40-41				
	(Many Mansions:)				
	0120:41-43				
	0341:46-47				
	0530: 3- 4				
	1841: 5				
	1841:38				
	1474:40-42				
	1934:46-47				
	1947:19-25				
	1951:46				
	(Cf: Heaven of Heavens:)				
	1953:27-35				De 10;14 1Ki 8:27
					Ne 9:6 Ps 148:4
					2Co 3:18
	(Foretelling His Departure, "I Go":)				
	1750:21-23				Jn 14:12,28;16:5
					Jn 16:10,16-19,28
					Jn 17:11,13;20:17
	1857:12-13	(Same as 1750:21-23, above)			
	1934:25-26	(Same as 1750:21-23, above)			
	1935: 9-10	(Same as 1750:21-23, above)			
	1952: 5-16	(Same as 1750:21-23, above)			

(John 14:2 Continued on next page.)

John 14:2 to 14:7

JOHN Chap:Verse	The URANTIA Book Page:Line	MATTHEW Chap:Verse	MARK Chap:Verse	LUKE Chap:Verse	Other BOOKS Chap:Verse
14: 2	1954: 7-17	(Same as 1750:21-23, above)			
	1962:32-33	(Same as 1750:21-23, above)			
	1964:10	(Same as 1750:21-23, above)			
	2055:30	(Same as 1750:21-23, above)			
14: 3	(Jesus' Promised Return to Earth:)				
	0227:18-27	24:27-37	13:32-33		Jn 14:28
		25:13			
	0409:10	(Same as 0227:18-27, above)			
	1319: 6- 8	(Same as 0227:18-27, above)			
	1915: 1-19	(Same as 0227:18-27, above)			
	1916:25-27	(Same as 0227:18-27, above)			
	1918:47-48	(Same as 0227:18-27, above)			
	(Going to Be with Jesus:)				
	1915:20-29				Jn 17:24
	1947:26-34				Jn 17:24
	1965: 2- 8				Jn 17:24
14: 5	1947:35-37				
14: 6	(Jesus as the Way, the Truth and the Life:)				
	0086:15-16				
	0242:24-26				
	1593:34				
	(Jesus as the Way, the "New & Living Way":)				
	0089:17-18				He 10:20
	0093:46				He 10:20
	0596:14,17				He 10:20
	1113:28				He 10:20
	1281:29				He 10:20
	1426:10				He 10:20
	1543:22-23				He 10:20
	1653:21				He 10:20
	1829:43-45	—	—		He 10:20 Jn 10:7,9
	2092:30				He 10:20
	(Jesus as Truth:)				
	0513:40				
	1101:39				
14: 7	1855:47				
	1947:39-41				

274

JOHN Chap:Verse	The URANTIA Book Page:Line	MATTHEW Chap:Verse	MARK Chap:Verse	LUKE Chap:Verse	Other BOOKS Chap:Verse
14: 7- 9	(Father is Revealed by Son:)				
	0028:14-15	11:27		10:22	Jn 1:18;6:45-46
					Jn 8:26;12:49-50
					Jn 14:20;17:6,25-26
	0093:46	(Same as 0028:14-15, above)			
	0109:28-33	(Same as 0028:14-15, above)			
	0196:10	(Same as 0028:14-15, above)			
	0232:42-44	(Same as 0028:14-15, above)			
	0233: 4- 5	(Same as 0028:14-15, above)			
	1324:23-32	(Same as 0028:14-15, above)			
	1328:38-41	(Same as 0028:14-15, above)			
	1331:21-22	(Same as 0028:14-15, above)			
	1608: 1- 2	(Same as 0028:14-15, above)			
	1710:15-16	(Same as 0028:14-15, above)			
	1750:14-15	(Same as 0028:14-15, above)			
	1855:46-47	(Same as 0028:14-15, above)			
	1947:42-47	(Same as 0028:14-15, above)			
	1965: 8-12	(Same as 0028:14-15, above)			
14: 9	(Who has Seen the Son has Seen the Father:)				
	0028:12-13				
	0074:42-43				
	0229:24				
	0361:18-19				
	1165:23-24				
	1176:24				
	1750:30-31				
	1786:39-40				
	1855:44-45				
	1857:15				
	1960:41				
14: 9-11	(Jesus and the Father are One:)				
	0028:19-20				Jn 1:1;5:18;10:30,38
					Jn 14:20;17:11,21-22
	0074:10-11	(Same as 0028:19-20, above)			
	0080: 3- 5	(Same as 0028:19-20, above)			
	0227:29-34	(Same as 0028:19-20, above)			
	0361:17-18	(Same as 0028:19-20, above)			
	0367: 5- 6	(Same as 0028:19-20, above)			

(John 14:9-11 Continued on next page.)

JOHN Chap:Verse	The URANTIA Book Page:Line	MATTHEW Chap:Verse	MARK Chap:Verse	LUKE Chap:Verse	Other BOOKS Chap:Verse
14: 9-11	1331:18-20	(Same as 0028:19-20, above)			
	1750:30	(Same as 0028:19-20, above)			
	1784:27	(Same as 0028:19-20, above)			
	1786:33	(Same as 0028:19-20, above)			
	1786:38-39	(Same as 0028:19-20, above)			
	1850:20-21	(Same as 0028:19-20, above)			
	1855:44	(Same as 0028:19-20, above)			
	1947:45-1948:3	(Same as 0028:19-20, above)			
	1985: 9-12	(Same as 0028:19-20, above)			
	2092: 2	(Same as 0028:19-20, above)			
14:12	("I Go to my Father: see John 14:2, above.)				
14:13-14	(Praying in Jesus' "Name":)				
	1454:22-23	7:7-8		11:9-10	Jn 15:7,16 Jn 16:23-24
	1619:12-15	(Same as 1454:22-23, above)			
	1638:18-23	(Same as 1454:22-23, above)			
•	1639:39-42	(Same as 1454:22-23, above)			
	1838:41-42	(Same as 1454:22-23, above)			
	1849:19-20	(Same as 1454:22-23, above)			
	1945:37-44	(Same as 1454:22-23, above)			
14:15	(If you Love Me, Keep My Commandments:)				
•	1206:38-39				Jn 14:23-24;15:10
	1573:10-18	—	—		Jn 14:23-24;15:10
	1945:46-47				Jn 14:23-24;15:10
	1953:36-38				Jn 14:23-24;15:10
14:16-18	(The Comforter, the "Spirit of Truth," The "New Teacher," Poured Out "On all Flesh":)				
	0241:41-42			24:49	Ek 11:19;36:26-27 Jn 14:26;15:26;16:7,13-14 Ek 11:19;36:26-27; Jl 2:28 Ac 2:2-4;16-18 Ga 4:6
	0365:32-33	(Same as 0241:41-42, above)			
	0379:36	(Same as 0241:41-42, above)			
	0382:10-14	(Same as 0241:41-42, above)			
	0596:31-32	(Same as 0241:41-42, above)			
	1328: 4- 5	(Same as 0241:41-42, above)			
	1328:22-25	(Same as 0241:41-42, above)			
	1340:24-27	(Same as 0241:41-42, above)			

(John 14:16-18 Continued on next page.)

JOHN Chap:Verse	The URANTIA Book Page:Line	MATTHEW Chap:Verse	MARK Chap:Verse	LUKE Chap:Verse	Other BOOKS Chap:Verse
14:16-18	1591:15-16	(Same as 0241:41-42, above)			
	1594: 3- 4	(Same as 0241:41-42, above)			
	1642:18-24	(Same as 0241:41-42, above)			
	1897:33	(Same as 0241:41-42, above)			
	1918:45-47	(Same as 0241:41-42, above)			
	1947:14-17	(Same as 0241:41-42, above)			
	1948: 9-24	(Same as 0241:41-42, above)			
	1948:34-36	(Same as 0241:41-42, above)			
	1951:45-48	(Same as 0241:41-42, above)			
	1953:22-26	(Same as 0241:41-42, above)			
	1954: 2	(Same as 0241:41-42, above)			
	1958: 7- 9	(Same as 0241:41-42, above)			
	1959:22-24	(Same as 0241:41-42, above)			
	1961:24-27	(Same as 0241:41-42, above)			
	2035:38-39	(Same as 0241:41-42, above)			
	2044:34-35	(Same as 0241:41-42, above)			
	2053:17-19	(Same as 0241:41-42, above)			
	2054:42-43	(Same as 0241:41-42, above)			
	2055: 9-11	(Same as 0241:41-42, above)			
	2057:21-22	(Same as 0241:41-42, above)			
	2061:10-13	(Same as 0241:41-42, above)			
	2061:20-21	(Same as 0241:41-42, above)			
	2062:43	(Same as 0241:41-42, above)			
	2064: 7	(Same as 0241:41-42, above)			
14:19-21	1948:27-33				
14:20	(Son Reveals Father, See John 14:7-9, above.)				
	(Jesus is "In the Father," See John 14:9-11, above.)				
	1454:14-15				Jn 15:4-7
14:21	0028:29	—	—		1Co 13:12
14:22	1564:23-24				
	1948:44-49				
14:23-24	1945:11				
	(If Love Me, Keep My Words, See John 14:15, above.)				
	(Keeping Words = Doing the Father's Will:)				
	0008:42	6:10;7:21	3:35	8:21	Jn 4:34;5:30
		12:50;26:39	14:36	11:2	Jn 6:38;7:17
		26:42,44	14:39	22:42	Jn 15:10,14
	0052: 1- 4	(Same as 0008:42, above)			

(John 14:23-24 Continued on next page.)

John 14:23 to 14:27

JOHN Chap:Verse	The URANTIA Book Page:Line	MATTHEW Chap:Verse	MARK Chap:Verse	LUKE Chap:Verse	Other BOOKS Chap:Verse
14:23-24	1200:41	(Same as 0008:42, above)			
	1221:33-34	(Same as 0008:42, above)			
	1303: 7	(Same as 0008:42, above)			
	1318:29-30	(Same as 0008:42, above)			
	1324:21-22	(Same as 0008:42, above)			
	1327:10	(Same as 0008:42, above)			
	1328:38-41	(Same as 0008:42, above)			
	1331: 9-10	(Same as 0008:42, above)			
	1417: 5- 7	(Same as 0008:42, above)			
	1453:43-44	(Same as 0008:42, above)			
	1500:27	(Same as 0008:42, above)			
	1511:47-48	(Same as 0008:42, above)			
	1514:35	(Same as 0008:42, above)			
	1569: 8- 9	(Same as 0008:42, above)			
	1574:21	(Same as 0008:42, above)			
	1582: 8	(Same as 0008:42, above)			
	1594:33-34	(Same as 0008:42, above)			
	1608: 1	(Same as 0008:42, above)			
	1615:22-23	(Same as 0008:42, above)			
	1769:42-44	(Same as 0008:42, above)			Ja 1:22-25
					Ja 2:17 1Jo 3:18
	1774:28	(Same as 0008:42, above)			
	1947:50-1948:1	(Same as 0008:42, above)			
	1968:21-24	(Same as 0008:42, above)			
	1968:33-34	(Same as 0008:42, above)			
	1972: 5- 7	(Same as 0008:42, above)			
	2078: 8	(Same as 0008:42, above)			
	2087:11	(Same as 0008:42, above)			
	2088:30	(Same as 0008:42, above)			
	2089:12-14	(Same as 0008:42, above)			
	2090: 1	(Same as 0008:42, above)			
14:25-26	1948:37-43				
14:26	(Comforter, Holy Spirit, See John 14:16-18, above.)				
14:27	(Jesus' Peace, Beyond all Understanding:)				
	0066:46-47			2:14	Pp 4:7 Jn 16:33
	1101: 6- 8			2:14	Pp 4:7 Jn 16:33
	1627:32-33			2:14	Pp 4:7 Jn 16:33
	1663:13-14			2:14	Pp 4:7 Jn 16:33

(John 14:27 Continued on next page.)

JOHN Chap:Verse	The URANTIA Book Page:Line	MATTHEW Chap:Verse	MARK Chap:Verse	LUKE Chap:Verse	Other BOOKS Chap:Verse
14:27	1954: 7- 9			2:14	Pp 4:7 Jn 16:33
	1954:28-47			2:14	Pp 4:7 Jn 16:33
	1955: 7- 9			2:14	Pp 4:7 Jn 16:33
	2042:13-14			2:14	Pp 4:7 Jn 16:33
	2054:43			2:14	Pp 4:7 Jn 16:33
	(Peace & Tribulation, See John 16:33, below.)				
	(Let Not Heart be Troubled, See John 14:1, above.)				
14:28	1934:25-26				
	(I Go Away, See John 14:2, above.)				
	(Jesus' Promised Return, See John 14:3, above.)				
14:29	1954:15-16				
14:30	(Prince of This World:)				
	0602: 5- 6				Jn 12:31;16:11
	0610: 4- 8	—	—		Jn 12:31;16:11
	1904:17-18				Jn 12:31;16:11
14:31	1954:16-17				Jn 14:28
15: 1- 5	(I am the Vine, You are the Branches:)				
	1945:24-37				
	1946:21-26				
	1965:41				
15: 2	(Purge of the Fruitless:)				
	1502:42-44	3:8-10		3:8-9	Jn 15:5-8,16
		7:16-20		6:43-44	Ep 5:9
		12:33		13:1-5	Ga 5:22-23
	1569: 6- 8	(Same as 1502:42-44, above)			
	1571:32-37	(Same as 1502:42-44, above)			
	1572:27	(Same as 1502:42-44, above)			
	1582:33-34	(Same as 1502:42-44, above)			
	1596:26-27	(Same as 1502:42-44, above)			
	1601: 8-10	(Same as 1502:42-44, above)			
	1714:36-38	(Same as 1502:42-44, above)			
	1830:39-45	(Same as 1502:42-44, above)			
	1917:30-32	(Same as 1502:42-44, above)			
	1945:40-47	(Same as 1502:42-44, above)			
	1946:21-26	(Same as 1502:42-44, above)			
	2054:36-39	(Same as 1502:42-44, above)			
15: 4- 7	(Abiding in Jesus:)				
	1945:31-40				Jn 14:20
	1454:14-15				Jn 14:20

JOHN Chap:Verse	The URANTIA Book Page:Line	MATTHEW Chap:Verse	MARK Chap:Verse	LUKE Chap:Verse	Other BOOKS Chap:Verse
15: 5- 8	(Requirement to Produce Fruit, See John 15:2, above.)				
15: 7	1945:37-40				Jn 14:13-14
	(Asking in Jesus' Name, See John 14:13-14, above.)				
15: 8	1945:40-44				
15: 9	1945:45				
	1279:37-39				Jn 17:18-23
15:10	(Keep My Commandments out of Love, See John 14:15.)				
15:10-11	1454:24-25				
15:11	1944:32-37				
15:12	(New Commandment, Love as I Love You, See John 13:34.)				
15:13-15	(God as a Friend)				
	1533:26				
	1534:11-12				
	1575:39-40				
	1861:28				
	1944:38-1945:4				
	2018:49-2019:2				
15:14	(See "Keeping Words," John 14:23-24, above.)				
15:15	1569:21				
15:16	1946: 6- 7				
	(Requirement to Produce Fruit, See John 15:2, above.)				
	(Ask in Jesus'Name, See John 14:13-14, above.)				
15:16-17	1945: 5- 9				
15:17	(Love One Another, See John 13:34, above.)				
15:18-20	1946:40-47				
15:20	1681:43-45	10:24-25		6:40	Jn 13:16
15:21	1946:48-1947:1				
15:22-26	1947: 4-17				Ps 35:19;69:4
	(Comforter/Spirit of Truth, See John 14:16-18, above.)				
16: 1- 4	1951:15-29				
16: 5	(I Go to Father, See John 14:2, above.)				
16: 5- 8	1951:34-43				
16: 5-16	2052:14-16				
16: 7	(Comforter, See John 14:16-18, above.)				
16:10	(I Go to Father, See John 14:2, above.)				
16:11	(Prince of This World, See John 14:30, above.)				
16:12-13	1951:44-46				
16:13-14	1951:47-48				
	(Spirit of Truth, See John 14:16-18, above.)				

JOHN Chap:Verse	The URANTIA Book Page:Line	MATTHEW Chap:Verse	MARK Chap:Verse	LUKE Chap:Verse	Other BOOKS Chap:Verse
16:14-15	1952: 1- 4				
16:15	1786:36-37				
16:16-19	(Jesus Foretells Departure, See John 14:2, above.)				
16:19-22	1952:13-25				
16:23-24	1952:26-28				Jn 16:26
	(Asking in Jesus' Name, See John 14:13-14, above.)				
16:25	1952:29-31				
16:26	1952:26-28				Jn 16:23-24
	(Asking in Jesus' Name, See John 14:13-14, above.)				
16:27	(The Father, Himself, Loves You:)				
	0039: 4- 5				
	1259:18				
16:27-28	1952:31-35				
16:28	1750:21-23				Jn 8:58
	(I Go to the Father, See John 16:5, above.)				
16:29-30	1952:36-37				
16:30	1855:45-46				
16:32	1954:19-23				
16:33	1102:29	9:2;14:27	6:50		
	(Peace & Tribulation:)				
	1533:29-31				Ac 14:22 Re 7:14
	1954:24-27				
	(Jesus' Peace, See John 14:27. above.)				
17: 1- 5	1963:30-1964:2				
17: 2- 3	1642:25-30				
17: 4	(Jesus' "Work:")				
	1615:22-23				Jn 4:34;5:17,36;9:4;19:30
	1649:30-31				Jn 4:34;5:17,36;9:4;19:30
	1812: 8-11				Jn 4:34;5:17,36;9:4;19:30
	1897:26				Jn 4:34;5:17,36;9:4;19:30
	1955:30-32				Jn 4:34;5:17,36;9:4;19:30
	1963:37-39				Jn 4:34;5:17,36;9:4;19:30
	2011: 3- 4				Jn 4:34;5:17,36;9:4;19:30
	(Doing Father's Will, See John 14:23-24,above.)				
17: 5	0074:18-19				
17: 6	(Son Revealed Father, See John 14:7-9, above.)				
17: 6-11	1964: 3-23				

John 17:11 to 18:18

JOHN Chap:Verse	The URANTIA Book Page:Line	MATTHEW Chap:Verse	MARK Chap:Verse	LUKE Chap:Verse	Other BOOKS Chap:Verse
17:11	(Jesus Goes to the Father:)				
	1750:21-23				Jn 14:2,12,28
					Jn 16:5,10,16-19,28
					Jn 17:13;20:17
	1857:12-13	(Same as 1750:21-23, above)			
	1934:25-26	(Same as 1750:21-23, above)			
	1935: 9-10	(Same as 1750:21-23, above)			
	1952: 5- 6	(Same as 1750:21-23, above)			
	1954: 7-17	(Same as 1750:21-23, above)			
	1962:32-33	(Same as 1750:21-23, above)			
	1964:10	(Same as 1750:21-23, above)			
	2055:30	(Same as 1750:21-23, above)			
	(Jesus and Father are One, See John 14:9-11, above.)				
17:12	1964:24-25				
	1966:35-37				
17:13	(Jesus Goes to Father, See John 17:11, above.)				
17:13-19	1964:27-39				
17:18	2044:31				
17:18-23	1279:37-39	—	—		Jn 15:12-17
17:20-23	1964:40-1965: 2				Jn 13:34
17:21-22	(See John 17:11, above, entries same as 0028:19-20)				
17:24	1965: 2- 8				
17:25-26	(Jesus Reveals Father, See John 14:7-9, above.)				
18: 1	1971:19-20				
18: 2	1973: 7-11				
18: 3	1973:29-36	26:47	14:43	22:47	
18: 4- 6	1974:11-20				
18: 7- 8	1974:34-38				
18:10-11	1974:41-1975:1	26:50-52	14:46-47	22:49-51	
18:12	1975: 4- 7				
18:13	1977: 5-11				
18:14	1847:39-41	—	—		Jn 11:49-50
18:15	1975:31-32				
18:15-16	1977:30-43				Jn 19:26-27
	1980: 7-16	26:58	14:54	22:54-55	
18:15-18	1551: 6- 8	26:69-75	14:66-72	22:55-62	
18:16-17	1551:15-17	26:69-72	14:66-70	22:56-57	Jn 18:25-27
18:17	1980:31-38	26:69-70	14:66-68	22:56-57	
18:18	1980:17-18				

JOHN Chap:Verse	The URANTIA Book Page:Line	MATTHEW Chap:Verse	MARK Chap:Verse	LUKE Chap:Verse	Other BOOKS Chap:Verse
18:19-23	1979:25-39				
18:24	1980: 1- 5	26:57	14:53		
18:25	1981: 3- 8	26:73-74	14:70	22:59-60	
18:25-27	1551: 6- 8	26:69-75	14:66-72	22:55-62	Jn 18:15-18
18:26-27	1980:39-43			22:58	
18:27	1981:13-14	26:74-75	14:72	22:60	
18:28	1986:12-14	27:2	15:1	23:1	
	1987:17-24				
18:29-30	1989:26-33				
18:31	1989:34-42				
18:33	1991: 2- 4				
18:33-35	1991:13-22	27:11	15:2	23:3	
18:33-37	1999:10-12	27:11	15:2	23:3	
18:36	(Jesus Kingdom Not of This World:)				
	1536:16				
	1702:36-37				
	1750:26				
	1758:28				
	1956:39-41				
	1991:23-28				
	2035:12				
18:37-38	1991:30-36	27:11	15:2	23:3	
18:38	1991:47-1992: 2			23:4	
18:39	1993:17-19	27:15	15:6	23:17	
	1993:32-34	27:17	15:9		
18:40	1993:25-29	27:16	15:7	23:19	
	1993:34-38		15:11	23:18	
19: 1	1995: 4- 6	27:26	15:15	23:23-25	
19: 2- 3	1995:12-17	27:27-31	15:16-20		
19: 4- 6	1995:19-23			23:22	
19: 5	1101:34				
	2000:15-21				
19: 6	1995:29-31			23:23	
	1996:43-46	27:24-25			
19: 7- 9	1995:36-43				
19: 9-11	1995:46-1996:10				
19:12-15	1996:14-28				
19:14-16	1997:26-28			23:25	

283

John 19:16 to 19:38

JOHN Chap:Verse	The URANTIA Book Page:Line	MATTHEW Chap:Verse	MARK Chap:Verse	LUKE Chap:Verse	Other BOOKS Chap:Verse
19:16	1995: 6- 6	27:26	15:15	23:23-25	Jn 19:1
	2001:29-30	27:26	15:15	23:24-25	
19:16-17	2004:21-22				
	2004:31-37				
19:18	2006:36-46	27:35	15:24	23:33	
	2007:15-16	27:38	15:27	23:33	
19:19	2005: 7- 9	27:37	15:24	23:38	
19:19-20	2007:22-36	27:37	15:26	23:38	
19:19-22	2005: 3-17	27:37	15:24	33:38	
19:23-24	(Casting Lots for Garments:)				
	1341:41-43	27:35	15:24	23:34	Ps 22:18
	2007:44-49	27:35	15:24	23:34	Ps 22;18
19:25	(Faithful Women:)				
	1403:35-36	27:55-56	15:40-41	8:2-3	Ac 1:14
				23:27,49	
				24:10	
	1671:20-26	(Same as 1403:35-36, above)			
	1678:28-1679:15	(Same as 1403:35-36, above)			
	1680:21-22	(Same as 1403:35-36, above)			
	1680:28-29	(Same as 1403:35-36, above)			
	2005:33-45	(Same as 1403:35-36, above)			
	2008:14-19	(Same as 1403:35-36, above)			
19:26	(Disciple "Whom Jesus Loved":)				
	1554: 1				Jn 13:23;20:2;21:7,20
	1554:22				Jn 13:23;20:2;21:7,20
19:26-27	1555:19-23				
	1977:30-43	—	—		Jn 18:15-16
	2009:43-2010: 4				
19:28-29	2010:39-42	27:48	15:36		
19:30	0240: 7				
	2011: 3- 5	27:50	15:37	23:46	
	(Jesus' Work, See John 17:4, above.)				
	(Give up Ghost:)				
	0954: 8				Ge 25:8+ Jb 3:11
					Je 15:9 La 1:19
					Jn 4:34;17:4
19:31-34	2011:19-29		15:42	23:54	Jn 19:42
19:38	2012:18-26	27:57-58	15:42-45	23:50-52	
19:38-42	1603: 6- 7				

JOHN Chap:Verse	The URANTIA Book Page:Line	MATTHEW Chap:Verse	MARK Chap:Verse	LUKE Chap:Verse	Other BOOKS Chap:Verse
19:39-41	2013:17-28	27:59-60	15:46	23:53	
19:41-42	2013: 6-11			23:53	
19:42	2011:19		15:42	23:54	Jn 19:31-34
20: 1	2025:30-39	28:1	16:1-2	24:1	
	2025:45-47		16:3-4	24:2	
20: 2	2027: 8-10	28:10	16:8,10-11		
	(Disciple Whom Jesus Loved, See John 19:26, above.)				
20: 3	2027:13-14				
20: 4- 9	2027:27-34			24:12	
20:10-17	2027:46-2028:2	28:7,10	16:7		
20:11-16	2026:32-49	28:5-6,9	16:5-6,9	24:4-8	
20:17	1676:17-18				
	2027: 4- 7	28:7,10	16:7		
	(Jesus Ascends to Father, See John 17:11, above.)				
20:18	2027: 8-12		16:10-11	24:9	Jn 20:2
20:19	2040:18-22		16:14	24:36-38	1Co 15:5
20:20	2040:37-38				
20:21	(The Great Commission:)				
	1051: 8	24:14 28:19-20	13:10 16:15	24:47	Ac 1:8
	1584: 4- 6	(Same as 1051:8, above)			
	1608:22	(Same as 1051:8, above)			
	1824:43-44	(Same as 1051:8, above)			
	1934:28-30	(Same as 1051:8, above)			
	1957:35-37	(Same as 1051:8, above)			
	1961:49	(Same as 1051:8, abpve)			
	2033:17-18	(Same as 1051:8, above)			
	2034: 2- 3	(Same as 1051:8, above)			
	2042: 8- 9	(Same as 1051:8, above)			
	2043: 3- 6	(Same as 1051:8, above)			
	2044:35-36	(Same as 1051:8, above)			
	2052:39-40	(Same as 1051:8, above)			
	2053:14-16	(Same as 1051:8, above)			
	2053:38-40	(Same as 1051:8, above)			
	2054: 5- 6	(Same as 1051:8, above)			
	2054:25-27	(Same as 1051:8, above)			
	2054:41-42	(Same as 1051:8, above)			
	2055:16-18	(Same as 1051:8, above)			
	2057:24-25	(same as 1051:8, above)			

JOHN Chap:Verse	The URANTIA Book Page:Line	MATTHEW Chap:Verse	MARK Chap:Verse	LUKE Chap:Verse	Other BOOKS Chap:Verse
20:22	0955: 3- 5				
20:24	2039: 3-14				
	2040:30				
20:25	1561: 3				
	2042:28-47	—	—		1Co 15:5
20:26	2042:47-2043:3				
20:27-29	2043:33-47				
20:28	1409: 2				
20:29	(Believing Without Seeing:)				
	0578:38-43				
	0579: 3				
	2043:46-47				
21: 1	2045:31-33				
21: 1- 2	1563: 6				
21: 2	1558:15				
21: 2- 3	2045:34-37				
21: 4	2046: 2- 7				
21: 5- 8	2046:13-26				
21: 7	1551: 1- 2				
	1555:25-27				
	(Disciple Whom Jesus Loved, See John 19:26, above.)				
21: 9-10	2046:37-41				
21:11	2046:45-46				
21:12-13	2047: 1- 7				
21:14	2047: 9-10				
21:15	2047:33-35				
21:15-17	1548:31				Jn 1:42
21:16	2047:40-42				
21:17	2047:46-2048: 3				
21:19	2048: 6				
21:20	(Disciple Whom Jesus Loved, See John 19:26, above.)				
21:20-22	2048: 7-12				
21:23	2048:13-15				

SECTION FOUR

The BOOKS of The BIBLE
(Including the Apocrypha)
Cross Referenced, in Alphabetical Order,
to *The URANTIA Book*.

* * * * *

A: The Book of ACTS.

ACTS Chap:Verse	The URANTIA Book Page:Line	Other BOOKS Chap:Verse
1: 4	2053:17-19	Lk 24:49
	2057:21-22	Lk 24:49
1: 4- 8	2055: 6-11	Mt 3:11 Mk 1:8 Lk 3:16;24:49
		Jn 1:33
1: 5	(Baptism:)	
	0947: 1- 2	Mt 3:6,11 Mk 1:4-5,8 Lk 3:3,7,16
		Jn 1:25-33
	0964:34	(Same as 0947:1-2, above)
	(Baptism of John:)	
	1502:11-14	(Same as 0947:1-2, above)
	1584:31-32	(Same as 0947:1-2, above)
	1593:11-13	(Same as 0947:1-2, above)
	(Baptism of the Spirit:)	
	1536:34-36	Mt 3:11 Mk 1:8 Lk 3:16 Jn 1:33
	2043:15	Mt 3:11 Mk 1:8 Lk 3:16 Jn 1:33
	2061:43-46	Mt 3:11 Mk 1:8 Lk 3:16 Jn 1:33
1: 6	1502: 2	
	2055:12-13	

Acts 1:8 to 1:14

ACTS Chap:Verse	The URANTIA Book Page:Line	Other BOOKS Chap:Verse
1: 8	(Receipt of Power:)	
	1187:18-20	
	1591:15-17	
	2057:21-22	
	(Baptism of Spirit, See Acts 1:5, above.)	
	(The Great Commmission:)	
	1051: 8	Mt 24:14;28:19-20 Mk 13:10;16:15
		Lk 24:47 Jn 20:21
	1584: 4- 6	(Same as 1051:8, above)
	1608:22	(Same as 1051:8, above)
	1824:43-44	(Same as 1051:8, above)
	1934:28-30	(Same as 1051:8, above)
	1957:35-37	(Same as 1051:8, above)
	1961:49	(Same as 1051:8, above)
	2033:17-18	(Same as 1051:8, above)
	2034: 2- 3	(Same as 1051:8, above)
	2042: 8- 9	(Same as 1051:8, above)
	2043: 4- 5	(Same as 1051:8, above)
	2044:35-36	(Same as 1051:8, above)
	2052:39-40	(Same as 1051:8, above)
	2053:14-16	(Same as 1051:8, above)
	2053:38-40	(Same as 1051:8, above)
	2054: 5- 6	(Same as 1051:8, above)
	2054:25-27	(Same as 1051:8, above)
	2054:41-42	(Same as 1051:8, above)
	2055:16-18	(Same as 1051:8, above)
	2057:24-25	(Same as 1051:8, above)
1: 9-11	2057:31-34	
1:12-14	2057:45-2058: 8	
1:13	(Eleven Apostles Named:)	
	1548: 2	Mt 10:2-4 Mk 3:16-19 Lk 6:13-16
1:14	(The Faithful Women's Corps:)	
	1403:35-36	Mt 27:55-56 Mk 15:40-41 Lk 8:2-3
		Lk 23:27,49;24:10 Jn 19:25
	1671:20-26	(Same as 1403:35-36, above)
	1678:28-1679:15	(Same as 1403:35-36, above)
	1680:21-29	(Same as 1403:35-36, above)
	2005:33-45	(Same as 1403:35-36, above)
	2008:14-19	(Same as 1403:35-36, above)

288

ACTS Chap:Verse	The URANTIA Book Page:Line	Other BOOKS Chap:Verse
1:15-23	2058: 9-16	
1:18	1998:49-50	
1:15-23	2058: 9-16	
1:18	1998:49-50	
1:26	2045:17	
	2058:17-20	
2: 1- 2	2059: 3-12	
2: 1- 4	2043:12-14	
2: 1-21	1187:18-20	
2: 1-42	2064: 7	Jn 14:26
2: 2- 4	(The Coming of the "Comforter," the "Spirit of Truth," the "New Teacher," the "Spirit Poured Out on All Flesh":)	
	0241:41-42	Lk 24:49 Jn 14:16-18,26;15:26 Jn 16:7,13-14 EK 11:19;36:26-27 Jl 2:28 Ac 2:16-18
	0365:32-33	(Same as 0241:41-42, above)
	0379:36	(Same as 0241:41-42, above)
	0382:10-14	(Same as 0241:41-42, above)
	0596:31-32	(Same as 0241:41-42, above)
	1328: 4- 5	(Same as 0241:41-42, above)
	1328:22-25	(Same as 0241:41-42, above)
	1340:24-27	(Same as 0241:41-42, above)
	1591:15-16	(Same as 0241:41-42, above)
	1594: 3- 4	(Same as 0241:41-42, above)
	1642:18-24	(Same as 0241:41-42, above)
	1897:33	(Same as 0241:41-42, above)
	1918:45-47	(Same as 0241:41-42, above)
	1947:14-17	(Same as 0241:41-42, above)
	1948: 9-24	(Same as 0241:41-42, above)
	1948:34-36	(Same as 0241:41-42, above)
	1951:45-48	(Same as 0241:41-42, above)
	1953:22-26	(Same as 0241:41-42, above)
	1954: 2	(Same as 0241:41-42, above)
	1958: 7- 9	(Same as 0241:41-42, above)
	1959:22-24	(Same as 0241:41-42, above)
	1961:24-27	(Same as 0241:41-42, above)
	2035:38-39	(Same as 0241:41-42, above)

(Acts 2:2-4 Continued on next page.)

ACTS Chap:Verse	The URANTIA Book Page:Line	Other BOOKS Chap:Verse			
2: 2- 4	2044:34-35	(Same as 0241:41-42, above)			
	2053:17-19	(Same as 0241:41-42, above)			
	2054:42-43	(Same as 0241:41-42, above)			
	2055: 9-11	(Same as 0241:41-42, above)			
	2057:21-22	(Same as 0241:41-42, above)			
	2061:10-13	(Same as 0241:41-42, above)			
	2061:20-21	(Same as 0241:41-42, above)			
	2062:43	(Same as 0241:41-42, above)			
	2064: 7	(Same as 0241:41-42, above)			
2: 4	2059:35-38				
	2060:16-19				
2: 5	2060: 2- 4				
2: 6-12	2060:15-19				
2:14-40	2060: 9-11				
2:16-18	(Outpouring of The Spirit, See Acts 2:2-4, above.)				
2:17	(Pour Out My Spirit on All Flesh:)				
	0241:41-42	Jl 2:28			
	0365:32-33	Jl 2:28			
	0379:36	Jl 2:28			
	0596:31-32	Jl 2:28			
	1954: 2	Jl 2:28			
	2035:38-39	Jl 2:28			
2:21	0038: 9-10				
	1454:40				
2:22-23	2066:35-37				
2:29-36	2092:40-42	Ac 2:29-36			
2:32-33	2066:38-41				
2:33	(The Trinity:)				
	0108:10-15	Mt 28:19	1Co 12:4-6	1Jo 5:7	
	0115:15-18	Mt 28:19	1Co 12:4-6	1Jo 5:7	
	0640:33-35	Mt 28:19	1Co 12:4-6	1Jo 5:7	
	1144:43-1145:2	Mt 28:19	1Co 12:4-6	1Jo 5:7	
	2061:47-2062:2	Mt 28:19	1Co 12:4-6	1Jo 5:7	
	2067:40	Mt 28:19	1Co 12:4-6	1Jo 5:7	
2:36	2066:39				
2:38-39	1954: 3- 6				
2:41	1549:28				
	2060:22-25				
2:41-42	2067:19-21				

ACTS Chap:Verse	The URANTIA Book Page:Line	Other BOOKS Chap:Verse
2:44	2067:22-24	
2:44-47	0976:25-27	
2:45	2067:31-32	
2:46-47	2066:24-26	
3: 2	1379: 4	
3:10	1379: 4	
3:14	1409: 2	
3:18	2066:37-38	
3:19-21	2066:41-44	
3:24	1062:18	
4:10-12	2069:10-11	
4:13	1548:20-21	
	2077:25	
4:24	1409: 7	
4:25-28	1725:11-18	
4:31-32	2066:26-30	
4:32	2065:32-33	
4:33	1957:13-14	
5: 1-10	0060:16	
5:17-18	2067:46	
5:19	0407:17-18	
	0865:26-28	
5:29-32	2069:10-11	
5:34	2067:47-2068: 3	
5:38-39	2067:47-2068: 3	
5:40	2068: 3	
7:32	1900:17-29	Mt 22:29-32 Mk 12:23-27 Lk 20:34-35
7:51-58	2068:15-17	
7:53	1241:13	
7:55-56	0148:46-47	
7:57-60	1411:37-39	
7:58	1411:44-46	
7:60	2018:46-47	
8: 1	2068:26	
8: 3-13	1616: 6-11	
8: 5	2049:12-13	
8: 5- 6	1557:36-38	
8:12	1557:36-38	
8:14-17	1557:38-40	

291

ACTS Chap:Verse	The URANTIA Book Page:Line	Other BOOKS Chap:Verse
8:14-25	1551:21-22	
8:32	1977:44-46	
8:40	1430:42-45	
9: 1-20	2091:32-34	
9: 3- 9	1099: 7- 8	
9:20	1099: 7- 8	
9:36-42	1428:41	
9:43	1428:42-43	
10: 1-48	1430:46	
10: 2	1333:40-41	
10: 7	1333:40-41	
	1430:45-46	
10: 9-16	1713:25-28	
10:22	1333:40-41	
10:34	(God is No Respecter of Persons:)	
	0027: 8	2Ch 19:7 Jb 34:19 Ro 2:11 Ga 2:6 Ep 6:9
	0036:43-44	2Ch 19:7 Jb 34:19 Ro 2:11 Ga 2:6 Ep 6:9
	0138:22	2Ch 19:7 Jb 34:19 Ro 2:11 Ga 2:6 Ep 6:9
	0454:17-19	2Ch 19:7 Jb 34:19 Ro 2:11 Ga 2:6 Ep 6:9
	1290:43-45	2Ch 19:7 Jb 34:19 Ro 2:11 Ga 2:6 Ep 6:9
	1468:30	2Ch 19:7 Jb 34:19 Ro 2:11 Ga 2:6 Ep 6:9
	1536:10	2Ch 19:7 Jb 34:19 Ro 2:11 Ga 2:6 Ep 6:9
	1608:20	2Ch 19:7 Jb 34:19 Ro 2:11 Ga 2:6 Ep 6:9
	1662:45-47	2Ch 19:7 Jb 34:19 Ro 2:11 Ga 2:6 Ep 6:9
	1731: 6- 8	2Ch 19:7 Jb 34:19 Ro 2:11 Ga 2:6 Ep 6:9
	1736:10-12	2Ch 19:7 Jb 34:19 Ro 2:11 Ga 2:6 Ep 6:9
	1831: 8	2Ch 19:7 Jb 34:19 Ro 2:11 Ga 2:6 Ep 6:9
	1909:35	2Ch 19:7 Jb 34:19 Ro 2:11 Ga 2:6 Ep 6:9
	1958:12	2Ch 19:7 Jb 34:19 Ro 2:11 Ga 2:6 Ep 6:9
	2047:37	2Ch 19:7 Jb 34:19 Ro 2:11 Ga 2:6 Ep 6:9
10:38	(Jesus Went About Doing Good:)	
	1102:27	
	1590:11	
	1770:24	
	1786:33	
	1875:23	
10:41	2031:34-35	
10:42	1409: 8	
11:16	(Baptism of the Spirit, See Acts 1:5, above.)	

ACTS Chap:Verse	The URANTIA Book Page:Line	Other BOOKS Chap:Verse
11:25-26	1492:18-19	
11:26	(Disciples First Called Christians at Antioch.)	
	1333:44-45	
	2068:27-28	
11:29-30	2067:34-35	
12: 1- 2	(Persecution of the Apostles:)	
	1553:21-32	Mt 20:23 Mk 10:39
	1958:25-26	Mt 20:23 Mk 10:39
	1958:33-34	Mt 20:23 Mk 10:39
	2048:36-37	
12: 7	0865:26-28	
12:1-2	1553:28-30	
12:17	0865:26-28	
13:24	(John Preached Baptism of Repentance:)	
	1502:11-20	Mt 3:2,6,11 Mk 1:4,8 Lk 3:3
		Jn 1:25-33
	1503:31	(Same as 1502:11-20, above)
	1510:26-27	(Same as 1502:11-20, above)
	1536:34-36	(Same as 1502:11-20, above)
	1584:31-32	(Same as 1502:11-20, above)
	1625:30-35	(Same as 1502:11-20, above)
13:26-39	2069:10-11	
13:33	(Only Begotten Son:)	
	0073:37	Jn 1:14,18;3:16,18 Ps 2:7
		He 1:5;5:5 1Jo 4:9
	0109:22	(Same as 0073:37, above)
	0232:33-35	(Same as 0073:37, above)
	0234: 7	(Same as 0073:37, above)
	0235: 6	(Same as 0073:37, above)
	0366:15	(Same as 0073:37, above)
	1522:43-47	(Same as 0073:37, above)
14:15	0021: 8-10	Ge 1:1 2Ki 19:15 Ne 9:6
		Ps 115:15-16 Is 37:16 Ac 14:15
	1011:32-33	(Same as 0021:8-10, above)
	1453:41-42	Jn 1:3
14:22	1521:13-14	
	1533:29-31	Jn 16:33 Re 17:4
	1935: 6-10	
14:27	2083:33-35	

Acts 15:1 to 20:35

ACTS Chap:Verse	The URANTIA Book Page:Line	Other BOOKS Chap:Verse
15: 5-12	1551:21-22	
15:11	1342:16-17	Lk 2:40
17: 2- 3	2092:40-42	
17: 4	1333:40-41	
17: 6	2077:26-27	
17:17	1333:40-41	
17:22-23	0962:15-17	
	2071: 2- 4	
17:24-31	2071: 4- 6	
17:25	0023:14-15	
	0035:38	
	0513:29	
17:26	0593:38-39	
17:27	0139: 7- 8	
17:28	(In Him Man Lives and Moves and Has Being:)	
	0022:40	
	0029:42	
	0035:28-29	
	0139: 8- 9	
	0646: 4- 5	
	1155:21	
	1283:11-12	
	1336:10	
	1900:29-30	
17:28-29	0025: 4	
18: 1- 5	1472:12-13	
18: 2	1473:48-50	
18: 7	1472:22-23	
18: 8	1471:48	
18:18	1473:48-50	
18:26	1473:48-50	
19: 1-10	1478:16-19	
19:20	1053:41	
19:29	1473:41-42	
20: 4	1473:41-42	
20:32	1820:41	
20:35	(More Blessed to Give Than to Receive:)	
	0316:39	

(Acts 20:35, Continued on next page.)

294

ACTS Chap:Verse	The URANTIA Book Page:Line	Other BOOKS Chap:Verse
20:35	1102:35-36	
	1131:48	
	1581:44-45	
21:37	1332:29	
22:12	1333:40-41	
22:24-29	1332:29-30	
23:31-33	1430:47-48	
24:15	1247:38	
24:16	1736:33	
24:27	1430:47-48	
26:18	1820:41	
28:25-27	1689:14-31	Mt 13:11-15;25:9 Mk 14:11-12
		Lk 8:10-11;19:26
28:31	1858:30	

* * * * * * * * * * *

B: The Book of AMOS.

AMOS Chap:Verse	The URANTIA Book Page:Line	Other BOOKS Chap:Verse
4:13	1065:38	
4:13	1066: 1	
5: 8	1065:38-40	
5:14-15	1392: 1- 3	
5:21-24	1066: 2	
7: 3	(God's "Repentance":)	
	0036: 1	Ge 6:6 Ex 32:14 Nu 23:19 1Sa 15:29
		Amos 7:6 Zc 8:14
	0058: 6	
	1131:48	
	1581:44-45	(Same as 0036:1, above)
	1063: 6- 7	(Same as 0036:1, above)
	1510:19	(Same as 0036:1, above)
7: 6	(God's Repentance, See Amos 7:3, above.)	
8: 7	1065:47	
9: 2	1065:42-44	
9: 4	1065:44-45	
9: 9	1065:48	

295

C: The ASSUMPTION of MOSES

AS. of MOSES Chap:Verse	The URANTIA Book Page:Line	Other BOOKS Chap:Verse
Lost	0596:21-24	Jd 9
	0601:30-32	Jd 9
10: 1- 2	0609:35-0610:2	Lk 10:18
	0611:11-20	Lk 10:18

*   *   *   *   *   *   *   *   *   *   *

D: The Book of BARUCH

BARUCH Chap:Verse	The URANTIA Book Page:Line	Other BOOKS Chap:Verse
1:15-2:10	1059:40-41	Jb 37:23
2: 9-5: 9	1076: 6- 9	
3:14	0630:26-27	
3:32-36	1444: 5- 6	Ge 1:1-31
6: 7	1241:17	

(Baruch, Chapter 6, is also known as "A Letter of Jeremiah.")

*   *   *   *   *   *   *   *   *   *   *

E: BEL and The DRAGON (Large SNAKE)

BEL & DRAGON Verse	The URANTIA Book Page:Line	Other BOOKS Chap:Verse
2-22	1042:30	Is 46:1 Je 50:2; 51:44
23	0946:23	
	0968: 2	

F: CANTICLES, or SONG of SOLOMON

CANTICLES Chap:Verse	The URANTIA Book Page:Line	Other BOOKS Chap:Verse
5: 2	0946:38-39	
5:10	1403:37-38	
	1566:18-19	
5:16	1403:37	
	1566:18	
6: 9	0946:38-39	

*   *   *   *   *   *   *   *   *   *   *

G: The FIRST Book of CHRONICLES

I CHRON. Chap:Verse	The URANTIA Book Page:Line	Other BOOKS Chap:Verse
1:32	1023:40-41	
10: 1-14	1072:19-20	
13:10	0060:16	
14:15	0988: 5- 7	
15:25-16:	1073:24-25	
16:31	1444:31-32	
16:34	0038:11-12	
	1444:32	
16:41	0038:11-12	
21: 1	(Satan Instigates David's Census)	
	0602: 1- 5	2Sa 24:1-4
	0968:11-12	2Sa 24:1-4
	1350:25-26	2Sa 24:1-4
	1599:10-12	2Sa 24:1
	1599:16-17	
21: 1- 7	0968:11-12	
21: 7	1350:25-26	
28: 6	1661: 7	
28: 9	0067:31	
29:11	1064: 1- 2	
	1064: 4- 5	
29:12	1064: 5- 7	

H: The SECOND Book of CHRONICLES

II CHRON. Chap:Verse	The URANTIA Book Page:Line	Other BOOKS Chap:Verse
2: 6	(Heaven of Heavens:)	
	0034: 2- 3	De 10:14 2Ch 6:18 1Ki 8:27
		Ne 9:6 Ps 148:4
	0044:33-34	(Same as 0034:2-3, above)
	0053:19-29	(Same as 0034:2-3, above)
	0553:26	(Same as 0034:2-3, above)
	1953:28-29	(Same as 0034:2-3, above)
5:13	0038:11-12	
6: 1	0033:38	
6:18	(Heaven of Heavens, See II Chronicles 2:6, above.)	
7: 3, 6	0038:11-12	
18: 6-27	1064:23	
19: 7	(No iniquity in God:)	
	0036:43	Ro 9:14
	(God is No Respecter of Persons:)	
	0027: 8	Jb 34:19 Ac 10:34 Ro 2:11 Ga 2:6 Ep 6:9
	0036:43-44	Jb 34:19 Ac 10:34 Ro 2:11 Ga 2:6 Ep 6:9
	0138:22	Jb 34:19 Ac 10:34 Ro 2:11 Ga 2:6 Ep 6:9
	0454:17-19	Jb 34:19 Ac 10:34 Ro 2:11 Ga 2:6 Ep 6:9
	1290:43-45	Jb 34:19 Ac 10:34 Ro 2:11 Ga 2:6 Ep 6:9
	1468:30	Jb 34:19 Ac 10:34 Ro 2:11 Ga 2:6 Ep 6:9
	1536:10	Jb 34:19 Ac 10:34 Ro 2:11 Ga 2:6 Ep 6:9
	1608:20	Jb 34:19 Ac 10:34 Ro 2:11 Ga 2:6 Ep 6:9
	1662:45-47	Jb 34:19 Ac 10:34 Ro 2:11 Ga 2:6 Ep 6:9
	1731: 6- 8	Jb 34:19 Ac 10:34 Ro 2:11 Ga 2:6 Ep 6:9
	1736:10-12	Jb 34:19 Ac 10:34 Ro 2:11 Ga 2:6 Ep 6:9
	1831: 8	Jb 34:19 Ac 10:34 Ro 2:11 Ga 2:6 Ep 6:9
	1909:35	Jb 34:19 Ac 10:34 Ro 2:11 Ga 2:6 Ep 6:9
	1958:12	Jb 34:19 Ac 10:34 Ro 2:11 Ga 2:6 Ep 6:9
	2047:37	Jb 34:19 Ac 10:34 Ro 2:11 Ga 2:6 Ep 6:9
20:15	0784:35	
23:11-17	1074:28-29	
25:27	1074:32-33	
26: 1	1074:32-33	
33: 1-20	1074:38-40	
33:19	0946: 3	
35:20-24	1074:44-46	
35:20-24	1387:15	

I: Paul's Letter to The COLOSSIANS

COLOSSIANS Chap:Verse	The URANTIA Book Page:Line	Other BOOKS Chap:Verse
1: 3	2064:36-37	
	2067: 7- 8	
1:14	1864:25-27	
1:15-16	0234: 2	
1:16-17	0045:34-35	
1:17	(God Before All Things:	
	0051:16-17	
	1409: 6	
	(In Him All Things Consist:)	
	0051:16-17	
	0098:32	
	0125:29-30	
	0467:27-28	
	0638:19	
	0646: 4- 5	1Co 8:6
	1150:42	Ro 11:36
	1409: 6- 7	
	1453:38	
2: 3	1409: 4- 5	
	1417: 8- 9	
2:12	2092:40-42	
2:17	1864: 8-11	
2:18	1897:23	
3: 1	(Right Hand of the Father:)	
	0064:33	Mt 22:44 Mk 16:19 Lk 20:42 Ps 110:1
	0239:45-46	Mt 22:44 Mk 16:19 Lk 20:42 Ps 110:1
	2057:35-42	Mt 22:44 Mk 16:19 Lk 20:42 Ps 110:1
3: 9-10	1131:47	
	1739: 8- 9	
3:11	0044:34	
	0646: 4- 5	
	1536:37	
	2033:14-15	
	2034: 1	
3:24	1820:41	
4:10	1461:45-46	

J: Paul's FIRST Letter to the CORINTHIANS

1 CORINTH. Chap:Verse	The URANTIA Book Page:Line	Other BOOKS Chap:Verse		
1: 9	0055: 1			
	2034: 4			
1:14	1471:48			
	1473:41-42			
2: 2	2069:10-11			
	2071:20			
2: 6-16	1199:10-21			
2: 8	1409: 1			
2: 9	(The Unimagined Future for Believers:)			
	0121:47-0122:2	Is 64:4		
	0269:45-47	Is 64:4		
	0501: 4	Is 64:4		
	1960:36-37	Is 64:4		
2: 9-16	1453:45-47			
2:10	(Spirit Searches All Things;)			
	0096:28			
	0313:34			
2:16	0191:34-40	Pp 2:5		
	0484:19-23	Pp 2:5		
	0553:46-48	Pp 2:5		
	1123:10-11	Pp 2:5		
3: 1- 2	1474:10-13			
	1736:26-28			
3: 6- 9	1286:19-20			
3: 9	1934:23			
3:11	2054:39-41	Ep 4:14-15	1Pe 2:2	2Pe 5:18
3:16	(God's Spirit Dwells in Humans:)			
	0026:27	1Co 6:19	2Co 6:16	
	0381: 2- 3	1Co 6:19	2Co 6:16	
	1181:14	1Co 6:19	2Co 6:16	
	1204:14-16	1Co 6:19	2Co 6:16	
	1453:38-39	1Co 6:19	2Co 6:16	
	1609:36-38	1Co 6:19	2Co 6:16	
	1841:22-23	1Co 6:19	2Co 6:16	
3:16-17	1204:14-16			
5: 7	0948:14-16			
6: 1- 7	1571: 7- 8			

300

I CORINTH. Chap:Verse	The URANTIA Book Page:Line	Other BOOKS Chap:Verse		
6:17	1204:21-27			
6:19	(Your Body is Temple of God's Spirit:)			
	0026:27	1Co 3:16	2Co 6:16	
	0381: 2- 3	1Co 3:16	2Co 6:16	
	1204:14-16	1Co 3:16	2Co 6:16	
	1609:36-38	1Co 3:16	2Co 6:16	
7: 1	0977:10-11			
7: 6	0977:14-15			
7: 7	0977:11			
7: 8	0977:11-12			
7: 9	0977: 6			
8: 4- 6	(One God, See Deuteronomy 6:4, below.)			
8: 6	0034: 5			
	0646: 4- 5			
10:13	0055: 1			
10:26	0051: 4- 5			
10:28	0051: 4- 5			
11:23-27	(The Rembrance Supper, Eucharist:			
	0984:17-18			
	1941:40-1943:14	Mt 26:26-29	Mk 14:22-25	
		Lk 22:19-20		
11:24	1942: 9-14	Mt 26:26	Mk 14:22	Lk 22:19
11:25	1941:41-47	Mt 26:27-28	Mk 14:23-24	Lk 22:20
11:26	1943: 5-11			
12: 4- 6	(Compare: Trinity Concept, See Acts 2:33, above.)			
12: 4-30	1591:41-45			
12: 6	0044:32			
	0646: 4- 5			
12:11	0096:30-31			
12:12-27	0052: 1- 4			
12:13	1536: 9-10			
	1541:38-40			
12:26	0619: 4- 5			
13: 1	0084:46			
13: 1- 8	1739:38-39			
13: 2	1619:36-38	Mt 17:20		

1st Corinthians 13:12 to 16:24

1 CORINTH. Chap:Verse	The URANTIA Book Page:Line	Other BOOKS Chap:Verse
13:12	(Know and Be Known:)	
	0028:29	Jn 10:14
	0078:32-33	Jn 10:14
	0078:42	Jn 10:14
	0503:20	Jn 10:14
	1235:36-39	Jn 10:14
13:13	2095:18	
13:32	0195:44	
14:14-15	1848:17-19	
15: 5	(Appearances:)	
	(--To Simon Peter:	
	2039:18-19	Lk 24:34
	(--To The Apostles:)	
	2040:18-22	Lk 24:36-37 Jn 20:19-23
	2042:28-47	Mk 16:14 Jn 20:26-29
15: 6	(--To Above 500:)	
	2050:33-44	
15: 7	(--To James:)	
	2032: 5-13	
	(--To All Apostles:)	
	2045:31-2047:10	Jn 21:1-14
	2047:25-2050:2	Jn 21:15-23
	2050: 4-20	Mt 28:16-20
15:11-22	2092:40-42	
15:12-20	2029:20-21	
15:28	0646: 4- 5	
15:35-38	0945:37-38	
15:42-50	1193:28-31	
15:44	0431:19	
15:45	1025:26	
15:45-49	1582:40-42	
15:58	1897:24	
16:19	1473:48-50	
16:20	2067:22	Ro 16:23

K: Paul's SECOND Letter to the CORINTHIANS

II CORINTH. Chap:Verse	The URANTIA Book Page:Line	Other BOOKS Chap:Verse
1: 3	0038:14	
	2064:36-37	
	2067: 7- 8	
3: 2	0301:42	
3: 6	0380:40	
3:17	(Where Spirit of The Lord is, There is Liberty:)	
	1135: 7- 8	
	1609:38-41	
	2063:28-29	
	2065:16	
3:18	1953:33-35	Jn 14:2
4: 4	0610: 9	
	0755:37	
5: 7	1897:25-26	
5:14-21	0228:24-29	Jn 3:16
5:17	(Old Things Pass Away; All Things Become New:)	
	0631:10-11	
	1103:30-32	
	1609:26-27	
	1739: 8- 9	
5:19	1083:43-44	
5:20	1571: 3- 4	
	1897:19-20	
6:16	(You are the Temple of the Living God:)	
	0026:27	1Co 3:16;6:19
	0381: 2- 3	1Co 3:16;6:19
	1204:14-16	1Co 3:16;6:19
	1609:36-38	1Co 3:16;6:19
6:18	1454:16-17	
7: 1	1610:10-12	
9: 6	2048:34-35	
9:15	1454:27	
10: 7	1897:14-15	
11:14	0754:15-16	
11:31	2064:36-37	
12: 2	0553:22-23	
13: 5	1474:22-23	

2nd Corinthians 13:11 to 13:14

II CORINTH. Chap:Verse	The URANTIA Book Page:Line	Other BOOKS Chap:Verse
13:11	(Be You Perfect:)	
	0021:30-31	Ge 17:1 Le 19:2 De 18:13 Mt 5:48 Ja 1:4
	0022:15-16	(Same as 0021:30-31, above)
	0086: 3	(Same as 0021:30-31, above)
	0086:11-12	(Same as 0021:30-31, above)
	0149: 3- 4	(Same as 0021:30-31, above)
	0290:20	(Same as 0021:30-31, above)
	0295:10-11	(Same as 0021:30-31, above)
	0297: 5- 6	(Same as 0021:30-31, above)
	0348:21	(Same as 0021:30-31, above)
	0411: 5	(Same as 0021:30-31, above)
	0449:14	(Same as 0021:30-31, above)
	0637: 8- 9	(Same as 0021:30-31, above)
	1091: 9-10	(Same as 0021:30-31, above)
	1165:24-25	(Same as 0021:30-31, above)
	1176:17	(Same as 0021:30-31, above)
	1444:42-43	(Same as 0021:30-31, above)
	1537: 2	(Same as 0021:30-31, above)
	1571:16-17	(Same as 0021:30-31, above)
	1573: 6- 7	(Same as 0021:30-31, above)
	1573:19-21	(Same as 0021:30-31, above)
	1574:45	(Same as 0021:30-31, above)
	1583:38	(Same as 0021:30-31, above)
	1584:28-29	(Same as 0021:30-31, above)
	1604:35-36	(Same as 0021:30-31, above)
	1784:43-44	(Same as 0021:30-31, above)
	1953:33-35	(Same as 0021:30-31, above)
	1961:33-34	(Same as 0021:30-31, above)
	(God of Love:)	
	1608:25	

L: The Book of DANIEL

DANIEL Chap:Verse	The URANTIA Book Page:Line	Other BOOKS Chap:Verse		
7:13	(Ancient of Days, See Daniel 7:9, above.)			
7:13-14	(The Son of Man as Seen by Daniel:)			
	1390:14-15			
	1498:31-33			
	1509:24			
	1510:35-36			
	1526:11-12			
7:14	1498:22-25			
7:22	(Ancient of Days, See Daniel 7:9, above.)			
7:27	1498:25-28			
	1865:29-31			
9:11	1511: 7			
11:31	1913:26-31	Mt 24:15-18	Mk 13:14-16	Lk 21:20-21
12: 1- 2	1534:41-42			
12: 2	0568:30			
12: 3	1445:50-1446: 2			
12:11	1913:26:31	Mt 24:15-18	Mk 13:14-16	Lk 21:20-21

*   *   *   *   *   *   *   *   *   *   *

M: The Book of DEUTERONOMY

DEUTER Chap:Verse	The URANTIA Book Page:Line	Other BOOKS Chap:Verse	
3: 1- 7	0779:10-11		
4: 2	1768:18-21		
4:12	0947:16		
4:15	1058:30-32		
4:24	1053:24	Ge 31:13+	
	(Jealous God:)		
	0057:36-38	Ex 20:5;34:14+	De 5:9;6:15+
	1597: 7-10	Ex 20:5;34:14+	De 5:9;6:15+
4:31	1157:19-21		
4:35	(None Else Beside Him:)		
	1009:33	De 4:39	
	1058:28	De 4:39	
	1444: 6- 7	De 4:39	
	(One God, See Deuteronomy 6:4, below.)		

DEUTER Chap:Verse	The URANTIA Book Page:Line	Other BOOKS Chap:Verse
4:35-39	0640:20-21	Mk 12:29-32
4:39	(One God, See Deuteronomy 6:4, below.)	
	(None Else Beside Him, See Deut. 4:35, above.)	
5: 4	0301:30-31	
5: 4- 5	1599:38	
5: 6-21	1599:38-40	
5: 7-21	(The Ten Commandments:)	
	0975: 5- 7	Ex 20:3-17
	1446: 6-10	Ex 20:3-17
	1802: 9-11	Ex 20:3-17 Mt 19:18-19 Mk 10:19
		Lk 18:20
5: 7	(No Other Gods Before Me:)	
	1781:47-50	
	(One God, See Deuteronomy 6:4, below.)	
5: 8	(No Graven Images:)	
	0044:26-27	
	0969:17-19	
	1600:23	
5: 9	(Jealous God, See Deuteronomy 4:24, above.)	
5:11	(Regard for God's "Name":)	
	0971:43-44	
5:12-14	(Keeping the Sabbath:)	
	1042:19-23	Ex 20:8-10
	(For Jesus' Use of Sabbath, see Matthew 12:1-14,	
	Mark 2:23-3:5, Luke 6:1-10 or John 5:5-9)	
5:15	1599:41-42	
5:16	(Honor Parents:)	
	1373: 4- 5	
	1712:21-42	Mt 15:1-9 Mk 7:5-13 Lk 11:37-41
5:17	(Do Not Kill:)	
	0796:45	
	1576:28	Mt 5:21-22
	1790:38	Jn 7:16-19
5:18	(Do Not Commit Adultery:)	
	1576:34	Mt 5:27-28
5:21	(Regard Property of Others:)	
	1822:30	

Deuteronomy 6:1 to 8:20

DEUTER Chap:Verse	The URANTIA Book Page:Line	Other BOOKS Chap:Verse
9:16-21	1637:24	
10: 5	0969:21-23	
10:12-13	1058:39-40	
10:14	(Heaven of Heavens, See 2nd Chronicles 2:6, above.)	
10:15	0028: 6	
10:17	1058:34-36	
	(God of Gods:)	
	0513:45	
	(Mighty & Terrible:)	
	1057:11	
10:20	1522:17-18	Mt 4:10 Lk 4:8
11:26-28	1071: 7- 8	
11:29	0945:24-27	
13: 1- 5	0954:40-42	
14: 2	(Chosen People, See Deuteronomy 7:6, above.)	
15: 6	1058:22-24	
15: 9	0962:35-36	
18:13	(Be Perfect, See 2nd Corinthians 13:11, above.)	
19:14	0781:46-47	
19:21	(Ancient Justice, an Eye for an Eye:)	
	0795:36-37	
	1577:17	Ex 21-24 Le 24:20 Mt 5:38-42
	1580: 1	Ex 21-24 Le 24:20 Mt 5:38-42
	1770:32	Ex 21-24 Le 24:20 Mt 5:38-40 Lk 6:29
21:10-14	0779:19-21	
23:14	1058:43-44	
25: 5- 6	(Providing an Heir:)	
	0919: 3- 4	Mt 22:24 Mk 12:19 Lk 20:28
	0926:12-14	Mt 22:24 Mk 12:19 Lk 20:28
	1900: 2-12	Mt 22:24 Mk 12:19 Lk 20:28
27: 5- 6	1004:30-32	
27:17	0781:47	
28: 1-37	1058:37-38	
28:15-53	1709:10-27	
28:54	0962:35-36	
28:56	0962:35-36	
28:58	1057:11	
29:10-15	0965:11-12	
29:27-28	0057:44-45	

DEUTER Chap:Verse	The URANTIA Book Page:Line	Other BOOKS Chap:Verse
30: 7	1058:45-46	
30:11-14	1685:50-1686: 6	
31:20	1822:30-31	
32: 1-43	1075:37-38	
32: 4	1057:23-24	
32: 8	0488:15	
	0491:34-35	
	1016:25	
32:15-17	1822:30-31	
32:35	0795:39-40	
	1597: 7-10	
32:39	1058:37-38	
33:27	0041: 3	
	0055: 6- 7	
	1057:17-18	
	1445:41-42	
33:27	1662:17-18	

*   *   *   *   *   *   *   *   *   *   *

N: The Book of ECCLESIASTES

ECCLES. Chap:Verse	The URANTIA Book Page:Line	Other BOOKS Chap:Verse
1: 1- 8	1118: 7-11	
1: 1-18	1070:46-48	
2:11-26	1118: 7-11	
2:12-17	1070:46-48	
3:14	0035:47-0036: 1	
3:20	(Dust to Dust:)	
	0026:36-37	
	0981:35	
4: 6	1674:35-36	
7: 9	1673:23-24	
9:10	1480:10	
9:11-12	0951:13-18	
12: 7	0026:36-38	

ECCLES. Chap:Verse	The URANTIA Book Page:Line	Other BOOKS Chap:Verse
12:13	(Fear God:) 1445:29-30 1676: 8- 9	
12:14	1445:24-25	

*   *   *   *   *   *   *   *   *   *   *

O: The First Book of ENOCH

ENOCH Chap:Verse	The URANTIA Book Page:Line	Other BOOKS Chap:Verse			
46: 1-71:17	1390: 3- 5	Mt 8:20+	Mk 2:10+	Lk 5:24+	Jn 1:51+
46: 1-71:17	1390:24-31	Mt 8:20+	Mk 2:10+	Lk 5:24+	Jn 1:51+
46: 1-71:17	1407:27	Mt 8:20+	Mk 2:10+	Lk 5:24+	Jn 1:51+
46: 1- 6	1501:23-28	Mt 8:20+	Mk 2:10+	Lk 5:24+	Jn 1:51+
48: 1- 7	1501:23-28	Mt 8:20+	Mk 2:10+	Lk 5:24+	Jn 1:51+
62: 1-15	1501:23-28	Mt 8:20+	Mk 2:10+	Lk 5:24+	Jn 1:51+
63:11	1501:23-28	Mt 8:20+	Mk 2:10+	Lk 5:24+	Jn 1:51+
69:27-29	1501:23-28	Mt 8:20+	Mk 2:10+	Lk 5:24+	Jn 1:51+
71:14,17	1501:23-28	Mt 8:20+	Mk 2:10+	Lk 5:24+	Jn 1:51+

*   *   *   *   *   *   *   *   *   *   *

P: Paul's Letter to The EPHESIANS

EPHES. Chap:Verse	The URANTIA Book Page:Line	Other BOOKS Chap:Verse
1: 3	2064:36-37 2067: 7- 8	
1:13	2034: 3	
1:23	0044:31 1409: 5	
2: 8	(Salvation through Grace by Faith:) 1204:46-47 1537:21-22 1610:18 1682:44-48	

Ephesians 2:12 to 5:9

EPHES. Chap:Verse	The URANTIA Book Page:Line	Other BOOKS Chap:Verse
2:12	1411:26	
	1414:48	
3: 9	0234: 2	
3:11	**0035:43-44**	
3:14-15	1861:25-27	Mt 12:50 Mk 3:35 Lk 8:21
3:16	**0381:24-25**	
3:19	**0381:27**	
4: 3	1591:30	
4: 3- 6	1487: 7	
4: 5	1985:10-12	
4: 6	(God "in All":)	
	0044:34	
	0051:15-16	
	0646: 4- 5	
	(One God, See Deuteronomy 6:4, above.)	
4: 8	**0341:11**	
4:10	**0044:31**	
4:13	1591:35-36	
4:14-15	2054:39-41	1Co 3:11 1Pe 2:2 2Pe 5:18
4:22	1131:47	
4:22-24	1739: 8- 9	
4:23-24	1193:14-17	
4:24	1131:47	
4:25	0619: 3-10	
4:30	**0096:32-33**	
5: 2	0977:47-0978: 1	
	0984:14:16	
5: 8	(Children of Light:)	
	1327:26-27	Mt 5:14-16 Lk 16:8 Jn 12:36 1Th 5:5
	1655:37-38	Mt 5:14-16 Lk 16:8 Jn 12:36 1Th 5:5
	1854:11-12	Mt 5:14-16 Lk 16:8 Jn 12:36 1Th 5:5
	1904:24-28	Mt 5:14-16 Lk 16:8 Jn 12:36 1Th 5:5
	1953:33	Mt 5:14-16 Lk 16:8 Jn 12:26 1Th 5:5
	2042: 2- 3	Mt 5:14-16 Lk 16:8 Jn 12:36 1Th 5:5
5: 9	(Fruit of the Spirit:)	
	0381:44-45	Ga 5:22-23
	1091:20	Ga 5:22-23
	1610:24-27	Ga 5:22-23

Ephesians 5:9 Continued on next page.)

EPHES. Chap:Verse	The URANTIA Book Page:Line	Other BOOKS Chap:Verse
	2053:44-45	Ga 5:22-23
	2054:29-33	Ga 5:22-23
	2062:40	Ga 5:22-23
	(For Requirement to Bear Good Spiritual Fruit, See Matthew 3:8-10, Luke 3:8-9, John 15:2, above.)	
5:21-32	1864:29-33	
5:23	1205:20-21	
5:31	1839:33-34	
6: 9	(God is No Respecter of Persons, See 2nd Chronicles 19:7, above.)	
6:11-17	2064:27-37	
6:12	0611:10	
	1938:20-21	Jn 13:1-3
6:16	0610:24-25	
6:18	1849: 2	Jn 4:23-24

* * * * * * * * * * *

Q: The FIRST Book of ESDRAS

I ESDRAS Chap:Verse	The URANTIA Book Page:Line	Other BOOKS Chap:Verse
1:25-38	1074:44-46	
1:45-58	1075: 7-11	
4:46	1856:21-24	

* * * * * * * * * * *

R: The SECOND Book of ESDRAS

II ESDRAS Chap:Verse	The URANTIA Book Page:Line	Other BOOKS Chap:Verse
1:30-32	1872:25-30	
	1908:42-49	
7:39-44	0009:41-0010: 4	

II ESDRAS Chap:Verse	The URANTIA Book Page:Line	Other BOOKS Chap:Verse
8:20	0021:30	Is 57:15
	0023:31-32	Is 57:15
	0034:30-31	Is 57:15
	0050:19	Is 57:15
	1069:33-34	Is 57:15

* * * * * * * * * * *

S: The Book of ESTHER

ESTHER Chap:Verse	The URANTIA Book Page:Line	Other BOOKS Chap:Verse
1: 2+	1481:22	
4: 1- 4	0976:29-32	
4:16	0976:16-17	
9:17-32	1379:14	

* * * * * * * * * * *

T: The Book of EXODUS

EXODUS Chap:Verse	The URANTIA Book Page:Line	Other BOOKS Chap:Verse
2: 1-10	0982: 9-12	
	1055:27-29	
2:16	0986:28-29	
3: 1	0945:24-27	
3: 2	(Angel of The Lord:)	
	0407:17-18	Mt 1:20;28:2 Lk 1:11 Ac 5:9 Ge 16:7+
	(Sacred Fire:)	
	0947:16	Ex 13:21-22;19:18 Nu 9:15-16 De 4:12+
3: 6	(I Am The God of Ancestors:)	
	1900:27	Mt 22:32 Mk 12:26 Lk 20:37
	1900:43-44	Mt 22:32 Mk 12:26 Lk 20:37
	1965:25	
3: 7	(God Knows our Sorrows:)	
	0049: 6- 8	
	1662:16-17	

EXODUS Chap:Verse	The URANTIA Book Page:Line	Other BOOKS Chap:Verse
3: 8	1054:46	
3:12	0945:24-27	
3:13-14	1152:21	
3:14	(I Am:)	
	0023:27-29	
	0034:32-33	
	1122:26-28	
	1965:26	
3:17	1054:46	
4: 3- 4	0946:23	Jn 3:14
4:14	1597: 7-10	
5: 1	(Lord God of Israel:)	
	0514:11	
	1053:40	
6: 3	(God Almighty:)	
	1058:42	
	(Yaweh/Jehovah:)	
	1053: 6- 7	
	1053:43	
7: 9-12	0946:23	Jn 3:14
7:13+	(Hardening of Pharaoh's Heart:)	
	1058:45	
	1738:34	
12: 1-28	1404:46-47	
12: 3- 5	0946:38	
12: 7	0982: 5- 6	
12: 8	1004:35-36	
12:12-13	0982: 5- 6	
12:16 +	1415:36	
12:22-23	0982: 5- 6	
13: 2	1352:37	
13:12-13	0981:44-45	
13:15	1352:38-40	
13:21-22	0947:16	
14: 8- 9	1056:16-17	
14:13	1704:11-12	
15: 3	1058:42	
15: 6	1058:43	
15:11	1058:29	

Exodus 16:1 to 20:16

EXODUS Chap:Verse	The URANTIA Book Page:Line	Other BOOKS Chap:Verse
16:14-15	1710:48-49	Jn 6:30-33
19: 3	0945:24-27	
19: 6	1536: 3	
19: 9	0947:17-19	
19:11-23	0945:24-27	
19:16	0947:17-19	
19:16-18	1599:38	
19:18	0947:16	
	1057: 7- 9	
20: 3-17	(The Ten Commandments:)	
	0975: 5- 7	De 5:7-21
	1446: 6-10	De 5:7-21
	1599:38-40	De 5:7-21
	1802: 9-11	De 5:7-21 Mt 19:18-19 Mk 10:19
		Lk 18:20
20: 3	(No Other Gods Before Me:)	
	1781:47-50	De 5:7
	(One God, See Deuteronomy 6:4, above.)	
20: 4	(No Graven Images:)	
	0044:26-27	De 5:8
	0969:17-19	De 5:8
	1600:23	De 5:8
20: 5	(Jealous God, See Deuteronomy 4:24, above.)	
20: 7	(Respecting God's Name:)	
	0971:43-44	De 5:11
20: 8-10	(Keep Sabbath Holy:)	
	1042:19-23	De 5:12-14
	(For Jesus' Use of Sabbath, See John 5:5-9, above.)	
20:10	0301:30-31	
20:11	1599:43-45	
20:12	(Honor Parents:)	
	1373: 4- 5	De 5:16
	1712:21-42	Mt 15:1-9 Mk 7:5-13 Lk 11:37-41
20:13	(Do Not Kill:)	
	0796:45	De 5:17
	1576:28	De 5:17 Mt 5:21-22
	1790:38	De 5:17 Jn 7:16-19
20:14	(Do Not Commit Adultery:)	
	1576:34	De 5:18 Mt 5:27-28

EXODUS Chap:Verse	The URANTIA Book Page:Line	Other BOOKS Chap:Verse
20:17	(Do Not Covet Property of Others:)	
	1822:30	De 5:21
20:24	0716:23-24	
20:25	1004:30-32	
21:24	(Retributive Justice, Eye for an Eye:)	
	0795:36-37	Le 24:20 De 19:21 Mt 5:38-42
	1577:17	Le 24:20 De 19:21 Mt 5:38-42
	1580: 1	Le 24:20 De 19:21 Mt 5:38-42
	1770:32	Le 24:20 De 19:21 Mt 5:38-40 Lk 6:29
21:30	0981:44-45	
22:18	0987:42-44	
22:24	(God's "Wrath":)	
	0057:44-45	Nu 11:33+ De 29:27-28+
	1597: 7-10	
23:10-19	1599:26-37	
23:25	1629:26-27	
24:12-18	0945:24-27	
24:17	1057:11	
25: 8- 9	0969: 3- 4	
25:20	0438:23	
28: 1- 3	0986:28-29	
29: 1	0978:30-31	
29:18	0977:47-0978: 1	
29:25	0977:47-0978: 1	
29:41	0977:47-0978: 1	
30:25-32	0312: 2	
31:13-16	1042:19-23	
32: 1-35	1637:24	
32:10	1597: 7-10	
32:14	(God's Repentance, See Amos 7:3, above.)	
33: 7	0969: 3- 4	
33:20	0025:17-18	
34: 6	0041: 3- 4	
	1444:18-19	
34:11-27	1599:24-37	
34:14	(Jealous God:)	
	0057:36-38	
	1597: 7-10	
34:20	1352:38-40	

317

EXODUS Chap:Verse	The URANTIA Book Page:Line	Other BOOKS Chap:Verse
34:23	1053: 6- 7	
35: 3	1042:19-23	
37: 1- 9	0969:21-23	
40: 1-33	0969: 3- 4	

* * * * * * * * * * *

U: The Book of EZEKIEL

EZEKIEL Chap:Verse	The URANTIA Book Page:Line	Other BOOKS Chap:Verse
1: 4	0438:41-43	
	0439: 2- 3	
1: 6	0438:27-30	
1:11	0438:27-30	
1:12	0439: 6- 7	
1:13-14	0439: 2- 3	
1:19-21	0438:35-38	
1:22	0438:41-43	
1:23	0438:27-30	
1:27	0438:41-43	
3:12	1536: 6	
5:16-17	0060:16-17	
10: 5	0438:23	
10: 9	0438:41-43	
10:16-17	0438:35-38	
10:19	0439: 6- 7	
10:21	0438:27-30	
11:19	(The New Spirit Within, "Spirit of Truth,":)	
	0241:41-42	Lk 24:49 Jn 14:16-18,26;15:26;16:7 Jn 16:13-14 Ek 36:26-27 Jl 2:28 Ac 2:2-4;16-18
	0365:32-33	(Same as 0241:41-42, above)
	0379:36	(Same as 0241:41-42, above)
	0382:10-14	(Same as 0241:41-42, above)
	0596:31-32	(Same as 0241:41-42, above)
	1328: 4- 5	(Same as 0241:41-42, above)

(Ezekiel 11:19 Continued on next page.)

EZEKIEL Chap:Verse	The URANTIA Book Page:Line	Other BOOKS Chap:Verse
11:19	1328:22-25	(Same as 0241:41-42, above)
	1340:24-27	(Same as 0241:41-42, above)
	1591:15-16	(Same as 0241:41-42, above)
	1594: 3- 4	(Same as 0241:41-42, above)
	1642:18-24	(Same as 0241:41-42, above)
	1897:33	(Same as 0241:41-42, above)
	1918:45-47	(Same as 0241:41-42, above)
	1947:14-17	(Same as 0241:41-42, above)
	1948: 9-24	(Same as 0241:41-42, above)
	1948:34-36	(Same as 0241:41-42, above)
	1951:45-48	(Same as 0241:41-42, above)
	1953:22-26	(Same as 0241:41-42, above)
	1954:14-15	(Same as 0241:41-42, above)
	1958: 7- 9	(Same as 0241:41-42, above)
	1959:22-24	(Same as 0241:41-42, above)
	1961:24-27	(Same as 0241:41-42, above)
	2035:38-39	(Same as 0241:41-42, above)
	2044:34-35	(Same as 0241:41-42, above)
	2053:17-19	(Same as 0241:41-42, above)
	2054:42-43	(Same as 0241:41-42, above)
	2055: 9-11	(Same as 0241:41-42, above)
	2057:21-22	(Same as 0241:41-42, above)
	2061: 2- 3	(Same as 0241:41-42, above)
	2061:10-13	(Same as 0241:41-42, above)
	2061:20-21	(Same as 0241:41-42, above)
	2062:39-44	(Same as 0241:41-42, above)
	2063:34-40	(Same as 0241:41-42, above)
	2064: 7	(Same as 0241:41-42, above)
	2065:40-43	(Same as 0241:41-42, above)
14:23	0036:40	
18: 1- 9	1076:26-27	
18: 2- 4	1630:22-25	
18:31	(New Heart, New Spirit, See Ezekiel 11:19, above.)	
28:14	0601:23-24	
28:15	0601:21-22	
28:16-19	0611:34-35	
28:17	0601:36-37	
28:19	0611:43-44	
33:31	1822:35-36	

319

EZEKIEL Chap:Verse	The URANTIA Book Page:Line	Other BOOKS Chap:Verse
34:23-24	1509:24	
36:26	1630:26-27	
36:26-27	(New Heart, New Spirit, See Ezekiel 11:19, above.)	
37:24-25	1509:24	
43:18-46:24	1076:27-28	

*   *   *   *   *   *   *   *   *   *   *

V: The Book of EZRA

EZRA Chap:Verse	The URANTIA Book Page:Line	Other BOOKS Chap:Verse
6:13	0977:47-0978: 1	
28:13	0492: 7	
31: 8- 9	0492: 7	

*   *   *   *   *   *   *   *   *   *   *

W: Paul's Letter to The GALATIANS

GALATIANS Chap:Verse	The URANTIA Book Page:Line	Other BOOKS Chap:Verse
1: 6- 9	1768:26-27	
1:19	1357: 5- 6	Mt 13:55;27:56 Mk 6:3;15:40
	1362: 1- 2	Mt 13:55;27:56 Mk 6:3;15:40
2: 6	(No Respecter of Persons, See 2nd Chronicles 19:7.)	
2:10	2067:22	Ro 15:26
2:11-14	1551:22-25	
2:16	(Justification by Faith, not Works:)	
	1610: 2-20	
	1682:46-48	
3: 6	1017:35	
3:13	1864:25-27	Lk 1:68
3:18	0773:32-33	
3:20	(One God, See Deuteronomy 6:4, above.)	
3:24	1682:46-48	

GALATIANS Chap:Verse	The URANTIA Book Page:Line	Other BOOKS Chap:Verse
3:26	(Children of God by Faith:)	
	0039:18-19	Is 56:5 Ro 8:14-17 Ga 4:6
		1Jo 3:1-2
	0067:32-33	(Same as 0039:18-19, above)
	0447:40-0448:35	(Same as 0039:18-19, above)
	1091:16-17	(Same as 0039:18-19, above)
	1112:41-42	(Same as 0039:18-19, above)
	1454:37	(Same as 0039:18-19, above)
	1603:37-40	(Same as 0039:18-19, above)
	1610: 2-20	(Same as 0039:18-19, above)
	1725:28	(Same as 0039:18-19, above)
	1861:29-30	(Same as 0039:18-19, above)
	1945:21	(Same as 0039:18-19, above)
	1957:36-37	(Same as 0039:18-19, above)
	1958:17	(Same as 0039:18-19, above)
	2053:14-18	(Same as 0039:18-19, above)
3:28	(Equality Before God:)	
	1536:37	
	1679:23-25	
	1957:45-46	
	2033:14-15	
	2034: 1	
4: 4- 5	1864:25-27	Lk 24:21
4: 4- 7	1860: 6- 8	Jn 1:12-13
4: 6	(Sons Of God, See Galatians 3:26, above.)	
	(Jesus' Spirit in You, See Ezekiel 11:19, above.)	
5: 7	1663: 2	
5:13	0613:37-38	
5:14	(Love Thy Neighbor as Thyself:)	
	1206:40-42	Mt 19:19;22:39 Mk 12:31,33
		Lk 10:27-28 Le 19:18 Ro 13:9 Ja 2:8
	1445:47	(Same as 1206:40-42, above)
	1446:11-12	(Same as 1206:40-42, above)
	1453:37	(Same as 1206:40-42, above)
	1600: 1- 3	(Same as 1206:40-42, above)
	1600:33-36	(Same as 1206:40-42, above)
	1769:26	(Same as 1206:40-42, above)
	1770: 4- 5	(Same as 1206:40-42, above)

(Galatians 5:14 Continued on next page.)

321

Galatians 5:14 to 6:18

GALATIANS Chap:Verse	The URANTIA Book Page:Line	Other BOOKS Chap:Verse
5:14	1805: 9-11	(Same as 1206:40-42, above)
	1809:25-27	(Same as 1206:40-42, above)
	1862: 8	(Same as 1206:40-42, above)
	1901:13-20	(Same as 1206:40-42, above)
	1950:17-18	(Same as 1206:40-42, above)
5:22-23	(Fruit of the Spirit:)	
	0381:44-45	Ep 5:9
	1091:20	Ep 5:9
	1610:24-27	Ep 5:9
	2053:44-45	Ep 5:9
	2054:29-33	Ep 5:9
	2062:40	Ep 5:9
	(For Requirement to Bring Forth Good Fruit, See Matthew 3:8-10 Luke 3:8-9 John 15:2, above.)	
6: 3	0549:11-12	
6: 7	(Reaping What is Sowed:)	
	0037: 1- 2	Jb 4:8
	1445:21-22	Jb 4:8
	14454:35	Jb 4:8
	2048:34-35	Jb 4:8
6: 9	(Be Not Weary in Well Doing:)	
	1740:43-44	2Th 3:13
	1808: 6- 7	2Th 3:13
	1897:36	2Th 3:13
6:10	(Serve Those in Household of Faith:)	
	1930:18-20	
	2042: 4- 6	

*   *   *   *   *   *   *   *   *   *   *

X: The Book of GENESIS

GENESIS Chap:Verse	The URANTIA Book Page:Line	Other BOOKS Chap:Verse
1: 1	(In Beginning The Gods Created:)	
	0021: 8-10	2Ki 19:15 Ne 9:6 Ps 115:15-16
		Is 37:16 Jn 1:1-14;6:32-35 Ac 14:15
	0513:43	(Same as 0021:8-10, above)
	1011:32-33	(Same as 0021:8-10, above)
	1053:41+	(Same as 0021:8-10, above)
	1444: 5- 6	
	1598:34-35	
1: 1-31	0836:44-45	
	(Use of Plural "Elohim":)	
	1053:28	
1: 2	(Spirit of God:)	
	0095:39-40	
	0096:10	
	1053:39	
1: 3	0655:28	
1: 6, 9	0660:13-15	
1:11	0667:33	
1:14-18	0837: 6- 9	
1:20	0669:15	
1:20-22	0691:24-30	
1:21	0679:10-26	
1:24	0686:21-37	
1:26	(God Said Make Man in Our Own Image:)	
	0078:15-16	
	0085:18-19	
	0110:40	
	0359:31-32	
1:26-27	(Man Made, See Genesis 2:7, below.)	
	(--In The Image of god:)	
	0025: 6	Ge 9:6
	0836:16-17	Ge 9:6
	1193:18	Ge 9:6
	1281:44	Ge 9:6
1:27	0975:46-47	
	1839:29	Mt 19:4 Mk 10:6
1:29	0851: 9	

GENESIS Chap:Verse	The URANTIA Book Page:Line	Other BOOKS Chap:Verse
1:31	1222:14-15	
2: 2- 3	0832:45	
	0837: 3- 4	
2: 6	0659:41-44	
	0823:19-20	
2: 7	(Man formed of Earth:)	
	0700:11	
	0707:41	
	0837:14-17	
	(The Breath of Life:)	
	0376:20	
	0404:17	
	0513:29	
	0932: 1- 2	
	0953: 6	
	(A Special Creation:)	
	0975:46-47	
2: 8	0584: 8	
2: 8-14	0583: 5- 7	
2: 9	0825:39	
2:10	0823:27	
2:15	0492:11	
2:16	0851: 9	
2:17	(Wages of Sin is Death:)	
	0529:18	
	0612: 1- 2	
	0842:37-38	
	(Tree of Knowledge of Good & Evil:)	
	0825:39	
	(Thou Shalt Not:)	
	0975:32-34	
2:18	(Not Good for Man to Be Alone:)	
	0283:27	
	1775:44-45	
	2055:21	
2:19-20	0831:31-32	
2:21-23	0837:10-17	
2:22	0975:46-47	
2:24	1839:33-34	Mt 19:4-5 Mk 10:6-8

GENESIS Chap:Verse	The URANTIA Book Page:Line	Other BOOKS Chap:Verse
3: 1	0841: 2-19	
3: 1- 4	0842:39-44	
3: 1- 5	0968: 3	
3: 1-17	0935:24-25	
3: 2	0851: 9	
3: 2- 3	0975:32-34	
3: 5	0826:24-25	
3: 6	0843: 1- 2	
3: 8	0437:11-12	
3: 8-11	0843: 9-11	
3: 8-19	0842:24-29	
3:15	0844:16-18	
3:16-19	0975:47-48	
3:17-19	0900:31-33	
3:18-19	0583:28-33	
3:19	(In Your Sweat Shall You Eat Bread:)	
	0751:47	
	0848: 3- 4	
	(Man Taken "Out of Dust":)	
	0026:36-37	
	0769:32-33	
	0837:14-20	
	0981:35	
	1240: 3- 4	
3:22-24	(The Tree of Life:)	
	0825:40-41	
	0845:29-35	
3:23-24	0492:11	
3:23-24	0844:28-31	
3:24	(East of Eden:)	
	0824:34	Ge 4:16
	0831:39	Ge 4:16
	0835:23	Ge 4:16
4: 2	0848: 7- 8	
4: 2- 5	0900:33-35	
4: 3- 5	0848:11-14	
4: 7	1445:21	
4: 8	0848:33-35	
4:10	0955:16	

Genesis 4:13 to 8:22

GENESIS Chap:Verse	The URANTIA Book Page:Line	Other BOOKS Chap:Verse
4:13-14	0849: 8- 9	
4:14-15	0763:29-30	
4:15	0849:12-16	
4:16	(Land of Nod:)	
	0758: 5	
	0849:17	
	0859:41	
	(East of Eden, See Genesis 3:24, above.)	
4:16-17	(Cain's Wife:)	
	0837:48-49	
	0849:20-22	
	1660:35-36	
4:24	1764:21-22	
5: 2	0828: 8-15	
5: 3	0849:46-0850: 1	
5: 5	0852:40	
5: 5-27	0858: 3- 6	
5: 5-31	0857:48-49	
5: 6	0850: 3	
5: 9	0850: 4	
5:24	0514: 7- 8	He 11:15
6: 2	(Sons of God took Daughters of Men:)	
	0851:34-41	
	0859:43-44	
	1660:36-38	
	(Not refer to Angels:)	
	1841: 3- 4	
6: 4	(Mighty Men of Old:)	
	0822:20	
	0856:38-41	
	0862:13-14	
	(Does Not Refer to Angels:)	
	1841: 3- 4	
6: 5- 8:19	0874:41-0875:17	
6: 6	(God's "Repentance", See Amos 7:3, above.)	
6:17	0060:17	
6:18+	0983: 8-11	
8:21	0977:47-0978: 1	

326

GENESIS Chap:Verse	The URANTIA Book Page:Line	Other BOOKS Chap:Verse
9: 6	(Who Sheds Man's Blood, Man Sheds His blood:)	
	0836:16-17	
	(Man Made in Image of God, See Genesis 1:26-27.)	
9: 9-17	0947:10	
9:29	0857:48-49	
	0858: 3- 6	
11: 1- 9	0858:11	
11:10-26	0857:48-49	
11:27-28	1481:21-22	
11:31	1598:23-24	
11:32	1019:10	
12: 1- 2	1019:12-14	
12: 3	2035:22	
12: 4- 5	1019:16	
12: 7	1023:32-33	
12: 8	1019:17-18	
12: 9-10	1019:23-25	
12:12-13	1023: 1- 2	
13: 1- 2	1019:28-29	
13: 5-12	1019:37-38	
13:14	1023:32-33	
13:17-18	1020: 1- 3	
14: 1-12	1020: 8- 9	
14:13-15	1020: 9-11	
14:16-20	1020:12-15	
14:18	(Melchizedek:)	
	1015: 7-1016:12	
	(--King of Salem:)	
	0389:27-28	He 7:1-2
	0491:43-44	He 7:1-2
	0584: 8- 9	He 7:1-2
	1015:26-30	He 7:1-2
	(--Priest of "El Elyon," Most High God:)	
	0491:43-44	Ps 110:4 He 7:1-3
	0514:15-16	Ps 110:4 He 7:1-3
	1015:21-23	Ps 110:4 He 7:1-3
	1016:18-25	Ps 110:4 He 7:1-3
	1085: 7- 8	Ps 110:4 He 7:1-3

(Genesis 14:18 Continued on next page.)

Genesis 14:18 to 17:1

14:18   (--Brought Bread and Wine:)
                 1018: 6- 7
14:18-20   1024: 3- 6
14:19-20   (Most High God:)
                 0488:15-0489:17   Nu 24:16   De 32:8   Ps 9:2   PM 7
                                   Mk 5:7   Da 4:17,25,32;5:21   He 7:1+
                 1053:10-14   (Same as 0488:15-0489:17, above)
                 1598:21-27   (Same as 0488:15-0489:17, above)
                 (See also Genesis 14:18, above.)
14:20   (Tithes:)
                 1016:16-17
14:22   (Most High God, See Genesis 4:18,19-20, above.)
15: 1   1023:32-33
15: 1- 3   1020:26-28
15: 2- 4   1021: 5- 6
15: 4- 5   1020:37-39
15: 6   (Belief Counted for Righteousness.)
                 1017:35
                 1020:39-40
15: 9-10   1018:11
15:12-16   1020:40-42
15:18   (Covenant with Abraham:)
                 0983: 8-11
                 1020:37
                 1023:32-33
15:18-21   1020:38-42
16: 6   0919: 1- 3
16: 7   0407:17-18   Mt 1:20   Lk 1:11
                 1053:39
17: 1   (Abraham's Age:)
                 1023:42-43
                 (Conversation with "El Shaddai":)
                 1023:32-33
                 1053:15
                 (Be You Perfect:)
                 0021:30-31   Le 19:2   De 18:13   2Co 13:11
                                Mt 8:45   Ja 1:4
                 0022:15-16   (Same as 0021:30-31, above)
(Genesis 17:1 Continued on next page.)

GENESIS Chap:Verse	The URANTIA Book Page:Line	Other BOOKS Chap:Verse
17: 1	0086: 3	(Same as 0021:30-31, above)
	0086:11-12	(Same as 0021:30-31, above)
	0148: 3- 4	(Same as 0021:30-31, above)
	0290:20	(Same as 0021:30-31, above)
	0295:10-11	(Same as 0021:30-31, above)
	0297: 5- 6	(Same as 0021:30-31, above)
	0348:21	(Same as 0021:30-31, above)
	0411: 5	(Same as 0021:30-31, above)
	0449:14	(Same as 0021:30-31, above)
	0637: 8- 9	(Same as 0021:30-31, above)
	1091: 9-10	(Same as 0021:30-31, above)
	1165:24-25	(Same as 0021:30-31, above)
	1176:17	(Same as 0021:30-31, above)
	1444:42-43	(Same as 0021:30-31, above)
	1537: 2	(Same as 0021:30-31, above)
	1571:16-17	(Same as 0021:30-31, above)
	1573: 6- 7	(Same as 0021:30-31, above)
	1573:19-20	(Same as 0021:30-31, above)
	1574:45	(Same as 0021:30-31, above)
	1583:38	(Same as 0021:30-31, above)
	1584:28-29	(Same as 0021:30-31, above)
	1604:35-36	(Same as 0021:30-31, above)
	1784:43-44	(Same as 0021:30-31, above)
	1953:34-35	(Same as 0021:30-31, above)
	1961:33-34	(Same as 0021:30-31, above)
17: 1- 9	1021: 6-10	
17: 2- 9	1052:24-26	
17:10-13	1021:14-15	
17:10-14	0982:46-47	
17:17	1023:42-45	
17:19	1021: 5- 6	
17:24	1023:42-43	
18: 1	1023:32-33	
18: 1- 5	1021:17-18	
18:11	1023:42-43	
18:16-19:29	1021:18-22	
18:25	1475: 7	
18:27	1053:39	

GENESIS Chap:Verse	The URANTIA Book Page:Line	Other BOOKS Chap:Verse
20: 1	1022:37-39	
20: 2	1022:40-42	
20: 2-11	1023: 1- 2	
20:12	0918:46	
21: 2- 3	1021: 5- 6	
21:22-23	1023: 4- 5	
21:33	0023:31	
	0946: 3	
22: 1	1738:37-41	
22: 1- 2	1023: 5- 7	
22: 1-10	(Human Sacrifice:)	
	0980:27-30	
	0981:36-38	
	1018:12-13	
22: 7- 8	0946:38	
22:11	1023:35-36	
22:14	0945:24-27	
22:15	1023:35-36	
23: 1	1023:42-43	
23: 2	1023:10	
23:17-20	1023:10-11	
24: 1- 4	1023:12-14	
25: 1	1023:40-41	
25: 7	1023:42-43	
25: 8	1023:15	
	(Give Up Ghost:)	
	0954: 8	Jb 3:11 Je 15:9 La 1:19 Jn 4:34
		Jn 17:4;19:30,42
28:12	1841:16-17	Jn 1:51
28:14	2035:22	
28:18	0944:30-31	
28:22	0969: 5- 6	
29:18-20	(Women Considered Property:)	
	0917:33-34	
	0924: 5	
31:13	(Ritual Vows:)	
	0965:11	
	(God Called "El":)	
	1053:24	

GENESIS Chap:Verse	The URANTIA Book Page:Line	Other BOOKS Chap:Verse
31:19	0944:31	
31:32-35	0944:31	
35:11	(Loins of Abraham:) 0836:28-29 (God Called "El Shaddai":) 1053:15	
37:19	1023:21-22	
37:23-28	1387:17-18	
37:34	0976:41-42	
38: 6-10	0926:12-14	Mt 22:24 Mk19:12 Lk 20:28
38:24	0796:25-26	
40:15	1055: 6	
41:41	1023:25-26	
45:21	1055: 6	
46: 3	0023:27-29	
49:25	(God Called "Almighty":) 1053:39 1058:42	PM 1 PM 1

* * * * * * * * * * *

Y: The Book of HABAKKUK

HABAKKUK Chap:Verse	The URANTIA Book Page:Line	Other BOOKS Chap:Verse
2: 4	1445:20-21 1682:41-42	

* * * * * * * * * * *

Z: The Book of HAGGAI

HAGGAI Chap:Verse	The URANTIA Book Page:Line	Other BOOKS Chap:Verse
2: 7	1965:32 2035:32-33	

AA: Paul's Letter to The HEBREWS

HEBREWS Chap:Verse	The URANTIA Book Page:Line	Other BOOKS Chap:Verse
1: 2	(Jesus, The Creator Son:)	
	0074:11-12	Jn 1:3
	0234: 3- 4	Jn 1:3
	0235:37-38	Jn 1:3
	0654: 1- 3	Jn 1:3
	1453:41-42	Jn 1:3
1: 3	0055:12	
1: 5	(God's Begotten Son:)	
	0073:37	Ps 2:7 Jn 1:14,18;3:16,18 Ac 13:33
		He 5:5 1Jo 4:9
	0109:22	(Same as 0073:37, above)
	0232:33-35	(Same as 0073:37, above)
	0234: 7	(Same as 0073:37, above)
	0235: 6	(Same as 0073:37, above)
	0366:15	(Same as 0073:37, above)
	1522:43-47	(Same as 0073:37, above)
1: 6	0422: 2- 3	
1:14	(Ministering Spirits:)	
	0147: 3	
	0285: 2	
2: 2	1241:12	
2: 3	2035:42	
2: 7	(Man Created a Little Lower Than The Angels:)	
	0441: 7	
	0445:20-21	
	1248:18-19	
2: 9-10	1407:12-13	
2:10	(All Things, See Colosssians 1:17, above.)	
	1409: 9	
2:10-11	0646: 4- 5	
2:14-18	(Jesus Personally Experienced Human Life:)	
	1407: 8-10	He 4:15
	1407:27-28	He 4:15
	1425:27-28	He 4:15
3:14	1897:20-21	
4:13	0049:13-14	
4:14-15	1408: 6- 8	

HEBREWS Chap:Verse	The URANTIA Book Page:Line	Other BOOKS Chap:Verse

4:15   Jesus Tested and Tried on All Points as We Are:)
          1313:17
          1314:13-14
          1314:45-46
          1403:18-19
          1407:34-35
          (Jesus Personally Experienced Human Life,
             See Hebrews 2:14-18, above.)

5: 5   (Begotten Son, See Hebrews 1:5, above.)

5: 6   (A Priest Forever, After Order of Melchizedek:)

1017: 9-10	Ps 110:4	He 5:10;6:20;7:17-21	
1024:17-18	Ps 110:4	He 5:10;6:20;7:17-21	
1310:26-31	Ps 110:4	He 5:10;6:20;7:17-21	

5: 7   1408:20-22

5: 9   1454:50

5:10   (A Priest Forever, See Hebrews 5:6 above.)

5:13-14 1736:26-28

6:20   (A Priest Forever, See Hebrews 5:6 above.)

7: 1   (Melchizedek:)
          1015: 7-1016:12
          (--King of Salem:)
          0389:28
          0491:43-44
          0584: 8- 9   Ge 14:18
          1015:26-30   Ge 14:18
          (--Priest of the Most High God:)

0491:43-44	Ge 14:18	Ps 110:4
0514:15-16	Ge 14:18	Ps 110:4
1015:21-23	Ge 14:18	Ps 110:4
1016:18-25	Ge 14:18	Ps 110:4
1085: 7- 8	Ge 14:18	Ps 110:4

          (--"El Elyon," Most High God:)
          0488:15-0489:17 Ge 14:19-20 Nu 24:16 De 32:8
                           Ps 9:2 Da 4:17,25,32;5:21 Mk 5:7
          1016:19-21   (Same as 0488:15-0489:17, above)
          1053:10-14   (Same as 0488:15-0489:17, above)
          1598:21-27   (Same as 0488:15-0489:17, above)

7: 1- 3   1024:13-16

333

Hebrews 7:2 to 10:19

HEBREWS Chap:Verse	The URANTIA Book Page:Line	Other BOOKS Chap:Verse
7: 2	(Paying Tithes to Melchizedek:) 1016:16-17	
7: 3	(Without Ancestors:) 1015: 7- 9 (Made Like Unto the Son of God:) 1015:40 (A Priest Continually, See Hebrews 5:6, above.)	
7: 4	(Paying Tithes, See Hebrews 7:2, above.)	
7: 5	(Loins of Abraham:) 0836:28-29 (Hereditary Priesthood:) 0992:38-39	
7: 6	(Paying Tithes, See Hebrews 7:2, above.)	
7:10	(Loins of Abraham, See Hebrews 7:5, above.)	
7:17	(A Priest Forever, See Hebrews 5:6, above.)	
7:21	1017: 9-10	
7:27	0984:14-16	
8: 5	1864: 8-11	
9: 4	0969:21-23	
9: 8	1543:22-23	
9:11-15	(Paul: Jesus as The Redeemer:) 1864:25-27	
9:11-28	(Paul's Explanation of Salvation:) 0228:24-29 0984:14-16	Jn 3:16 Ro 5:6-21 2Co 5:14-21 He 13:12 1Jo 4:9 1Co 5:7 Ep 5:2 He 7:27;10:10-18 He 13:12
9:22	(Without Blood, No Remission of Sins:) 0060:31-32 0716:25	
9:23	0300: 3	
9:28	2003: 7	
10: 1	1864: 8-11	
10:10-18	0984:14-16	
10:12	(Right Hand of The Father:) 0064:33 0239:45-46 2057:39-42	Mt 22:44 Mk 12:36; 16:19 Lk 20:42 Ps 110:1 Ro 8:34 Cl 3:1 1Pe 3:22 (Same as 0064:33, above) (Same as 0064:33, above)

HEBREWS Chap:Verse	The URANTIA Book Page:Line	Other BOOKS Chap:Verse
10:20	(Jesus as The New and Living Way;)	
	0089:17-18	Jn 14:6
	0093:46	Jn 14:6
	0596:14,17	Jn 14:6
	1113:28	Jn 14:6
	1281:29	Jn 14:6
	1426:10	Jn 14:6
	1543:22-23	Jn 14:6
	1653:21	Jn 14:6
	1829:43-45	Jn 14:6
	2092:30	Jn 14:6
10:30	0795:40	
10:34	0542:24-25	
11: 1	1091:34-35	
11: 5	0514: 7- 8	Ge 5:24
	0623: 2- 5	Ge 5:24
11:10	(City with Foundations Built and Made by God:)	
	0501:42	
	0542:26	
	1474:42-43	
	1935: 1	
11:16	(A Better Country, a Heavenly one:)	
	0542:27	
	1570:10-12	
11:27	(Seeing the Invisible:)	
	0363:28-29	
	1121:10-11	
	1401: 2	
12: 2	2091:28-29	
12: 5-10	1661:39-48	
12: 5-11	1608: 5- 8	
12: 9	(Father of Spirits:)	
	0481:40	
	1640: 4	
	1796:13	
12:10	0039:12-13	
12:14	1105: 3- 4	
12:22	0525:24	

HEBREWS Chap:Verse	The URANTIA Book Page:Line	Other BOOKS Chap:Verse
12:22-23	(Assemblies of Paradise:)	
	0489:43-44	
	0495:20-21	
	0539:36-40	
13: 5	1750:32	
13:12	0228:24-29	
	0984:14-16	
13:20	(Language of a "Blood Cult":)	
	0984:10	
	(Jesus as the Great Shepherd;)	
	1409: 8	

* * * * * * * * * * *

BB: The Book of HOSEA

HOSEA Chap:Verse	The URANTIA Book Page:Line	Other BOOKS Chap:Verse
1: 7	1066:19-20	
1:10	1446:14	
	1661: 9-10	
2:19-20	1066: 9-11	
2:23	1066:15-16	
6: 6	1066: 8	
	2049:13-14	
8: 7	1445:35-36	
10:10	1066:13-14	
11: 1	1341:41-43	Mt 2:15
13: 4	1066:20	
13:14	1446:12-13	
14: 4	1066:11-12	
14: 4	1066:17-18	

CC: The Book of ISAIAH

ISAIAH Chap:Verse	The URANTIA Book Page:Line	Other BOOKS Chap:Verse
1: 4	2087:12	
1:16-17	1392: 4- 6	
1:18	1066:38-41	
	1445:37-39	
2: 2	0945:24-27	Jn 4:21
2: 4	1769:29	
5: 8	1074:26	
6: 2	(Seraphim:)	
	0418:18	
	(Angels' Wings:)	
	0438:23	
6: 6	0418:18	
6: 8	1805:21	
6: 9-10	(Use in Prophecy:)	
	1341:41-43	Mt 13:35
	(Hearing & Seeing without Perception:)	
	1689:14-31	Mt 13:35 Mk 4:11-12 Jn 12:37-40
	1902:47-1903:1	Mt 13:35 Mk 4:11-12 Jn 12:37-40
6:11	1071: 3	
7:14	(Virgin Birth:)	
	1341:41-43	Mt 1:22-23
	1348: 6- 7	Mt 1:23
8:18	0945:24-27	Jn 4:21
9: 1- 2	1341:41-43	Mt 4:13-15
9: 2	(Jesus as Light:)	
	0447:38-39	Mt 4:16 Lk 1:79;2:32 Jn 1:4-9;5:35 Jn 8:12;9:5;12:35-36,46 1Jo 2:8
	0513:31	(Same as 0447:38-39, above)
	0590:33	(Same as 0447:38-39, above)
	1104:14-15	(Same as 0447:38-39, above)
	1181: 7- 8	(Same as 0447:38-39, above)
	1353:38-39	(Same as 0447:38-39, above)
	1458:33-35	(Same as 0447:38-39, above)
	1671:10-11	(Same as 0447:38-39, above)
	1795: 1	(Same as 0447:38-39, above)
	1965:31	(Same as 0447:38-39, above)
	2035:28-29	(Same as 0447:38-39, above)

ISAIAH Chap:Verse	The URANTIA Book Page:Line	Other BOOKS Chap:Verse
9: 6	(Prince of Peace:)	
	0591:33	
	0597:13	
	0766:47	
	1025:25-26	
9: 6- 7	1858:27-28	
10:20	1074:24-25	
11: 1	1341:41-43	Mt 2:23
	1946: 1- 2	Mt 2:23
11: 1-10	1858:27-28	
11: 2	(Adjutant Mind Spirits:)	
	0378:24-27	
	0401:40-42	
	0402:23	
	0402:32	
	0402:36	
	0402:39	
	0402:44	
11: 3	0378:41	
11: 9	1444: 9-10	
12: 2	(Jehovah, YAHWEH, as a Concept of God:)	
	1053:43	
	1066:37-38	
	1445:17-18	
12: 2- 3	1795:41	
14: 3	1066:34-36	
	1445: 1- 2	
14:12	(Lucifer:)	
	0601:38-40	
	0602: 1	Mt 4:3-11 Mk 1:13 Lk 4:3-11
	1327:26-27	Lk 16:8
14:13-14	0489:41-43	
	0490: 4- 5	
20: 1	0876:38	
25: 4	1662:23-24	
26: 3	1731:43	
26: 4	1053:43	
26: 8	0836:20-21	
26:19	0568:30	

ISAIAH Chap:Verse	The URANTIA Book Page:Line	Other BOOKS Chap:Verse
28: 2	0060:15	
28:17	1066:34	
29: 6	0060:15	
29:13	1712:36-38	Mt 15:1-9 Mk 7:5-13 Lk 11:37-41
30:15	1444:44-46	
30:21	(Spirit Says "This is the Way":)	
	0383:17	
	1066:36-37	
	1287: 1	
	1664:24-25	
31: 5	1074:36	
31:33	1071:10	
32: 2	2035:24-25	
32:15-17	1601:30-32	Jn 1:12-13
33:22	1536: 3- 4	
35: 4	1597: 9-10	
37: 1- 2	0976:29-32	
37:16	(God Created Heaven and Earth:)	
	0021: 8-10	Ge 1:1 2Ki 19:15 Ne 9:6 Ps 115:15 Is 45:18
	1011:32-33	(Same as 0021:8-10, above.)
40: 3- 5	(The Voice in the Wilderness:)	
	1501:29-35	Mt 3:3 Mk 1:2-3 Lk 3:4-6 Jn 1:23
	1502:28-29	Mt 3:3 Mk 1:3 Lk 3:4-6 Jn 1:22-23
40:11	(Feed Flock Like a Shepherd:)	
	1069:20-22	
	2035:25-26	
40:12	0027:40-42	
	0081:37-38	
40:15	1068:45	
40:18	1392:14	
40:22	0027:42-43	
	1392:14	
40:26	0027:43-45	
	1392:15-17	
40:28	0023:31	
40:29	1069:22-23	
	1392:18	
	1662:24-25	

Isaiah 40:31 to 45:20

ISAIAH Chap:Verse	The URANTIA Book Page:Line	Other BOOKS Chap:Verse
40:31	1069:23-25	
	1444:46-1445: 1	
41:10	(Fear Not, Be Not Dismayed:)	
	1069: 8	
	(--I will Strengthen and Uphold You:)	
	1392:19-21	
	1445: 2- 4	
41:13	1392:21-22	
	1769:27-28	
41:17	1069:39	
42: 1	1509:24	
42: 1- 4	1341:41-43	Mt 12:18-21
42: 3	1662:26	
42: 7	2035:26-28	
43: 1	1069:11-12	
43: 2	1069:12-13	
	1662:27-28	
43: 4	1069:13	
43: 6- 7	1661: 7- 9	
43: 7	1069:41	
43:10-11	1392:23-25	
43:21	1069:42	
43:25	0039:16-18	
	1069:42-43	
44: 3	1796: 4- 7	
44: 6	(The First and Last:)	
	0034: 6- 7	Re 1:8,11,17;21:6;22:13
	0115:19	Re 1:8,11,17;21:6;22:13
	1069: 4- 5	Re 1:8,11,17;21:6;22:13
	1069:34-35	Re 1:8,11,17;21:6;22:13
	1408:48-49	Re 1:8,11,17;21:6;22:13
45:12	1069: 3	
45:18	(God Created Heaven and Earth, See Isaiah 37:16.)	
	(--Not in Vain, to be Inhabited:)	
	0021:18-20	
	1069: 4	
	(--None Else Beside Me:)	
	1445:30-33	

ISAIAH Chap:Verse	The URANTIA Book Page:Line	Other BOOKS Chap:Verse
45:21	1069: 9	
45:21-22	1445:30-33	
45:24	1682:34-35	
46: 1	1042:30	
46:10	(See End from Beginning:)	
	0034:26	
	(My Counsel Shall Stand:)	
	0035:42-43	
48:16	0095:39	
48:22	1445:39	
49:15	1069:38	
49:15-16	1069:14-16	
51: 5	1682:35-36	
51: 6	1069: 6- 7	
51: 8	1069: 7- 8	
51:16	1069:16-17	
53: 1	1902:45-46	Jn 12:37-43
53: 3	(Man of Sorrows:)	
	1103: 3	
	1425:21	
	1766:31	
	1954:44	
53: 3- 4	1341:41-43	Mt 8:17
	2019:39-40	
53: 7	1977:44-46	
54:13	1711:31-32	Jn 6:45
55: 1	(Jesus as the Water of Life:)	
	0381: 5- 9	Mt 5:6 Jn 4:10,13-14; 6:35; 7:37-38
		Re 7:16-17
	1613: 3- 5	(Same as 0381:5-9, above)
	1711: 4- 5	(Same as 0381:5-9, above)
	1712: 8- 9	(Same as 0381:5-9, above)
	1954: 3- 6	(Same as 0381:5-9, above)
	1965:30	(Same as 0381:5-9, above)
	2035:39-40	(Same as 0381:5-9, above)
	2054:19-21	(Same as 0381:5-9, above)
55: 1- 3	1206:35-37	Mt 5:6

ISAIAH Chap:Verse	The URANTIA Book Page:Line	Other BOOKS Chap:Verse
55: 2	(Jesus as the Bread of Life:	
	1711: 1- 4	Mt 5:6;26:26 Mk 14:22 Lk 22:19
		Jn 6:35,48,51,58 Re 7:16-17
	1711:14-16	(Same as 1711:1-4, above)
	1711:38-43	(Same as 1711:1-4, above)
	1712: 8-16	(Same as 1711:1-4, above)
	1942: 9-16	(Same as 1711:1-4, above)
	1965:29	(Same as 1711:1-4, above)
	2054:19-20	(Same as 1711:1-4, above)
55: 6	1850:31-32	
55: 7	(Abundantly Pardon:)	
	0038:10	
	0039:16	
55: 7	1069:17-19	
	1446: 2- 4	
55: 9	1068:46-47	
	1444:16-17	
56: 5	(Servants Made Sons & Daughters of God:)	
	0039:18-19	Jn 1:12 Ro 8:14-17 Ga 3:26;4:6
		1Jo 3:1-2
	0067:32-33	(Same as 0039:18-19, above)
	0447:40-0448:35	(Same as 0039:18-19, above)
	0191:16-17	(Same as 0039:18-19, above)
	1112:41-42	(Same as 0039:18-19, above)
	1454:37	(Same as 0039:18-19, above)
	1603:37-40	(Same as 0039:18-19, above)
	1610: 2-20	(Same as 0039:18-19, above)
	1725:28	(Same as 0039:18-19, above)
	1861:29-30	(Same as 0039:18-19, above)
	1945:21	(Same as 0039:18-19, above)
	1957:36-37	(Same as 0039:18-19, above)
	1958:17	(Same as 0039:18-19, above)
	2053:14,38	(Same as 0039:18-19, above)
56: 7	1890:24-25	Mt 21:12-13 Mk 11:15-17 Lk 19:45-46
		Jn 2:14-16
57:15	(The One Who Inhabits Eternity:)	
	0021:30	2Ed 8:20
	0023:31-32	2Ed 8:20

(Isaiah 57:15 Continued on next page.)

ISAIAH Chap:Verse	The URANTIA Book Page:Line	Other BOOKS Chap:Verse
57:15	0034:30-31	2Ed 8:20
	0050:19	2Ed 8:20
	1069:33-34	2Ed 8:20
	(--Who Dwells in a High and Holy Place:)	
	0118:29-30	
	(----And Also With Those of a Contrite and Humble Spirit:)	
	1070: 5- 6	
	1444:28-30	
	1676:46-47	
57:20-21	1674:43-44	
57:21	1445:39	
58: 3- 4	1656:14-17	
58: 3- 6	0976:16-17	Mt 9:14 Mk 2:18-20 Lk 5:33
58: 5	0976:29-32	
58: 5- 7	1656:18-24	
58: 8-12	1656:25-37	
58:11	1070: 7- 9	
59: 1	1069:35-36	
59:19	1070: 9-10	
60: 1	1066:43-44	
60: 1- 3	1629:28-32	
61: 1	1066:44-47	
	1363:27-30	
	1391:41-43	
	1686: 8-11	Lk 4:17-19
	(Preach Good Tidings To Meek:)	
	1594:12-13	Mt 11:5 Lk 4:18;7:22;14:13
	1608:15-24	Mt 11:5 Lk 4:18;7:22;14:13
	1859:39-40	Mt 11:5 Lk 4:18;7:22;14:13
	(Freeing Spiritual Captives:	
	1328:14-15	Lk 4:18
	1570:23-24	Lk 4:18
	1662:28-29	Lk 4:18
	2035:29-31	Lk 4:18;24:27
61: 2	1391:43-45	
	1662:29-30	
	1686:11	

ISAIAH Chap:Verse	The URANTIA Book Page:Line	Other BOOKS Chap:Verse
61: 3	1391:45-47	
	2035:31-32	
61: 7	2035:33	
61:10	(Joyful Soul:)	
	1066:47-1067: 2	
	1445:41	
	1682:36-38	
63: 9	(In Your Afflictions He is Afflicted:)	
	0029:33	
	0039:14	
	0053:24	
	1067: 2- 3	
	1203: 5- 6	
	2019:39-40	
63:16	(God as Father of Israel:)	
	1445: 5	
	1590:31	
64: 4	(Man's Inability to Perceive Paradise:)	
	0121:47-0122:2	1Co 2:9
	0269:45-47	1Co 2:9
	0501: 4	1Co 2:9
	1960:36-37	1Co 2:9
64: 8	1590:31	
65:17	1500:41-42	
65:24	(God's Foreknowledge:)	
	0049:16-17	Mt 6:8
	1577:31-32	Mt 6:8
66: 1	1069:45-46	
66: 1- 2	1532:41-45	
66: 5- 8	1532:45-1533: 3	
66:12-14	1533: 4- 7	
66:22	1500:41-42	
	1914: 1	
66:22-23	0600: 2- 6	

DD: The Book of JAMES

JAMES Chap:Verse	The URANTIA Book Page:Line	Other BOOKS Chap:Verse
1: 4	1091: 9-10	
	(Be Perfect, See Genesis 17:1, above.)	
1: 5	0310:43	
1:13-14	1738:37-41	
1:17	(Father of Lights as Name of God:)	
	0023:14	
	0035:40	
	1702:42	
	(All Good Gifts from Father of Lights:)	
	0041: 2	
	1454: 9-10	
1:17	(--In Whom No Variableness, No Shadow of Turning:)	
	0035:38-41	Ml 3:6
	0058:35	Ml 3:6
	0137:43	Ml 3:6
	0138: 1- 2	Ml 3:6
	1454:10-11	Ml 3:6
1:20	1673:12-15	
1:22-25	1769:42-44	Mt 12:50 Mk 3:35 Lk 8:21 Jn 7:17
2: 8	(Love Neighbor as Self, See Galatians 5:14, above.)	
2:17	(Requirement for "Works," See "Doing the Father's Will," Mathew 6:10, Mark 3:35, Luke 8:21 or John 4:34, above.)	
	(Requirement to Bring Forth Good Fruit, See Matthew 3:8-10, Luke 3:9, or John 15:2, above.)	
2:19	(One God, see Deuteronomy 6:4, above.)	
2:23	(Belief Counted for Righteousness:)	
	1017:35	
	(Friend of God:)	
	0028:30-31	
3: 8	0317:11	
	1640:19-22	
4:12	0046:46	
5:15-16	1849:13-14	
5:16	0983:32-33	

EE: The Book of JEREMIAH

JEREMIAH Chap:Verse	The URANTIA Book Page:Line	Other BOOKS Chap:Verse
3:23	0945:24-27	
5:25	1445:39-40	
6: 1- 8	1074:37	
7:11	1890:24-25	Mt 21:12-13 Mk 11:15-17 Lk 19:45-46
		Jn 2:14-16
9:23	1822:34-35	
9:24	0038:12-13	
	(Know God:)	
	0067:31	
10: 6- 7	1067:31-32	
12: 1	1067:43	
12: 2	1677: 3- 4	
15: 5- 6	1074:37	
15: 9	0954: 8	Jn 19:30
17: 7	1444:21	
17: 9	1609:44-46	
17: 9-10	1630:16-19	
21: 3- 7	1067:27-28	
23: 5	1946: 1- 2	
23: 6	1682:39	
23:23	0045:11-12	
23:23-24	0044:29-30	
23:24	1444:30-31	
24:7	1440:24-25	
26: 4-15	1709:29-48	
27: 6	1067:47-1068: 1	
29:13	(Seek Me With All Your Heart & You Shall Find Me:)	
	1440:22-23	Mt 7:7 Lk 11:9
	1445:33	Mt 7:7 Lk 11:9
	1619:13-14	Mt 7:7 Lk 11:9
	1838:42	Mt 7:7 Lk 11:9
31: 3	(Loved With Everlasting Love:)	
	1446:14-15	
	(I Have Drawn Thee, "Spirit Gravity":)	
	0026:29	Jn 3:14-15; 6:44; 8:28; 12:32
	0082:24-29	Jn 3:14-15; 6:44; 8:28; 12:32

(Jeremiah 31:3 Continued on next page.)

JEREMIAH Chap:Verse	The URANTIA Book Page:Line	Other BOOKS Chap:Verse
31: 3	0084:12-20	Jn 3:14-15; 6:44; 8:28; 12:32
	0139:43-44	Jn 3:14-15; 6:44; 8:28; 12:32
	1067:40-41	Jn 3:14-15; 6:44; 8:28; 12:32
	1190:17-18	Jn 3:14-15; 6:44; 8:28; 12:32
	1750:15	Jn 3:14-15; 6:44; 8:28; 12:32
	1904:20-21	Jn 3:14-15; 6:44; 8:28; 12:32
	2019:19-25	Jn 3:14-15; 6:44; 8:28; 12:32
	2084: 8- 9	Jn 3:14-15; 6:44; 8:28; 12:32
31:13	2035:31-32	
31:15	1341:41-43	Mt 2:17-18
31:29-34	1630: 4-12	
31:33	1340:24-25	
31:34	0067:31	
32:19	1067:43-45	
32:27	1067:28-29	
32:35	1387:10-11	
33:16	1682:39	
36: 3	1770:47	
38: 2- 3	1068: 1- 2	
	1075: 7- 8	
38: 4- 6	1710: 1- 3	
38: 6	1068: 2- 3	
39: 1- 9	1075: 8-11	
46: 2	1075: 3	
50: 2	1042:30-31	
51:29	0569:15-17	
51:44	1042:30	

*   *   *   *   *   *   *   *   *   *   *

FF: The Book of JOB

JOB Chap:Verse	The URANTIA Book Page:Line	Other BOOKS Chap:Verse
1: 1- 5	1662:40-43	
1: 1-42:17	1043:38-39	
	1662:38-40	

Job 1:6 to 23:9

JOB Chap:Verse	The URANTIA Book Page:Line	Other BOOKS Chap:Verse
23:10	0049:10-11	
26: 7	0055:15-16	
	0055:26-27	
27: 1-31:40	1664: 9-11	
28:26	0047:10	
28:28	(Fear of the Lord is Beginning of Wisdom:)	
	0766:32-33	Ps 111:10 Pv 1:7;9:10
	1444:41	Ps 111:10 Pv 1:7;9:10
	1675:43-44	Ps 111:10 Pv 1:7;9:10
32: 2	1061: 1- 2	
33: 4	0095:39-40	
33:24	1060:42-43	
33:26-28	1060:39-45	
33:27-28	1440:26-28	
36: 4	0048:46	
36:26	0033:39-0034: 2	
	1059:46-47	
37:16	0048:45-46	
37:23	(We Cannot Find Him Out:)	
	0033:35	
	1059:47	
	(God of Power, Judgment & Justice:)	
	1059:40-41	
38: 1	1664:21-22	
38: 7	0087:38-39	
38:25	0047:10	
42: 6	1663:10	

*   *   *   *   *   *   *   *   *   *   *

GG: The Book of JOEL

JOEL Chap:Verse	The URANTIA Book Page:Line	Other BOOKS Chap:Verse
2:28	(Pour Out My Spirit on All Flesh:)	
	0241:41-42	Lk 24:49 Jn 14:16-18,26;15:26
		Jn 16:7,13-14 Ek 11:19;36:26-27
		Ac 2:2-4,16-18 Ga 4:6

(Joel 2:28 Continued on next page.)

Joel 2:28 to 3:21

JOEL Chap:Verse	The URANTIA Book Page:Line	Other BOOKS Chap:Verse
	0365:32-33	(Same as 0241:41-42, above)
	0379:36	(Same as 0241:41-42, above)
	0382:10-14	(Same as 0241:41-42, above)
	0596:31-32	(Same as 0241:41-42, above)
	1328: 4- 5	(Same as 0241:41-42, above)
	1328:22-25	(Same as 0241:41-42, above)
	1340:24-27	(Same as 0241:41-42, above)
	1591:15-16	(Same as 0241:41-42, above)
	1594: 3- 4	(Same as 0241:41-42, above)
	1642:18-24	(Same as 0241:41-42, above)
	1897:33	(Same as 0241:41-42, above)
	1918:45-47	(Same as 0241:41-42, above)
	1947:14-17	(Same as 0241:41-42, above)
	1948: 9-24	(Same as 0241:41-42, above)
	1948:34-36	(Same as 0241:41-42, above)
	1951:45-48	(Same as 0241:41-42, above)
	1953:22-26	(Same as 0241:41-42, above)
	1954: 2	(same as 0241:41-42, above)
	1958: 7- 9	(Same as 0241:41-42, above)
	1959:22-24	(Same as 0241:41-42, above)
	1961:24-27	(Same as 0241:41-42, above)
	2035:38-39	(Same as 0241:41-42, above)
	2044:34-35	(Same as 0241:41-42, above)
	2053:17-19	(Same as 0241:41-42, above)
	2054:42-43	(Same as 0241:41-42, above)
	2055: 9-11	(Same as 0241:41-42, above)
	2057:21-22	(Same as 0241:41-42, above)
	2061:10-13	(Same as 0241:41-42, above)
	2061:20-21	(Same as 0241:41-42, above)
	2062:43	(Same as 0241:41-42, above)
	2064: 7	(Same as 0241:41-42, above)
2:28-29	1954: 2	Jn 1:10-13
2:32	0038: 9-10	
	1454:40	

HH: The FIRST Letter of JOHN

I JOHN Chap:Verse	The URANTIA Book Page:Line	Other BOOKS Chap:Verse
1: 1	0074:14-16	
	0227:33	Jn 1:14
1: 3- 7	1861:29	
1: 9	1736:32	
2: 8	(Jesus as Light, See Isaiah 9:2, above.)	
3: 1	0039:18-19	
	0448: 5- 6	
3: 1- 2	(Becoming Sons of God, See Isaiah 56:5, above.)	
3: 2	0448: 7- 8	
	(We Shall Be Like Him:)	
	1454:30-31	
3:11	1554:37-42	
3:18	1769:42-44	Mt 7:21; 12:50 Mk 3:35 Lk 8:21
		Jn 7:17; 14:23-24
3:20	(God's Omniscience:)	
	0048:43	
	1855:45-46	
3:23	1554:37-42	
4: 4,6	0045:14	
4: 7	(True Love is From God:)	
	1289:21	
4: 7-19	(Divine Parental Love:)	
	1486:37-38	
	1608: 8-15	
4: 7-21	(John's View of Love:)	
	1554:37-42	
4: 8	(God is Love:)	
	0026:17	1Jo 4:16
	0038:45	1Jo 4:16
	0050:34	1Jo 4:16
	0075:25,35	1Jo 4:16
	0075:47	1Jo 4:16
	0648:23	1Jo 4:16
	1004:20	1Jo 4:16
	1429: 7	1Jo 4:16
	1486:37	1Jo 4:16
	1782:22	1Jo 4:16

I JOHN Chap:Verse	The URANTIA Book Page:Line	Other BOOKS Chap:Verse			
4: 9	0228:24-29	Jn 3:16			
	(Only Begotten Son, See Hebrews 1:5, above.)				
4:11	2053:16	Jn 15:12			
4:12	0139: 8				
4:12-13	1453:38-39				
	1664:25-26				
4:13	0045: 6- 7				
4:16	(God is Love, See I John 4:8, above.)				
	(Dwelling in Love:)				
	0045:14-15				
4:18	0552:31				
4:19	(God Loves and Can Be Loved:)				
	0028:28-31	Jn 10:14			
	1285:26-28				
	1486:37-38				
5: 4	(Faith Overcomes World:)				
	0059:42-43	Jn 1:12-13			
	0383: 2	Jn 1:12-13			
	1601:27-29	Jn 1:12-13			
5: 7	(The Trinity:)				
	0108:10-15	Mt 28:19	Ac 2:33	1Co 12:4-6	
	0115:15-18	Mt 28:19	Ac 2:33	1Co 12:4-6	
	0640:33-35	Mt 28:19	Ac 2:33	1Co 12:4-6	
	1144:43-1145:2	Mt 28:19	Ac 2:33	1Co 12:4-6	
	2061:47-2062:2	Mt 28:19	Ac 2:33	1Co 12:4-6	
	2067:40	Mt 28:19	Ac 2:33	1Co 12:4-6	
5:11	0035:37				
5:11-12	2097:18-20				
	(Eternal Life:)				
	0044: 5- 6	Jn 3:15-16; 5:24-25,39-40; 6:40,47			
		Jn 10:10; 11:25-26			
	1113: 7- 8	(Same as 0044:5-6, above)			
	1567: 3- 5	(Same as 0044:5-6, above)			
	1649:39-43	(Same as 0044:5-6, above)			
	1711:12-13	(Same as 0044:5-6, above)			
	1750:16-17	(Same as 0044:5-6, above)			
	1792: 4- 5	(Same as 0044:5-6, above)			
	1829:44-45	(Same as 0044:5-6, above)			

(I John 5:11-12 Continued on next page.)

I JOHN Chap:Verse	The URANTIA Book Page:Line	Other BOOKS Chap:Verse
5:11-12	1843: 9-10	(Same as 0044:5-6, above)
	1861:23	(Same as 0044:5-6, above)
	1965:33-34	(Same as 0044:5-6, above)
	2035:38	(Same as 0044:5-6, above)
	2053:36-37	(Same as 0044:5-6, above)
5:18	0610:25-26	
5:19	0045:14	

*   *   *   *   *   *   *   *   *   *   *

II: The SECOND Letter of JOHN

II JOHN Verse	The URANTIA Book Page:Line	Other BOOKS Chap:Verse
5	1554:37-42	

*   *   *   *   *   *   *   *   *   *   *

JJ: The THIRD Letter of JOHN

III JOHN Verse	The URANTIA Book Page:Line	Other BOOKS Chap:Verse
1	1473:41-42	

*   *   *   *   *   *   *   *   *   *   *

KK: The Book of JONAH

JONAH Chap:Verse	The URANTIA Book Page:Line	Other BOOKS Chap:Verse
1: 3	1428:14-15	
1:17	1428:16-17	
3: 5	0976:29-32	
4:11	1767:44-45	

353

LL: The Book of JOSHUA

JOSHUA Chap:Verse	The URANTIA Book Page:Line	Other BOOKS Chap:Verse
1: 5	1059:34-35	
2:10	0779:12	
2:11	0044:26-27	
3:11	1053:40	
3:13	1053:40	
4: 1- 9	1502:44-46	
6:20	1879: 3	
6:26	0981:11-12	
8: 1-29	0779: 8-10	
12: 7-24	1505:35-36	
24:15	1710:25-26	
24:19	1059:38-39	
	1059:43-44	
24:27	0945: 9-10	

* * * * * * * * * * *

MM: The Book of JUDE

JUDE Verse	The URANTIA Book Page:Line	Other BOOKS Chap:Verse
3	1006: 3- 4	
6	0602:16-18	
9	(Archangel Michael:)	
	0409:26	
	(Dispute over Moses' Resurrection:)	
	0596:21-24	AM
	0601:30-32	AM
24	0096: 4- 5	
	1820:16-18	

NN: The Book of JUDGES

JUDGES Chap:Verse	The URANTIA Book Page:Line	Other BOOKS Chap:Verse
2:13	1042:36-37	
3: 5- 6	1071:41-43	
4:10-16	1387:16	
4:16	0785: 1- 2	
9:23	1060:35-36	
10: 6	1042:36-37	
11:30-39	0980:41-44	
21:10-11	0784:37-39	
21:11	0779:12	

*   *   *   *   *   *   *   *   *   *   *

OO: The FIRST Book of KINGS

I KINGS Chap:Verse	The URANTIA Book Page:Line	Other BOOKS Chap:Verse
7: 8	1073:39	
8:12	0033:38	
8:27	(Heaven Of Heavens:)	
	0034: 2- 3	De 10:14 2Ch 2:6; 6:18 Ne 9:6 Ps 148:4
	0044:33-34	(Same as 0034:2-3, above)
	0553:19-29	(Same as 0034:2-3, above)
	1953:28-29	(Same as 0034:2-3, above)
9:15	1073:39-41	
9:26-27	1073:41-42	
11: 3	1073:42	
11:50	1042:36-37	
16:23-24	1073:49	
16:30-33	1064:20	
16:34	0981:22-26	
17: 1	1064:15	
17: 1-19:21	1363:39	
18:17-40	1065: 8- 9	
18:40	1064:18-19	

I KINGS Chap:Verse	The URANTIA Book Page:Line	Other BOOKS Chap:Verse
19:12	1664:24	
19:16	1064:22	
19:19-20	1064:22	
20:23	1054:17-19	
21: 1-16	1065:12-13	
	1074: 5- 8	
21:17-24	1074: 8- 9	
21:25-26	1064:20	
21:27	0976:29-32	
22: 7-28	1064:23	

*   *   *   *   *   *   *   *   *   *   *

PP: The SECOND Book of KINGS

II KINGS Chap:Verse	The URANTIA Book Page:Line	Other BOOKS Chap:Verse
1: 3- 2:11	1363:39	
2: 1-15	1064:22-23	
2:11	0514:12-13	
	1212:24	
10:15-28	1074:12-14	
11:12-18	1074:28-29	
14: 8-29	1074:15-16	
16: 6	1055: 6	
17: 4- 6	1074:21-24	
17:10-16	0946: 3	
17:13	0986:28-29	
18: 4	0946:23	Jn 3:14
	0969:21-23	
19:15	0021: 8-10	Ge 1:1 Ne 9:6 Ps 115:15-16 Is 37:16
19:22	1053:39-40	
21: 1-18	1074:38-40	
21: 3, 7	0946: 3	
23:13	1043:10	
23:29	1387:15	
23:29-30	1074:44-46	
25: 1-17	1075: 8-11	

QQ: The LAMENTATIONS of JEREMIAH

LAMENTS Chap:Verse	The URANTIA Book Page:Line	Other BOOKS Chap:Verse
1:19	0954: 8	Jn 19:30
3:33	(God Does Not Afflict Willingly:)	
	0038:13-14	
	1067:41-42	
	1662:14	
	1664:27-28	
4:20	1341:41-43	Mt 26:56

*   *   *   *   *   *   *   *   *   *   *

RR: The Book of LEVITICUS

LEVITICUS Chap:Verse	The URANTIA Book Page:Line	Other BOOKS Chap:Verse
1: 1-9:24	0974:12-16	
1: 3	0978:30-31	
1: 9	0977:47-0978: 1	
3:17	0955:18	
6:16	0978:37-38	
6:29	0978:37-38	
7:22-25	0955:18	
10: 1- 2	0974:34-35	
11: 1-47	0974:24-27	
11: 7- 8	0975:12-13	
12: 2- 8	(Uncleanliness & Purification for Childbirth:)	
	0935:36-38	Lk 2:22-24
	1352:40-47	Lk 2:22-24
12: 6- 8	1354:18-19	
13:45	0976:11	
15:19-20	0936: 8-11	
17:11	0932:41-43	
18: 9	0918:46-47	
19: 2	(Be You Holy--Perfect, See Genesis 17:1, above.)	
19:18	(Love Neighbor as Self, See Galatians 5:14, above.)	

Leviticus 19:34 to II Maccabees 15:36

LEVITICUS Chap:Verse	The URANTIA Book Page:Line	Other BOOKS Chap:Verse
19:34	0787:38-39	
20:27	0987:42-44	
21: 9	0796:25-26	
22:18-25	1888:26-27	
23: 7 +	1415:36	
23:39-43	1793:43	
24:17	1576:28-29	
24:20	(Retaliation, Eye For Eye, Tooth For Tooth:)	
	0795:36-37	Ex 21:24 De 19:21 Mt 5:38-42
	1577:17	Ex 21:24 De 19:21 Mt 5:38-42
	1580: 1	Ex 21:24 De 19:21 Mt 5:38-42
	1770:32	Ex 21:24 De 19:21 Mt 5:38-42 Lk 6:29
24:21	1576:28-29	
25:23	1064:37-38	
26: 1	0969:17-19	
26:14-39	0976: 3- 4	
27: 1-34	0981:45-47	

*   *   *   *   *   *   *   *   *   *   *

SS: The FIRST Book of MACCABEES

I MACCABEES Chap:Verse	The URANTIA Book Page:Line	Other BOOKS Chap:Verse
4:52-59	1374:14	

*   *   *   *   *   *   *   *   *   *   *

TT: The SECOND Book of MACCABEES

II MACCABEES Chap:Verse	The URANTIA Book Page:Line	Other BOOKS Chap:Verse
1:18-22	(Sacred Fire:)	
	0777:44-46	
	0947:26-27	
2: 1,10	(Sacred Fire, See II Maccabees 1:18-22, above.)	

UU: The Book of MALACHI

MALACHI Chap:Verse	The URANTIA Book Page:Line	Other BOOKS Chap:Verse
3: 1	1627: 7- 8	Mt 11:7-10 Lk 7:24-27 Jn 1:6-7
		Jn 5:32-35
3: 6	(God Changes Not:)	
	0035:38-41	Ja 1:17
	0058:35	Ja 1:17
	0137:43	Ja 1:17
	0138: 1- 2	Ja 1:17
	1454:11	Ja 1:17
4: 2	2035:34-35	
4: 5- 6	1499:24-27	
	1754:21-22	Mt 11:14; 17:10-13 Mk 9:11-13

*   *   *   *   *   *   *   *   *   *   *

VV: The Prayer of MANASSEH

MANASSEH Verse	The URANTIA Book Page:Line	Other BOOKS Chap:Verse
1	(God Called "Almighty":)	
	1053:39	Ge 49:25+
	1058:42	Ge 49:25+
5	1597: 7-10	
7	(God Called "Most High":)	
	0488:15-0489:17	Ge 14:19-20+ Nu 24:16+ De 32:8+
		Ps 9:2; 110:4 Da 4:17,25,32;5:21
		Mk 5:7 He 7:1-3
	0491:43-44	(Same as 0488:15-0489:17, above)
	0514:15-16	(Same as 0488:15-0489:17, above)
	1015:21-23	(Same as 0488:15-0489:17, above)
	1016:18-25	(Same as 0488:15-0489:17, above)
	1053:10-14	(Same as 0488:15-0489:17, above)
	1053:40	(Same as 0488:15-0489:17, above)
	1085: 7- 8	(Same as 0488:15-0489:17, above)
	1598:21-27	(Same as 0488:15-0489:17, above)

WW: The Book of MICAH

MICAH Chap:Verse	The URANTIA Book Page:Line	Other BOOKS Chap:Verse
3:11	1067: 8- 9	
	1677: 5- 7	
4: 1-10	1858:27-28	
4: 3	1769:29	
4: 4- 5	1067:10-12	
5: 2	1341:41-43	Mt 2:5-6
6: 6- 8	1067:13-18	
	1392: 7-13	
6: 8	1676:45	
7:18	1608:25	

* * * * * * * * * * *

XX: The Book of NAHUM

NAHUM Chap:Verse	The URANTIA Book Page:Line	Other BOOKS Chap:Verse
1: 2- 6	0060:15-16	
1: 7	0041: 3	

* * * * * * * * * * *

YY: The Book of NEHEMIAH

NEHEMIAH Chap:Verse	The URANTIA Book Page:Line	Other BOOKS Chap:Verse
9: 6	0021: 8-10	
	0055:14	
	(Heaven of Heavens, See I Kings 8:27, above.)	
	(The Creator Preserves All:)	
	1445: 5- 6	
10:31	1042:19-23	

ZZ: The Book of NUMBERS

NUMBERS Chap:Verse	The URANTIA Book Page:Line	Other BOOKS Chap:Verse
3: 5-10	0986:33-34	
3:13	1352:37	
3:47-48	1352:38-40	
5:12-31	0795:16-25	
6: 2- 8	0965:11	
9:15-16	0947:16	
10: 1- 7	0794: 5	
10:33	0945:24-27	
11:33	0057:44-45	
12: 3	1575:12-13	
14: 8	0028: 6	
16:22	1057:16-17	
18: 1-10	0986:28-29	
18:16	1352:38-40	
19: 1-22	0992:29-30	
21: 1- 3	1071:44-45	
21: 8- 9	0946:23	Jn 3:14
23:19	(God Does Not Repent:)	
	0036: 1	Ge 6:6 Ex 32:14 1Sa 15:29 Am 7:3,6 Zc 8:14
	0058: 6	(Same as 0036:1, above)
	1063: 6- 7	(Same as 0036:1, above)
	1510:19	(Same as 0036:1, above)
24:16	(Most High God, See Prayer of Manasseh 7, above.)	
26:65	1828:32-33	
27:16	1057:16-17	
30: 2-15	0965:11-12	
31: 1- 2	0784:40-41	
31: 3-18	0784:36-39	
31: 7	0779:13	
35: 6,11	0775:19	
35:30	1576:28-29	
35:31	0796:16-17	

AAA: The Book of OBADIAH

OBADIAH Verse	The <u>URANTIA</u> Book Page:Line	Other BOOKS Chap:Verse
16	0037:25-26	
	0611:45	
21	1858:27-28	

*   *   *   *   *   *   *   *   *   *   *

BBB: The FIRST Book of PETER

I PETER Chap:Verse	The <u>URANTIA</u> Book Page:Line	Other BOOKS Chap:Verse
1: 3	2064:36-37	
1: 3- 4	1820:41	
1: 4	1113:29	
1: 8	1454:32-33	
1:17	1731: 6- 8	
1:19	1864:25-27	
2: 2	(Growing in The Spirit;)	
	1474:10-13	1Co 3:1-2
	1736:26-28	1Co 3:1-2 He 5:13-14
	2054:39-41	1Co 3:1-2 Ep 4:14-15 2Pe 5:18
2: 9	(Chosen People:)	
	0600: 7-10	
	1334:23	
2: 9-10	1731:11-21	
2:16	0613:37-38	
2:21-23	2091:41-42	
2:23	1609:11-14	
3: 9	1454: 6	
	1580: 8- 9	Mt 18:14
3:12	(God Hears and Watches Over the Righteous:)	
	0055:10-11	
	0095:21-23	
3:19	0610:33	

I PETER Chap:Verse	The URANTIA Book Page:Line	Other BOOKS Chap:Verse
3:22	(Right Hand of God:)	
	0064:33	Ps 110:1 Mt 22:44 Mk 12:36;16:19
		Lk 20:42 Ro 8:34 Cl 3:1 He 10:12
	0239:45-46	(Same as 0064:33, above)
	0418: 6- 7	(Same as 0064:33, above)
	1317:34-1318: 3	
	2057:35-42	(Same as 0064:33, above)
4:19	(Faithful Creator)	
	0034: 5	
	0055: 4	
	1453:40-41	
5: 8- 9	1897:24	
5:13	1461:45-46	

*   *   *   *   *   *   *   *   *   *   *

CCC: The SECOND Book of PETER

II PETER Chap:Verse	The URANTIA Book Page:Line	Other BOOKS Chap:Verse
1: 4	1609:35-36	
1: 8	0067:32	
2:11	0419:33-34	
3: 8	0153:28-29	
3: 9	0039: 8- 9	
	1454: 6	Mt 18:14
3:10	(The End of the Earth:)	
	0599:45-48	Is 65:17;66:22 Mt 24:35 Mk 13:31
		Lk 21:33 Re 21:1-2
	1500:40-45	(Same as 0599:45-46, above)
	1914: 2	(Same as 0599:45-46, above)
3:13-14	0600:17-21	
3:18	(Grow in Grace:)	
	2054:39-41	1Co 3:1-2 Ep 4:14-15 1Pe 2:2
	(--And in Knowledge of God:)	
	1917:30	
	0067:32	

DDD: Paul's Letter to PHILEMON

PHILEMON Verse	The URANTIA Book Page:Line	Other BOOKS Chap:Verse
24	1461:45-46	

*   *   *   *   *   *   *   *   *   *   *

EEE: Paul's Letter to The PHILIPPIANS

PHILIPPIANS Chap:Verse	The URANTIA Book Page:Line	Other BOOKS Chap:Verse	
2: 1- 6	1205:20-21		
2: 5	(Adopt The Mind of Jesus:)		
	0191:34-40	1Co 2:16	
	0484:19-23	1Co 2:16	
	0553:46-48	1Co 2:16	
	1123:10-11	1Co 2:16	
2: 5- 8	1408:14-18		
2: 9	1409: 3		
3: 5	1332:28		
3: 8	0067:32		
3:12	2090:28		
3:13-14	1736:24-26		
4: 3	0301:45		
4: 6	1640:42-46		
4: 7	(Peace of God Which Passes All Understanding:)		
	0066:46-47	Lk 2:14	Jn 14:27; 16:33
	1101: 6- 8	Lk 2:14	Jn 14:27; 16:33
	1627:32-33	Lk 2:14	Jn 14:27; 16:33
	1663:13-14	Lk 2:14	Jn 14:27; 16:33
	1954: 7- 9	Lk 2:14	Jn 14:27; 16:33
	1954:28-47	Lk 2:14	Jn 14:27; 16:33
	1955: 7- 9	Lk 2:14	Jn 14:27; 16:33
	2042:13-14	Lk 2:14	Jn 14:27; 16:33
	2054:43	Lk 2:14	Jn 14:27; 16:33
4:11	1336:14		

FFF: The Book of PROVERBS

PROVERBS Chap:Verse	The URANTIA Book Page:Line	Other BOOKS Chap:Verse		
1: 7	(Fear of Lord, Beginning of Knowledge/Wisdom:)			
	0766:32-33	Jb 28:28	Ps 111:10	Pv 9:10
	1444:41-42	Jb 28:28	Ps 111:10	Pv 9:10
	1675:43-44	Jb 28:28	Ps 111:10	Pv 9:10
1: 8	1046:27-29			
1:24-29	1639: 3- 7			
3: 5- 6	1445:18-20			
3:11-12	1662:12-14			
3:18	0946: 4			
4: 7- 8	1481:28-31			
4:18	1445:49-50			
8:31	0028: 6			
8:36	1445:23-24			
9:10	(Fear of Lord is Beginning of Wisdom, See Proverbs 1:7, above.)			
11:30	0946: 4			
13: 7- 8	1822:25-29			
13:12	0946: 4			
13:15	(The Way of Transgressors is Hard:)			
	0611:48			
	0844:41			
14:12	(A Way that Seems Right, But Leads to Death:)			
	0842:45-48			
	1566:32			
14:14	1674:29-30			
14:29	1673:18-19			
15: 1	(A Soft Answer Turns Away Wrath:)			
	1555:40-41			
	1673:20			
	1687: 3			
15: 1-33	1046:46			
15: 3	0048:46			
15: 4	0946: 4			
15:13-17	1674:30-33			

365

Proverbs 16:1 to 31:31

PROVERBS Chap:Verse	The URANTIA Book Page:Line	Other BOOKS Chap:Verse
16: 8	1674:33-34	
16:18	1223: 7- 8	
16:18	1444:43-44	
16:25	1566:32	
16:32	(Self-Control Better than Control of Many Others:)	
	0317: 8-11	
	1444:44	
	1609:22-23	
17: 1-28	1046:46	
17: 6	(Civilized Man Loves Grandchildren:)	
	0750:38-39	
	0940:29-30	
17:22	(Merry Heart Like Good Medicine:)	
	1445:28-29	
	1674:34-35	
18:16	1478:12-13	
18:24	(Who Would Have Friends Must be Friendly:)	
	1439: 3- 4	
	2055:22-23	
19:11	1673:21	
20: 1-30	1046:46	
20:27	1674:26-27	
21: 3	2049:13-14	
21:13	1639:11-12	
22: 1- 4	1046:21	
22: 8	1445:35	
22:17-24:22	1046:46-47	
23: 5	1046:31-32	
23: 6	0962:36-38	
23: 7	1445:25-26	
25:28	1673:21-22	
27: 4	1673:22	
28: 1	1674:42-43	
28: 9	1638:28-29	
29:22	1673:23	
30: 6	1768:18-21	

GGG: The Book of PSALMS

PSALMS Chap:Verse	The URANTIA Book Page:Line	Other BOOKS Chap:Verse
1: 1- 6	1047: 1- 3	
1: 6	1444:40-41	
2: 1- 3	1725:12-15	
2: 4- 5	1725:19-21	
2: 7	(Begotten Son, See Hebrews 1:5, above.)	
2: 8	1725:21-22	
2:11	1725:27-29	
2:12	1725:29-30	
	1725:33-34	
3: 2	0992:26	
4: 5	1704:12-13	
5: 9	1677: 9-10	
6: 8	1829:23	
8: 2	1890:32	Mt 21:15-16
8: 5	(Mankind Made a Little Lower than Angels:)	
	0441: 7	
	0445:20-21	
	(--And Crowned with Glory and Honor:)	
	1444:39-40	
9: 2	(Most High as God:)	
	0488:15	
	1016:25	
9: 9	1662:18-19	
10: 3	1822:32	
10:16	1536: 6	
12: 2	1677: 9-10	
16: 6	1674:27-28	
19: 1	1107: 6- 7	
	1222:14-15	Ge 1:31
19: 1- 3	1444:10-12	
19: 6	0045: 3- 5	
19: 9	0036:40-41	
19:12-13	1640:16-17	
20: 6	2010:28-29	Mt 27:46 Mk 15:34
21: 8	2010:29	Mt 27:46 Mk 15:34
22: 1	2010:30	Mt 27:46 Mk 15:34
	2010:35-36	Mt 27:46 Mk 15:34

Psalms 22:18 to 34:17

PSALMS Chap:Verse	The URANTIA Book Page:Line	Other BOOKS Chap:Verse
34:18-19	1445:42-44	
35: 9	1445:41	
35:13	0976:16-17	Mt 9:14 Mk 2:18-20 Lk 5:33
35:19	1947:13	Jn 15:22-25
36: 5	0055: 1- 2	
36: 6	1445: 6- 7	
36: 8- 9	1445: 7- 8	
37: 1	1445:22	
37: 4- 5	1639:34-36	
37: 5	1445:44-45	
37:11	1445:34-35	
37:16	1674:28-29	
	1822:32-33	
38: 1- 2	0990:19	
41: 3	1662:19-20	
43: 5	1445:40	
46: 1	0041: 7- 8	
	1444:21-22	
46: 4	0488:30-32	
46: 6	1725:35-36	
47: 2	1536: 5	
51:10	(Create In Me A Clean Heart:)	
	1769:24	
	(--And Renew a Right Spirit Within Me:)	
	1340:26-27 Ek 36:26-27	
	1640:15-17	
	(The New Spirit Within, See Ezekiel 11:19, above.)	
55:22	1704:14-15	
62: 8	1704:15-16	
62:10	1822:33-34	
66:18	1445:23	
68: 4	1053:41	
68: 5	0022:28-30	
68:20	0041: 6	
69: 4	1947:13	Jn 15:22-25
69:28	0409:33	
69:30-31	1640:46-48	
71:22	2087:12	

PSALMS Chap:Verse	The URANTIA Book Page:Line	Other BOOKS Chap:Verse
72:12	1639:37	
72:12-13	2035:22-23	
72:17	2035:23-24	
72:19	1444:36-37	
74: 2	0945:24-27	
76: 1- 2	1016:14	
77:19	0033:35-36	
80: 4	0421:45	
80: 7	0421:45	
80:14	0421:45	
80:19	0421:45	
82: 5- 8	1794:43	
82: 6	(Children of the Most High:)	
	1373:30	
	1475: 9	
	1661: 5- 6	
	(Faith Children of God, See Isaiah 56:5, above.)	
83:18	(Yahweh or Jehovah as Name of God:)	
	1053: 6- 7	
	1053:43	
84: 3	1536: 4- 5	
84:11	1445:29	
86:15	0038: 8- 9	
89: 2	0055: 4	
89: 6	1063:36	
89:19-37	1858:27-28	
89:26	0022:28-30	
90: 2	0023:31	
90: 4	0036: 3- 4	
	0153:28-29	
90:10	0858: 5	
91: 1	0055: 7- 8	
	0488:37-39	
	1445:45-46	
	1704:16-17	
91:10-12	1519:34-38	Mt 4:5-7 Lk 4:9-11
92: 1- 2	1445: 8-10	
92: 1- 4	1640:38-41	
92: 5	1444:12	

PSALMS Chap:Verse	The URANTIA Book Page:Line	Other BOOKS Chap:Verse
94: 1	0795:39-40	
94: 1-15	1590:27-30	
94: 9	0027:21-22	
96:10	1444:31-32	
96:11	1444:31	
97: 6	1444:33-34	
100: 3	(Be God Conscious:)	
	0024: 9	
	(God Made Us, We Are His:)	
	1444:34-35	
100: 5	1444:35-36	
102:17	1639:37	
103: 8	1444:18	
103:13	0022:28-30	
103:13-14	1662:20-22	
103:14	0049:15	
	1240: 3- 4	
103:17	0038:10-11	
	1444:23-24	
103:17-18	1446:13	
103:19	1858:26	
104: 2	0021:11-12	
104:24	1444:13	
104:30	0376:10-11	
	(God Sends Forth Creators:)	
	0055:13	
	(God Renews:)	
	0055:24-25	
107: 1	0038:11-12	
107: 8	(A Call to Praise God for His Goodness to People.)	
	1444:37-38	Ps 107:15,21,31
	1454:27-28	Ps 107:15.21,31
107:15	(A Call to Praise, See Psalms 107:8, above.)	
107:21	(A Call to Praise, See Psalms 107:8, above.)	
107:31	(A Call to Praise, See Psalms 107:8, above.)	
109: 6	0602: 1- 2	

PSALMS Chap:Verse	The URANTIA Book Page:Line	Other BOOKS Chap:Verse
110: 1	(Jesus' Relationship to God & Man:)	
	0064:33	Mt 22:43-44 Mk 12:35-36 Lk 20:42-44
	1902: 2- 3	Mt 22:43-44 Mk 12:35-36 Lk 20:42-44
	(Jesus Cited This to Deny He was Son of David:)	
	1348: 5- 6	Mt 22:43-44 Mk 12:35-36 Lk 20:42-44
	1901:40-1902:6	Mt 22:43-44 Mk 12:35-36 Lk 20:42-44
	(Right Hand of the Father:)	
	0064:33	Mt 22:44 Mk 12:36; 16:19 Lk 20:42
		Ro 8:34 Cl 3:1 He 10:12 1Pe 3:22
	0239:45-46	(Same as 0064:33, above)
	0418: 6- 7	(Same as 0064:33, above)
	2057:39-42	(Same as 0064:33, above)
110: 4	(Melchizedek Priesthood:)	
	0514:15-16	
	1017: 8- 9	
	1024:17-18	He 7:17,21
111: 4	0041: 6	
	1444:24-25	
111:10	(Fear of Lord as Beginning of Wisdom:)	
	0766:32-33	Pv 1:7;9:10 Jb 28:28 Ps 111:10
	1444:41	Pv 1:7;9:10 Jb 28:28 Ps 111:10
	1675:43-44	Pv 1:7;9:10 Jb 28:28 Ps 111:10
113: 1-118	1794:39	
115:15	0021: 8-10	Ge 1:1 Is 37:16 Lk 19:15
118: 1- 4	0038:11-12	
118: 9	1704:17-18	
118:22	1894:23-24	Mt 21:42-44 Mk 12:10 Lk 20:17-18
118:26	1882:12-13	Mt 21:7-9 Mk 11:7-10 Lk 19:35-38
		Jn 12:12-14
119:165	1446: 5- 6	
119:172	0055: 1	
119:67	1662:15	
119:71	1662:15-16	
119:86	0055: 4	
119:89-90	0055: 2- 4	
121: 1	0945:24-27	
121: 4	0055: 8- 9	
121: 8	1372:33-34	
132:17	1353:17-18	

PSALMS Chap:Verse	The URANTIA Book Page:Line	Other BOOKS Chap:Verse
136: 1- 3	1444:32	
136: 1-26	0038:11-12	
136: 2,26	1444:32	
138: 2	1536: 5- 6	
139: 2- 3	0049:11-13	
139: 7	0044:27-28	
	1444:27	
141: 3	1640:19	
143:10	0024:11	
145: 3	(God's Greatness Unsearchable:)	
	0033:36	
	1444:13	
145: 8	(God is Gracious and Compassionate:)	
	0038: 8- 9	
	0041: 6	
	1444:24-25	
145: 9	1444:25-26	
145:11-13	1858:26	
145:13	1445:10-11	
145:17	0036:39	
145:18	1445:27	
147: 3	(He Heals Broken Hearts, Binds Spiritual Wounds:)	
	0041: 6- 7	
	1444:26	
	1662:22-23	
147: 4	(God Knows the Stars by Name & Number:)	
	0049: 2- 3	
	0165:46-47	
	1444:14	
147: 5	(God's Understanding is Infinite:)	
	0033:36	
	(--And His Power is Great:)	
	1444:15	
148: 4	(Heaven of Heavens:)	
	0034 2- 9	De 10:14 1Ki 8:27 2Ch 2:6; 6:18 Ne 9:6
	0044:33-34	(Same as 0034:2-3, above)
	0553:19-29	(Same as 0034:2-3, above)
	1953:28-29	(Same as 0034:2-3, above)

HHH: The Book of REVELATION

REVELATION Chap:Verse	The URANTIA Book Page:Line	Other BOOKS Chap:Verse
1: 4	(Seven Spirits Before the Throne:)	
	0184: 2	Re 3:1; 4:5; 5:6
	0189: 9-16	Re 3:1; 4:5; 5:6
	0378:21-29	Re 3:1; 4:5; 5:6
	0401:31	Re 3:1; 4:5; 5:6
	1269:31	Re 3:1; 4:5; 5:6
1: 8	(I Am The Alpha & Omega, The Beginning & End, The Source and Destiny:)	
	0034: 6	Re 1:11,17;21:6;22:13 Is 44:6
	0115:19	Re 1:11,17;21:6;22:13 Is 44:6
	1069: 4- 5	Re 1:11,17;21:6;22:13 Is 44:6
	1069:34-35	Re 1:11,17;21:6;22:13 Is 44:6
	1408:48-49	Re 1:11,17;21:6;22:13 Is 44:6
1: 9	1555:35-36	
1:11	(Alpha & Omega, See Revelation 1:8, above.)	
1:17	(First & Last, See Revelation 1:8, above.)	
1:18	0034:12:13	
1:20	1255:24	
2: 7	(Who Has Ears, Listen to The Spirit:)	
	0096:36-37	Re 2:11,17,29; 3:6,13,22
	(Tree of Life:)	
	0825:30-0825:32	Ge 3:22,24 Re 22:2,14
2:10	1454:33-34	
2:11	0096:36-37	Re 2:7,17,29; 3:6,13,22
2:17	0096:36-37	Re 2:7.11,29; 3:6,13,22
	(New Name:)	
	0538:14	Re 3:12
	1188:41	Re 3:12
	1191:45	Re 3:12
	2062:22	Re 3:12
2:29	0096:36-37	Re 2:7,11,17; 3:6,13,22
3: 1	(Seven Spirits, See Revelation 1:4, above.)	
3: 6	0096:36-37	Re 2:7,11,17,29; 3:13,22
3: 8	(The Open Door:)	
	1567: 3- 5	Jn 3:15-16
	1652:43-45	
	(Whosoever Will May Enter, See Revelation 22:17.)	

REVELATION Chap:Verse	The URANTIA Book Page:Line	Other BOOKS Chap:Verse
3:12	(Temple Coming Down From Heaven:)	
	0622: 6	Re 21:1-2
	0622:19-20	Re 21:1-2
	(New Name, See Revelation 2:17, above.)	
3:13	0096:36-37	Re 2:7,11,17,29; 3:6,22
3:15-16	1715:30-31	Jn 6:61-62
3:20	(I Stand at Door and Knock:)	
	0026:29-31	
	1765:31-32	
	1829:38-42	
3:21	1935: 4- 5	
3:22	0096:36-37	Re 2:7,11,17,29; 3:6,13
4: 2	0513:13-15	
4: 4	(The Four & Twenty Elders:)	
	0378:29-34	Re 4:10; 5:8,14
	0513: 9-13	Re 4:10; 5:8,14
	1251: 7- 9	Re 4:10; 5:8,14
	1251:31-43	
4: 5	(Seven Spirits of God, See Revelation 1:4, above.)	
	(Lightenings, Thunderings & Voices:)	
	0378:35-36	
4: 6	(Sea of Glass:)	
	0486:27	Re 15:2
	0487: 7-11	Re 15:2
	0521:44	Re 15:2
	0534:44	Re 15:2
	0539:27-31	Re 15:2
4: 6- 8	0378:42-43	
4:10	(Four & Twenty Elders, See Revelation 4:4, above.)	
5: 6	(Seven Spirits of God, See Revelation 1:4, above.)	
5: 8	(Four & Twenty Elders, See Revelation 4:4, above.	
	(Harp of God:)	
	0539:30,33	Re 14:2; 15:2
5:14	(Four & Twenty Elders, See Revelation 4:4, above.)	
7: 2- 3	0590:29	
7:11	1251:31-43	
7:14	(Great Tribulation:)	
	0538:27-28	
	1533:29-31	Jn 16:33 Ac 14:22

REVELATION Chap:Verse	The URANTIA Book Page:Line	Other BOOKS Chap:Verse
7:16-17	(Water of Life, See Isaiah 55:1, above.) (Bread of Life, See Isaiah 55:2, above.)	
8: 2	1255:34	
8: 6	1255:34	
9:11	0602: 9	
10: 1	0422: 4	
12: 3- 4	0608:17-19	
12: 7	(War in Heaven:) 0606: 7-19 0608:44-45 0756:11	
12: 7- 8	(The Dragon Prevailed Not:) 0606: 8- 9 0608:37-0609: 7 0609:20-23 0609:35-45	
12: 8	(--And Has No Place in Heaven:) 0609:11 0611:42	
12: 9	(Old Serpent Cast Out:) 0611: 4- 6 0611:25-29 (--And His Angels Cast Out With Him:) 0611:11-20	
13:16-18	0538:39	
14: 2	0539:30,33	Re 5:8; 15:2
14: 3	1251:31-43	
14: 9	0538:39	
15: 2	(Sea of Glass, See Revelation 4:6, above.) (Harps of God:) 0539:30,33	Re 5:8; 14:2
15: 3	1311:49-1312: 2	
16: 2	0538:39	
17:14	0240:11-12	
19: 4	0421:44	
19: 6	0046:37	
19:10	0419:37-39	

REVELATION Chap:Verse	The URANTIA Book Page:Line	Other BOOKS Chap:Verse
19:13	(The Word of God:)	
	0111: 4	Jn 1:1-2,14
	1409: 5- 6	Jn 1:1-2,14
19:14	0370:19-20	
19:16	0240:11-12	
19:20	0538:39	
20: 1- 2	0602:14-15	
20: 1- 3	0611:11-20	
20:12	0301:45	
21: 1- 2	(New Heavens and New Earth:)	
	0599:45-48	Is 65:17; 66:22 Mt 24:35 Mk 13:31 Lk 21:33 2Pe 3:10
	1500:40-45	(Same as 0599:45-48, above)
	1914: 1- 4	(Same as 0599:45-48, above)
	(--A New Jerusalem:)	
	1913:46-47	Re 3:12
	(--With Temple, Coming Down From Heaven:)	
	0622: 6	Re 3:12
	0622:19-20	Re 3:12
21: 4	0299:44-46	
21: 4- 5	0631:10-11	
21: 6	(Alpha & Omega, See Revelation 1:8, above.0	
21:23	0519:33	
22: 2	(Tree of Life:)	
	0825:30-0826:32 Ge 3:22,24 Re 2:7; 22:14	
22: 3- 4	0299:40-42	
22: 5	0299:42-43	
22: 8- 9	0419:37-39	
22:13	(Alpha & Omega, See Revelation 1:8, above.)	
22:14	0825:30-0826:32 Ge 3:22,24 Re 2:7; 22:2	
22:16	(Bright & Morning Star:)	
	0237: 4- 5	
	0306:36-0307:1	
	0376:12-14	
	0406:26-31	

REVELATION Chap:Verse	The URANTIA Book Page:Line	Other BOOKS Chap:Verse
22:17	(Whosoever Will May Come:)	
	0039: 7	Mt 16:24-25 Mk 8:34-35 Lk 9:23-24 Jn 3:15-16
	1102:18-19	(Same as 0039:7, above.)
	1205: 1- 2	(Same as 0039:7, above.)
	1567: 3- 5	(Same as 0039:7, above.)
	1750:16-17	(Same as 0039:7, above.)
	1820:44-45	(Same as 0039:7, above.)
	1829:44-45	(Same as 0039:7, above.)
	(Water of Life, See Isaiah 55:1, above.)	
22:18-19	1768:26-27	

*   *   *   *   *   *   *   *   *   *   *

III: Paul's Letter to The ROMANS

ROMANS Chap:Verse	The URANTIA Book Page:Line	Other BOOKS Chap:Verse
1:16	(Gospel For Jews & Gentiles:)	
	1584:18	
	1909:35-36	
1:20	0027:45-46	
2: 4	(The Goodness of God Leads Us to Repentance:)	
	0041: 1	
	0552:30	
	1610:15-16	
	1675:31-32	
2: 9	1725:26-27	
2:11	(God is No Respecter of Persons:)	
	0027: 8	2Ch 19:7 Jb 34:19 Ac 10:34 Ga 2:6 Ep 6:9
	0036:43-44	(Same as 0027:8, above)
	0138:22	(Same as 0027:8, above)
	0454:17-19	(Same as 0027:8, above)
	1290:43-45	(Same as 0027:8, above)
	1468:30	(Same as 0027:8, above)
	1536:10	(Same as 0027:8, above)

(Romans 2:11 Continued on next page.)

ROMANS Chap:Verse	The URANTIA Book Page:Line	Other BOOKS Chap:Verse
2:11	1608:20	(Same as 0027:8, above)
	1662:45-47	(Same as 0027:8, above)
	1731: 6- 8	(Same as 0027:8, above)
	1736:10-12	(Same as 0027:8, above)
	1831: 8	(Same as 0027:8, above)
	1909:35	(Same as 0027:8, above)
	1958:12	(Same as 0027:8, above)
	2047:37	(Same as 0027:8, above)
3:21- 4: 5	1682:32-1683: 3	
3:23	1660:39	
3:27-28	1610: 3- 8	
3:28	1682:46-48	
3:29-30	0640:20-21	
3:30	(One God, See Deuteronomy 6:4, above.)	
4: 3	1017:35	
5: 1	(Peace With God Through Faith in Jesus:)	
	1454:31-32	
	1610: 4-12	
	1682:46-48	
5: 10	1083:43-44	
5: 6- 9	2003: 7- 9	
5: 6-21	0228:24-29	Jn 3:16
5:12-19	(Views of the Origin of Sin & Evil:)	
	1660:31-34	
	1660:48-1661: 2	
6:23	(The Wages of Sin is Death:)	
	0529:18	
	0612: 1- 2	
	0975:40-41	
	(--But God Gives Eternal Life:)	
	0023:14-15	
	1409: 8	
	1957:26-27	
8: 1-17	1610:21-23	
8: 2	0382:46-0383: 2	
8: 9	1474:33	
8: 9-16	1601:18-37	Jn 1:12-13

ROMANS Chap:Verse	The URANTIA Book Page:Line	Other BOOKS Chap:Verse
8:14	(Those Led by Spirit are Sons of God:) 0096:39 0381:27-28	
8:14-17	(Power to Become Sons of God:) 0039:18-19	Is 56:5 Jn 1:12 Ga 3:26;4:6 1Jo 3:1-2
	0067:32-33	(Same as 0039:18-19, above)
	0447:40-0448:35	(Same as 0039:18-19, above)
	1091:16-17	(Same as 0039:18-19, above)
	1112:41-42	(Same as 0039:18-19, above)
	1191:16-17	(Same as 0039:18-19, above)
	1454:37	(Same as 0039:18-19, above)
	1603:37-40	(Same as 0039:18-19, above)
	1610: 2-20	(Same as 0039:18-19, above)
	1725:28	(Same as 0039:18-19, above)
	1861:29-30	(Same as 0039:18-19, above)
	1945:21	(Same as 0039:18-19, above)
	1957:36-37	(Same as 0039:18-19, above)
	1958:17	(Same as 0039:18-19, above)
	2053:14,38	(Same as 0039:18-19, above)
8:16	(The Spirit Tells Our Spirit: We Are Sons of God:) 0381:37-38 1107:17-18 1642:20-24	
8:21	(From Bondage to Liberty:) 1609:28-29 1610:19-20 1861:30 2033:16-17	
8:26-27	(Prayer In The Spirit:) 0096:37-38 1849: 3- 4	Mt 6:5-13 Mk 11:24 Lk 11:2-4
8:27	0079: 3	
8:28	(All Things Work Together for Good:) 0055: 9-10 0548: 7- 8 0616:38-41 1306:44-46	

ROMANS Chap:Verse	The URANTIA Book Page:Line	Other BOOKS Chap:Verse
8:34	2092:40-42	
	(Right Hand of the Father, See 1Pe 3:22, above.)	
8:35-39	1608:28-34	
8:37	2084: 9	
8:38-39	1101:10-12	
9:26	1091:16-17	
10:12	1909: 1	
10:13	0038: 9-10	
11:33	0034: 3- 4	
11:36	1150:42	
12: 2	(Be Transformed by Renewal of Mind:)	
	1205:20-21	
	1609:30-34	
12: 3	0549:11-12	
12:17	1580: 8- 9	
12:18	1956: 5- 6	
12:19	0795:39-40	
12:21	(Overcome Evil With Good:)	
	1580: 8- 9	
	1739:12-13	
	1770:20	
	2064:31	
13: 1	0046:40	
13: 9	(Love Thy Neighbor as Thyself:)	
	1206:40-42	Mt 19:19;22:39 Mk 12:31 Lk 10:27-28 Le 19:18 Ga 5:14 Ja 2:8
	1445:47	(Same as 1206:40-42, above)
	1446:11-12	(Same as 1206:40-42, above)
	1453:37	(Same as 1206:40-42, above)
	1600: 1- 3	(Same as 1206:40-42, above)
	1600:33-36	(Same as 1206:40-42, above)
	1769:26	(Same as 1206:40-42, above)
	1770: 4- 5	(Same as 1206:40-42, above)
	1805: 9-11	(Same as 1206:40-42, above)
	1809:25-27	(Same as 1206:40-42, above)
	1862: 8	(Same as 1206:40-42, above)
	1901:13-20	(Same as 1206:40-42, above)
	1950:17-18	(Same as 1206:40-42, above)

ROMANS Chap:Verse	The URANTIA Book Page:Line	Other BOOKS Chap:Verse
14: 7	(None Lives or Dies To Himself:)	
	0647:29-30	
	1227:23-25	
	2055:21-22	
14:17	(The Nature of The Kingdom:)	
	0382: 1- 3	
	1536:47-49	
	1727:10-11	
14:22	1091:32	
15: 6	2064:36-37	
15:13	1454:32-33	
15:26	2067:22	Ga 2:10
15:30	0096:32	
16: 3	1473:48-50	
16:16	2067:22	1Co 16:20
16:23	1473:41-42	

* * * * * * * * * * *

JJJ: The Book of RUTH

RUTH Chap:Verse	The URANTIA Book Page:Line	Other BOOKS Chap:Verse
4:10	0917:33-34	

* * * * * * * * * * *

KKK: The FIRST Book of SAMUEL

I SAMUEL Chap:Verse	The URANTIA Book Page:Line	Other BOOKS Chap:Verse
1: 3	1053:41	
	2064:35-36	
1:11	2064:35-36	
2: 2	1063:35-36	
2: 3	1063:38-39	

I SAMUEL Chap:Verse	The URANTIA Book Page:Line	Other BOOKS Chap:Verse
2: 7- 8	1063:26-28	
2: 8	1062:38-39	
2:10	1063:39	
7: 3- 4	1062:33-34	
7:10	0947:19-21	
9: 8-10	0986:33-34	
10: 1	1072:11-12	
11: 1-11	1072: 3- 5	
11:15	1072: 6- 7	
12:10	1042:36-37	
12:22	1063:19	
14: 6	1063:43-44	
15: 3	1768: 8-10	
15:22	2049:13-14	
15:29	(God Does Not Repent:)	
	0036: 1	Ge 6:6 Ex 32:14 Nu 23:19 Am 7:3,6 Zc 8:14
	0058: 6	(Same as 0036:1, above)
	1063: 6- 7	(Same as 0036:1, above)
	1510:19	(Same as 0036:1, above)
15:32-33	1062:36-37	
15:35	(God "Repented," See I Samuel 15:29, above.)	
16: 1-13	1072:38-42	
16: 7	1576:29	
17: 1-51	0785: 8-10	
17:14	1060:35-36	
18:22-27	1072:46	
18:25	0785: 4- 5	
21: 3- 6	1655: 2- 5	Lk 6:3-4
22: 1- 2	1072:21-22	
23: 1- 5	1073:19-20	
25:42	1072:47	
27: 2- 3	1072:17-18	
28: 7-19	0988: 9-11	
28: 7-25	1646:10-12	
28:18	1072:26	
29: 1-11	1072:18-19	
29:11	0034: 8- 9	
31: 1- 4	1495:16-17	
31: 1- 9	1072:19-20	

LLL: The SECOND Book of SAMUEL

II SAMUEL Chap:Verse	The URANTIA Book Page:Line	Other BOOKS Chap:Verse
2: 1- 4	1072:28-37	
3: 3	1072:47	
5: 3	1073: 4- 5	
5: 6- 7	1073: 6- 7	
5:10	(Lord God of Hosts:)	
	0421:45	
	1073:10	
5:17-25	1073: 8- 9	
5:20	1073:14-15	
5:24	0988: 5- 7	
6: 1-17	1073:24-25	
7:12-16	1858:27-28	
7:14	1661: 6- 7	
7:22	1063:22-23	
8:11-12	1073:26-27	
11:14-17	1073:31	
11:27	1072:49	
12:16	0976:16-17	Mt 9:14 Mk 2:18 Lk 5:33
12:21-23	0976:16-17	
15: 2- 6	1073:31-34	
15:27	0986:33-34	
21: 1- 2	1073:17-19	
21: 3- 9	1073:21-23	
21:23	0976:16-20	Mt 9:14 Mk 2:18 Lk 5:33
22:14	1016:25	
22:14-15	0947:19-21	
22:26	1063:39-40	
22:31	0034: 8	
23: 5	1063:19-20	
24: 1	1599:10-12	
24: 1- 4	(Numbering The People:)	
	0602: 1- 2	1Ch 21:1-5
	0968:11-12	1Ch 21:1-5
	1350:25-26	1Ch 21:1-5
	1599:16-17	1Ch 21:1-5
24:10	1350:25-26	
24:14	1063:42-43	

384

MMM: The Book of SIRACH

SIRACH Chap:Verse	The URANTIA Book Page:Line	Other BOOKS Chap:Verse
1: 4	0402:44-0403: 8	
11:18-19	1822:25-29	

*   *   *   *   *   *   *   *   *   *   *

NNN: Paul's 1st Letter to The THESSASLONIANS

I THESSA. Chap:Verse	The URANTIA Book Page:Line	Other BOOKS Chap:Verse			
1: 5	0380:43-44				
4:16	0409:24				
5: 5	(Children of Light:)				
	1327:26-27	Mt 5:14-16	Lk 16:8	Jn 12:36	Ep 5:8
	1655:37-38	Mt 5:14-16	Lk 16:8	Jn 12:36	Ep 5:8
	1854:11-12	Mt 5:14-16	Lk 16:8	Jn 12:36	Ep 5:8
	1904:24-28	Mt 5:14-16	Lk 16:8	Jn 12:36	Ep 5:8
	1953:33	Mt 5:14-16	Lk 16:8	Jn 12:36	Ep 5:8
	2042: 2	Mt 5:14-16	Lk 16:8	Jn 12:36	Ep 5:8
5:15	1580: 8- 9				
5:21	1454:35				

*   *   *   *   *   *   *   *   *   *   *

OOO: Paul's 2nd Letter to The THESSALONIANS

II THESSA. Chap:Verse	The URANTIA Book Page:Line	Other BOOKS Chap:Verse
1: 7	0422: 3	
3:10	0773:32-33	
3:13	1740:43-44	Ga 6:9
	1808: 6- 7	Ga 6:9
	1897:36	Ga 6:9

PPP: Paul's FIRST Letter to TIMOTHY

I TIMOTHY Chap:Verse	The URANTIA Book Page:Line	Other BOOKS Chap:Verse
1: 1	1965:42	
1:17	0025: 3- 4	
2: 4	0039: 7- 8	
2: 5	1594:48	
2:11-12	1679:36-38	
6: 8-11	0976:25-27	
6:12	(Fight the Good Fight of Faith:)	
	1766:20-21	2Tm 4:7
	1829:17-18	2Tm 4:7
	2018:36-37	2Tm 4:7
	(Eternal Life, See I John 5:11-12)	
6:15	0240:11-12	
6:16	(Light Which No Man Can Approach:)	
	0025:22-23	
	0027:38-39	

*   *   *   *   *   *   *   *   *   *   *

QQQ: Paul's SECOND Letter to TIMOTHY

II TIMOTHY Chap:Verse	The URANTIA Book Page:Line	Other BOOKS Chap:Verse
2:14	(Do Not Strive About Words:)	
	1577:18-19	
	1593: 5	
	1932:20	
	1956: 7- 8	
2:19	0363:42	
2:24-25	(Don't Strive, Teach Gently, See II Timothy 2:14, above.)	
4: 7	(Certain Victory for Those Who Finish the Race:)	
	0365:29-31	
	1237:24	
	(--Or Fight the Good Fight of Faith, See I Timothy 6:12, above.)	
4:19	1473:48-50	

RRR: Paul's Letter to TITUS

TITUS Chap:Verse	The URANTIA Book Page:Line	Other BOOKS Chap:Verse
1: 5	1438:30-31	
1:10-16	1436:16-18	
2:14	1864:25-27	
3: 5	0380:36-37	
3:12	1471:39-40	

* * * * * * * * * * *

SSS: The Book of TOBIT

TOBIT Chap:Verse	The URANTIA Book Page:Line	Other BOOKS Chap:Verse
4:15	(The Negative "Golden Rule," Do Not Do To Anyone That Which You Would Hate Have Done to You:)	
	1445:47-48	Mt 7:12 Lk 6:31
	1454:35-36	Mt 7:12 Lk 6:31
	1464:37-38	Mt 7:12 Lk 6:31
	1571:11-12	Mt 7:12 Lk 6:31
	1585:29-32	Mt 7:12 Lk 6:31
	1650:15-1651:21	Mt 7:12 Lk 6:31
	1771: 2- 3	Mt 7:12 Lk 6:31
	1931:23-24	Mt 7:12 Lk 6:31
	1949:43-1950:28	Mt 7:12 Lk 6:31

* * * * * * * * * * *

TTT: The Book of WISDOM of SOLOMON

WISDOM Chap:Verse	The URANTIA Book Page:Line	Other BOOKS Chap:Verse
1: 6	0402:44-0403: 8	
1: 6- 7	0403:25-27	
1: 6- 9	0103:39-44	
13: 2	0944:19-24	

387

UUU: The Book of ZECHARIAH

ZECHARIAH Chap:Verse	The URANTIA Book Page:Line	Other BOOKS Chap:Verse
3: 1- 2	0602: 1- 2	
3: 4	1682:39-41	
3: 8	1946: 1- 2	
6:12	1946: 1- 2	
7:11-13	1638:22-27	
8:14	0058: 6	Mt 21:2-5
	(God's "Repentance," See Nu 23:19, above.)	
9: 9	1341:41-43	Mt 21:4
	(King Arrives Riding an Ass:)	
	1881:16-18	Mt 21:4-5 Jn 12:14-15
	1884:49-50	Mt 21:4-5 Jn 12:14-15
	1885:38-39	Mt 21:4-5 Jn 12:14-15
11:12	1341:41-43	Mt 26:15;27:9-10
13: 6	1677:10-11	
13: 7	(Shepherd Smitten, Sheep Scattered:)	
	1962:13-18	Mt 26:31 Mk 14:27
	1976:34	Mt 26:31 Mk 14:27
14: 6- 9	1858:32-33	
14: 9 +	1590:31	

*   *   *   *   *   *   *   *   *   *   *

VVV: The Book of ZEPHANIAH

ZEPHANIAH Chap:Verse	The URANTIA Book Page:Line	Other BOOKS Chap:Verse
1:12	2081:27-32	
2: 3	1570:31	Mt 5:5
	1574:19-24	Mt 5:5

The End

MATTHEW

1:1-17-1344.1
:20-25-1347.4
2:1-12-1352:1
:13-23-1353.10
3:1-10-1501.6
:11-17-1503.7 & .8
4:1-11-1492.8
:12-17-1535.8
:18-22-1524.1
5:1-28-1570.3-.6
:39-41-1770:2-4
:44-48-1571:2 & 3
6:1-8-1576.6
:9-13-1620:1
:14-15-1638.4
:16-26-1577:5-7
:25-34-1823.5
7:1-2-1639:1
:3-6-1571:4 & 5
:7-11-1618.2
:13-14-1828:7
:15-27-1571:6 & 7
:28-29-1630:7
8:1-4-1643.4
:5-13-1647.1
:14-15-1631:3
:16-1631.3
:19-22-1801.2
:23-34-1694.5 & .6
9:2-8-1666.9
:9-13-1540.3
:14-17-1655.7
:18-27-1698.0 & .1
:32-34-1713.4
:37-38-1681:8
10:2-7-1681.4
:7-16-1800.1
:16-22-1584:2
:24-37-1681.4
:39-1575:4
:42-1764:3
11:1-19-1626.8
:20-23-1807:4
:25-29-1627:5
:30-1766:3
12:1-8-1653.6
:9-14-1664.7
:22-39-1713.4
:46-50-1721.6
13:1-15-1688.1
:16-17-1807:3
:18-23-1689.2
:24-48-1693.4
:55-58-1686.9
14:3-12-1508.12
:13-34-1700.2-.5
15:1-20-1712.3
:21-28-1734.0 & .1
16:1-6-1744.2
:13-20-1745.3
:21-28-1759.7
17:1-13-1752.1 & .2
:14-23-1757.5 & .6
:24-27-1743.1
18:1-10-1761.8
:12-35-1762.1
19:3-15-1838.5 & .6
:16-30-1801.2 & .3
20:1-16-1804:1-4
:17-19-1871.4
:20-28-1867.0
20:29-34-1873.5
21:1-11-1880.3
:12-16-1888.1
:23-46-1891.2-.4
22:1-14-1894.5
:15-46-1899.2-.4
23:1-39-1905.0 & .1
24:1-51-1912.0 & .1
25:1-13-1915:5
:13-29-1916.3
26:3-5-1924.4
:6-13-1878.1
:14-16-1924.4
:17-19-1933:4-5
:21-30-1940.4 & 5
:31-35-1962:1-3
:36-46-1968.3
:47-58-1973.3
:59-68-1982.3 & .4
:69-75-1980.2
27:1-2-1985.5
:3-10-1997.1
:11-1991:2 & 4
:12-14-1990:7
:15-23-1993.5
:24-31-1994.6-.8
:32-2006:2
:33-44-2006.2 & .3
:45-54-2010.5
:55-56-2008:3
:57-66-2012.0 - .2
28:1-2025:4 & 5
:2-4-2023:3
:5-10-2025.4
:11-15-2023:3 & 4
:16:17-2050.3
:19-20-2053:1

MARK

1:1-15-1501.6-.9
:16-20-1524.1
:21-39-1629.2-.5
:39-45-1643.4
2:1-12-1666.9
:14-17-1540.3
:18-28-1653.6 & .7
3:1-6-1664.7
:7-8-1669:1
:22-30-1713.4
:31-35-1721.6
4:1-41-1688.1-.5
5:1-20-1695.6
:21-43-1698.0 & .1
6-1-5-1683.6-.9
:7-9-1583.9
:17-30-1508.12
:31-53-1700.2-.5
7:1-30-1712.3 & .4
8:11-30-1744.2 & .3
:31-38-1759.7
9:1-13-1752.1 & .2
:14-37-1755.4-.8
:38-41-1764.2
:42-47-1761.8
10:2-16-1838.5 & .6
:17-31-1801.2 & .3
:32-34-1871.4
:35-45-1867.0
:46-52-1873.5
11:1-10-1880.3
:15-18-1888.1
:25-26-1638:4
:27-33-1891.2
12:1-12-1893.4
:13-37-1899.2-.4
:38-40-1907:1
:41-44-1883.4
13:1-37-1912.0-.2
14:1-2-1924.4
:3-9-1878.1
:10-11-1924.4
:12-16-1932.2
:18-26-1940.4 & .5
:27-30-1962:1-3
:32-42-1968.3
:43-54-1973.3
:55-72-1982.2 & .3
15:3-5-1990:7
:6-19-1993.5 & .6
:22-32-2006.2 & .3
:33-39-2010.5
:40-41-2008:3
:42-47-2012.0 & .1
16:1-11-2025.4
:12-13-2034.5
:14-2040.2
:15-2043:1
:16-2053:3
:19-2057.5

LUKE

1:5-66-1345.2 & .3
:57-80-1496.0
2:1-38-1350.7-.9
:39-40-1356:3-5
:42-1374:1
:43-45-1381.3
:46-51-1383.6
3:3-22-1501.6-.8
:23-38-1344.1
4:1-13-1512.3
:16-31-1684.8 & .9
:31-41-1629.2 & .3
:42-44-1634.5
5:1-11-1628.1
:12-15-1643.4
:17-26-1666.9
:27-32-1540.3
:33-39-1655.7
6:1-5-1653.6
:6-11-1664.7
:13-16-1548.0
:20-49-1570.3
7:1-10-1647.1
:11-17-1645.6
:18:23-1507:3
:19-35-1626.8
:36-50-1651.5
8:1-3-1678.1
:4-15-1688.1 & .2
:16-18-1692:0
:19-21-1721.6
:22-39-1694.5 & .6
:40-56-1698.0 & .1
9:1-3-1583.9
:10-17-1700.2
:18-21-1745.3
:22-27-1759.7
:28-36-1752.1
:37-45-1755.4- .6
:46-48-1761.8
:49-50-1764.2
:51-56-1788.0
:57-62-1801.2
10:1-11-1800.1
:13-14-1807:4
10:16-1801:1
:17-24-1806.6
:25-37-1809.1
:38-42-1797.8
11:1-13-1618.2 & .3
:14-23-1713.4
:27-28-1722:3
:29-1714:4
:33-1570:5
:34-36-1577:6
:37-54-1825.1
12:1-53-1819.3- .6
:54-56-1744.2
13:1-9-1830.4
:10-17-1835.3
:18-21-1693.4
:22-30-1828.3
:31-35-1872:1-4
14:1-24-1833.1 & .2
:25-35-1869.2
15:2-32-1850.0 & .1
16:1-31-1853.2 & .3
17:2-1761:2
:11-19-1827.2
18:1-8-1618.2
:9-17-1838.5 & .6
:18-30-1801.2 & .3
:31-43-1871.4 & .5
19:1-10-1873.6
:11-27-1875.8
:28-44-1880.3
:45-48-1888.1
20:1-8-1891.2
:9-19-1893.4
:20-44-1899.2- .4
:46-47-1907:1
21:1-4-1883.4
:5-33-1912.0- .2
22:2-6-1924.4
:8-13-1932.2
:15-18-1937.2
:19-23-1940.4 & .5
:24-30-1940:1
:32-34-1962:2-3
:35-36-1944:2
:39-46-1968.3
:47-54-1973.3
:54-62-1980.2
:63-65-1984.4
:67-68-1986:2
:69-71-1982.3
23:1-23-1989.2- .5
:24-25-1996.8
:26-38-2004.0- .3
:39-49-2008.4 & .5
:50-56-2012.0 & .1
24:1-12-2025.4
:13-35-2034.5
:36-46-2040.2
:47-51-2057.5

JOHN

1-1-3-74:2
:9-590:3
:12-13-1601:2
:14-227:4
:18-28:2, & 64:5
:19-36-1503.8 & .9
:35-51-1524.1 & .2
2:1-12-1528.4 & .5
:14-16-1888.1
:18-22-1895:2
3:1-13-1601.6
3:26-36-1507:1
4:5-41-1612.5 & .6
:46-53-1644.5
5:1-25-1649.3
6:1-21-1700.2- .4
:22-61-1709.2 & .3
:61-70-1715.5
7:1-36-1788.1 & .2
:37-44-1795.6
:45-53-1792:3
8:2-11-1792.3
:12-59-1794.5- .7
9:1-34-1811.3 & .4
10:1-21-1818.2
:23-40-1815.5
11:1-16-1836.4
:17-54-1842.0- .3
:55-57-1878.1
12:1-11-1878.4
:12-19-1880.3
:20-50-1902.5
13:1-30-1938.3 & .4
:31-35-1944:2 & 3
:37-38-1962:2 & 3
14:1-26-1946.3 & .4
:27-31-1954:2
15:1-26-1944.1- .3
16:1-30-1951.6
:32-33-1954:3
17:1-26-1963.1
18:1-15-1973.3
:15-18-1980.2
:19-24-1978.1
:25-27-1980.2
:29-38-1989.2 & .3
:39-40-1993.5
19:1-15-1994.6 & .7
:16-25-2004.1- .3
:26-27-2009:6
:28-34-2010.5
:38-42-2012.0 & .1
20:1-18-2025.4 & .5
:19-24-2040.2
:25-29-2042.5
21:1-23-2045.1 & .2

By Randy Moser, 713 Fort Hall, American Falls, Idaho 83211.
Based on my BIBLICAL QUOTATIONS & Duane Faw's PARAMONY

KEY: 1:1-17-1344.1=Chapter 1, Verse 1-17 on page 1344, Section 1
7:1-2-1639:1=Chapter 7, Verse 1-2 on page 1639, Paragraph 1

The URANTIA Book, °1955 by URANTIA FOUNDATION.

JUNE, 1985

APPENDIX: Randy Moser's PARALLEL
of *The URANTIA Book* and the four Gospels

NOTES

NOTES